≺ ≻

THE FRENCH IDEA OF FREEDOM:
THE OLD REGIME AND THE
DECLARATION OF RIGHTS
OF 1789

THE MAKING OF MODERN FREEDOM

General Editor: R. W. Davis

THE
FRENCH IDEA OF FREEDOM
THE OLD REGIME AND THE DECLARATION
OF RIGHTS OF 1789

≺ ≻

Edited by Dale Van Kley

STANFORD UNIVERSITY PRESS
STANFORD, CALIFORNIA

Stanford University Press
Stanford, California
© 1994 by the Board of Trustees of the
Leland Stanford Junior University
Printed in the United States of America

CIP data appear at the end of the book

Stanford University Press publications
are distributed exclusively by Stanford
University Press within the United
States, Canada, Mexico, and Central
America; they are distributed exclusively
by Cambridge University Press throughout the rest of the world.

<ＸＸＸ>

Series Foreword

THE STARTLING AND MOVING events that swept from China to Eastern Europe to Latin America and South Africa at the end of the 1980s, followed closely by similar events and the subsequent dissolution of what used to be the Soviet Union, formed one of those great historic occasions when calls for freedom, rights, and democracy echoed through political upheaval. A clear-eyed look at any of those conjunctions—in 1776 and 1789, in 1848 and 1918, as well as in 1989—reminds us that freedom, liberty, rights, and democracy are words into which many different and conflicting hopes have been read. The language of freedom—or liberty, which is interchangeable with freedom most of the time—is inherently difficult. It carried vastly different meanings in the classical world and in medieval Europe from those of modern understanding, though thinkers in later ages sometimes eagerly assimilated the older meanings to their own circumstances and purposes.

A new kind of freedom, which we have here called modern, gradually disentangles itself from old contexts in Europe, beginning first in England in the early seventeenth century and then, with many confusions, denials, reversals, and cross-purposes, elsewhere in Europe and the world. A large-scale history of this modern, conceptually distinct, idea of freedom is now beyond the ambition of any one scholar, however learned. This collaborative enterprise, tentative though it must be, is an effort to fill the gap.

We could not take into account all the varied meanings that freedom and liberty have carried in the modern world. We have, for example, ruled out extended attention to what some political philosophers have called "positive freedom," in the sense of self-realization of the individual; nor could we, even in a series as large as this, cope with the enormous implications of the four freedoms invoked by Franklin D. Roosevelt in 1941. Freedom of speech and freedom of the press will have their place in the narrative that follows, certainly, but not the boundless calls for freedom from want and freedom from fear.

We use freedom in the traditional and restricted sense of civil and political liberty—freedom of religion, freedom of speech and assembly, freedom of the individual from arbitrary and capricious authority over persons or property, freedom to produce and to exchange goods and services, and the freedom to take part in the political process that shapes people's destiny. In no major part of the world over the past few years have aspirations for those freedoms not been at least powerfully expressed; and in most places where they did not exist, strong measures have been taken—not always successfully—to attain them.

The history we trace was not a steady march toward the present or the fulfillment of some cosmic necessity. Modern freedom had its roots in specific circumstances in early modern Europe, despite the unpromising and even hostile characteristics of the larger society and culture. From these narrow and often selfishly motivated beginnings, modern freedom came to be realized in later times, constrained by old traditions and institutions hard to move, and driven by ambition as well as idealism: everywhere the growth of freedom has been *sui generis*. But to understand these unique developments fully, we must first try to see them against the making of modern freedom as a whole.

The Making of Modern Freedom grows out of a continuing series of conferences and institutes held at the Center for the History of Freedom at Washington University in St. Louis. Professor J. H. Hexter was the founder and, for three years, the resident gadfly of the Center. His contribution is gratefully recalled by all his colleagues.

                                                            R.W.D.

≺ ≻

Acknowledgments

Several foundations have generously supported The Making of Modern Freedom series, and two in particular have supported this volume. The National Endowment for the Humanities provided funding for planning meetings and also sponsored the autumn 1991 conference where the volume was first discussed. It largely took shape in the fifth of our annual Institutes in the spring semester of 1992. The Institutes, which bring the authors together as Fellows of the Institute for the History of Freedom, have been fully funded by the Lynde and Harry Bradley Foundation. We are grateful for all the support we have received, including the strong backing we have always enjoyed from Washington University.

R.W.D.

The indebtedness incurred in the course of editing a book, I have found, is even greater than that incurred by writing one. Space allows me to acknowledge only the chief of these debts here.

My first debt is to the Center for the History of Freedom at Washington University in St. Louis and to its present and past directors, Richard W. Davis and J. H. Hexter respectively. It was the Center that conceived of the need for a volume on the French Declaration of Rights of 1789; and it was the Center that brought three other contributors besides myself—Raymond Birn, Thomas Kaiser, and Kent Wright—to St. Louis during the spring semester of 1992 to give this idea expression. Our indebtedness to the Center extends to our luncheons, witness as these were to a high-spirited rewriting of the script of the 1992 American presidential election as well as to discussion of the 1789 French Declaration of Rights.

Second is the debt to this volume's other contributors, who could not help editing this book as well as writing chapters for it. To them I am grateful not only for their criticism and improvement of my own written contributions but for their help in conceptualizing the volume as a whole—so much so, indeed, that the introduction to this volume represents very much a collaborative statement. I am also grateful to the critics of the draft chapters at the first conference in November 1991: Gail Bossenga, Jack Censer, Marvin Cox, Colin Lucas, Pierre Manin, Sarah Maza, Douglass North, and John Pocock. Their presence made for the most profitable and exciting discussion of the Old Regime and its relation to the French Revolution in which I have personally taken part.

I owe a very personal debt of gratitude to the Pew Charitable Trusts and its Evangelical Scholarship Initiative, whose support of my scholarship during the year following my stay at the Center, 1992–93, allowed me to finish the remaining editorial work with much greater dispatch than would otherwise have been possible. Finally, neither my editorship of a volume having to do with the French Revolution nor my own chapter for that volume would have been conceivable without generous and frequently subsidized access to Chicago's Newberry Library and its magnificent—and still underused—French Revolution Collection, beginning with a National Endowment for the Humanities fellowship there during the year 1983–84. David Bien and Raymond Birn are similarly indebted to that collection and to N.E.H. fellowships for parts of their contributions to this volume. They may not have procrastinated as shamelessly as I have, allowing research done there in 1984 to lie unexploited in noteboxes until this moment. But I am sure they join me in hoping that the Newberry's staff thinks, as I do, that even—or most especially—scholarly debts are better paid late than never!

D.V.K.

CONTRIBUTORS

Keith Michael Baker
Stanford University

David A. Bell
Yale University

David D. Bien
University of Michigan

Raymond Birn
University of Oregon

Thomas E. Kaiser
University of Arkansas, Little Rock

Shanti Marie Singham
Williams College

Dale Van Kley
Calvin College

J. K. Wright
University of Chicago

≺ ≻

THE FRENCH IDEA OF FREEDOM: THE OLD REGIME AND THE DECLARATION OF RIGHTS OF 1789

Declaration of the Rights of Man
and of the Citizen

THE REPRESENTATIVES OF the French people, constituted as the National Assembly, considering that ignorance, disregard, or contempt for the rights of man are the sole causes of public misfortunes and the corruption of governments, have resolved to set forth, in a solemn declaration, the natural, inalienable, and sacred rights of man, so that the constant presence of this declaration may ceaselessly remind all members of the social body of their rights and duties; so that the acts of the legislative power and those of the executive power may be the more respected, since it will be possible at each moment to compare them against the goal of every political institution; and so that the demands of the citizens, grounded henceforth on simple and incontestable principles, may always be directed to the maintenance of the constitution and to the welfare of all.

Consequently, the National Assembly recognizes and declares, in the presence and under the auspices of the Supreme Being, the following rights of man and the citizen:

Article 1. Men are born and remain free and equal in rights. Social distinctions can be based only on public utility.

Article 2. The aim of every political association is the preservation of the natural and imprescriptible rights of man. These rights are liberty, property, security, and resistance to oppression.

Article 3. The source of all sovereignty resides essentially in the nation. No body, no individual can exercise authority that does not explicitly proceed from it.

Article 4. Liberty consists in being able to do anything that does not injure another; thus the only limits upon each man's exercise of his natural rights are those that guarantee enjoyment of these same rights to the other members of society. These limits can be determined only be law.

Law

Article 5. The law has the right to forbid only actions harmful to society. No action may be prevented that is not forbidden by law, and no one may be constrained to do what the law does not order.

Article 6. The law is the expression of the general will. All citizens have the right to participate personally, or through their representatives, in its formation. It must be the same for all, whether it protects or punishes. All citizens, being equal in its eyes, are equally admissible to all public dignities, positions, and employments, according to their ability, and on the basis of no other distinction than that of their virtues and talents.

Article 7. No man may be accused, arrested, or detained except in cases determined by the law and according to the forms it has prescribed. Those who solicit, expedite, execute, or effect the execution of arbitrary orders must be punished; but every citizen summoned or seized by virtue of the law must obey at once; he makes himself guilty by resistance.

Article 8. The law must lay down only those penalties that are strictly and evidently necessary, and no one may be punished except by virtue of a law established and promulgated prior to the offense, and legally applied.

Article 9. Every man is presumed innocent until he has been found guilty; if it is considered indispensable to arrest him, any severity not necessary to secure his person must be strictly repressed by law.

Expression

Article 10. No one must be disturbed because of his opinions, even in religious matters, provided their expression does not trouble the public order established by law.

Article 11. The free expression of thought and opinions is one of the most precious rights of man: thus every citizen may freely speak, write, and print, subject to accountability for abuse of this freedom in the cases determined by law.

Gov and taxation

Article 12. To guarantee the rights of man and the citizen requires a public force; this force is therefore instituted for the benefit of all, and not for the personal advantage of those to whom it is entrusted.

Article 13. A common tax is indispensable to maintain the public force and support the expenses of administration. It must be shared equally among all the citizens in proportion to their means.

Article 14. All citizens have the right to ascertain, personally or through their representatives, the necessity of the public tax, to consent to it freely, to know how it is spent, and to determine its amount, basis, mode of collection, and duration.

Article 15. Society has the right to demand that every public agent give an account of his administration.

Article 16. A society in which the guarantee of rights is not secured, or the separation of powers not clearly established, has no constitution.

Article 17. Property being an inviolable and sacred right, no one can be deprived of it, unless legally established public necessity obviously demands it, and upon condition of a just and prior indemnity.

Translated by Keith Michael Baker. Reprinted from Baker, ed., *The Old Regime and the French Revolution* (Chicago, © 1987 by the University of Chicago), by permission of the University of Chicago Press.

Introduction

DALE VAN KLEY

TODAY MOST NATIONAL constitutions begin with or somewhere contain an explicit declaration of the rights of citizens. That these declarations are often very ineffective barriers against social and political oppression there can be no doubt. One of the world's longest and most detailed declarations of rights, that of Uganda drafted in the 1960s, did not prevent Idi Amin's assault on the whole concept of human dignity in the decade that followed; nor did specific provisions in favor of freedom of belief and expression and against arbitrary arrest and imprisonment in Eastern European constitutions prevent these rights from being routinely flouted until quite recently.[1] Yet if, in the duc de La Rochefoucauld's renowned estimation, "hypocrisy is the homage that vice renders to virtue," then perhaps declarations of human rights are the homage that even the most tyrannical of regimes are today forced to render to the principle of human worth and dignity.[2] And if in the last analysis hypocrisy is preferable to undisguised vice, then even paper-thin acknowledgments of human rights are surely preferable to principled contempt for them. At the worst, such acknowledgments buttressed by world opinion have prevented the very worst from happening; at best, as in South Africa in the 1990s, they have been a factor in change for the better.

But declarations of individual rights are an essential feature of modern political culture quite apart from the protection, or lack of it, that they afford to individuals against each other or their governments. No matter how tyrannical or benign they may be, just about all governments today except perhaps for a few Islamic states claim ultimately to derive their legitimacy, not from the sanction of the gods above or from the binding wishes of heroic ancestors in the past, but from the individual components below—from their "citizens," in other words, as bearers of "rights." Whether they accord the rights of political participation or not, therefore, modern states are also expressly "constituted," which is to say that they feature a written "constitution" allocating the people's power among various agencies and organs and somewhere declaring its "rights," making if possible an exhaustive list of them. Indeed, the expressed declaration of individual "rights" has increased in importance in proportion as governmental "sovereignty" has been derived from them. For legislation thus legitimated has in some respects proven more "sovereign" and less limited than royal promulgation derived from, but also bounded by, divine and natural law.

In the history of these developments, the French Revolution at the end of the eighteenth century occupies a special place. Giving us the notion of a total and decisive break with the past, the French Revolution virtually invented the related notions of "nation" and the "citizen," adopted and discarded four of the world's first written "constitutions," and promulgated three sets of declarations of rights.[3] Of these, the first one, the Declaration of the Rights of Man and the Citizen of 1789, is the French Revolution's best known utterance. It has therefore been chosen as the subject of this volume in the series on The Making of Modern Freedom.

By 1789, to be sure, England and Edmund Burke looked proudly back to Magna Carta, the Petition of Right, and a bill of rights; while even the young American Declaration of Independence and the individual states' various declarations and bills of rights preceded the French Declaration by a decade or more. All these Anglo-Saxon precedents were already there for the French to emulate, eschew, or surpass in 1789. Yet not even the American states' declarations of rights entirely broke with the notions that the rights in question were peculiarly English rights—even if enunciated against the English—or that they derived their force in part from their status as property inherited from the past. Very conscious of breaking from the American example in these respects, the French deputies of the Estates General reborn as the National Assembly of 1789 tried hard, in the words of one of their number, not to receive lessons from others but rather "to give them" to the rest of the world, not to proclaim the rights of Frenchmen but those "for all times and all nations."[4] And although less different from American states in this respect, the French National Assembly also clearly intended its declaration not only to protect individual rights from government, but also to serve as a foundation for a new government.

It was for these reasons, perhaps, that the French historian Jacques Godechot dared to assure a largely Anglo-Saxon audience in 1975 that the French declaration had been "the principal vehicle of the ideas of liberty and equality around the globe."[5] "Influence" of the sort here alleged is of course notoriously difficult to chart, as some nations, mainly Commonwealth ones, have simply incorporated British "laws and customs" piecemeal into their constitutions; some as in Central and South America seem to have followed the American examples of detailed declarations of rights cast in an indigenous judicial language; and some—many, but still only some—feature declarations bearing the clear and "universal" imprint of 1789, most notably in Western Europe and in the former French colonies of Asia and Africa.[6] Suffice it to say that, faced in 1948 with a choice between a draft "covenant" in the American mode and a "universal declaration" in the idiom of 1789, the United Nations opted for the latter, as well it might have done, being an agency of all nations if not for all times.[7]

Not the least remarkable feature of the French Declaration is that these intentions realized the universal form that they did. It is of course proverbial that little of lasting literary value either has or is ever likely to come from a committee. That skepticism concerning committees was shared by the comte de Mirabeau on 18 August 1789 when, having failed to synthesize numbers of competing draft declarations to the National Assembly's satisfaction as head of a committee of five, he allowed that "among all human affairs I know of only one where despotism is not only good but also necessary, and that is in composition; the words 'committee' and 'composition' scream in fright at the prospect of being linked to one another."[8] If then it was not likely that a committee would produce a declaration fit for "all times and all places," how much less so a tumultuous assembly numbering nearly twelve hundred deputies deliberating article by article on a draft declaration originally composed by a committee? In the end, however, that is quite literally what happened. Rejecting Mirabeau's proposal to postpone the task of composing a declaration until after writing the constitution, the Assembly passed over all draft declarations despotically composed by individuals, some of them illustrious, only to adopt as a basis for discussion one of the more lackluster drafts —that of another committee, the Assembly's sixth bureau, on 19 August. Seven days, two or three verbal slugfests, ninety motions, sixty amendments, and at least a hundred opinants later, the Declaration of the Rights of Man and of the Citizen as we know it emerged from the hands of the National Assembly, whose members still thought of it as provisional and incomplete.[9]

That things turned out so well would seem reason enough for continued rejoicing, even at this late date. Yet, what had been a source of national pride at the time of the centennial of the French Revolution and the young Third Republic in 1889 has become the occasion of some soul searching in France on the occasion of the recent bicentennial. Where Emile Boutmy, writing at the turn of the last century, proudly asserted the uniquely French and eighteenth-century origins of the Declaration in response to Georg Jellinek's valorization of the document's Germanic and Reformational roots, French historians writing at the end of the twentieth century have tended to regret precisely the lack of Anglo-Saxon origins of their founding event. If very few of them have followed Pierre Chaunu into historiographical counter revolution, calling into question the worth of the Revolution as a whole, many have "thought" and even rethought the Revolution, calling into question parts of it heretofore sacrosanct in French liberal thought. Those parts are the supposedly liberal beginnings including the Declaration of Rights of 1789.

Much of that rethinking has of course come in response to the vicissitudes of Marxism in France. First came the gradual impact of Anglo-Saxon historiography's empirical assault on the (more or less) Marxian paradigm for the French Revolution as a capitalist "bourgeois" revolution, sending historians in want of a new paradigm back to Alexis de Tocqueville's classic *The Old Regime and the French Revolution*, as well as stimulating interest in high culture and politics as independent actors in the historical drama. The result has been a search for political and cultural continuities between the Old Regime and the French Revolution in addition to the administrative centralization and social leveling that Tocqueville underscored. Then came the publication in translation of Solzhenitsyn's *Gulag Archipelago* in advance of the spectacular collapse in Eastern Europe of Marxian socialism itself, indicting not only Soviet socialism's later stages but also the totalitarian origins of the Bolshevik Revolution in 1917. In France where a native school of socialist historians had long regarded 1789 as the distant harbinger of 1917, a renewed interest in the very beginnings of the French Revolution has given rise to a tendency to see in them the seeds of the proto-totalitarian Terror of 1793.

Together these developments have spelled a search for the origin of
the Revolution's more totalitarian phases in the political culture of
the Old Regime.

In agreement with Tocqueville on the long-term development of
administrative centralization and its dislocation of the Old Regime's
corporate society, François Furet, the most self-consciously Toc-
quevillian of this group of historians, has tried to account for the sen-
sation of revolutionary rupture by insisting on the novelty of revolutionary politics, substituting as it did oratory for the routine exercise
of power and enshrining national sovereignty in the place of monarchical sovereignty. Yet the long shadow of monarchical absolutism is
visible for Furet even in the political culture of the Revolution itself,
inasmuch as the revolutionaries expected the national will to be as
unitary and undivided as the monarchy's had been in principle and
hence found themselves conceptually incapable of construing disagreement as anything but "faction." The result was the politics of
ideological purity and purge that made for the eventful character of the
years from 1789 to 1794, and most especially the Terror of 1792–94.[10]
Applying this perspective to the Declaration of Rights in particular,
Marcel Gauchet has persuasively argued that before it was a text the
Declaration was an act, an act justifying the seizure of royal power
rather than self-defense against it, with the consequence that the revolutionaries ensnared themselves in "the trap of power" from the very
outset. Unlike the American declarations, concerned above all to
make individual rights and civil society immune to power, the French
Declaration's main purpose was to use abstract individuals and their
rights as the constituent elements of a new and unlimited power. The
result, for Gauchet as for Furet, was the construction of a sovereignty
so collective as to effect an identification of citizenry with their government archaically reminiscent of the virtual identity of Old Regime
nation with its king.[11]

The same interpretational tendencies are visible in recent works
written from the perspective of political science and the traditional
history of ideas, as opposed to the newer interest in political culture.
Blandine Barret-Kriegel, for example, has pointed her finger at René
Descartes and the Cartesian legacy in France. Unlike the natural
law school of Thomas Hobbes and John Locke, which objectively
grounded rights in nature and natural law, the Continental school of
natural rights theorists including Jean-Jacques Rousseau and the baron

de Montesquieu inherited the radical separation of human thought
from physical nature characteristic of Cartesian dualism, producing a
subjective and voluntaristic version of rights much more dependent
on societal conventions than on an objective nature. Hence, in her
opinion, the accent on the rights of the citizen as opposed to natural
man in the French Declaration of Rights. Hence, too, the close relation
of these rights to the creation of a constitution — and their vulnerabil-
ity to change by subsequent regimes supposedly based on them.[12]
Philippe Raynaud has similarly insisted that "the natural and imprescriptible rights of man" in the Declaration of Rights take second
place to positive law and the legislative will — the "law" being of
course the "expression of the general will," in the Declaration's most
Rousseauian article. By allowing, he argues, for representation and
specifying only that the law ought not to permit privilege, the Declaration tended to remove even Rousseau's strictures of generality as to
the law's object and source in the whole people. Only the law's self-ev-
ident, quasi-Cartesian rationality remained by way of a guarantee for
rights; yet even this criterion was designed to reinforce obedience
rather than limit it.[13]

   To be sure, this post-Marxian, civil, and "legicentric" reading of
the Declaration—to translate a word coined by Stéphane Rials—has
not gone unchallenged, even in France. Having shared it for awhile,
Stéphane Rials for one has recently come to insist on the Lockean and
more liberal accents of the text. Recalling that natural rights are after
all "declared, exhibited, recognized, and not constituted" by the Declaration, he has concluded that after all has been said and done the Declaration's natural man "does not disappear into . . . the citizen."[14]
That small note of dissent is worth listening to, if only to attenuate
what might seem too arrogant about a group of American historians
coming to the rescue of a text now treated as suspect in the country of
its origin. For that is the general tenor of this volume focused sharply
on the text of the Declaration of the Rights of Man and of the Citizen
of 1789.

   This volume treats mainly of the origins of the Declaration in the
political thought and practice of the preceding three centuries that
Tocqueville roughly designated as the "Old Regime," regarding the
Declaration as the end and culmination of that Old Regime. The
origins emphasized, then, are overwhelmingly French, although political theorists who figure prominently in previous volumes in this se-

ries — Hugo Grotius, James Harrington, John Locke, or James Madison—put in occasional and important appearances. In many of the chapters, moreover, Old Regime law and lawyers occupy pride of place. This prospective, French, and legal orientation surely speaks volumes about the deep influence that the post-Marxian revisionist reinterpretation of the French Revolution in France has had on American and British historians, including the ones represented in this volume. All are deeply indebted to this school of thought; some have importantly contributed to it. The effect of a year's collaborative effort at understanding the text of the Declaration of Rights in the light—or darkness—of the Old Regime has nonetheless been to nuance the nature of the continuities routinely seen between the two, and that in three distinct ways.

First, most of the chapters of this volume begin and end with the writing of the Declaration of the Rights of Man and of the Citizen itself. That is to say that, although all these chapters look upstream toward long-term origins, some more distant than others, all also pay attention to the point of final confluence in 1789. For all these contributors, as for Gauchet, the Declaration was an act as well as a text, an act anchored in a particular time and place which conditioned— arguably made possible—this very attempt at a declaration for "all times and all places." The effect of this approach is to restore an immediacy and contingency to a text that has begun to seem a little like the predestined product of multi-secular if not eternal political-cultural decrees.

Thus, as Keith Baker's blow-by-blow account of the Assembly's debates preceding its composition shows, the idea of a declaration of rights was far from a foregone conclusion, seeing that on two occasions the deputies seriously entertained the suggestion that they should not adopt a separate declaration at all and, on another, narrowly rejected a proposal to compromise the aesthetic simplicity of a declaration with a parallel declaration of duties. Given the nature of these debates, the fact of a separate declaration of rights was by itself fraught with meaning, already committing the deputies of the National Assembly to a more radical course of action than if they had not decided to write one at all. Thus too, if Dale Van Kley is correct, the universal and timeless kind of declaration that the Assembly decided to write was itself contingent, hardly thinkable until the events of the preceding three months had discredited France's competing versions of a "usable past" as either "despotic" or "aristocratic" or both. Under the circumstances, the Declaration's silence about the French past was perhaps more eloquent than explicit condemnations of "despotism" or "aristocracy" would have been.

If the Declaration's silence spoke more loudly against the "aristocratic" past than against the "despotic" one, that was in part due to changes in the legal profession—a profession that sent more delegates to the National Assembly than any other sent. For in the several decades preceding the Revolution, as David Bell's chapter shows, barristers increasingly called for rights secured by legislation that could have only come from the king, in contrast to the "imprescriptible rights" protected by the courts that they had earlier urged *against* the monarchy. Yet that discovery of the monarchy's potential as reformist legislator clashed with the monarchy's simultaneous rediscovery of its identity as quasi-feudal—and to that extent, "aristocratic"—suzerain. For, as Thomas Kaiser's chapter shows, the monarchy increasingly turned to the "feudal" exploitation of the royal domain in order to cope with its ever more desperate fiscal situation, reversing its earlier sponsorship of anti-feudal juristic thought. These contingencies, if they help explain Louis XVI's inability to decide whether he was the "first servant of the state" or the "first gentleman of the realm," also probe the structural limits of the contingent. Could a monarchy so fiscally dependent on forms of privilege, as David Bien's chapter also shows, have really taken the side of commoners against the "privileged" orders, as some royalist publicists claimed that it wanted to do?

Kent Wright's chapter, in any case, ranges farther afield, finding the origins for the notions of sovereignty and the separation of powers in the distant sixteenth century, but even he shows how the various strands of the Declaration's constitutional program contingently came together in the summer of 1789 in a fledgling statement of a modern and uniquely French republicanism. Traumatic memories of the sixteenth century, especially of Protestant and ultra-Catholic challenges to monarchical order with the help of the newly invented printing press, also haunt Raymond Birn's chapter on the subject of religious toleration and the freedom of the press. Yet the very different forms assumed by the Declaration's two articles devoted to those rights—the one on toleration being more tortuous and restrictive than the one on the freedom of the press—are hardly intelligible except in the light of the divergent histories of tacit permissions for books and tacit toleration of Protestantism after 1750.

Long-term origins and the conjuncture of 1789—the encounter of these two was productive, not only of meaning, but of a plurality of meanings which tend to remain resistant to attempts at overall coherence, be it that seemingly conferred by the events of the later Revolution. Where Marcel Gauchet tends to stress the Declaration's "strong coherence" over its "constitutive equivocation," the authors represented in this volume tend to see ambiguity more readily than coherence, or rather several possible coherences—it is not claimed that the text is incoherent—rather than any single one.[15] Hence the second of this volume's general orientations, an inclination to read the Declaration as a calculated compromise evident in its textual tensions.

The textual ambiguity in question is, to be sure, an artful one, such as one would have expected from a generation of men of the law still educated in classical rhetoric. And indeed, in none of their deliberations did they neglect a classical quest for aesthetic unity in potent combination, perhaps, with a neo-Catholic catechetical simplicity that would enable the entire faithful citizenry, even those on the margins of literacy, to understand their rights. If for example Alexandre de Lameth carried the day on Articles 4 and 5, it was because his two proposed articles "more energetically" expressed in two articles what the Sixth Bureau's draft had tried to say in four. Although not different in substance from other motions on the table, Bishop Talleyrand of Autun's proposal for what became Article 6 prevailed because he had "found a happier formulation."[16] Yet the fact that this formulation artfully stitched together fragments from individual projects as divergent as those by the abbé Emmanuel-Joseph Sieyès, the Norman barrister Jacques Thouret, and the Sixth Bureau is perhaps warning enough that more than purely aesthetic considerations were involved, that a conscious attempt was made to find formulas that would do the bidding of twelve hundred deputies already divided by profound disagreements.[17]

Was the Declaration mainly concerned to limit an existing power or to institute a new one? In asking that question, Keith Baker calls attention to a kind of constitutional ambivalence running throughout the whole Declaration, which could be read as justifying a balanced and limited constitutional monarchy on the one hand or a radically

democratic polity vested with unlimited power on the other. That ambiguity or tension is not unlike the one, touted by Van Kley, between
those articles protecting individual and constitutional liberty arising
from "patriotic" or parlementary discourse and those having to do
with the rights of equality coming from the monarchical or absolutist
side of the pre-revolutionary debate. Both of these are in turn closely
related to the tension detected by David Bell between legislation and
something like prescription as the best protection of rights that the
Declaration still calls "natural and imprescriptible." And although
Wright tends to discern a kind of proto-"republican" coherence where
most other contributors see through the Declaration's textual trans-
parencies more darkly, even his account of the Declaration's composition makes it clear that many of its provisions were the result of a seesaw battle between the Assembly's emergent moderate and more radical political factions.

More than "merely rhetorical," these textual tensions reflected
social as well as political divisions. The text of the Declaration itself
pitted "natural rights" on the one hand against "society" and its
"utility" on the other. Attuned though it may generally be to "discourse" and its many changes, this volume means to take no stand in
favor of discursive against social history. For if, in Bien's chapter, the
Old Regime's society of privileged corporations dialectically prepared
the terrain for the new society of individual rights to equality, it also
paradoxically bequeathed a legacy of social conflict about what equality was which was inscribed in the Declaration as well. Thus, for example, behind the brouhaha over the word *"capacité"* in Article 6 in
Van Kley's account of the debate of 21 August, there clearly lay tensions between the "natural" right of equality, placing noble and commoner on a par, and social and economic "capacity," possessed by the
"well born" in unequal measure. Kaiser's chapter, too, is a story about
the conflict between natural rights and society, in this case between
the language of natural rights and what remained of "feudal" society,
a conflict that did not end with the legislation of 4 August 1789 or the
drafting of the rather ambiguous Article 17. The same tension between natural rights and society makes another appearance in Birn's
account of the origins of Articles 10 and 11, here in the form of the
natural rights to freedom of religious conscience and written expression in conflict with a still Catholic society's worries about public
order. The results, again, were the Janus-faced Article 10 which, as
Birn points out, is susceptible of a punitive as well as a liberal reading.

But it is Shanti Singham's chapter on blacks, Jews, and women that points to the Declaration's largest single ambiguity involving the relation between natural rights and society. Did the Declaration's natural rights cross these boundaries of race, gender, and religion or not? If only some natural rights applied to some of these groups, which ones in either case? In leaving this issue unaddressed, the Declaration of Rights implicitly raised fundamental questions about prevailing conceptions of both human nature and society, whether homogeneous or diverse, that were debated at the time and remain unresolved today.

Yet a third area where current revisionism sustains a little revision in this volume has to do with the continuities between the French Old Regime and the Revolution. It is not the fact of such continuities that is in question here. All of the contributors to this volume are *dix-huitièmistes* or specialists in the Old Regime rather than in the Revolution proper and, like Tocqueville, are on the lookout for ways in which the Revolution might have been unwittingly more continuous than discontinuous with the "Old Regime" that it invented, inventoried, and tried hard to bury. What is rather in question is whether the nature of the Old Regime can be reduced to monarchical absolutism, or even whether the Old Regime's many critics of absolutism can be reduced to philosophes or the Enlightenment. The Old Regime consisted not only of absolutism but also of "resistance to oppression," going back to the Fronde in the seventeenth century and the religious civil wars of the sixteenth century. And if, in the words of the deputy Bertrand Barère in 1789, the Declaration of Rights would be the product of "the lights (*lumières*) of a whole century," those "lights" included Jansenists and *dévots* as well as philosophes, and that century abounded in barristers and churchmen as well as men of letters.[18] It is hence the diversity and heterogeneity of the Old Regime legacy that this volume collectively tends to underscore, a heterogeneity that, in new internal combinations, may to some degree account for the obvious discontinuity and instability of the Revolution itself.

At the center of this dialectic of continuity and discontinuity from Old Regime to Revolution stands David Bien's chapter on royal fiscality, corporate privilege, and the pervasiveness of "rights" in France. Where Tocqueville already paradoxically argued that by undermining the social hierarchy and corporate privilege the monarchy nurtured the revolutionary quest for the rights of equality, thereby digging its own grave—a dynamic corroborated on a rhetorical level in Van Kley's chapter—Bien even more paradoxically argues that by in fact *reinforcing* social hierarchy and corporate privilege for fiscal purposes, the monarchy also nurtured the development of a sense of equal rights within these many privileged corporations. Hence perhaps the most paradoxical of all continuities from Old Regime to Revolution, that from Old Regime privilege to revolutionary right. At the same time, however, intense competition both within but especially between more or less privileged groups and corporations fostered an equally pervasive resentment of social inequality, perhaps explaining the very brittle and individual character of French revolutionary right. In spite of or perhaps because of these corporate origins, the French Declaration, in notable contrast to its American precedents, proposed no right of association.

Other chapters play variations on the theme of a various Old Regime and its connection to Revolution. The absolute monarchy's legislative "good pleasure" did not lack defenders, as Bell and Van Kley variously show, but its judicial or "patriotic" critics remained just as prolific, and it took the dialectical union of the arguments of both— or so the argument goes—to make for revolutionary ideology and the whole Declaration of Rights. Or not quite, perhaps, because neither side of that debate does justice to the contribution of physiocracy and its quest for transparent rationality—the language of reason—that also plays an important part in the Declaration of Rights, as Baker shows. The physiocrats also defended the "natural rights" of property against "feudalism," just as some defenders of absolutism had already done in the seventeenth century. But so did some eighteenth-century defenders of feudal property in opposition to both absolutism and the physiocrats, as Kaiser's chapter shows. Thus were the natural rights of property far from unknown to the most old-regimist jurists in the Old Regime, nor would arguments from prescription remain unknown to the most revolutionary jurists of the Revolution.

And was, finally, the implicit exclusion of blacks, Jews, and women from the text of the Declaration of Rights as continuous with the whole Old Regime as has been generally supposed? On the one hand, as Singham implies, there were numbers of traditions variously rooted in the Old Regime, Jansenist and Protestant among others, that produced defenders of the rights of all three of these groups. Their voices could be heard on the periphery of the discussion of natural and social rights, even if they did not make it into the text of the Declaration itself. On the other hand, part of what these groups either gained or endured at the hands of the Revolution came, not from the Old Regime, but from revolutionary ideology's anti- "aristocratic" reaction to all that recalled the Old Regime's legitimation of particularity and difference. Subjected to the Revolution's attempt to force all the Old Regime's diverse and differently privileged subjects into the mold of a common citizenship, blacks and Jews, whose differences were arguably cultural, fared a little better than women, whose differences were unalterably biological.

In conclusion, then, the Old Regime was not of one piece, its diverse pieces entered contingently into the Declaration, and the Declaration was therefore intrinsically ambiguous. Thus, just as it is hardly licit to absolutize absolutism in the Old Regime at the expense of recurrent regional, frondish, and religious resistance, so it would not seem to be licit to privilege a unitary or neo-absolutist reading of the "general will" or national sovereignty in the Declaration to the exclusion of the "right to resist oppression." And no more than absolutism ever entirely succeeded in occupying the inner space or "conscience" of the king's officially docile subjects in the Old Regime did the lawful "citizen" ever replace the "natural" man—or even woman—in the Declaration of the Rights of Man and of the Citizen.

But why belabor these points, it may well be asked, especially since they do not exactly add up to a new account of the origins of the French Revolution? Simply for this reason, that the Declaration, thus interpreted, acts as a much better harbinger of how France actually turned out in the nineteenth and twentieth centuries than it does on the assumption that it systematically subordinated the private individual to public power, "natural" rights to societal ones, or the right of resistance to the duty of obedience. For France did not after all turn into some kind of proto-totalitarian state, or one in which authority invariably got the better of liberty.

To be sure, and as everyone knows, the "liberal" Revolution of 1789–91 gave way to the reign of the omnipotent Convention and its terroristic committees between 1793 and 1794, while the Thermidorian return to moderate constitutionalism in 1795 gave way to Bonapartist dictatorship between 1799 and 1815. And at times it must have seemed—and so it seemed to Tocqueville as Second Republic gave way to Second Empire in 1851—as though postrevolutionary France were forever condemned to oscillate pointlessly between the despotism of a putative "people" and that of one man.[19] That that was so was in part due to the fact, as Tocqueville well knew, that the French quest for the right balance between public and individual liberty—the first of the Declaration of Right's internal tensions—was complicated and crisscrossed by the quest for social equality—the second of these tensions. For until the invention of a decentralist—and quintessentially French—anarchism in the latter part of the nineteenth century, the quest for social equality tended to issue into the strengthening of governmental authority, whether that of a popular assembly or of a single person.

Yet none of these regimes survived indefinitely, nor of course did they go uncontested during their brief seasons in the sun. On the contrary, revolutions and rumors of revolution punctuated the authoritarian monotony of the nineteenth century, just as that monotony also exacted its revenge on revolutionary exhilaration—and both with such regularity that the resultant cycle ought to be regarded as normal for France, as the episodic working out of the logic already visible in the Declaration of the Rights of Man and the Citizen. As early as on the morrow of that Declaration in 1789, the revolutionary National Assembly had no sooner begun to act out a "high" reading of its role as mouthpiece of the "general will" and agent of national sovereignty—to arrogate to itself, or so it seemed, the integral powers of the monarchy—than it faced frondist challenges to its authority from a Jean-Paul Marat on its left and some of the monarchy's formerly patriotic opponents on the right—the two being in many respects overlapping—each of course sure that it spoke for a legal or moral majority against an assembly at once "despotic" and "aristocratic." And not many years after the ink was dry on the Assembly's abolishment of the old provinces and judicial bailiwicks in an attempt to create a unitary nation, its successor, the Convention, faced regional challenges to its authority, some flaring into civil war. And that is in some sense how things would remain in France, notwithstanding Montagnard terrors and Bonapartist authoritarianisms. For it is arguably just these apparently incompatible yet somehow symbiotic quests for order and freedom, authority and spaces off limits to it, that constitute the texture of modern French political culture and its unique idea of freedom.

Hence the title of this volume, arrived at tentatively and in conclusion to a collaborative effort and not in advance of it. French freedom, if it may be spoken of in the singular, would then seem to occupy a point equidistant from that of its Anglo-Saxon neighbors on the one side and its Germanic ones on the other. Anglo-Saxon "liberty"—English and American—has specialized in the defensive protection of the concrete rights of individuals, groups, and regions from public authority; and *The German Idea of Freedom* as memorably described by Leonard Krieger has consoled itself with an inner or higher moral autonomy for the individual while leaving the realization of concrete or material rights to the "prince" or state; the French idea of freedom has somehow tended to do both at once.[20]

At its most internally coherent, the Declaration could be read as proposing a uniquely French kind of republicanism that, as Wright argues, saw the individual's freedom from the state as compatible enough with the state's collective freedom from each individual. An inner purity of will and a zone of personal autonomy, individual freedom, in this view of things, was not incompatible with a very strong and bureaucratic state. That compatibility depended of course on enough "citizens" convincing themselves that they themselves had made the laws and that the laws they obeyed therefore represented the impersonal will of all rather than the personal authority of anyone in particular—the famous French *horreur du face-à-face*. But when, as it cyclically happened, enough Frenchmen perceived that this always precarious Rousseauian state of affairs had ceased to obtain, and that collective authority had collapsed into purely personal power, then it was that an individual, social, or regional "right to resist oppression" that had never been relinquished in the meantime was ever ready to take the field against "despotism," just as in days of yore. French freedom, moreover, not only alternated these freedoms cyclically but juggled them simultaneously, meaning that no regime could ever assume total allegiance, whether officially revolutionary, Bonapartist, or monarchist.[21]

In taking this tortuous course, finally—and in thus bedeviling all attempts to define it—the French quest for freedom was faithful in its frondish way to an Old Regime monarchy which had been absolute enough to unite the realm's many parts and parcels occasionally against it but never absolute enough for them to do without it as the realm's only symbol of unity. Nor of course was it unfaithful to the spirit of the Declaration of the Rights of Man and of the Citizen of 1789, which both transformed and projected just this ambivalence between resistance and authority, between "man" and the "citizen."

To go beyond this cursory characterization is to try to define the indefinable, to do gross violence to the very texture of French freedom, to engage in a self-defeating enterprise. Faced with indefinable Frenchness, it would seem better to throw up one's hands and say, with Tocqueville, that

when I consider this nation in itself, I find it . . . indocile by temperament, more readily accommodating itself to the arbitrary and even violent empire of a prince than to the free and regular government of its principal citizens; today the declared enemy of all obedience, but tomorrow subservient with a sort of passion that even those nations most made for servitude cannot muster; easily led by the leash so long as no one resists, yet ungovernable as soon as the example of resistance is somewhere given; always fooling its masters who either fear it too much or too little; never so free that the prospect of enslaving it is hopeless, yet never so enslaved that it might not break its yoke.[22]

PART I
Context

≺ ≻

Old Regime Origins of Democratic Liberty

DAVID D. BIEN

HOW COULD A FRENCH SOCIETY SO conditioned in its habits by despotism, privilege, even "feudalism" have produced, and resonated to, the Declaration of the Rights of Man and of the Citizen? Why did the principles of liberty and equality emerge from a people accustomed to act only with the state's permission and according to laws that breathed inequality? In 1789 the French themselves had an answer: the new principles developed within but in opposition to the old order. The Declaration opened a new era by negating the previous one. That view, of course, has a good deal of truth in it — no one would deny that 1789 brought vast changes. The purpose of this chapter, however, is not to ask about the changes, but rather to look for less obvious lines of continuity between the old and the new societies. This is a search within the Old Regime for some largely unrecognized sources of the Declaration. Finding the Declaration's origins in that old society will require probing its widespread routines and customary patterns of thinking, the usually unstated assumptions that were shaped in a long interaction between the French and a particular kind of state. Readers of Tocqueville will recognize the framework, although perhaps not the specific question or the answer. I want to investigate continuities to explain something about the presence of liberty and democracy in 1789, not their absence.

Before proceeding, a word about the ideas in the Declaration of the Rights of Man and of the Citizen, or at least my understanding of what those ideas are. Briefly, three principles form the essence of the Declaration: equality is one, and the two others are conceptions of liberty—first, liberty as protection from authority, the freedom to think and do what one wants, the guarantee of independence; and then, liberty as participation, as sharing in sovereignty and the general will, and in the making of law. Liberty as protection against authority appears in ten of the Declaration's seventeen articles (2, 4, 5, 7–11, 16, 17), liberty defined as participation in four articles (3, 6, 14, 15), and equality also in four (1, 6, 13, 14). The three principles fitted together more easily than one might think, and together they formed the package, democracy.

≺ I ≻

The Feudal Background

Curious though it may seem, the place to begin the search for democracy's origins is with its supposed opposite in 1789, that is, with feudalism and its legacy. Within feudalism can be found the three main ideas of the Declaration of the Rights of Man.

As we know, feudalism came from the joining of two institutions, vassalage and the fief.[1] Vassalage was the honorable tie of personal dependency that linked unequal but free men within a narrow elite. It was spread through the top stratum of society first by the initiative of Carolingians desiring to administer an empire, and then by initiatives from below when disorders and local warfare forced many of the remaining independent landowners to look for protection. The fief was the temporary grant to a vassal of the use of land and the revenues of a lesser jurisdiction, this to sustain the follower and to permit him to provide full-time service to his lord. A momentous change came when, in the tenth and eleventh centuries, the fief ceased to be a temporary grant, revocable, essentially the property of the lord, and largely entered instead into the patrimony of the vassal. The change occurred unnoticed in that non-literate society where law was custom, and where the person or family that exercised some function or occupied one or another piece of land was presumed to have done it forever and therefore to have the right to continue to do it forever. It was a society that did not accept change, one where the definition of bad law was innovation. But it was also a society that changed with surprising speed precisely because illiterate. In the absence of written documents, the archives existed only in minds and memories (short because lives were short). Thus, when for practical reasons or even from accident something new was done, it was easy to suppose that it must always have been done. No document proved the reverse. *Ad hoc* arrangements quickly hardened into law.

This explains what happened with the fief. When lords, for convenience and not wanting to discourage new fidelities, began to accept the sons of vassals to succeed their fathers in that role, soon no one could actually remember that anything else had been done. After several such transfers society came to expect that the vassal would follow his father as vassal *and* as holder of the fief. And at some point in the tenth century the unwritten law began to hold that a lord could no longer revoke the fief or deny it to the vassal's son. It then appeared that its revenues and functions belonged more to the vassal than the lord, and that the obligations and payments the vassal owed were only the traditional tribute he paid for a property really his own. This was the situation when lawyers reappeared in the eleventh century to record a feudal contract that, thought to be very old, was in fact relatively new. Whereas in the past the agreement between lord and vassal had been short, expressed in an oath of all-out and full-time support that was at once vague and strong, now the agreement grew in length as it diminished in strength. The later contract specified how long a vassal should serve militarily at his own expense (forty days a year); how many times he had to go to the lord's court, or pay money aids for his ransom (one), his daughter's marriage (one), and so on. As ownership shifted and the fief moved to the center of a relationship once more purely personal, it became important to be exact about what was owed in order to be exact about what was *not* owed. Although vassalic obligations remained and would be important as a basis for later state-building, it is at least as important that the obligations were limited, that the fief appeared to belong to the vassal, and that intrusion into it by higher authority seemed to involve innovation, thus violation of the law and injustice. In this lay the basis for the idea of authority limited by law, the moral basis for rights against authority, for rights as protection of the individual.

It is worth keeping in mind too that the fief was not simply land. The fief was also jurisdiction, or public authority and government as those terms were then understood. Every vassal was a judge, always over his peasants and over his own vassals as well, if he had any. He was responsible too for military levies. Thus, when the fief was assimilated to the vassals' patrimony, so was much of what we think of as government. Government fragmented into small pieces was wholly confused with private property. This meant, of course, that when kings tried later to recover and centralize authority, their attempts would seem to be attacks on private property. And for the vassals, the feudal "rights" they would defend were very broad because notions of what constituted property were so broad.

If feudal decentralization gave rise to the first of the three controlling ideas of the Declaration of the Rights of Man, rights against authority, the long interaction of vassals with higher authorities in the process of feudal state-building contributed much to developing the other two. Feudal state-building was possible because rights continued to exist at all levels in the hierarchy, and the lord had as much right to the remaining vassalic obligations as did vassals to the strict limits on these obligations. By moving slowly, invoking need, and using persuasion, great lords, and especially kings as theoretical feudal overlords, were able bit by bit to expand their powers. A by-product of this process was the gradual association of liberty with participation, that is, with the involvement of an elite in making decisions. The initiative came from above. The strength of any seigneur after the tenth century depended on his having the physical and moral force such that his vassals, when called, would actually appear and share in "finding" the law, fighting, or both. The company of numerous and prominent vassals visibly helping to make a decision imposed itself on what passed then for public opinion, and implied the moral and physical force sufficient to execute the decision. Lords who were successful in gathering their vassals both built their own strength and launched a history that could end in constitutionalism and representation. For the vassal, of course, such participation carried a price: it diminished his independence, and he was expected to supply moral and material support to enforce the decision he helped to make. Thus, participation could be expensive the first time, and it also supplied a precedent that made similar support difficult to refuse in similar situations later. Once instituted and habitual, however, participation also became the guarantee that the rest of what was not specifically conceded to higher authority was secure in the hands of the participant. Sharing in power was a protection. Within developed feudalism, then, there appeared also the second of the two meanings of rights that we are after, that is, rights as participation.

Finally, there is equality. The sources for that idea are diverse. There was a Christian equality, but because its rewards and punishments were in another world, it is not entirely germane here. Certain ideas of equality appeared also in the system of discipline practiced in the schools from the late sixteenth and seventeenth centuries, and in various bureaucratic structures, especially military, after the mid- to late seventeenth century. Those practices, however, reflected a principle of *émulation* or competitive striving between individuals to determine some rank order or hierarchy based on merit. That sense of equality, although not inconsistent with democracy (it too is in the Declaration of Rights, Article 6), is not the one needed here. More relevant in this context is a notion of equality coming out of the later practices of feudal state-building. As with participation, the initiative came from above. When vassals assembled and opined, there had to be some way to know what the opinions added up to collectively. As feudal councils developed into larger representative bodies, that continued to be true. At some undefined point in the evolution, mere acclamation was not enough. To make hard, perhaps painful decisions, voting was necessary, along with the principle by which the vote of a majority carried the decision and bound the dissenting minority to it. But for votes to be counted and added together to form a majority, each vote had to be understood as exactly equal in nature to every other—qualitatively unequal votes can only be weighed or assessed, not counted. Further, for the minority to acquiesce in the decision of the majority required that the minority members perceive in the majority the same interests as their own. The strongest leaders and states were able to force into existence the representative institutions where majorities could decide, minorities accepted the decision, and the voice of representatives bound constituencies. For the system to work representation had to be by units understood to be equal to one another. When the important parts of society were too diverse for that kind of representation in a single body, the solution to the problem lay in a filtration of the elites into separate but internally homogeneous bodies. Thus, Lords and Commons in England, three estates in France, four in Sweden, and so on. However it was done, a principle of equality was essential to the functioning of the system.[2]

Three ideas, then, eventually converged. The result was not always a democracy—sometimes the ideas, through disuse, simply went away and were replaced by others; sometimes they were confined within an elite. Special circumstances were needed to spread the ideas widely and to give them a democratic twist. To understand those circumstances requires thinking about some features of French development that were both like and unlike models for development in other countries.

≺ II ≻

Paying for War: The French State
in Comparative Perspective

The modern European state was rooted in war. Or more precisely, in
meeting the costs of war, whose weight grew always heavier from the
late sixteenth century. Wherever states chose to compete by arms,
governments had to find resources for military establishments that
were making unprecedented demands. The demands were so large, in
fact, as to transform not only the problem but the states themselves.

The new financial situation, it appears, came from the convergence of several causes. First, armed forces increased in sheer size. In
the case of France the army numbering not more than 50,000 in the
1550s attained wartime peaks of 150,000 in the 1630s and the extraordinary figure of 400,000 for a short time in the War of the Spanish Succession and again in the Seven Years War. To the army must be added
the navy, Richelieu's and Colbert's creation in the seventeenth century. But the mere growth in numbers of men under arms does not tell
the whole story of cost. Men by themselves, after all, were relatively
cheap. The more serious problem was that changes in the nature of
warfare drove up the overhead expenditure.

With naval warfare the point is obvious: investing in, maintaining,
and supplying ships added high fixed costs disproportionate to the
number of men involved. But in France the larger share of the rapidly
expanding expenditures went to the army. The reason lay in the new
tactical formations at the heart of Michael Roberts's long "military
revolution" completed toward 1660.[3] As battle squares of massed soldiers gave way to fighting in long, thin lines stretching over several
miles, the linear formations demanded a new soldier. That soldier had
to have knowledge and a kind of conditioning; he should respond to
orders almost reflexively, moving quickly from marching column to
line in varying situations. Constant drill was an obsession, along with
discipline—how much easier to break and run when facing the
enemy in a line only three deep. The way to form good soldiers was to
work on them intensively in numerous and small training units. Each
of those units needed higher personnel with experience, who served
long only with pay and the prospect of pensions. Once trained, the soldier was valuable; he had then to be kept the year round and, so far as
possible, insulated from the surrounding society—thus barracks, and

uniforms that made deserting difficult. In war the new army lived not off the land but in camps, and there it had to be supplied: tents and beds for officers; food, wine, and water for everyone; ovens to cook 50,000 or more loaves of bread a day; vast quantities of forage for a dense population of horses. Often the supplies had to come from home, raising questions of transport for long, heavy baggage trains. From these needs in France came a program from the 1680s to build and keep open military roads to the theaters of war. Fortresses too were built or rebuilt in large numbers, mainly to protect the lines of supply. With fortresses of course came garrisons, a much larger artillery, and more engineers who understood sieges. To oversee and coordinate it all, and to keep the voluminous records, there appeared a rapidly expanding bureaucracy of civilians.

And so, regular costs for armed forces went up rapidly, and even in peacetime they were the main object of government spending. In France, through most of the seventeenth and the entire eighteenth century the armed forces never absorbed less than 60 percent of annual non-debt expenditure in peacetime. In war military spending took over 80 percent of the then-expanded outlay (again exclusive of debt payments), and ran at a level about twice as high as in peace. That doubling of military costs obviously made the frequency and duration of wars matter enormously, and it is easy to imagine the strain on resources in a world where war continued to be as common as peace. Under Louis XIV, during the second half of Louis XV's reign, and under Louis XVI, France was at war about one year in two. And when the French were fighting, of course, so normally were the British, the Hapsburgs, and the other European powers.

The result was an arms race, regular war, and huge expense. There were dropouts from the race—the Spanish in the seventeenth century, the Poles in the eighteenth—but most states believed they had to compete. As if to validate Machiavelli's dictum that the more one looks at his enemy the more one resembles him, they fielded armies and sometimes launched navies that were recognizably alike in their organization, equipment, and new demands on society. By a process of imitation the warring states began to borrow practices and forms from one another, and to build heavy military and administrative superstructures. But for language, the personnel in one might have moved to another without noting large differences between war offices, proliferating *bureaux*, and training camps where war was the business.

The picture is different, however, when one begins to examine how the states that were to compete, or even to survive independently, tried to support their military establishments. Those states had to extract resources from poor societies and to concentrate a much larger share of the resources on military and related administrative expenditure. The needs were modern, the resources were not. From this central fact came policies and practices that historians have identified as Mercantilism.

Mercantilism, defined loosely as the states' efforts to find the new resources they needed, was never a single body or thing. It varied from place to place with the different characteristics of societies; it was the *ad hoc* arrangements that worked not here and there, but here as opposed to there. For rulers and their ministers were in a hurry, concerned less to transform their societies according to universal principles and some fixed model than to field an army for the coming campaign. They grabbed what they could and quickly, and in doing so, they came to terms with the distinctive cultures to which they also belonged. The problem of finding the means for war, confronted almost simultaneously in societies that were very uneven and unequal, in fact had the effect of reinforcing differences between them, freezing old ones and creating new ones. In contrast to administrative and military development, there was no single path to social modernity.

In Eastern Europe, in the absence of important mercantile and urban wealth, the bureaucratization and militarization of nobilities and a deepening serfdom were a cheap if brutalizing response to the problem. Serfdom, of course, had appeared earlier, as a tendency everywhere east of the Elbe since the late Middle Ages. In that non-Malthusian world of thin, scattered populations and plentiful land which even the periods of early modern demographic growth could not fill, serfdom reflected the efforts of an agrarian elite to fix and to control a scarce labor supply. Poland had serfdom, even though by the eighteenth century it had almost no state. But wherever in the east the new state did grow, it reinforced and spread peasant servitude. In regions lacking mobile wealth, where taxes grew heavier without producing much and credit operations were impossible, the state was unable to pay cash for the large and permanent army and the apparatus to maintain it. The only alternative was to use force, and to redefine social and economic obligation and legal status in terms the state could use. For many peasants, especially in Russia, this meant adding to forced labor for their masters that for the state, as in building Saint Petersburg and a navy, or making iron in the Urals. At best it was likely to mean the requisitioning of their grain and unpaid military service added to already heavy seigneurial obligations.

But no less important than serfdom is that in the statist societies of Eastern Europe the model of servitude spread upward, with the difference that in the upper ranks it was called service. Toward 1600 in the poorer Prussian lands a pacifist and constitutionalist nobility had been using representative institutions to dictate to rulers; by the eighteenth century most of that nobility was already formed into the well-known body whose highest allegiance was to the state and whose members found prestige in carrying out orders. Thus transformed, nobilities could be trusted to do locally what more expensive civilian bureaucracies might do in the west. And the nobles, once secure in their revenues and control at that level, could accept and internalize the state's new definition of their role, especially the military role. In Russia by the mid-eighteenth century it was thought a reform when the noble's required service for the army was reduced to only twenty-five years. And it was Prussia and Russia that early in the eighteenth century issued Tables of Ranks defining and grading social standing by state service, thereby implying that with failure to serve that standing might disappear. If the reality was not quite that, it is nonetheless clear that new practices and ideas were being formed that did not resemble those in the west. In the military regimes to the east the state was acting directly on society, to force and to shape it in its own image. Unable to buy an army, the states had either to abandon the race or to generate a military force cheaply by tightening bonds of subordination and trying to militarize the society. Independent rights and the institutions to express them were a luxury no longer conceived.

But in the west resources were different and other solutions possible. A denser population—by comparison to the east, much of the west *was* Malthusian—meant that force, applied internally, was more for repressing disturbances than to compel service. There, where people were plentiful, the free market in persons and competition for subsistence guaranteed tenants to landowners and cheap labor to manufacturers. For the state this was both threat and opportunity: from the prosperity of the landowners might come renewed feudal disorder; from the affluence of the manufacturers came expanding cities and a new kind of wealth to use. What was clear, however, was that these societies had resources that the state could hope to draw on to finance armed forces. But how to do it? One part of the answer, but only a part, was new and heavier taxes. Levied first on persons accustomed to paying, and increasingly, toward the end of the seventeenth century, on the landed elite as well, they raised state revenues dramatically. But the limits to taxation were reflected in popular rebellions, in the irritation and active or passive resistance of the upper classes, and at times, also, in the sheer exhaustion of resources to tax. And the state was insatiable, as the cost of its enterprise went up. In that age of chronic warfare the state could not live on taxes alone. The solution—the one that fundamentally distinguished west from east—lay in the availability of the mobile wealth that, if nowhere taxed very effectively, could be borrowed. In the west states could buy the men and supplies they needed for war, even if they had to pay for them on time. Here they could finance the military establishment through credit, building large and ever growing royal or national debts on an unprecedented scale.

It was England that did this most conspicuously and successfully, establishing a structure of state credit on its new constitution and parliamentary system at the end of the seventeenth century. Heavier indirect taxes and the new Land Tax were not nearly enough. With budget deficits a way of life, the solution was to borrow, and regularly. New taxes were levied in part to assure payment of the interest on a permanent state debt, soon called "national." P.G.M. Dickson's study of the "financial revolution" shows all this in rich detail, how from the 1690s the British developed techniques and practices of public borrowing that allowed them to raise sums entirely disproportionate to their annual tax revenues.[4] Nor did the heavy borrowing imply a government in distress—when needed in the eighteenth century, the money was gotten quickly and easily, at ever lower rates of interest. From the 10 percent that the hard-pressed Crown once paid, the rate of interest fell in stages to 3 percent by the 1730s, and thereafter it never rose often or very much.[5] Even so, investors at home, and the Dutch as well, appeared eager to place funds with the English state for a low return. For the government that was essential, the interest on its debt a burden it could bear. Public credit did for England what bureaucratization and militarization did for the emerging east European states.

Many in England, and a few elsewhere, recognized at the time that the bases of that system of public credit were political and constitutional. The Revolution of 1688 was more than accidentally related to its development. Seen in one way, of course, that revolution was no more than the seizure of power by English landed groups resembling the French middle and upper noblesse. But far more important here is that the constitutional settlement gave rise to institutions and attitudes that, while limiting the Crown, strengthened the state. Not all landed aristocracies were capable of that. The explanation seems to lie in a long past conditioned by two features, the precocious power of the Crown in a relatively unified realm and the slowly growing participation by the elite. Here was the classic case of feudal state-building. Norman kings, as invaders visible to their followers and applying the practices they brought from politically-advanced Normandy, had considerable advantages. They saw vassals, made royal needs clear, and forced into existence the representative institutions that could help. Because the English feudal state was relatively strong and unified, eventually those institutions became national. Their use strengthened Tudor "despots," and the inability to use them is what fatally weakened the early Stuarts.

English development, of course, was far from smooth. The king's bad will or seeming innovation easily aroused the indignation and resistance of conservative and touchy vassals. It was not hard for some or all of the elite to imagine that the king demanded too much, overstepped his bounds, and violated law. There were renewed conflicts over rights, and episodic violence that became collective as Parliament's role expanded in the late medieval and early modern periods. Such battles between kings and parts of elites, however, were not uniquely British.

What *was* uniquely British, and here very important, is the widespread and routine assumption that the existence of the state and national community was normal. Conditioned alike by their past, all parties to even violent conflict shared that view, which did not even require stating. The dialogue of politics and, later, of revolution simply supposed it. If the central issues in England were persistent and not at all trivial—despotism, what limits to set on king and state—they were comparatively narrow in their range. From very early the British could assume the functioning community whose establishment was at issue on the Continent. Sure early that state power was real, and that in one way or another it would be exercised, they debated and fought over its form and organization, absolutist or constitutional and representative. More than economic development, it is this central political and institutional fact that explains why the first modern revolution (despite its seemingly archaic ideology) came in the mid-seventeenth century to England alone—throughout that country men knew what had to be controlled or seized, and that the state's organization or form dictated how, not if, its power was to be felt.

In 1688 the resistance that was as national as the Crown won finally and definitively. The triumph of constitutionalism was the triumph of the landed elite, which proceeded to root itself in the very structure of the state. Now this elite was no longer willing, as in the old days, merely to react to decisions already made and to confine its role to consenting or resisting. Henceforth through Parliament it would itself make the decisions, or share actively in making them, even administrative ones. The German kings arrived in the eighteenth century to discover laws that limited the kinds of wars they might fight. Above all, Parliament controlled taxation and the purposes for which it was raised. The Crown's sometimes successful efforts to get its own way by corrupting and buying members of Parliament in a sense reflect the same reality, for the kings knew where power lay and had now a shrewd sense of what needed to be bought. But this triumph of the elite, as noted above, did not weaken the state. The heated and extended rhetoric and new laws that guaranteed the rights of individuals against the state should not obscure this, for in England those rights did not extend into areas that might hinder the state's work. In fact, individual rights once assured, the rest and main part of what this aristocracy called liberty seemed in line with what the state needed. In short, rights as protection or independence seemed reasonably harmonious with rights as participation.

The English, then, defined a part of their liberty within the national community. That liberty meant participation as much as it did independence. One might even say that the English elite lived by the habits and attitudes that Rousseau announced later, although then for whole nations rather than elites: liberty is obedience to a law that we prescribe to ourselves. Lest this sound too abstract and idealistic, we should note quickly that those attitudes were visible in works and had practical effect. Having set down fundamental laws, assured in its control and able to apply the policies designed for its interests (imperialism, a large navy, regular war with France), the national corporation of the propertied proceeded to impose on itself heavy taxes that were perceived as consistent with the elite's peculiar understanding of liberty. The Land Tax, voted in the 1690s, required that squires pay to the state an additional one-fifth of their incomes from land. There was grumbling, but what astonishes is that most paid it and the tax became permanent. When men like themselves, the elected directors of the corporation, acted in Parliament, there was now no mental basis for resisting. Throughout the land the propertied were at last within the corporation, limited and constrained by laws perceived to be of their own making.

And so, it might now be said that the British elite had developed habits that implied belief in two of the three general principles that were in the French Declaration of 1789, that is, in the two meanings of liberty. The third principle, equality, was similarly implicit in the system of representation arising within late feudal state-building. At the level of those voting for representatives were not just people, but people on larger properties, the more or less equal holders of one or more whole pieces on the checkerboard of land that made up the political establishment. Then, in Parliament, the system of voting supposed equality between members within each of two Houses. Persons who were not equal, that is, the overwhelming majority of the population, were simply unseen and read out of the system. The political system was no doubt messier than I am making it sound. There was corruption, faction, party divisions, the things British historians tell us about. For all that, seen from across the channel, the operating principles not of British society as a whole, but of and within the political elite alone, in fact look quite democratic. All the essential ideas were there.

The consequences of the long evolution into "elite democracy" were several. One is easier to identify than another. Aristocratic democracy prepared the transformation of public credit that made the English the strongest state in eighteenth-century Europe. With the decision to create a national debt after 1688, and the establishment of the Bank of England, the credit machinery was in place. What made it run, however, was that Parliament guaranteed it, assuring investors that the interest would be paid and that the capital was secure. From the 1690s confidence spread in the investing public.[6] Investors could see in Parliament men of property like themselves debating issues openly and participating in making, or at least checking, the decisions that mattered. Above all, the Parliament that spoke for them oversaw the budget and controlled taxes which its members themselves paid. There was the guarantee that underlay the formal assurances—real power exercised by men who could not repudiate a national debt without denying principles of property and rights that conditioned equally their own thinking and interests. It was they collectively, not individuals, who could and would vote to raise the levers of taxation to see that investors were paid, making certain that nothing happened to their money and its promised return. Secure in this feeling, investors accepted the ever lower rates of interest.

At the top, then, was a real community of the well-to-do having its own general will. Some members were representatives; all at least voted. They projected an image of responsibility. Together they formed the community that permitted the state to live by borrowing the wealth its subjects produced. But what did that "success" story at the top mean for the whole society? Here is another consequence of England's institutional evolution. In England a precociously strong state made possible the "liberal" state that could stand back, free its economy, and avoid much direct intervention in the society, that is, intervention to shape the society in ways needed to serve the state. The self-operating society of investors was quite adequate to the purpose. For this reason the English government failed to follow lines of policy through which, as we shall see, the state in France actively, if often unintentionally, formed society there. Successive governments in France, lacking a Parliament and thus a guarantee to investors that their interest would be paid (in full and approximately on time), were led for reasons of state credit to create and steadily to reinforce the honeycomb of corporate institutions that covered the country. Then, once committed to that system, the French state could not be indifferent to the fate of those bodies.

To understand the appearance of contrasting forms in government and society in France, it is useful to look more closely at the distinguishing marks of French problems and development. The problems of the French state were the same as elsewhere, larger in scale because its aims—maritime and imperialist as well as traditionally continental and military—were more diverse. Yet its resources were larger too. As late as 1750 one of every five to six Europeans was French; the country was densely populated and comparatively rich. With these resources France should have been able to solve the problem of how to support the new military and administrative structures, and fairly effectively. But how was it to be done? The east European model for the interaction of state and society does not fit, no matter that the French state was absolutist in form. French absolutism never acted on society so directly, never shaped a culture in which service and obedience replaced rights. For no matter its form, the French state was in a society that had other resources to draw on, provided other options. By contrast to Eastern Europe, and like England, France had important cities and much mercantile, as well as agrarian, wealth. Thus, like England also, it had a population whose money it might borrow. In the end it is the English case that is germane.

But that parallel is not exact. The English, as just noted, used finally a constitutional and parliamentary system to supply taxes and credit, but such mechanisms did not exist in France. There was no French Parliament, nor did the persons who counted want one. They had instead a deep distrust of English-style constitutionalism that seemed to them dangerous and retrograde. The strength of those feelings and reasons for them emerge from the two national histories, so similar in many ways yet diverging permanently at critical points. The lessons of the past would be different in France.

If local political development in the two feudalized countries began almost simultaneously—that in England was no more than an offshoot from Normandy's—the national states grew at different times, France's later. That timing posed problems that were to leave a large legacy in habits and ideas. In the eleventh and twelfth centuries, when the feudal state was being implanted through the whole country in England, similarly compact and reasonably uniform states (for the day) appeared in France, but within provinces where they crystallized around local leaders instead of the then inconspicuous king. After Normandy came a number of others, including the king's own "province" in the Ile de France. This meant that when from the late twelfth century the royal state did begin to expand and slowly to become national, the king took over units that were already formed, where laws, customs, and identities had hardened and been fixed. The elite with which kings had later to deal comprised men who were Normans or Burgundians before they were French, and whose liberties under the feudal contract were provincial or even more local in origin. For the king this was partly an advantage in that resistance to him, when it came, was unlikely to be massive. Habits of cooperation between provinces, each with its own varying rights, laws, and identity, were slow to develop, and individual provinces could be appeased or pacified in sequence.

But the disadvantages for the state are equally obvious. In France, assemblies of the elite from throughout the country were difficult to convoke, and even when they began to meet more regularly in the late thirteenth and early fourteenth centuries, they did not become representative bodies of deputies who made decisions and whose consent bound constituencies at home. Unlike the English Parliament, these assemblies remained devices for public relations, for giving publicity to the king's need and the aid he required. The serious negotiations took place later, at the local level, where a single policy could not fit all cases. There the privileges and liberties for whose confirmation individuals and communities might be persuaded or forced to pay again and again were bewildering in their variety. Local law and circumstance dictated the highly variable amounts of money that could be extracted. In addition, by developing when it did, the wider royal state had not only constraints but opportunities not present in England earlier. By then law faculties were supplying the men and a revived money economy the means that permitted the Crown to buy the services of a bureaucratic personnel able to conduct the negotiations. The earliest and small beginning of bureaucratization gave an alternative, a way of getting at the country that would not have existed if the French national state had been formed at the same time as the English. In France royal officials could imagine by-passing the elite. It is this that underlay the drift toward the famous late medieval bargain described by Tocqueville, the tacit understanding by which the elite gave up pretensions to political participation in exchange for privilege, exemptions, the right not to be taxed.

Even so, the sixteenth and early seventeenth centuries seemed to offer the possibility that French and English forms might converge. Population growth and rising rents from land shifted greater wealth and power to the rural elite, and it appeared that the state might have to come to terms with that elite, conceding it a share of political power in return for its support and the use of its resources. Notions of contract, the king fully under law, and an attenuated popular sovereignty for which the magistracy was to speak were all bandied about. But so was the idea of tyrannicide, not easily distinguishable from simple regicide. And in the end the ideas would seem subversive, discredited by being linked with what later generations imagined as perhaps their nation's darkest hour. The long civil and religious wars, that seemed to tear apart and nearly to destroy France, horrified posterity, and in the eighteenth century popular histories, those in almanachs, for example, dwelt still on the terror, the arson, murders, and brutality. In that context ideas of constitutionalism and representation sounded selfish or worse, a cover for dark and unworthy motives. What evidently saved France, and only with the greatest difficulty, was a series of strong kings and the absolute state. What worked in England—a Parliament and government operating by negotiation, national elites participating by right in forming decisions—to the French those things seemed out of a past better forgotten. In fact, it was the terrible events of the 1640s in England that were most consistent with French expectations. Revolution and civil war followed inevitably whenever two equal powers, king and Parliament, coexisted in a state. The Parlement of Paris grew furious when its enemies compared it to Parliament. Naturally the absolutist administrators and financiers shared the perception, and Mazarin impressed it permanently in the mind of his pupil, the young Louis XIV.[7] In France, the felt need was for integration, and national representation seemed disintegrating.

≺ III ≻

Royal Borrowing: Building the Old Regime

With or without a national representative body, however, French kings would have to borrow. From the 1550s to 1789, every year brought a budget deficit, vast in war and still large in peace. The result was the need for loans on a wholly new scale. But borrowing directly from the public posed problems for the king. Short-term loans were usually available, but insufficient. Financial officers issued notes payable on specific revenues in three or six months, and in quiet times the notes were renewed easily and circulated like currency. Used in moderation, short-term loans were as effective in France as elsewhere. But in periods of financial crisis officials wrote more and more notes, so many that finally it was obvious to holders that most could not be paid. Then, with the value of the paper plummeting, it was useless to write more. That situation of depreciated paper always announced some kind of bankruptcy. Collapse followed the government's efforts to stretch short-term loans and to make them do what they were not suited for, that is, stand in the place of long-term loans.

Those failed efforts, in turn, take us to the fundamental flaw in royal credit—the inadequacy of long-term borrowing.

That inadequacy was structural and built into the regime. Although absolutism made the king powerful in some ways, it could not make him a good credit risk. Without a Parliament he was free to administer as he wished. Unfortunately for his credit, he was also free not to pay his creditors. From the sixteenth century the king contracted long-term loans by selling his bonds (*rentes*) directly to the public through the Hôtel de Ville of Paris. But under repeated pressure royal governments first delayed paying the interest, then arbitrarily reduced its rate, and sometimes reduced also the capital. No representative body defended the investors. But lenders to the king did have a recourse: the lesson they learned was to advance him no fresh funds except at interest rates that reflected the risk they ran. Through the eighteenth century the French king's long-term borrowing directly from the public was at about double the rate of interest that English governments paid, and double the rate also at which individuals other than kings could find money in France on the security of real property. The result for the French state was a permanent and circular problem: lack of confidence among lenders made interest charges heavy, the heavier charges in turn added to deficits, larger deficits caused additional borrowing at high rates, snowballing debt charges finally set off the next bankruptcy, and the bankruptcy renewed investors' fears and led to higher interest. When debt charges of all kinds regularly absorbed between one-third and two-thirds of the royal revenues (the smaller share each time after a new bankruptcy), the interest rate was a critical matter. Perhaps there was no way out. In any event, it is certain that absolutism and state credit did not mix well.

Even so, the old order lasted until 1789. Although bankruptcies came at intervals, they did not come every year. It may be useful, therefore, to recast a large question. We are accustomed to asking why the Old Regime ended, but here it is equally interesting to ask why, in spite of everything, it survived as long as it did. The explanation is not obvious. Finding it requires looking beneath the surface to identify a large number of sources for low-cost state credit that are easy to overlook. Governments found ways to supplement regular loans with others that cost less and were slower to dry up in difficult times. Those loans, often disguised as something else, are usually called "expedients." Together they grew into a system by which the king borrowed through intermediaries, through persons and bodies whose credit with the lending public was stronger than his. This system, which provided roughly one-third of total state borrowing and at a rate of interest well below what the English paid, does much to explain how the regime weathered its financial storms so long.[8]

Beyond the use of intermediaries, the system relied in varying ways on three other operating principles: the creation or strengthening of privilege, the alienating of royal revenues, and the forming or reinforcement of corps. Consider the three in sequence. Privilege was of course the legal guarantee of favors. It often consisted in exemptions from the taxes and fees paid by others, sometimes in direct access to a higher court for a lawsuit, or a prominent rank when marching in processions. Some privileges gave the exclusive right to an occupation: collecting taxes or fees, judging, administering, manufacturing, and selling. Usually such functions were embedded in venal offices, but not always. Guild masters by the tens of thousands owned monopoly rights to make and sell things in designated markets without purchasing offices. Privilege could come from a place of residence or from membership in the clergy. But diverse as they were, all privileges were alike in being a property. And because this was a kind of property that kings could make (and unmake), it is perhaps not surprising that privilege came to play a large role in royal finance and credit. Practiced administrators knew that privilege was useful at two levels. First, individuals or groups advancing capital to acquire or preserve revenues and property would pay more, or accept a lower interest, if privileges were included. And the same persons or groups, once enjoying privileges, would pay again and again to buy off threats of revocation and to have their special rights reaffirmed. At the one level there appeared over time a large body of creditors who, having advanced capital directly to the king for one thing or another, received a part of their interest in the form of privileges. Then, at a second level, were the larger number of people from whom the privileged persons borrowed in turn. The privileged, as intermediaries between the king and that larger lending public, borrowed on their own credit the funds to make up the price required by the king for a purchase or confirmation. Because at most times the intermediaries' credit was good, the king could demand and get large sums exceeding the personal means of his direct creditors. French kings, far from struggling against privilege, found in it a resource they could not do without.

The next operating principle was the alienation of various royal revenues, old and new. The idea was to assign a revenue as the permanent interest on capital advanced right away. The king retained the right to recover the revenue by paying back the capital, but because his need was always to borrow more, he did not normally reimburse anything. Lenders found the arrangement advantageous because, rather than depending on the king's good will for the payment of their interest, they often controlled the source of that payment themselves. The interest rate varied by period, by the security of the revenue, and by the extent of other advantages (such as privileges) that supplemented or partially replaced the payment in money. The large and better-known regular taxes, heavily alienated in the past, were easily diverted and inspired little confidence; they were not much used to secure new loans through privileged intermediaries after the great bankruptcy that ran from 1709 to 1726. Only the collectors advanced capital against the direct taxes (for the purchase of expensive offices) and received for interest a small percentage added permanently to those taxes. The indirect taxes were partially committed to the payment of a low and badly-paid interest (called *gages*) on the investments of all magistrates and some administrators in offices.

Almost entirely alienated were the revenues belonging to the king as theoretical feudal overlord. The essence of feudal monarchy was justice, and in the growing royal court system lay a great financial opportunity. The courts were ever busier. No doubt some of the increase in business would have occurred anyway, as jurisdictions penetrated deeper into society to regulate and record affairs involving businesses, land transactions, families, and so on. That happened almost everywhere in the west. But in France, with its multiplying privileges and other distinctive properties, such as offices, there were more legal acts to record and more possibilities for dispute. The society was highly litigious. Indeed, the king had done much to make it so, selling to one person or group the right to collect a fee or tax, and to another person or group the right to be exempt from it. Both sides were frequently in court, and a judgment was less an ending than the occasion for opening a series of appeals that lasted for years. In all the litigating, and even in the mere recording, there was work for an army of people who were not judges. They were attorneys (*procureurs*), court clerks, sergeants-at-arms and process servers, auctioneers of movable and immovable goods, treasurers to hold funds pending the court's decision, keepers of accounts, inspectors of keepers of accounts, the ubiquitous notaries, and others. For each function only the king could authorize the activity and fees to be paid. If he had chosen to do it, he could have paid officials a salary to do the work, and thereby have kept the revenues for himself. Instead he created and sold offices for each kind of work, and in the process alienated the multiple revenues permanently to officers in exchange for capital sums that, like the rest, entered into the royal debt.

Under the heading of capitalized royal revenues might be put also at least one that the king had never in fact possessed, but that, following the example of fellow monarchs, he might have taken over and made his own. That unrealized revenue was the tax never imposed on the lands and income of the clergy. The government thought it better to leave that revenue in the hands of the clergy, to let the clergy tax itself, and to have it use a large part of the proceeds to pay the interest on loans that the corps contracted for the king. In this sense, the clergy was a kind of self-funding royal bank. The operations of provincial estates and municipalities were much the same. By constantly renewed contracts with the king the estates of Languedoc, for example, had the right to collect the direct taxes in the province. Most of the yield went, in turn, to pay interest and reimbursements on funds owed by the province in the king's behalf. The portion left to cities from the dues (octrois) levied on goods entering or leaving a municipality was in part for the support of debts that were really the king's. Wherever one looks, money that might have shown up as disposable income in an annual royal budget was funneled through individuals and corps, large and small, to sustain payments on loans.

This takes us to the ubiquitous corps. They included the clergy, local estates, municipalities, hundreds of bodies of officeholders, thousands of guilds. The survival of so many privileged bodies through the era of the Enlightenment seems anachronistic, until one notices their unspecified and modern role in state credit. The corps lent to the king, and outside investors lent to the corps, all at rates of interest that even the English had to envy. Authorized in each case by the king, the corps governed themselves, living by constitutions or statutes set into letters patent and registered in the courts. The statutes regulated how the administrators or leaders were chosen, often by fellow members in an election. Those leaders, usually called *sindics*, ran the corps' affairs in consultation with their colleagues, who assembled periodically to review routine operations or to decide special matters as they arose. Decisions were by majority vote among equal members. The bodies ranged enormously in size, from the very large clergy through still-substantial corps—the silkworkers at Lyon numbered 6000 or more—down to middle-sized corps of office owners and municipalities, reaching finally at the lower end some smalltown guilds with a handful or less of master artisans. Governance in the very large corps and some of the others was oligarchical, but within themselves the oligarchies operated by practices essentially the same as in the democratically-run middling and small bodies.

The corps were invaluable to governments needing to borrow in a hurry. First, the members were vulnerable to threats to their privileges and related property, and then, because clustered in corps, they were also accessible to a state unable to track down scattered individuals. At intervals the government approached the corps with demands for fresh capital in return for new privileges, additional revenues, or merely the confirmation of existing rights. The minister or his agent opened talks with the *sindic,* and each side began by explaining its needs and pleading limited resources. The negotiators made offers and counter-proposals, and after a time arrived at some tentative agreement. Ordinarily they compromised on a sum set somewhere below the state's original demands but above what the corps first said it could pay. In fact, both parties had a stake in fixing an amount that they believed the members could raise quickly. A good deal of realism went into the discussion. The *sindic* then took the proposal to the assembly. There the members of the corps, already informed of developments by the *sindic,* proceeded to debate, to vote, and usually to ratify the agreement. By the terms of that agreement the government then knew how much it was supposed to receive, and when the money should arrive. And because the commitment to paying was collective and corporate, the government did not face the difficult problem of dealing with individual members who did not pay or paid late. That task belonged entirely to the corps.

But all that was only on paper. What mechanism assured that the funds agreed on would actually come in? Here is where the corps' organization had a further and profound effect. More than merely convenient for negotiating agreements, the corps imposed, and members absorbed, a kind of discipline that guaranteed payment by most. It was crucial to the success of the operation that the decision to advance the capital was collective, that the corps as a whole obligated itself to getting the money together, and that the decision was taken by majority vote among equal members. This was the procedure that gave legitimacy to coercion. There was of course a good interest-based incentive impelling the majority to apply pressure to laggards. Unpaid sums might otherwise be spread as an additional charge on those who had already paid. But the effect of the procedures was also moral, and thus practical in a different sense. Because the vote in the corps was among equals—within the corps all full members voted and all had precisely the same interest to protect—the majority had no qualms about generalizing their will and imposing it on dissidents. And on the other side it was difficult to resist the decision made by a majority composed of persons just like oneself. In this situation anyone refusing to pay could not charge the decision-making authority with ill will or opposing interests or failure to understand. As a result, the number of members who did not pay was quite small. What emerges within the particularist French corps is the operation of democratic and communitarian principles resembling those at work in the British political elite.

One piece completed the structure of French state credit built on corps. The corps borrowed directly from the public. As individuals, of course, members of certain corps often borrowed the capital they needed from friends or relatives. They did this on the security of real property, like an office they might have just purchased. But when times were bad and money scarce, even normally solvent and credit-worthy members with the best of intentions were unable to find enough of their own or others' cash to meet the state's demands. It was then that the corps, acting as a unit and a legal person, intervened. It sold its own bonds to outsiders, and established a loan in the name of all the members jointly. In this way the corps simultaneously eased the burden on financially-distressed members and supplied the whole of the promised funds to the king. In return the government assigned something of value to the corps, so that it could pay the interest on the collective loan. Sometimes the new resource was additional gages, paid this time not to individuals but directly to the institution. In other cases the officers obtained increases in the state-regulated fees that clients had to pay them, and the increases were then pooled to make a fund for paying the corps' creditors. With the corps whose members did not actually own their places or borrow for the king individually—clergy, provincial estates (sometimes), and others—all the loans were corporate. For their capital advances those corps obtained regular confirmations of their privileges in contracts that also renewed their rights to collect various taxes. From about the mid-seventeenth century, then, the corps themselves, and not just their members, were instruments of state credit, their corporate debts largely the debts of the king.

To understand the success of the corps in mobilizing credit in a wider public, however, it is the perspective of the investor that matters. What made the corps seem an attractive and safe location for investing one's funds? Consider first the kinds of guarantees found in the corps whose members owned offices. On entry, the newcomer signed a register affirming his equal responsibility with the other members for supporting the collective loans, an obligation that remained so long as he belonged to the corps. That responsibility did not extend to everything he owned—the corps developed very early the practice of limited liability—but the value of his and the others' offices and any gages still owing formed a visible and large collateral that stood behind the loan and reassured lenders. Since total default by a corps was unlikely—it never happened, so far as I know—the real risk was non-payment or late payment of interest, especially by those corps that depended on gages coming from the king. But here too the risk was slight: the corps had to pay its creditors even if the king did not pay the corps. The assurance of payment lay in the collective governance of the corps by assemblies. In a crisis the members met and voted to assess themselves the sums needed to make up the amount owing to the corps' creditors. What impressed investors was the mechanism for making decisions that were collective, binding on all by majority vote. The decision appeared to express the self-interest of privileged officers who acted in a rational and orderly way. The procedure ruled out actions that were idiosyncratic, possibly tied to transitory passions of small factions or individual dissidents. The very impersonality of the decision-making was critical. For investors, lending to the corps seemed far safer than lending to willful and often unpredictable individuals, even (or especially) a king.

Corps whose members did not receive gages inspired equal or greater confidence. In them too the members (some or all) met in assemblies to discuss and vote, and to oversee the corps' financial situation which included payment of interest on corporate loans. The members of those corps did not ordinarily have to dip into their own pockets to deal with crises set off by the king's failure to pay. Their corporate incomes came instead from revenues that did not depend on the king. The corps composed of officers who lived on fees from clients took a share of those fees. Guilds received their revenues from entry fees. The clergy imposed taxes (*décimes*) on its own members, and the taxes collected by provincial estates were guaranteed to them by contracts with the king. In these cases the investors' money and the interest on it seemed safe because the corps not only ran its own affairs but controlled its income independently.

What emerges, then, is the curious situation in France where a modern kind of investment led to extending and reinforcing the seemingly traditional, even "feudal," regime of privilege and corps. To complete the analysis, return for a moment to privilege. For their capital the possessors of privilege knew they were entitled to various revenues. But threats to revenues, and to roles and even exemptions, were frequent. They came variously from interlopers who sought the income without paying and the function without expertise; from other corps to whom the government sold overlapping functions; and from a state whose administrators undermined old exemptions and tried sometimes to recover its mortgaged revenues without any or much reimbursement or to open occupations to a kind of free market in persons. The threats and attacks then promptly and inevitably activated the further feature of privilege, namely, that it was generally (except for noble privilege) embedded in independent corps. The corps organized to resist attacks on privilege, and took their causes into the king's own courts to protect themselves. From this came some of the frequently noted and troublesome characteristics of the old society— egoistic corps everywhere in noisy conflict, defending selfish privilege and obstructing the "public interest."

But what is easily missed in this description of conflict and blockage is that those were precisely the conditions that comforted investors. For it was the combativeness of the corps, their resistance to intruders from outside or above, that in preserving their own privilege protected also the investments of the lenders to the corps. Thus, it was the old or "feudal" order that often provided an essential mechanism for mobilizing royal credit in an expanding capitalist economy. It is highly doubtful that a regime simultaneously absolutist and more individualist could have done the same.

The system of credit built on the regime of privilege and corps was, therefore, a technical success. It provided one-third or more of the loans that the state had to have, many of them in difficult times when another kind of borrowing was impossible. It also supplied the funds at a remarkably low rate of interest. A survey in 1779 showed that the net annual charge to the state for 600 million livres invested in offices was only about 1 percent (omitting, of course, the cost in privileges).[9] Much of that, however, was for old capital, and what eighteenth-century governments always needed was fresh funds. Again the figure is striking: as intermediaries, the corps borrowed at 4½ percent to 5 percent the new money for which the king by himself had to pay nearly 10 percent. A further sign of the corps' strong credit was that through the century, even to the end, those bodies reimbursed the full face value of their bonds to any holder who asked for it.

The result, then, was the spread and reinforcement of the corps. To investors, they looked like so many thousands of mini-parliaments, each operating by most of the practices that established credit on a national scale across the channel. In both countries corporate institutions reduced the risk to lenders by eliminating the personal and arbitrary element from the management of money. But, of course, the difference between France and England is more obvious than the similarity. Here were two states seeking a common end—borrowing for war—in societies with kinds of resources that were roughly alike. But because the governing regimes were different, constitutionalist-representative as opposed to absolutist, the states, when acting on the societies, developed them in opposite directions, the one toward individualism and the other more deeply into the society of corps and privilege.

Several illustrations will complete the comparison. One is already evident and requires only to be stated: France had more than 50,000 officials owning offices and clustered in corps; England had no system of venal offices at all. A second example is in the diametrically opposed evolutions of the two national clergies. Until the 1660s both the English and French clergies were corps; both were governed in autonomous representative assemblies (that in England was called Convocation); each taxed itself separately from the rest of society and made independent contributions to the Crown. Then in England, in 1664, the clergy quietly made a deal and gave up its separate taxation.[10] Henceforth a clergyman paid the same taxes as his fellow subjects, and participated, or failed to participate, in political life as an individual, like everyone else. That deal pleased Parliament which, reaching to monopolize the grant of revenues to the king, no longer had to fear Convocation's passing money to a king on its own (as it had to the "tyrant" Charles I in 1639). This was the situation in which the eighteenth-century clergy could dissolve as an independent corporate body. Now without its fiscal role, Convocation suspended meetings in 1717 and through the century did not meet again. In France, the history of the clergy was exactly the reverse. The Assembly of the Clergy continued to meet regularly, called together by the king every three or five years, the last time in 1788. As time passed, in fact, the French clergy became tougher and tighter, defending its immunities and exemptions, and battling as a corps the worsening threats posed by unsympathetic secular administrators, judges, Jansenists, Protestants, and philosophes.

The fates of English and French guilds show the same sharp contrast. In England the creation of guilds appears to have ended after the mid-seventeenth century, and the functions of the remaining ones diminished to very little in the liberal economic atmosphere of the eighteenth century. In France, on the other hand, Colbert extended the guilds everywhere in the 1670s, and after 1745 almost 1900 of them paid to buy off useless offices of inspectors that the government forced on them.[11] Turgot notwithstanding, the members of most of these bodies continued to meet, to vote, to defend their monopolies as best they could—and to pay the interest on debts which largely explain their continuing existence. In short, then, the regime of privilege and corps appears to have been peculiarly French and to have reflected a particular kind of state.

≺ IV ≻

The Old Regime as Education for Democracy

It is time to return to the question: why did French society resonate as it did to the Declaration of the Rights of Man and of the Citizen? The answer seems now to lie in the conditioning of ideas and habits by the long operation of distinctive institutions. It is easier to deduce the relevant patterns of thinking, however, than to show them; for most basic notions are more felt and lived than articulated; they are the

consensual ideas that parties to quarrels share and, thus, do not have
to specify. For this chapter the consensual ideas of interest are those
underlying conflicts preceding the French Revolution. Disagreements
were sharp and sharpening; they involved parlements and absolutist
administrators, military men and financiers, merchants and guild
members, curés and bishops, and others with diverging, even opposing, interests and social prescriptions. Obviously the nature of the
conflicts and their consequences are extremely important. At the
same time, however, even the parties who most detested one another
shared certain things; they were recognizably participants in a common culture. In that culture privileges and corps pervaded the atmosphere, and were familiar to all. It would not be surprising, therefore, if
the old forms shaped ideas about rights and community more than
contemporaries said, or even knew.

The chapter began with the proposition that the Declaration's
essence was in three principal ideas—liberty as protection, liberty as
participation, and equality. We might look first for the idea of rights
involving protection of the individual against authority. One place to
look is among the many persons who had something to lose, or at
least to exchange, early in the Revolution. These were the owners of
privilege and related property, together with their creditors. It appears
that Article 17 of the Declaration was written in a form intended particularly to soothe them. The article began by stating flatly that property was "an inviolable and sacred right," and went on to say that
no property could be taken away except for some "legally established
public necessity," and then only "upon condition of a just and prior
indemnity." That guarantee of an indemnity sounded all through
France, heard by the hundreds of thousands of persons who owned
the privileges that the Revolution abolished. Most of those and other
lenders to the king were reimbursed or absorbed uneventfully into
the list of recognized state creditors. In those cases no disputes occurred to generate documents that might have revealed the thinking
about rights. Fortunately for us, however, decisions were not always
made so smoothly. Complications did arise from time to time, especially with the *officiers ministériels*.

The right level of reimbursement of those offices was difficult to
determine, for several reasons. First, their capital value was a fairly
fixed multiple of revenues whose amount had been rising. The officers' income came wholly from fees, and with inflation and increased

economic activity in the decades before 1789 the revenues increased, driving up the price of those offices substantially. This meant that recent acquirers paid more for their offices than had their senior colleagues. And all paid considerably more than had the original purchasers much earlier. Discussions also took place over what portion of the purchase price was for the clientele rather than the office, and what (if any) indemnity should compensate an ex-officer for the loss of his monopoly over work and a profession. Finally, there was the matter of the low valuations that the occupants placed on their offices in 1771. In that year an edict required these and other officials to declare the value of their offices to establish the base for a new tax, the *centième denier*. The tax called for a 1 percent annual levy and a turnover fee of nearly 5 percent based on the office's declared value. The officers had an obvious stake in undervaluing their property to reduce the tax; they gathered by corps, as the edict required, and agreed on a common, and low, price. At the time they never dreamed that the threat the abbé Terray wrote into the edict—in the event of reimbursement the officers were to receive only the amount they declared —could have had effect. How could the old state reimburse anything? But in the Revolution the inaccurate declarations became a cause for alarm when some deputies to the National Assembly, thinking to reduce the nation's heavy costs, wanted to reimburse only the declared sums.

There followed an outpouring of printed and unprinted petitions and memoranda when the officers tried to define (and expand) their property for reimbursement. The petitioners included rich Parisian stockbrokers and notaries; attorneys (*procureurs*), bailiffs, and process-servers; auctioneers of movable goods; and, at the bottom, a mass of wigmakers. Whole corps made their cases in writing. To analyze the words, ideas, and themes I read a sample (about fifty) of the petitions and other communications.[12] They regularly invoked Article 17 of the Declaration to defend what they called hereditary and patrimonial property in the name of sacred and inviolable rights. Such references, however, could be brief because, in fact, no one was attacking property in itself. Occupying more space were arguments about the nature of the particular property. For example, was an office like a house, reimbursable at its current market value, or should the owner get back only what he paid his predecessor, or worse, what someone had once paid the state? Facing a loss, the officers used the word "robbed" ("*dépouillé*") to describe their situations as "fathers of families" near ruin, their children reduced to hunger, dowries threatened or lost, and so on. While there was still a chance, the officers, agreeing that venal judicial offices were a terrible thing and should go, tried to save their own places and corps (said to assure competence, discipline, and financial responsibility). Later, with reimbursement impending, they insisted that their offices had a higher value because they mixed work with money. The ten *procureurs postulans* in the sovereign financial court (*chambre des comptes*) at Aix-en-Provence, after the almost ritual quoting of Article 17, explained that their property was as much in studies, tests, and capacity as in money, and that "the ownership of thought" is the noblest property of all. We used "the efforts of our minds" to expand the value of our property, they said.[13] Their colleagues in Aix, the attorneys in the parlement, pursued the same theme, adding that the state's "sacred social debt" required paying an indemnity to compensate the loss of their "natural and imprescriptible right to seek a subsistence through assiduous labor."[14] For the stockbrokers of Lyon, it was harder to replace an occupation or profession than it was a house, because "man is not endowed with a universal aptitude"; unlike some who sought offices for a placement of capital or for honorific distinctions, they did it to work, to support families, and to avoid "a fatal idleness."[15]

It will come as no surprise that the words "just" and "justice" (in the sense of equity) appeared from time to time in the documents. The master wigmakers of Dijon invoked justice and humanity against the ruin of families, and justice alone to assure compensation for the destruction of a property that they might have supposed beyond attack. The Declaration, they said, demanded such justice.[16] The stockbrokers at Lyon stated that "the sacred law of property" guaranteed them a "just" reimbursement, and the attorneys in the Parlement of Aix thought they could demand "the rights and consideration guaranteed to them by Justice."[17] There is no need to go on, except to note that in these and other instances where the petitioners called for justice, they meant a justice more commutative than distributive. The notion that justice was the maintenance of varying and qualitatively different rights existing in some kind of chain from top to bottom simply did not appear. The language was close to Hobbes, for whom justice was nothing more than covenants kept. In dozens of contexts the arguments of the *officiers ministériels* converged on a single point: all of them owned something of value, something the state had created and sold, and with the abolition of the one kind of property they had the right to a money equivalent. The privileges abolished in August 1789 were properties differing from one another only quantitatively; all were measurable on the single scale defined by money.

The case of the stockbrokers of Paris is worth mentioning specifically, for two reasons. It made explicit an idea—the contract with the state—that was everywhere implied, and it shows the shared assumptions that underlay the views of bitter opponents. The Paris stockbrokers had been operating on simple commissions for many years when Calonne decided to make their places into venal offices in 1786. In an operation that brought in six million livres to the state, sixty brokers paid for the offices and received, in addition to the old fees paid by their clients, annual gages or interest at 4½ percent on the new capital. Two years later Loménie de Brienne, having learned that the offices were more lucrative than thought—they were selling between individuals for twice what the state had received—threatened to create additional offices to share in the high revenues. Under that pressure the brokers agreed at a meeting to renounce their gages in return for the minister's agreeing not to add the new offices. At the Revolution, however, with talk widespread about the sanctity of property, the brokers remembered the property they had lost. Now they told the story of how Calonne with his "absolute will" forcibly extracted from them a loan (their payments for the purchase of the offices), and how the "minister-despot" Brienne then took away their legitimate interest on that loan. Simple equity required that the present government pay the back interest on money its predecessor borrowed. The brokers showed how the promise of gages had been essential to their own borrowing to purchase the offices. Everything, therefore, had depended on mutual respect for what they called the "formal contract" that sealed their purchases.[18]

On the other side was Gérard-Maurice Turpin, an absolutist administrator whose job before 1789 was to investigate office-owning tax collectors. When he responded to the brokers in 1790, as *agent* of the Treasury, his answer was scathing: it was terrible that the needs of the state ever led the king to sell privileges at all, but even worse that he sold them to blackmailers like the stockbrokers. The king did not borrow from the brokers, and so he owed them no interest, thus no gages. Instead the king sold them a right that was his to dispose of

whenever and however he wished. With his decision to sell the functions as offices in 1786, the deal was made and the transaction was
complete. The brokers had no automatic right to receive interest on
the price of objects they purchased; the only claim they retained was
the right to be reimbursed if the king ever suppressed the offices.[19]

In the debate the brokers were probably right, at least in practical
terms. In 1786 the promise of gages helped the brokers to find lenders
with money for the purchase of the expensive offices. Turpin's view,
perhaps correct from a narrowly legal standpoint, excluded consideration of the credit networks and mechanisms that inspired confidence
and made privileged intermediaries effective as borrowers for the king.
The ideas in opposition—absolutism against a kind of credit-based constitutionalism—are of course interesting. But equally interesting here
is what the absolutist Turpin and the brokers in their new offices and
corps shared. Both sides agreed that privilege and functions were simple
commodities in a market, objects to be sold and borrowed against; and
that acquiring them gave one legal guarantees to reimbursement if the
property were recalled or abolished. Both sides assumed property rights
tied to the diffusion of privileges through society.

Similar ideas, implicit when not explicit, ran through the rest of
the documents making up the dossier of the *officiers ministériels*.
Most of the officers invoked the interests of their own creditors who
had advanced funds for the purchase of state-created property that
once seemed as secure as land. They stated or assumed that the property at issue was one whose circulation the king had authorized. Most
striking in the petitions, however, is that all the owners supposed a
reciprocal relationship between themselves and the state. Sometimes
they invoked a contractual relationship with the king or government
explicitly: the attorneys at the Parlement of Aix referred to the "reciprocal contract" with the government that came from their paying the
centième denier, and sixty-one attorneys in the *présidial* of Riom insisted that the king by his silence about the high sales price of their offices "had so to speak contracted again with each acquirer" for that
price. Most officers, it is true, did not use the term "contract." More
typical were the wigmakers of Paris who referred only to precise and
explicit documents (*actes formels*) that should have protected them
from ruin.[20] But whatever the language, something like contract was
involved, and the state was a party to it. Ideas of property, and the
rights protecting it, were of course not uniquely French, nor was the

idea of contract (stated or unstated). But only the French state had taken on widespread obligations to maintain agreements with individuals and corps, and only the French state would be held responsible by wigmakers, stockbrokers, and so many others for violations of their property rights. Far more than elsewhere, the right to property in France supposed defense not just against other individuals and groups, but equally against the state.

How deep into society did the ownership of state-created property go? In 1789 at least 60,000 persons owned some kind of office, and perhaps twice as many others loaned money to the officers for the purchases. Among the 300 secretaries of the king in the Grande Chancellerie of Paris, forced to add capital to their offices in 1743, 165 paid by borrowing from 226 persons.[21] The full record, including other forced loans and receipts for the purchases of the Chancellerie offices, would push the list of creditors on the individual offices much higher. Then there were the guilds. Following the edict of February 1745, which created offices of inspectors and controllers for each corps to buy and unite to itself, 1871 *communautés* made the payments. Early in 1793 the provisional general director of the liquidation referred to 40,000 indemnities paid or to be paid to members still active in the same trades. There must have been many more. And the guilds had corporate creditors nearby: 644 (35 percent) of the corps borrowed from outsiders to pay for the offices after 1745. Twenty Parisian guilds borrowed from 726 persons.[22] Others invested in the large privileged corps. The Estates of Languedoc had over 9000 creditors in the 1780s, the clergy more than twice as many.[23] Probably one could make an inventory of all owners and investors in privileges and corps, but it has not been done. It is clear, however, that the list would be extensive, and it would go rather far down into the society. It would have to include the 32 wigmaker-barbers at Sedan in the Ardennes who signed a petition in October 1791. They spoke of their misery and the need for proper reimbursement. Without that reimbursement their creditors, all artisans and workers in that impoverished town, would similarly fall into misery.[24] Even after discounting for hyperbole, it is clear that ownership and investment were not confined to a capitalist elite, and that the rights associated with property in the distinctive French system of state credit were spread unusually far across and into the society. It was, in a sense, a society of archivists, composed of individuals and families guarding hundreds of thousands of documents that assured their state-created properties. This was a society for which Article 17 was no intellectual abstraction. People knew what it was about.

The Declaration's other two essential ideas, equality and liberty as participation, were in practice joined. We saw in section 3 how their linkage solidified the corps and permitted them to act by voting. The connection between equality and participation was, of course, at the heart of Rousseau's analysis of community and what held it together, although it is worth emphasizing that in their ubiquitous corps the French lived those ideas before Rousseau wrote them down. But what were the questions and issues that in practice drew members of corps together, permitting the habits of participation as equals to form?

Early in the Revolution many corps, agreeing that the abolition of corps and privileges was proper for the others, argued that their own was useful and should form an exception. The argument made in each case was that a particular corps was essential for recruiting and disciplining persons engaged in an important occupation. All kinds of *officiers ministériels* made.the point. The attorneys at the *Châtelet* of Paris spoke of their "exact and rigorous" discipline that required a "meeting point and community" to protect clients against chicanery. The corps verified the aspirant's knowledge and also his moral character about which, the procureurs stated, every company is very "touchy" (*délicate*). They described rules that empowered two elected officials, the *procureurs de communauté*, to handle complaints, demanding that the wayward member conform or even make restitution, if need be. When the member failed to heed the community's warning, the officials handed him over to the magistrates for punishment. All that was in the statutes. In practice, however, the actual disciplining of members seems not to have occupied the corps much. The records for the *procureurs* at the Châtelet cover hundreds of meetings from 1768 to 1783. The officials reported on everything that occurred involving the company, but there was not a single instance where the subject of disciplining a member came up. Perhaps the 240 *procureurs* at the Chatelet were uniformly dispute-free and honest, though one wonders.[25]

What attracted the attention of members and drew them together much more consistently was financial matters. All the corps had revenues and expenditures to oversee, and nearly all had long-term debts to manage. The debts were large and small. The great corps of the clergy and provincial estates between them owed about 300 million livres in 1789. Loans made by the corps of officers and guilds ranged widely in amount. The 300 secretaries of the king in the Grande Chancellerie, whose offices alone were worth thirty-six million livres, had collectively borrowed another twenty-four million for the government. Credit operations on that scale were unique for the corps of officers, but other debts were significant, for example, the 1.6 million owed by the bailiff-auctioneers (*huissiers-priseurs*) of movable goods at the Chatelet of Paris. Lower in the scale came small corps, like the attorneys in the *chambre des comptes* of Aix with a debt of 55,000, and near the bottom were the wigmakers of Sedan who said they had together borrowed 800 livres for the king "under the guarantee of our properties [in offices] and on which we are still paying the interest." By the thousands the corps took on collective obligations to buy off supernumerary offices or masterships, to have their privileges reconfirmed, to pay for the right to collect new or larger fees, and so on. In 1789 most corps had debts.[26]

For any corps, no matter its size, acquiring a debt and then dealing with it necessarily involved meetings and a joint, visible agreement by the members to support it. On such occasions all members were convoked, and normally a substantial number appeared to hear proposals and reports on negotiations, to share in making the decision, and finally to sign a register recording their assent. This was the procedure both for authorizing the collective loan and, later, for resolving difficulties that arose over how to pay the interest. The secretaries of the king in the Grande Chancellerie left a full documentation that shows frequent assemblies to which all the members were called at the several stages. In 1755 and 1758, for example, they met a number of times to arrange loans for the king, and then through the 1760s the handling of those loans continued to bring them together. With gages arriving two to three years late, a new tax reducing gages and interest by 10 percent after 1764, and an annual loss on their 1755 loan—on its twelve million livres the corps received new gages at 4 percent, but paid its creditors 5 percent—the members gathered repeatedly to assess themselves the sums necessary to complete the payments to more than a thousand creditors.

The circumstances requiring members to meet in the *sénéchaussée* of Grasse were worse than that. There the magistrates had taken on the usual collective debt to purchase redundant offices created during the second half of Louis XIV's reign. For a time all went well: the government paid to the corps, as gages on the unfilled offices, the exact sum that the corps paid its creditors as interest. But trouble began later when the government sharply reduced the gages. To continue paying the corps' creditors at the original rate, the magistrates met and decided to assign two-thirds of the income from their own offices (the emoluments and *épices*) for the purpose. Then, by 1780, when that court's business slowed, the common fund for the interest was insufficient. At another meeting the magistrates diverted the remaining one-third of their income to the creditors, and from that time on they worked purely for the honor of the thing. In another *sénéchaussée* (Armagnac) the magistrates similarly assigned their revenues to the payment of interest, in this case on 30,000 livres in accumulated loans contracted to meet the cost of a long jurisdictional battle with the Parlement of Toulouse. The court authorized the loans by decisions taken at five separate meetings between 1774 and 1788. In the late 1780s the bailiff-auctioneers in Paris gathered a number of times as they tried to decide what new and higher level of fees would project an image of their solidity to potential investors in a projected new loan of two million livres.[27]

Making and managing debt were the main, but not the only, affairs that brought the corps' members together. We saw that the abbé Terray required all the officers (except those in the high sovereign courts) to assemble and to agree on a value for their offices in each corps as the basis for paying the *centième denier*. Some corps, like the attorneys at the Chatelet in 1781, met to discuss proposals for new fee schedules, and many assembled when their privileges were contested and threatened. Then there were the meetings for elections and to hear the periodic financial reports. Even without meetings officers and guildsmen would have remained well aware of their memberships, since it was through the corps that they made their contributions to the state (contributions the heavier because belonging to the corps made the members both accessible to state officials and of a known level of wealth). Moussu, the *lieutenant civil* in the *bailliage et présidial* of Chaumont, illustrates a magistrate's payments: against gages of 44 livres (less than one-half of 1 percent on the capital), he paid annually through the corps 180 livres for the *capitation* tax, 100 livres for the *centième denier*, and another 96 livres for his personal share in the debts and charges of the company.[28]

There were meetings, then, and enough pressures of various kinds to build and preserve the participatory sense in members. But it would be wrong to exaggerate. Most meetings were routine, dull, and in the larger corps participated in only by councils of insiders composed of elected officials, former officials, and some senior members. These were the persons who oversaw regular operations involving revenues and expenditures, the pooling of designated fees or portions of fees, collections of sums owed by members, interest payments on loans, and dozens of small items. Elections drew more of the members, but even then the turnout was usually low, candidates often pre-selected and uncontested. The corps of attorneys at the Chatelet worked that way. There sixteen to eighteen of the 240 members met often, and once a year those officials named sixty others, or one-quarter of the membership, to elect the new officials. Typically only fifteen to twenty of those designated actually appeared to cast votes in elections that were contested only twice in fifteen years. Thus, in quiet times participation by the majority of members was fairly low. Further, there is no reason to think that the members took pleasure in paying taxes and charges, that they enjoyed having their income reduced or, like Moussu, reaching into their pockets for cash to make up the sum that the corps owed. And yet, what is striking is that in a crisis the majority reappeared at meetings. When, episodically, issues and fundamental questions involving fresh obligations or the defense of privilege arose, the distinctive principles and practices of democratic functioning within the corps came to life. For the average member, that occasional personal participation, the vicarious involvement through the work of elected representatives, and the permanent need to support (and contain) financial obligations understood to be of his own making, preserved his feel for participation and the collective life. Montlevaud, *maître des comptes* in the *chambre des comptes* of Paris, expressed the feeling when he asked reimbursement of his office at the evaluation price "to which, as member of the *chambre*, I subjected myself by voting freely."[29]

Finally, as already noted, with participation came also the equality essential to the corps' workings. That equality needs comment and illustration. First, it is important to identify what was distinctive in the notion of equality generated through the corps. All eighteenth-century European societies, even marked as they were by huge inequalities of class, status, and occupation, nonetheless provided social settings where individuals came together informally with persons roughly like themselves. There friends or acquaintances shared not only drink, but a vocabulary, jokes, resentments; they were equals with a sense of the sameness between them and of a culture that separated them from others. But in France those loose and "natural" forms of association with their feelings of social equality were enormously reinforced and focused by the regime of corps that filtered people with a finer grid, and in addition imposed a formal structure over relationships between peers. The institutions associated persons alike socially and identical in occupation, who shared not only a general culture but memberships, rights, privileges, kinds of property. In the corps practical pressures required equality for taking group action, for sustaining collective obligations, and, as we shall see, for protecting the members' property. The equality in the corps was strong and principled, sometimes even oppressive, but in any event very different from merely rubbing shoulders in a neighborhood café or in a salon.

In practice, however, the process of filtration by the corps into homogeneous social and occupational groups was not perfect. Although the members were equal in rights and obligations inside a corps, outside it there were some differences between them. They could vary in talent, energy, age, and to a certain degree in wealth. Some members worked harder or better than others, as at Bourg-en-Bresse where one-third of the attorneys handled three-quarters of the business. In 1782 among 972 Parisian wigmakers, 271 (28 percent) could not pay their personal shares of twenty-six livres toward the corps' contribution to a fund intended to repair that year's naval losses at sea. The secretaries of the king, who paid 120,000 livres for an office, were in quite another financial world, but they too included rich and poor, at least as the terms were defined at that level. When approached to give to the navy's fund, too, the corps sent a circular letter to members soliciting opinions on how to respond. One of the answers is particularly interesting here. Guénard, not himself in financial difficulty, worried whether some of his colleagues would be able to pay. "The first third of the company," he wrote, "is composed of millionaires, another third of comfortably-off persons living nobly, [but] the third in fact of persons who are in tight circumstances."[30] At all levels there were some members of corps who had trouble meeting their obligations in difficult times.

Faced by that fact, both the government and the corps had a large

stake in papering over those differences and in assuring the formal
equality between members inside the corps. The government needed
that equality (and the solidarity that went with it) to raise money
through the corps, and members needed the same things to make secure the value of their individual investments. The assumptions by
both sides are implicit in the regular operation of the corps; they can
be deduced from the records of negotiations and payments, meetings,
votes, collections from members, collective loans, the corps' management of their own finances. Again, however, explicit descriptions
of the principle of operation and how it worked are rare. But once in a
long while there are indications of it, invariably in response to some
threat by the government to the members' equality. Such threats, always lifted when the corps was able to raise money through the old
system, left as residue an occasional remark about equality.

In 1689 the government issued an edict creating various new
offices of attorneys with the additional function of setting fees and
arbitrating disputes over them. Two of the offices were for the corps
at the *chambre des comptes* of Aix. That creation would have profoundly irritated the members for two reasons. One was that the
twenty-one attorneys had joined to purchase and retire exactly similar
offices only fourteen years earlier, and had borrowed 7000 livres collectively to do it. Even more disturbing was the privilege that the edict
conferred on individuals who purchased the offices. "To facilitate the
sale," purchasers were to acquire the right to exercise the occupation
of attorney "with exemption from contributing to the debts." That exemption, of course, destroyed the equality between members and
ended the joint responsibility of all members for the corps' obligations.
The government evidently knew it, its intent having been "to force
the community . . . to purchase the new offices and unite them to the
corps." Frightened by the prospect of the sale to individuals, the attorneys did what the government wanted. After remonstrating and negotiating a slightly reduced price, they borrowed together another 3850
livres to purchase and retire the new offices. Stimulated by the government's threat to create unequal members with a right not to share in
the corporate obligations, then, the corps used the principles of equality and solidarity to find the money and to pay—as the government
knew it would.[31]

The ideas at work among administrators appear again in three proposals for squeezing money from the guilds in 1691. The first proposal
would have required all entering guild masters to take chancellery

letters as if officers named by the king, and of course to pay a fee; the second was a scheme to turn all the guilds' elective positions (*sindics, gardes, jurés*) into venal offices for the state to sell. The third plan envisaged creating and selling fourteen to sixteen additional masterships in each guild. In all cases it was expected that the guilds would raise money to buy off the creations and fresh obligations through lump-sum payments. Supporters of the first proposal thought the guilds could get up six million livres quickly by assessing their members, diverting cash they had on hand, or borrowing. Since the aim was to raise money by encouraging payments for exemptions, the provisions of the proposals were in a sense irrelevant.

Nonetheless, the debate over substance was vigorous and interesting. The proponents of the first plan attacked the second by arguing that selling the offices in guilds "would be the ruin of elections that we derive from the prudence of our forebears and which form the basis for all our statutes." It was elections and competition between equals (*émulation*) that guaranteed discipline. The hope of being chosen made every master want to appear worthy of the choice by adhering to the statutes. The *mémoire* that developed these views went on to compare the guilds to the parlements and other superior companies, "because the former being all masters and equals, as the latter are officers, there are none who do not wish to appear equal in merit and honesty, and they all unite against the one whose conduct is not regular, as if against a rotten member who could injure the other parts of the corps." By contrast, selling the elective offices, thus institutionalizing inequality between masters, would increase corruption when the masters who owned the right to inspect the others, now their inferiors, demanded money of them and made deals. The inevitable result when equality disappeared was the destruction of community and "an incurable wound."[32]

A last example shows better the pressures to maintain equality that arose inside a corps, from the members themselves. The corps is the Grande Chancellerie, and the episode its long confrontation with the abbé Terray over a loan in 1770 and 1771.[33] Terray, faced by severe economic crisis and the very real possibility of general government bankruptcy, had to find money quickly. He looked for help to the privileged corps, the Grande Chancellerie conspicuous among them. Early in 1770 an edict authorized the secretaries of the king to raise twelve million livres either individually or by a collective loan, as they preferred. At a meeting on 30 March the Grande Chancellerie voted in favor of the collective loan, because they knew that many colleagues were unable then to find the funds to cover personal shares amounting to 40,000 livres. But 1770 was not like 1755, when the Grande Chancellerie raised twelve million livres easily in less than two months. This time after two months only 886,000 livres had come in. The Chancellerie's officers explained the slowness in filling the loan by the corps' diminished credit resulting from the government's failure to pay the interest through the 1760s, and by the competition from multiple loans that other institutions launched simultaneously. They could also have invoked the general economic conditions.

But Terray, an impatient man in the best of times, was in no mood to wait. He first threatened the corps in blunt terms, and then moved to a plan that cut straight through the traditions and unwritten rules that had always guided negotiations between royal ministers and the corps. By the order in council of 15 May Terray raised the official price for the offices from 110,000 to 150,00 livres, and used that higher price to apply pressure to the richer members—Terray wrote them separate letters—demanding that they pay the whole 40,000 livres individually and right away, regardless of what their colleagues did. At the same time he withdrew the option of a collective loan guaranteed by all 300 members. The new strategy divided the officers into two groups: those paying the full 40,000 livres as individuals received new gages and were declared free of the collective obligation for any new loan; others with less resources, after paying only 10,000 livres each, could then band together to make a collective loan for the rest of the money. That loan, however, was unlike any other in the Chancellerie or elsewhere: it involved the "poorer" secretaries of the king only and was intended to be temporary, paid off by successors when they entered the offices. Terray, then, attempted to fragment the company, taking what he could get quickly from the richer members and freeing them from the internal corporate pressures and solidarity that earlier financial ministers had found useful. Terray's solution was essentially individualistic. The episode extended over nearly a year and a half, and no less than twenty meetings of the Grande Chancellerie. There were deadlines, renewed threats, and dogged efforts by the corps to get Terray to reverse himself and to restore the collective loan for all. Only in 1771 did the two sides come together. In the end Terray had his twelve millions and the Grande Chancellerie the broader loan that saved the principles of solidarity and collective responsibility.

The importance of the Grande Chancellerie's story here, however, is less in finance than in the language and routine thinking displayed by this Old Regime corps. The theme of equality runs through most of the minutes of meetings during the struggle with Terray. On 29 May 1770, the issue came up at a special meeting attended by 119 of the secretaries. There Le Bègue, the *premier sindic*, after stating that in present circumstances some members could pay and others could not, explained that "it is not possible, without attacking the essence of a company, to establish a distinction between subjects who are rich and others who are not, and to have the ones experience a different fate from the others." The company, he went on, "being able to decide only according to the situation of the largest number," had to ask the king's favor for citizens who did not make money from their offices. The entire corps then approved a statement to the effect that the order in council of 15 May broke "the solidarity of the loan in collective name," and would create a ruinous inequality between those who could and could not make the major financial effort. The result would be to diminish the price of the offices, and to make any collective loan impossible by removing from its guarantee the offices that were least encumbered, "and destroying the solidarity which is the base of public confidence." At a meeting on 9 June the *sindic* told of having explained to Terray that "the unanimity which has always been in the company is precious to it, and necessarily furnishes the basis of its credit, which the company has used only to fulfill engagements contracted in the service of the king and the state." On 30 June the corps approved a new letter pointing out how easy it was to restore the collective loan by making all in the company equal. Le Bègue on 12 July amplified the theme: reestablishing the collective loan was essential, but it could be effective "only insofar as the condition of the members of the company is entirely equal, not only relative to the amount of the finances in their offices, but for the solidarity of their obligations contracted with relation to the public." He assured the minister that a restored collective loan for all would speed up the payment of the twelve million. On that day the company approved telling Terray that *all* the members wanted the collective loan, to keep the offices uniform, and thereby to restore life to the borrowing.

Meeting on 16 July, the company again voted the loan in common, and twelve days later the officers and commissaires, in a joint letter to the controller general about how essential it was to keep all offices identical to one another in value, emphasized once more how failure to do that would lead to selling off the offices at a low price. In October the Chancellerie reminded Terray of its collective loans in 1755 and 1758, and the relation of their solidarity to those successes. Finally, in January 1771 as a favorable breakthrough approached, Le Bègue summarized the situation: only a collective loan could raise all the money needed, but the collective loan was illusory if limited to those who could not pay the 40,000 livres. Now he proposed that all who had paid 40,000 livres should shift 30,000 of it into the common loan. By this arrangement, all offices being priced equally at 120,000 livres, the loan would succeed. Le Bègue advised Terray that this was certain to get him the money faster than would "the most rigorous actions," and that the company was most anxious to avoid the "schism" already developing from the resentments among persons who, having paid the 40,000 livres, could not resell the office for the extraordinary sum of 150,000. Finally, in June 1771 the company approved a letter asking urgently that all offices be fixed at 120,000 livres, and stating that this was the general view in the company, denied by a few members only. These were the arrangements, then, that appeared in the order in council of 30 September 1771. All the members were equal again, and equally responsible to the Grande Chancellerie's creditors for the security of their funds.

And so, pressure to maintain equality came from inside, from the members, and it was effective. Similar pressures help to explain the collective borrowing elsewhere. The pattern was widespread in all the corps of officers from whom the government demanded capital to support *augmentations de gages*: the capital in one office had to remain exactly the same as in all the others. The corps did not accept extra and unequal placements in their own offices by the richer members, and it tried to avoid driving the less well-off members to sell their places at a loss. What everyone knew more or less consciously was that a kind of Gresham's law controlled the market for offices and memberships, that is, that the lowest price at which any place sold was likely to be the price for all, and that the loss for the poorer members would be compounded for the richer if they had put supplementary funds in their offices. In general, then, three strong interests converged on the policy for keeping the members equal inside the corps. The state relied on it to provide the solidarity that permitted the corps to raise money. Lenders to both individual members and to the corps found in equality and collective responsibility the assurance that their funds were safe. And, as we have just seen, the members themselves wanted equality to protect their own investments. Those interests joined to foster practices that became habitual and, unless under attack, were not specified or reflected upon. The idea of equality was "normal" and so deeply ingrained that it seems not even to have been particularly sentimentalized.

≺ V ≻

Conflicts and Consensus: Toward a Conclusion

Finally, two related points before a brief summary. First, the picture of the corps to this point could seem too tidy, perhaps even idealized. Although the oligarchical tendencies in larger corps have been mentioned, solidarity and consensus have been the center of attention. Such a picture can easily downplay the real divisions that existed in a number of corps. Consider the Parisian guilds studied by Steven L. Kaplan.[34] In twenty or so there appeared not only the familiar split between masters and journeymen-workers, but serious divisions and inequalities between kinds of masters who were in principle equals. Masters in those guilds fell into one of three groups: the *anciens* or senior members, *modernes* who were members with five, ten, or fifteen years seniority (depending on the guild), and *jeunes* who were new. The *anciens* with the current and former officers formed an inner circle that dominated decision-making and administration in the corps. They oversaw most business themselves or carried it out with the aid of a few hand-picked members drawn from the other groups. The insiders imposed limits on the role of general assemblies, and themselves selected the candidates to succeed them in guild offices. From their power base and largely unscrutinized by the wider membership, the elite sometimes siphoned off funds; they were said to favor friends and relatives and to persecute others when inspecting shops and goods, in tax assessments, in regulating recruitment of workers, or in arranging access to raw materials. Many masters were entirely excluded from the exercise of power. Some were silent, indifferent or cowed, and their ideas unknown. A surprising number, however, were moved to resist in one way or another. Kaplan presents a rich documentation for the disputes, petitions, protests, lawsuits, and movements that the high-handed behavior of the guild oligarchs occasioned. The resentments evidently ran deep, were strongly felt, and noisily expressed. And the visible divisions common in the larger guilds were not unknown in the more sizable corps of officers and also in the clergy.

The second point is that where they existed, the movements of protest and resistance were set in ideas, and gave rise to language, reflecting the same model of democratic community that the corps represented. Once more the secretaries of the king provide an example.[35] We saw that through the 1760s the corps was regularly assessing its members sums to make up for the gages and interest that the government failed to pay. At the large annual meeting to hear the financial report on 6 May 1769, the 186 members in attendance voted unanimously to renew the assessments and to continue to press the government for an indemnity to cover the Chancellerie's losses. Two days later a second meeting was held, at which each member was supposed to sign the deliberation to renew the personal contributions. It had been understood that the second meeting would also take up the means (proposed by the *sindics*) for avoiding such contributions in the future. Expectation of that discussion drew a crowd. Of 300 members, 223 attended, that is, almost all who lived close enough to get there. The senior members who led the governing group (an inner circle of twelve composing the Cabinet) began by announcing that "observations" made to the leaders since the last meeting required them to ask the company to suspend deliberations on the means for avoiding future contributions. The record does not indicate whose observations they were. Whether in response to this stifling of debate or by pre-arrangement, Pidansat de Mairobert, a liberal publicist and soon-to-be activist in the movement opposing Maupeou and Terray, rose to demand structural change in the Grande Chancellerie. Speaking "before his turn," Mairobert insisted that for the company to make a better-reflected decision in matters of such importance required that the members gather with the dean (the senior secretary of the king) in smaller groups where they would select "commissaires." These commissioners or agents, to be chosen by the "columns of service" by which the secretaries were listed for alternating periods of work, should then be in touch with the *sindics* before meetings, learning what was coming up for discussion and reporting back to each "column" individually on the expected subjects for deliberation.

The dean spoke against Mairobert's proposition, which he said was contrary to practice and did not conform to the governing regulation of 1672; he went on to say that the officers and *sindics*, deriving their power from that regulation, were themselves the company's commissaires. As such, they reported on important affairs to the whole company, which was then free to suspend judgment when the members thought that an affair required further reflection. The company's members had the right to assemble among themselves, however they wished, to confer on common affairs. And, the dean went on, the *sindics* and former officers would always see only honor and duty in taking account of their colleagues' verbal or written opinions, and in reporting on those opinions to the whole assembly. But to divide the company by "columns" whose composition shifts every year, and to make particular chambers of those lists, would be to divide the company which is "a pure essence." Naming commissioners by columns would necessarily revoke the powers that the members had given their *sindics*.

Discussion then followed. Some members rallied to a compromise view developed by one of the two Paporet brothers then in office, both lawyers. Paporet conceded that to name permanent agents other than the *sindics* would violate the regulation, but sometimes there were affairs so important that the company should charge some of its members with developing opinions on proposed alternatives to a decision recommended by the leadership. In those cases it could be useful to report to the columns. Finding a remedy to the present ill, Paporet concluded, was such an affair. The debate having ended, opinions were gathered, and Paporet's proposal drew the support of 48 members. The other 175 favored the existing practice consistent with the regulation. The majority view, as reported in the register, was that the elected *sindics* were the formally established agents of the corps; they should continue to report to the company after receiving the enlightened opinions (*lumières*) of colleagues; and they were bound to delay action for further reflection whenever an Assembly, comprising a quorum of thirty, decided that they should. The constitutional issue, then, raised issues of representation and wider participation by a normally silent constituency only a short time before the struggle with Terray began. Even these "*bourgeois gentilshommes*," who had purchased their expensive offices only to become nobles, were being familiarized with the categories for revolutionary discussion, and the inner council was sensitized to the possibility of control from below.

Similar resentments spread in the artisans' world, directed against unrepresentative and "corrupt" *sindics*, *gardes*, and *jurés*. There too the dialogue was between insiders and outsiders who wanted to be in. The wigmakers again provide examples. In the 1760s a creation of new masterships ignited rebellion by the newer members in Paris against their leaders. For the senior members the issue was simple: the newer members were rebels violating the law; they "had no right to assemble or deliberate." The newer members gave a heated and democratic response. The *sindics* were only the temporary agents of the masters:

When it is a question of some act that would oblige each of the members of the community or might bear prejudice against individual members, the mission of the *sindics* necessarily ends. They must convoke *all* the parts of the community, and the decision on the course of action to take must result from the plurality of the votes of all the members.[36]

At the Revolution those ideas echoed in wigmakers who were not masters at all. These were mainly persons who rented the privileges from master-proprietors. At Versailles the renters complained bitterly about a clique of corrupt despots who secretly sold the rights to practice to mere workers with no formal titles to produce on their own. No one should ever be admitted "without a legal convocation of all the concerned members." The renters went on to say that they were the largest part of the community, paid dues, but were not permitted to attend the important meetings. They insisted that it is "only just that every individual who pays the charges be admitted equally to the prerogatives," and that he have the same "right to know the destination and use of his share, and even of the whole fund." To that end the guild's accountants must convoke general assemblies where they were to report on finances, and other affairs should never be decided in any meeting where less than a majority of those with voting rights were present. In Paris the renters opened a thoroughly radical statement by speaking of how they had been subjected to all the community's orders without having been its members.[37]

The list of corps where one part of a membership excluded another includes some great corps like the clergy, some (although not most) of the corps of venal officers, and, as we have seen, the larger guilds.

Questions of exclusion, inclusion, accountability, and representation generated ideas and a vocabulary soon to be heard in revolution. In fact, the ideas rooted in the divisions in corps probably spread and contributed to the breakdown of the old order more broadly. The matter is worth pursuing.[38] It is not, however, the subject of this chapter. More important here is that the persons on the edge of the corps, excluded from governance and moved to resist, were conditioned by the same model for community that served both the insiders and the undivided corps. The terms of angry exchanges involved the democratization of community and the exercise of power within it. Those who were outside did not ordinarily argue for the right to be independent of bodies they thought oppressive, but for full membership in them. They wanted to be inside and to participate as equals. The fact of conflicts, even bitter ones, should not obscure the image of community that parties in opposition shared.

The conclusion, then, is that the Declaration of the Rights of Man and of the Citizen appeared in a French society well prepared to understand it. The Declaration's three essential ideas, available more or less anywhere in the legacy of feudalism, could not have been received, combined, and spread in the same way by other societies. Absolutisms with less developed economies necessarily militarized their societies, teaching habits of service and subordination but not liberty (in either sense) or equality. In England the ideas were absorbed, but confined to an elite. There, in an advanced economy, a "democratic" community at the top, national in scale, exercised power through Parliament and mobilized resources for the state through borrowing. The confidence and financial success that the constitutional regime inspired, however, meant that in the rest of society there was no need for smaller corporations to sustain state credit. In England they either atrophied or were never created. In France, by contrast, an absolutist state in an advanced economy (like England's) but with bad credit, found intermediaries who could borrow for it as cheaply as did the English state. The result was the extension and reenforcement of privilege and corps, the proliferation of state-created properties and institutions through society at all levels. The paradoxical outcome for France, however, was that the absolutist regime supplied the models for rights, community, and democratic functioning, and brought those models into the routine lives and habits of the largest part of the population. Then, in 1789, when the shells of the corps burst and hundreds of thousands of privileges were invalidated and reimbursed, the models and the habits peculiar to a long experience remained. Right away they were applied to the broader sphere of state and society. The Declaration, therefore, marked a transfer as well as a destruction.

The theme, then, is continuity amid discontinuity. What continued, however, was a kind of conflict as well as consensus. After 1789 the whole society became in a sense one enlarged corps of the Old Regime type. But all was not harmony and bliss in the vast new corps of equal members called citizens. Divisions reappeared not unlike those in the larger corps of the Old Regime. As before, voting required equality, but equality on what basis? What constituted membership in the society-corps? Mere citizenship? A certain wealth? Education? Ideology? Virtue? Sex? Whom to include, and therefore whom to exclude? Where should the line be drawn between insiders and outsiders? If the circle of inclusion was too wide, voters could be imagined too unequal and diverse in their interests for the significance of a majority among them to be clear and acceptable. Then control could easily fall to Jacobin or Napoleonic authoritarianism. But if the circle was too tight, the pressures for inclusion could build, leading toward renewed revolution. No solution was easy to find in a society so saturated with ideas of rights, participation, and equality, where elections in nearly 40,000 communes continued to place within sight of everyone the democratic model (working badly or well, but working nonetheless under all regimes). In a distinctively French political culture the questions of how to apply the Declaration's ideas remained at the heart of politics for a long time.

But that is another story. Here it is enough to observe that the Declaration, which marked the destruction of an old order while codifying the new, reflected also a fundamental continuity. With the Declaration of the Rights of Man and of the Citizen ideas and habits coming from inside the regime of privileges and corps entered the fully public sphere, where they went on conditioning the terms of discourse and conflict.

From the Lessons of French History to Truths for All Times and All People

The Historical Origins of an Anti-Historical Declaration

DALE VAN KLEY

ADOPTED PROVISIONALLY BY an impatient National Assembly on 27 August 1789, the Declaration of the Rights of Man and of the Citizen was the French Revolution's inaugural statement. Ironically, it was also the Revolution's most lasting utterance, surviving all subsequent constitutions to which in principle it stood as prolegomenon. Whether this immortality is the Declaration's vindication or indictment, whether it survived because of its textual virtue or by virtue of default, having doomed its entire constitutional offspring to untimely death, has remained controversial ever since.

Conservatives from the outset blamed the Revolution's subsequent violence and instability on the Declaration's abstract and antihistorical form. Instead of reaffirming, complained Edmund Burke as early as 1790, their "real" and historic rights resplendent with "pedigree and illustrating ancestors," the French National Assembly's deputies of 1789 had set out in quest of an "abstract perfection," enunciating rights which were as "morally and politically false" as they were "metaphysically true." Having schooled themselves in the "political metaphysics" of the French Enlightenment, especially Rousseau, the French revolutionaries had suicidally spurned their own history as though they were a "people of yesterday" with "everything to begin anew."[1]

To the charge of anti-historical utopianism, which despite its association with Burke is as much French as English, there was added another: that the French Declaration unduly subordinated individual liberties to the national state and public law. Pointing a finger again at the influence of Rousseau and the French Enlightenment, the

nineteenth-century French historian and literary critic Hippolyte
Taine complained that the French declaration contains "nothing
similar to the precise declarations of the American constitution . . .
which circumscribe the territories where the State may not enter,
because they are reserved to the individual." In deadly combination,
Taine declared, with the Declaration's abstract and utopian features,
its accent on the sovereign state and legislation transformed its various articles into "so many daggers pointed at human society," justifying at once the "spontaneous anarchy" of 1789 and the dictatorial
terror of 1793.[2]

Recent scholarship has enhanced the sophistication and explanatory force of this conservative indictment by combining it with
Alexis de Tocqueville's classic thesis of monarchical continuity
amidst revolutionary change. Just as the Revolution in Tocqueville's
reckoning completed the monarchy's centuries-long attempt to centralize France's governmental administration, so to François Furet
did the Revolution transfer an absolute and indivisible notion of "sovereignty" from the monarchy to the nation.[3] And lest the resultant
case seem contradictory—the Revolution being credited with both
renouncing the past and perpetuating it—both Furet and Marcel
Gauchet following Tocqueville have underlined the paradoxical nature of the Revolution's relation to the past: that the apparently timeless individuals and their equal "metaphysical" rights functioned
as building blocks for a new "sovereignty" fully as collective as the
royal one, effecting a virtual identification between citizenry and its
government reminiscent of the unity of Old-Regime nation with its
king.[4]

In sharp contrast to this conservative critique, both liberal and socialist defenses of the Revolution have generally insisted on the fundamental similarity between the American and French declarations.
For F. A. Mignet, writing under the Restoration, the drafting of a declaration of rights was "ever the first step" by "a people rising from
slavery," making the French Declaration altogether "similar" to the
American ones.[5] And in reaction to conservative historiography's indictment of the Enlightenment and Rousseau, both liberal and socialist histories of the Revolution have tended to minimize the role of
ideas in general to the benefit of concrete events and contingent "circumstances," and therefore to interpret the Declaration of Rights less
as an ideological manifesto than as a transparent reflection of those

circumstances. For Taine's contemporary Alphonse Aulard, defending both philosophical positivism and the French Third Republic, the
Declaration's generalities should be read less for the deputies' plans
for the future than as the restrospective "death certificate of the Old
Regime, just as the Americans had drawn their declaration of rights
. . . against the King of England and the despotic system."[6] Endorsing
this judgment, the great Marxian historian Georges Lefebvre added
that "for the members of the National Assembly . . . there was nothing abstract or even properly philosophical in such generalization, for
under each article they mentally aligned concrete particularities from
which they had suffered."[7]

Both liberal-socialist and conservative historiographical traditions,
it may be noted, presuppose a sharp distinction between thought and
action, ideas and circumstances. And despite liberal historiography's
emphasis upon the contingent event, both traditions have as a whole
downgraded contingency in their accounts of the coming of the Revolution, regarding it as "inevitable," whether as a result of "abuses" or
"ideas." But is there no middle way, it might be asked, between ideas
and events? Might not ideas themselves have been among the "circumstances" surrounding the composition of the Declaration of the
Rights of Man and of the Citizen, interacting with each other and
events in quite contingent ways?

Some such mediating approach will be attempted in what follows.
Certain competitive ways of thinking about the French realm or "nation" and its history, it will be argued, came to the point of ultimate
confrontation in the summer of 1789, interacting with "events" in
such a way as virtually to exclude France and French history as possible reference points in a declaration of rights. Hence the Assembly's
attempt at timeless universalisms in 1789. These timeless universalisms, however, at best papered over the competitive readings of
French history and the issues that underlay them. These issues hence
persisted in the form of competitive constitutionalisms and interpretations of the Declaration of Rights itself. Yet the same ideological circumstances that gave rise to the Declaration's "metaphysical" form
—so the argument continues—militated against any moderate or
"historical" interpretation of the Declaration, increasing the likeli-
hood that the National Assembly would assume the inheritance of
undivided sovereignty, much to the immediate detriment of individual rights.

This argument relies primarily on the evidence of pamphlets. Unlike the *cahiers de doléance* drafted by the electoral assemblies for the Estates General in 1789, the pamphlets appeared continuously from the beginning of the prerevolutionary crisis of 1787 to the drafting of the Declaration of Rights, and therefore provide a longer look at the development of revolutionary ideology.

≺ I ≻

The American Precedents

Is the French Declaration either so different from or similar to the American precedents as these opposing theses imply? The sharp contrast that Gauchet and Furet following Taine have drawn between the French Declaration's conflation of individual rights with public powers and the American constitution's distinction between the two stands out a little less saliently than might be expected, especially if we consider the various states' declarations or bills of rights which were available in translation to the French as models. Like the French declaration, the American declarations routinely juxtapose articles of individual or civil liberties such as the "enjoyment of life and liberty" and principles concerning the nature and distribution of public powers which are technically constitutional.[8] And as in the French declaration, individual rights in the American declarations are sometimes hedged about with public provisos. In matters of religion especially, the New England states' declarations went much farther than did the French declaration in protecting the rights of *governments* to impose duties on individuals.[9]

It remains true, however, that in comparison to the French declaration the American declarations generally prefer dispersed "people" to the more cohesive "nation," eschew the formidable term "sovereignty" in favor of mere "power," contain fewer references to the "law," and relate the purpose of law to the traditional notion of the "general good" or "common weal" in apparent innocence of the Rousseauian notion of the "general will."

It is abstract principles or criteria—the "nation" and its "sovereignty," the "general will" and the "law," "common utility" or "public necessity" and the "law," and last but not least "natural rights"—that doubtlessly give the pithier French declaration its abstract or "metaphysical" cast, which indeed sets it apart from its American predecessors. In sharp contrast to the detailed Anglo-Saxon parochialisms of the American declarations, what with their reverent references to "the common law of England" and specific strictures against "general warrants," nothing except the preamble's reference to "the French people" and its "National Assembly" obviously situates the French declaration in place or time.[10]

That these qualities of timelessness and universality are hardly inadvertent in that declaration, that they were indeed intended by its authors to distinguish the French declaration from the American precedents, fairly leaps off the record of the debates preceding and accompanying its adoption by the National Assembly. Although numerous deputies anticipated Burke in warning of the dangers of "a metaphysical exposition and abstract definitions" and despite advice in favor of a declaration of "factual verities" in the English style, the National Assembly's choice of a working draft pointedly passed over drafts closely modelled after the American ones and fell instead on a pretty "metaphysical" one that owed much to a draft by the abbé Joseph-Emmanuel Sieyès.[11] And although probably not many deputies agreed with Rousseauian deputy Jean-Baptiste Crenière's judgment that the American declarations were "absurd," most of them eschewed the comte de Sillery's plea for a declaration specific to time and place in favor of Pétion de Villeneuve's call for a declaration, "not ... for France alone, but for man in general."[12]

≺ II ≻

The Prerevolutionary 'Déjà Vu'

Not the least among the ironies of the French Revolution is that this first among anti-historical revolutions began as a dozen or more Old Regime crises had begun before it, with a confrontation between the ministry and the parlements apropos of the monarchy's insolvency and need for new taxes, and with both parties appealing to or at least evoking some segment of the French past.[13]

Confronted in 1786 by his chief finance minister, Charles-Alexandre de Calonne, with the news that the government's debt and annual deficit called for "constitutional" remedies, Louis XVI on Calonne's advice convoked an Assembly of Notables to consider a series of reform measures, among them a new land tax or "territorial subvention" and the creation of advisory provincial assemblies to help apportion it. The purpose of convoking a hand-picked Assembly of Notables was in part to disarm in advance the Parlement of Paris, which would eventually have had to register any new tax and was bound to oppose it if it came directly from the ministry.

But the notables refused to play the role of rubberstamp assembly. Encouraged by Calonne's predecessor and ministerial rival, the Genevan Protestant banker Jacques Necker, they disbelieved the deficit and demanded to see the monarchy's fiscal accounts. Believers in the baron de Montesquieu's famous typology of monarchy as dependent on social hierarchy, they objected to the novel form of the proposed provincial assemblies—delegation was to be based on property qualifications alone—and called for the restoration of honorific distinctions among nobility, clergy, and commons. And although they accepted the principle of equality of taxation, they doubted their own constitutional authority to assent to new taxes, and invoked the authority of the parlements, even the long defunct representative body called the Estates General. Nagged by the notables and pilloried in the pamphlets, Calonne fell from power and fled to England in the spring of 1787, the first of the Revolution's many exiles.

This first phase of the prerevolutionary crisis was accompanied by the appearance of pamphlets that not only reflected but to some degree shaped the debate between Calonne and the notables. Stimulated on the notables' side by the meeting of a "national" assembly, erudite enquiries into the history of "national assemblies" purported to demonstrate that such assemblies had existed at the beginning of the monarchy and had once involved the whole French "nation." As it developed, this archival pamphleteering became more audacious, ending with the assertion of the constitutional principle of something like national legislative authority and a call to "citizens" to acquire a "knowledge of their [political] *rights*, which are intimately related to that of the duties of man."[14] On the other side, some pamphleteers rose to Calonne's defense, justifying his land tax and socially undifferentiated assemblies in the name of the principles of equality, utility, and the general good. In a phrase that anticipated the last clause of the future Declaration of Rights's sixth article, one pamphleteer argued that delegates to the proposed provincial assemblies "ought not be differentiated except by their virtues, capacity, and ability to make themselves useful." And although these principles seemed opposed to French history to the extent that they stood opposed to "antique prejudices" in favor of "odious privileges," they were not incompatible with a royalist past inasmuch as it was the king who had gradually "destroyed all the particular [feudal and clerical] dependencies"—or most of them at least, except for the ones that Calonne now proposed to abolish.[15]

By the time the pamphlets no longer had either Calonne or the Assembly of Notables to advise, then, they had invoked two French histories against each other: one a political or constitutional history of France bewailing the rise of monarchical or ministerial "despotism" at the expense of a once free "nation"; the other a social and institutional history of France celebrating the rise of civic equality sponsored by a centralized monarchy at the expense of aristocratic "privilege" and feudal particularism. Implicit in these histories, moreover, were two very different conceptions of rights: the one proclaiming the whole "nation's" public or constitutional freedom on the basis of the principles of precedent and sovereignty; the other defending individuals' equality by virtue of the considerations of utility, reason, and the general good.

This pattern of a politically radical but socially conservative pamphlet pitted against a socially radical but politically conservative one continued, becoming even more salient during the parlementary stage of the prerevolutinary debate.

In July 1787, having dismissed the notables without obtaining their endorsement, the new first minister, Loménie de Brienne, archbishop of Toulouse, sent a revised version of Calonne's proposals to the Parlement of Paris for its "registration." Some of these proposals—for provincial assemblies, for example, revised to accommodate the distinction between orders—survived the gauntlet of parlementary registration, but it was otherwise with edicts establishing Calonne's revamped land tax and a new stamp tax. Like the notables, the *parlementaires* accepted—or at least did not object to—the principle of equality of taxation but, also like some of the notables, pleaded their own incompetence to approve of such fundamentally new taxes and formally appealed to the authority of the "nation" convened in the long-defunct Estates General. Caught offguard, Brienne and his ministerial cohort, Chancellor Lamoignon, retaliated with outmoded weaponry: an attempt to force registration of the contested edicts in the king's presence—a *lit de justice* assembly—on 6 August 1787, and the exile of the recalcitrant magistrates to a provincial city, Troyes, shortly later.

Negotiations and a compromise brought the exiled Parlement back to Paris in September. But this compromise, too, unraveled when on 19 November a supposedly advisory "royal session" (*séance royale*) in the king's presence degenerated into another *lit de justice* assembly and forced registration of five successive years of government loans, and the Parlement again remonstrated against this assembly. The ministry then arrested two of the most outspoken magistrates, whereupon the Parlement publicly remonstrated against the monarchy's practice of extra-judicial or "arbitrary" arrests and the use of "sealed letters" (*lettres de cachet*). Not to be outdone, the ministry upped the ante by having the king publicly accuse the *parlementaires* of aspiring to transform the monarchy into a self-interested "aristocracy of magistrates." The conflict continued to escalate until, getting wind that the ministry was contemplating an anti-parlementary coup similar to the one perpetrated by Chancellor Maupeou in 1771, the magistrates unanimously swore an oath on 3 May 1788 not to accept positions in any makeshift replacement for the Parlement, and also to defend their version of the monarchy's "fundamental laws." This fledgling but still historically oriented declaration of rights, the Revolution's first, now included the freedom of the individual from arbitrary arrest as well as the "nation's" right to consent to taxation in periodic Estates General.

These events signalled the crisis point of the Old Regime's last parlementary-ministerial set-to. The government made yet another attempt to arrest parlementary ringleaders who, forewarned, took refuge in the Parlement's assembled chambers, provoking a siege of the *Palais de justice* by royal troops not unlike the one apparently attempted by the monarchy against the National Assembly in July 1789. This marathon "session of thirty hours" ended only after the two magistrates identified themselves and submitted to arrest. In yet another *lit de justice* assembly on 8 May the ministry unveiled its own "constitutional" solution: a national "plenary court" (*Cour plenière*) amalgamating representatives of provincial parlements with a curtailed Parlement of Paris which would henceforth register whatever royal edicts and declarations the monarchy sent it. Although Brienne and Lamoignon did not, like Maupeou, profess to end venality of office, they abolished both torture in criminal procedure and the remaining seigneurial courts, thereby adding "feudal" or seigneurial rights to the widening public discussion of legitimate rights. The ministry then sent first the Parlement of Paris on vacation *sine die* and after it the provincial parlements as each protested in turn against the "military" registration of the May edicts.[16]

≺ III ≻

The Patriotic Pamphlet

These events precipitated an avalanche of mainly anonymous pamphlets—more than a thousand between July 1787 and the end of September 1788—some of them against but most of them sympathetic to the parlements. The great bulk of these pro-parlementary or "patriotic" pamphlets, as they were then called, were inexpensively printed *arrêts* and remonstrances of the various parlements themselves; more interesting, however, are the many anonymous pamphlets which, written by simple *avocats* more often than by magistrates, drew out the most radical implications of the long legacy of parlementary constitutionalism. Although some pamphlets persisted in seeing the office-owning or venal parlementary magistracy as the nation's best and only legitimate representative—the constitutional successor, in effect, of presumably ancient national assemblies—most reflected the weakened position of the Parlement of Paris after Chancellor Maupeou's constitutional coup of 1771, and hence followed the Parlement of Paris itself in appealing to the Estates General as the nation's most direct mouthpiece.[17] And although many pamphleteers, like most of the Parisian magistrates themselves, had probably not envisioned the purview of a revived Estates General as embracing much more than the monarchy's fiscal administration, the appeal to the "nation" encouraged them and others to enlarge this agenda, and to imagine the Estates General reconfirming or perfecting France's presumably "historical" constitution. With varying degrees of clarity, then, and more distinctly than while the Assembly of Notables met, patriotic pamphlets espoused some degree of national legislative sovereignty and the separation of constitutional powers. And to the extent that they defended the right of magistrates and barristers to speak and of pamphlets to appear, patriotic pamphlets also stood for the rights of individual liberty and the freedom of the press.

It was only in the recent past, in the patriotic view of events, that these public and individual rights had fallen victim to despotism. Indeed, these partial harbingers of revolutionary ideology are relentlessly historical, reading French history as a crescendo of usurpations of national constitutional rights by the forces of "ministerial" if not monarchical "despotism." They are also pervasively defensive, fearful of human fallibility and its "desire to dominate." The many villains of patriotic history included Charles VII, Louis XI, Richelieu, Mazarin, and Louis XIV; the all-too-few heroes were Charlemagne, Louis XII, and Henry IV. Yet this history had more than negative value, because the historical record bore faithful "witness" to the existence of these rights, a precious and consoling confirmation of the dictates of natural law. At its most radical, the patriotic pamphlet might frankly express preference for a republican form of government, or it might frontally assault the whole notion of divine-right monarchy.[18] But the bias of its outlook was political and constitutional, not social, and its respect for the historical institutions and corporate texture of Old-Regime France would eventually make it unseaworthy in revolutionary waters.

The most widely read patriotic pamphlet of the prerevolutionary period was probably the comte Emmanuel d'Antraigues's *Mémoire sur les Etats-généraux*, which appeared in 1788 and went through fourteen editions.[19] A certain danger attends taking this *Mémoire* as exemplary of patriotic discourse. For d'Antraigues himself later emerged as an outspoken defender of the nobility's separate "constitutional" identity in the Estates General, making it seem as though, for him at least, patriotic discourse had never been more than a rhetorical smokescreen for noble interests. Yet his *Mémoire* is just as plausibly evidence of how powerful and pervasive that discourse was, to the point of temporarily overwhelming a Catholic nobleman's sense of social self-interest. And as d'Antraigues was also a serious student of Rousseau's *Social Contract*, his *Mémoire* also illustrates the degree to which patriotic discourse successfully assimilated some of the most anti-historical elements in the eighteenth-century French Enlightenment.

To be sure, d'Antraigues began, the "essential rights of societies" were "written by the hand of God on the hearts of men," and it would be "terrible" to suppose that Frenchmen had "no other titles to their national liberty than those covered by eight centuries of archival dust." It was nonetheless those remote records that, enlightened by the "heart of a free man," revealed "the precious remains of our first institutions," and suggested the project of "restoring among us those national institutions that surrounded us in the cradle."[20] The national institutions in question were of course those of the Frankish conquerors of Gaul who, "gathered around a king they had elected," had met annually in "august assemblies." Endowed with "legislative authority," an assembly's "general wish [*voeu général*] dictated the law." The king's role was limited to presiding over these assemblies and executing the laws; he was punished for disobeying them. The whole Frankish nation retained these free institutions and political "rights" through the reign of Charlemagne, the greatest of French kings, after which they fell victim to feudal confusion and then to royal conquest.[21]

An imperfect restoration of these national assemblies took place in the late Middle Ages in the form of the Estates General which, though no longer able to convene the whole nation, carefully bound delegates to the wishes of their constituents by means of written mandates. Under Philip V the Estates promulgated an early "declaration of our rights" solemnizing, among other things, the king's promise not to raise taxes without the consent of the Estates. The parlements acquired their final form during the same period and, although not literally representative of the nation or successors of earlier legislative assemblies, became a "national judicial corps by the decrees of the Estates General," and a legitimate defender of the nation's interest in the absence of the Estates themselves. In an obvious reference to recent events, d'Antraigues reminded Frenchmen that the parlements had just tried to restore their "imprescriptible rights," only to be "menaced with an entire destruction . . . pursued by the ministers into their own sanctuary, and forced to abandon it to military force."[22]

Yet the fate that had now befallen the parlements had long bedeviled the defenders of the nation. Neither the Estates General nor the parlements had been able to protect Frenchmen's "imprescriptible rights" from the modern monarchy's drive toward "absolute power." That drive, in d'Antraigues' estimation, was "unfortunately inevitable," seeing that "the desire to dominate is the foible of the human heart" and that those "destined by the laws for the throne were of all men the most subject to error."[23] The descent into despotism began under Charles VII who established a permanent militia with the tax called the *taille*; but it was Louis XI who, combining "a tyrant's character with a scoundrel's heart, endowed despotism with all of its energy." The benign but all too brief reigns of Louis XII and Henry IV were not enough to reverse the trend because, however well-intentioned some kings were, their ministers never were. Indeed, it was under the "tyranny" of Richelieu and the "knavery" of Mazarin that despotism took systematic form—became "ministerial despotism" in short—representing "the last extreme of absolute power" and the "corruption of despotism itself." Thus did these ministers forge the "chains" of Louis XIV's long reign and the "incredible pretention, always maintained by ministers," that the king reigned as a sort of "divinity."[24] And thus also had one despotic usurpation led to another until, "fallen into the deepest degradation," Frenchmen—with d'Antraigues as their guide—turned to a more distant past "to search among the tombs of our forefathers for the hope of a national resurrection."[25]

D'Antraigues himself was not without guides, and the ones he appealed to along the way give a fair indication of the ideological makeup and ancestry of the patriotic pamphlet. Such paradoxes as that "man is born free" while bearing the "essential rights of societies" announce the inspiration of Jean-Jacques Rousseau's *Social Contract*, although it remains uncited as such. Vaguely Rousseauian too are the appeals to the nation's "general will" or "general wish" as the source of all law. Unlike Rousseau's "general will," however, which regenerated and replaced particular wills, d'Antraigues's designated those areas where particular wills conveniently coincided; and his quest for the remote Merovingian past took abrupt leave of the *Social Contract*'s timeless truths.[26] That quest led to Montesquieu's *Spirit of the Laws* and to the historical works of the comte Henri de Boulainvilliers. Yet d'Antraigues was not slavishly dependent on these sources either, seeing that his thesis of legislative sovereignty is quite foreign to Montesquieu while his "nation" is clearly much larger than Boulainvilliers's exclusively noble affair.[27]

A few unobtrusive citations from a two-volume work entitled the *Maximes du droit public françois* point to d'Antraigues's chief cache of anti-absolutist ammunition.[28] It was principally from this source that he derived such theses as that kings did not reign by virtue of special divine grace, that coronation oaths proved that French kingship had once been elective, that the Estates General might convene themselves without royal authority, and that the absolutist *lit de justice* ceremony had once been a national deliberative assembly.[29]

Originally published in reaction to Chancellor Maupeou's short-lived purge and "reform" of the French parlements in 1771, the *Maximes* was therefore part of the "patriot" pamphlet literature that was provoked by that event and that reappeared under the same banner during the prerevolutionary crisis. It was the work of four or five Jansenist barristers, possibly including the future revolutionary constituent Armand-Gaston Camus, and it represents the *summa* of a whole century of polemicizing by Jansenists in alliance with the parlements against the papal bull *Unigenitus* which had condemned the doctrines of predestination and efficacious grace. And indeed, d'Antraigues's *Mémoire* incidentally professed a view of divine grace as restrictive as any condemned by that bull.[30] But judicial Jansenism's case against Bourbon absolutism drew deeply in turn not only from parlementary constitutionalist literature going back to the seventeenth-century Fronde and before, but also from Calvinist "monarchomach" pamphlets of the sixteenth century. Accordingly d'Antraigues subscribed to a constitutionalist version of French history first articulated by the Protestant polemicist François Hotman in 1574; explicitly cited Hotman's *Francogallia* in one place; and, though a Catholic, allowed that the religious wars of the sixteenth century and the "protestant religion" in particular had "conserved liberty and energy in France during the reign of princes most minded to destroy them."[31]

From both Protestant and Jansenist sources, finally, d'Antraigues arguably acquired a "political Augustinianism," a defensive distrust of all political power but especially executive power which embodied the concupiscent "desire to dominate."[32] In his case this distrust armed itself with the "binding mandate" whereby unanimity among all of the "nation's" parts and parcels was required before their collective "will" might be regarded as "general." Designed to prevent delegates' undue compliance with the royal will, such a law would have prevented a nation's undue compliance with a legislature's mere majority, at which point d'Antraigues's constitutionalism made some contact with Rousseau's. What is hardly Rousseauian—but what is also politically Augustinian—is d'Antraigues's tendency to regard laws as "verities," eternally true even if history also bore a contingent "witness" to them.[33]

Together these "verities" would have made up d'Antraigues's—

and the patriot pamphlet's—ideal declaration of rights, which would have highlighted the constitutional rights of a certain separation of governmental powers, the responsibility of ministers to the nation, and the participation of all "citizens" in the election of delegates and in the formulation of law or what he sometimes called the "general will."[34] Among individual rights, d'Antraigues's declaration would have protected those to freedom from arbitrary arrest and to liberty of expression—perhaps even to public religious expression—but above all the rights to own property and to consent to taxation.[35]

≺ IV ≻

The Ministerial Pamphlet

The patriotic purity of d'Antraigues's *Mémoire* is compromised by a little alien content. Examples are the momentary dismissal of historical erudition as "useless," the judgment of feudalism as "dangerous," the condemnation of hereditary nobility as a "plague," and the definition of commoners or the Third Estate as "really the whole nation"—and therefore entitled to a doubled representation in the Estates General, the clergy and nobility being only "dependencies" or "political divisions."[36] These socially radical judgments were far more typical of what might be called the "ministerial" pamphlet that, until late in 1788, remained antithetically opposed to the "patriotic" thesis. As used here, the term "ministerial" refers to pamphlets that in fact took the side of the ministry, whether subsidized by ministers or not, and which in doing so displayed several common traits.[37]

The ministerial pamphlet typically attacked its adversary's implicit acceptance of corporate privilege with a conception of the nation as an association of individuals with equal rights. The accent was on equality rather than rights, however, making the rights in question social or civic rather than political, and singling out the rights of a just distribution of the tax burden and equal access to all social positions and places as opposed to "privilege" in either domain. While supporting Brienne's "grand bailiwick" courts as replacements for the parlements, for example, one anonymous pamphlet called for greater access to the judiciary for commoners; although exalting royal authority to the skies, another called for the doubling of the Third's delegation to the Estates General and the revocation of the Ségur Law of 1781 disbarring commoners from the officers corps.[38] For the ministerial pamphlet, therefore, the nation already consisted mainly of "the most useful and numerous portion of men"—that is, the Third Estate—and that long before the abbé Emmanuel-Joseph Sieyès's *What Is the Third Estate?* made this definition famous.[39]

Like the patriotic pamphlet that opposed it, the ministerial pamphlet subscribed to a version of French history, but a very different version it was! For where the typical patriotic pamphlet had bemoaned the rise of "ministerial despotism" at the expense of the primitive Frankish constitution, the typical ministerial pamphlet celebrated the rise of royal power which had effected the civil liberation of the Third Estate from the twin hydras of "aristocratic domination" and "feudal anarchy." Far from attesting to any fixed constitution limiting the exercise of monarchical power, French history in the ministerial conception of events tended rather to demonstrate the empirical necessity of absolute royal power, without which history unfailingly degenerated into one damned feudal thing after another. "That one commands, and that all the rest obey," was "the soul of our constitution," and followed naturally from French history's "spectacular proof that the absolute independence of the master is the rampart of the subjects' liberty."[40] The ministerial pamphlet's historical heroes were therefore precisely the "patriotic" pamphlet's villains: "Charles VII maintained the first standing troops, and Louis XI took our kings off [the Estates'] payroll," and "behold [royal] authority on a firm footing and the monstrous colossus of clergy and nobility, which threatened it, on the precipice of its ruin. Richelieu gave it the last push."[41] For all its social radicalism, then, ministerial discourse remained wedded to a very uncompromising view of royal sovereignty; indeed, it restated the *thèse royale* in language as brittle and willful as any before it. "The essence of a monarchical state is that the sovereign power resides in only one man": thus the anonymous *Je m'en rapporte à tout le monde*, adding that "the turbulent centuries of feudalism have proved to us only too well just how much that unity is essential to the general happiness."[42]

Yet this ministerial pamphleteering's continuing commitment to integral royal absolutism was not incompatible with selective appeals to the authority of the philosophes, most notably to the anti-"aristocratic" Rousseau and to the Voltaire who thought the "tyranny of the

one" preferable to "that of a *corps*."[43] In fact, what remained in prerevolutionary France by way of a *bona fide* "philosophic" community
tended to side with the ministry against pro-parlementary patriots.
Textual evidence of that tendency is perhaps the comparative absence,
in ministerial pamphlets, of appeals to natural rights, or in other words
to "nature" as a source of rights, and the marked preference for
the more utilitarian appeal to historical "necessity," to the people's
"happiness"—indeed, to "utility" and "preference" as such. When,
as would soon happen, ministerial language's "general happiness" or
"welfare" became the "general will," it did not have to change much
in order to become Rousseauian in a different sense than in d'Antraigues's to connote the people's real interest whether they perceived it as such or not.

One notable exception to this rule was the physiocratic school of
economic and political thought which readily invoked the natural
rights of surety and property but that, ever since Anne-Robert Turgot's brief tenure as controller-general in the mid 1770s, had looked to
the ministry and the monarchy as the ideal agent for reform. The physiocratic tradition's hesitancy between the language of utility and
that of natural rights is exemplified by the marquis de Condorcet,
who thought that equality under the monarchy's tranquility brought
greater utilitarian "advantages" than "aristocracy, which knew no re-
pose until it had destroyed all, even the memory of the rights of
man."[44]

While no single pamphlet epitomized the ministerial field in quite
the same way as d'Antraigues's *Mémoire* did the patriotic genre, one
pamphleteer dominated ministerial discourse to a greater degree than
anyone did on the patriotic side: namely the disbarred barrister and
journalist Nicolas-Simon-Henri Linguet. A Jansenist's son who wrote
pamphlets in favor of Jesuits, would-be philosopher who wrote against
"the fanaticism of the philosophes," barrister who polemicized all his
life against the bar and the parlements, and prisoner of the Bastille
who defended the cause of "despotism," Linguet threw himself body
and soul into the defense of the ministry and the monarchy, producing
thirteen or fourteen pamphlets as well as his periodical *Annales politiques* which continued to appear until the end of 1788.[45] "As to the
ministers," he avowed, "it is true—very true—that it is their cause
that I defend; yet it is also my own principles I maintain."[46] Those

principles, he explained, consisted in dedication to "*true public welfare*" and the "true *advantages* of the *people*," and an "involuntary
aversion for *aristocracy*" including the English constitution.[47]

It was not "ministerial despotism," in Linguet's estimation, but
rather "corporate consciousness" (*esprit de corps*) that was the real
enemy facing France in 1788. This corporate consciousness was "in
every respect more redoubtable and terrible to both prince and subject
. . . than ministers without capacity . . . because whereas ministers die
or are replaced, this mentality never dies." Whereas the "blind incorporation, as it were, of all wills into a single one" was advantageous to
—even the essence of—certain professions like the military where
"success depends on rapid obedience," it was the nemesis of "the liv-
ery of justice" whose "essence was on the contrary that of reason and
reasoning." And that corporate consciousness was, alas, now suffocat-
ing France in the form of her parlements, what with their tentacles
having a horizontal hold on each of her provinces combined with a ver-
tical grip on a whole segment of society from the ennobled magistracy
on top to the merest *greffier* on the bottom.[48]

Was Linguet contradicting himself, enjoining "obedience" on subjects in general while blaming it in the case of the magistrates? Only a
little, since obedience to a corps in his opinion too often meant disobedience to the king, and nothing, least of all a corps, had any place in
Linguet's opinion between individual subjects and their king. Linguet
hence had little patience with Montesquieu's much vaunted "intermediate *corps*," the first of which had been medieval "feudal government" featuring an aristocracy of "subaltern tyrants" that had reduced
the monarchy to impotence and the people to "a flock of slaves." Happily, the monarchy eventually recovered its sovereign "rights," in the
process restoring the social "liberty" of the people, and demonstrating
that the "people cannot be happy, free, or tranquil except to the extent
that the sovereign is free from everything that can impede the exercise
of absolute power." There was therefore no king, thought Linguet,
"not even Louis XI himself, who was not entitled to our gratitude—
and yet some dare these days to try to inspire us with horror for so advantageous a government!"[49]

Those ungrateful denouncers of despotism were of course the
parlementary magistrates, who had long played that role. But not so
long as *parlementaires* thought—not so long, for example, as had the
Estates General which, having enjoyed no more independence from

royal authority than did the Parlement, had formerly met to advise the king at his good pleasure albeit with mainly "pernicious effect." How much more insufferable, then, the pretensions of an originally bourgeois magistracy whose proper business was only the administration of private justice and whose institutional "genealogical tree" dated only to King Philip the Fair and the stabilization of his heretofore ambulatory court in 1302. Alas! These *parlementaires* had unfortunately if recently become nobles indeed; and after having been Burgundians under Charles VII, Leaguers under Henry IV, *frondeurs* under Louis XIV, and Jansenists under Louis XV, they were now trying to foist an aristocratic Estates General on good King Louis XVI and the poor people of France.[50]

That it was an "aristocratic" Estates General that the Parlement had in mind was revealed to Linguet by its *arrêt* of 25 September in favor of the "forms of 1614," which he took to mean that the clergy, nobility, and Third Estates would have three equal delegations and votes, with each able to veto the others' decisions. Thus the Parlement's version of a balanced constitution more English than England's because, counting the king, this French constitution would have four parts instead of England's mere three, thereby enabling "a single one to prevail over three." As a checkmate to this aristocratic general will Linguet moved the "*utility* of the [ministry's] reforms of 8 May" and the "demonstrated *necessity* of the preponderance of the throne," and as an antidote to this monstrous "*quadrature*" he proposed the united "*interest* of the king and the Third Estate."[51]

Obviously, Linguet was not very interested in constitutional arrangements, particularly if they involved limitations on royal authority. Linguet was just as indebted to Rousseau as was d'Antraigues, but his Rousseau was not the theoretician of popular sovereignty but rather the critic of "aristocracy" and "intermediate bodies." As Darlene Gay Levy has observed, Linguet tended to equate the "general will" with the king's will; like Rousseau, he tended to see all varieties of "balanced" constitutions as so many disguises for "partial" and "aristocratic" self-interest.[52] Linguet's rights, then, were social rights rather than political or even natural ones: the rights to life and property, to be sure, but most especially *equal* rights as opposed to privileges. Hence his lifelong demand for accessible and affordable "civil justice" for commoners and, in 1789 at least, something like proportional representation for the Third Estate in the realm's chief institutions including the Estates General. In one of his last and most incendiary prerevolutionary publications, the *Avis aux Parisiens*, Linguet characteristically urged commoners to demand that they henceforth constitute three-fourths of the personnel of the parlements and no less than seven-eighths of the deputies of the newly convoked Estates General, which might then make common cause with the king against "the clergy, the nobility, and the magistracy leagued together."[53]

Yet the precociously revolutionary tone of this anti-aristocratic rhetoric does not obscure a traditional royalism for which Linguet eventually paid with his head. And however *sui generis* Linguet may have been, his royalism clearly points to precedents other than Rousseau. Linguet was hardly indebted to the pamphlet defense of Chancellor Maupeou and Company in 1771, seeing that he himself had contributed four or five pamphlets to that cause and so in 1787–88 needed only to quote himself.[54]

But the ancestry of the late-eighteenth-century ministerial pamphlet is itself just as hoary as that of the patriotic pamphlet. For behind the pamphlet defenses of Brienne and Lamoignon in 1788 and Maupeou in 1771 lay a vast hinterland of apologies for absolutism, ranging from the episcopacy's defense of royal authority against the Jansenist parlements in the decades just before 1770 to Jean Bodin's high definition of sovereignty in reaction to the challenge of Protestant monarchomachy in the sixteenth century.

All these languages still spoke through Linguet, whether he was aware of it or not. His occasional swipes at Jansenists and his erstwhile defense of Jesuits recalled the *parti dévot*'s defense of the monarchy and the bull *Unigenitus* in the 1750s and 1760s, while his abhorence of Montesquieu, the English constitution, and the whole notion of mixed government echoed Jean Bodin's influential characterization of sovereignty as "indivisible" in the sixteenth century. Linguet's perverse defense of "despotism" found a pedigree in the abbé de Saint Pierre's apologia for enlightened "*despoticité*" in the 1720s, while his excoriation of "feudalism" and "aristocracy" harked back to seventeenth-century royalist historiography's celebration of the monarchy's triumph over "feudal anarchy" and "aristocratic usurpation," to say nothing of the proto-philosophic marquis René-Louis d'Argenson's more recent judgment that "democracy is as much the friend of monarchy as aristocracy is its enemy."[55] Nothing, finally, was more conspicuous in Linguet's language than the appeals to "utility," "necessity," "interest," and the "general good," appeals that had long figured prominently in justifications for monarchical high-handedness, from medieval legists' casuistry of *ratio necessitatis* (reason of necessity) and *ratio publicae utilitatis* (reason of public utility), to the physiocrats' utilitarian defense of the necessity of a "tutelary authority."[56]

≺ V ≻

The National Synthesis

Although the integral absolutism of Linguet's ministerial pamphlets looked a little anachronistic after the royal declaration convoking the Estates General, they were in other respects quite precocious. Among the first pamphleteers to hurl the charge of "despotism" back in the face of the magistracy— thereby conflating "despotism" with "aristocracy"—he also advised his pro-parlementary readers that "if you are determined at all costs to topple the throne, at least raise the entire nation on its debris."[57] That advice was prophetic: the final three months of 1788 witnessed a revolutionary conflation of the hitherto opposed charges of "despotism" and "aristocracy" toward which, although coming from opposite directions, Linguet's pamphlets and d'Antraigues's *Mémoire* both pointed the way. Those pamphlets which, beginning in late 1788, began to identify "despotism" and "aristocracy" *together* as the twin *bêtes noires* of the apocalypse might well be called "national" pamphlets, following the name invented by a perspicacious pamphleteer who thought he descried the formation of a "national party" between the parlementary and royalist ones in 1788.[58]

Patriotic and ministerial pamphleteers had of course all along held much in common. Indeed, without some shared assumptions of which they were probably unaware, debate between them would scarcely have been possible. For both, France was already a "nation" consisting of "citizens," rather than a "realm" consisting of the king's "subjects." And although they urged different rights against each other, both spoke the language of rights as well as of duties. Both perforce addressed themselves to public opinion on the implicit assumption that its authority somehow stood above that of either the king or the Parlement. What began to force patriotic and ministerial languages further together, however—what gave birth, in other words, to the "national" pamphlet—were the unprecedented institutional developments of late August and early September 1788 that dragged the whole debate into ideological *terra incognita* where no workable version of French history clearly pointed the way. The institutional developments in question had of course to do with the monarchy's imminent bankruptcy and the resultant convocation of the Estates General.

By finally securing the convocation of the Estates General, the parlements' resistance together with the monarchy's fiscal impasse challenged the very premises of Bourbon absolutism, exposing those pamphleteers like Linguet who had been defending it in such unmeasured terms. Although the monarchy itself maintained the fiction, it became increasingly difficult to suppose that the king would do no more than "consult" with "his" assembled nation and then do as he best saw fit. Yet by registering the royal declaration of convocation on 25 September "according to the forms of 1614," the Parlement of Paris exposed itself to highly "aristocratic" misunderstanding, embarrassing patriotic publicists who had been defending advanced parlementary constitutionalism until then. Whatever the Parlement may have meant by the "forms of 1614," it was easy for ministerial pamphleteers like Linguet to read the Parlement's ruling as meaning numerically equal delegations by the three estates voting separately and therefore as a telltale manifestation of "aristocratic" self-interest.[59] That reading grew more plausible in early December in the wake of a second meeting of the Assembly of Notables. Called by the new finance minister Jacques Necker to advise him on the forms of convocation and composition of the Estates General, this assembly in majority not only interpreted the "forms of 1614" to mean what anti-parlementary pamphleteers had maliciously speculated it meant, but also laid it down that not even the assembled nation could change these forms.[60]

It was at this stage of the debate that a segment of noble opinion began to claim that the distinction between the orders and corporate voting were part of France's historic "constitution." Reinforcing the association between historical constitutionalism and the cause of "aristocracy," the *Mémoire des princes*, signed by the king's younger brother Artois and several princes of the blood, impoliticly tied the throne to the defense of this aristocratic "constitution," prematurely defended "feudal" rights and forms of property, and clumsily threatened the Estates General with a noble schism if the princes' views on these and other matters did not prevail. Under these circumstances, the ground became increasingly untenable for such defenders of parlementary constitutionalism as the celebrated barrister Jean-Baptiste Target, who, while continuing to interpret the Parlement's intentions on 25 September in the best possible light, had soon to acknowledge the existence of, not one, but "two dangerous enemies [that] menace the happiness and the liberty of Nations: ministerial Despotism and the Aristocracy of the highest classes." Like other national pamphleteers, he too called for the doubling of the Third Estate's delegation and the vote by head.[61]

The condemnation of both "despotism" and "aristocracy" entailed the condemnation of both patriotic and ministerial versions of French history. If French history bore witness neither to a lost constitutional freedom in need of restoration nor to the civil benefits of a strong monarchy, it was clearly good for nothing, at best a record, in the abbé Sieyès's words, of the long "night of [aristocratic] barbarity and ferocity" pierced only by a few rays of "pure despotism."[62] It is this global condemnation of all of history—or at least all of French history—this spirit of studied anti-erudition, that is conspicuous as a leitmotif in the "national" pamphlets after 25 September and that is one of their defining characteristics. "It is the salvation of France and not of the archives that we must heed," advised ex-Jesuit Joseph-Antoine Cérutti; "History is not our code," repeated the "enlightened" Protestant pastor Rabaut de Saint-Etienne. "What does it matter to us what our fathers did?" asked Jean-Nicolas Desmeuniers, impatiently summing up the case against history in late 1788. To come up with a workable constitution was attended with difficulties enough, he deemed, "without adding to them an obscure erudition almost always sustained with false or equivocal facts." Even d'Antraigues, whose *Mémoire* circulated under vaguely "national" auspices, felt obliged to warn that the study of history "would be catastrophic to him who believed . . . that we have no other titles to our national liberty than those that, during eight centuries, have been covered with the dust of the archives."[63]

These condemnations of both "despotism" and "aristocracy" and of the tyranny of historical erudition arose too suddenly and simultaneously in late 1788 to have been entirely spontaneous, and they betray the organizational influence of the many Parisian clubs which sprang up in the politically fertile soil exposed by the receding royal censorship. Among these clubs, the notorious Committee of Thirty was perhaps the chief institutional base of the "national party." Recruiting its members from both patriotic and ministerial camps, it forged a political agenda consisting of an enlarged (at least doubled) delegation for the Third Estate, the vote by head as opposed to the vote by order, the elimination of noble influence in the election of the Third's delegates, and the granting of wide powers to delegates as opposed to restrictive or "binding" mandates. And like the patriotic and ministerial "parties" before it, the national party pressed this agenda by means of pamphlets, to which it now added model *cahiers* for the upcoming Estates General.

Undergirding this whole agenda was the synthesis of the hitherto opposed patriotic thesis of the nation's legislative sovereignty with the ministerial antithesis of the nation as consisting in equally entitled commoners. The casualties of this synthesis were obviously the thesis of monarchical sovereignty and the conception of the nation as made up of privileged and corporate groups. And at the very center of this synthesis was the abbé Sieyès's famous *What Is the Third Estate?*

Sieyès reached this point of "national" synthesis dialectically, as had the "national party" as a whole. The first prerevolutionary pamphlet he wrote—although not the first published—contained a strong statement of the thesis of national sovereignty, yet envisioned a united three orders seizing sovereign power in the name of the nation from royal ministers. His second pamphlet, written under the impact of the Parlement of Paris's ruling of 25 September 1788 and the second Assembly of Notables, excoriated the principle of "privilege," even honorific privilege, and all but excommunicated the nobility from the nation, yet breathed nary a word about national sovereignty. His *What is the Third Estate?* finally put these two theses together with a combination of Cartesian clarity and Rousseauian passion, vesting the nation with almost limitless power vis-à-vis all positive law, defining the nation in opposition to all privileged groups and individuals, and prophetically urging the Third Estate to seize the occasion of the meeting of the Estates General to peremptorily declare itself the nation at the expense of both royal ministers *and* the privileged orders.[64]

To justify these revolutionary measures, Sieyès like Linguet invoked the language of "utility" and "necessity." Because the Third

Estate contained all that was "useful" to the nation, it was of para-
mount "necessity" to recognize its will as that of the nation itself. So
defined, Sieyès's nation was the "master" to change all positive laws
—the same claim that apologists of absolutism had always made for
the king. Yet d'Antraigues's natural law and natural rights were not
absent from Sieyès's language either. "Natural law" both gave birth
to and limited the nation; while "rights" resided within individuals,
"where an all powerful hand has etched them . . . in deathless characters." Bringing together the very different emphases in Linguet and
d'Antraigues, Sieyès's rights were both natural and positive, both political and civil, clearly including the political right to participate
in the making of the law and the right to social equality under the
law. The totality of both collective and individual rights in *What is
the Third Estate?*—of national sovereignty, of law as an expression
of the general will, of equality under the law—began to resemble
the future Declaration of Rights. But above all Sieyès deployed the
language of "will"—*volonté, vouloir, voeu, désir*—at the heart of
which lay the Rousseauian concept of the "general will." As befits
his work of synthesis, Sieyès's understanding of the "general will"
seems equidistant from Linguet's and d'Antraigues's. Like Linguet's
and unlike d'Antraigues's, Sieyès's "general will" excluded rather
than embraced privileged corporate wills; but like d'Antraigues's and
unlike Linguet's, it arose from many wills rather than descending
from the royal will, being expressed by the majority of equally entitled individuals.[65]

But what seems so clear at the center of this "national" synthesis
was inevitably more ragged around the edges. Recruiting informally as
it did from formerly patriotic and ministerial constituencies alike, it
was bound to contain the tendencies of both, more or less pronounced
in individual cases. Although for example Sieyès's future colleague on
the Constitutional Committee, Jean-Nicolas Desmeuniers, agreed
with Sieyès that the nation would do well to have "a single interest, a
single will," his constitutional scheme of things obviously had room
for a clergy and a titled nobility, whose separate interests might be
components of rather than obstacles to the formulation of a "general
interest."[66] And although its denunciations of particular corporate interests and its insistence on "a sole interest, which is the interest of
all," were fully as emphatic as in Sieyès's pamphlets, Rabaut de Saint-
Etienne's *Considérations sur les intérêts du Tiers-état* barely avoided

remaining in the ministerial mode, holding as it did that "our common center is the general interest represented by the king."[67] And not
only did the national consensus contain both patriotic and ministerial
tendencies, but the national pamphlet remained outnumbered by its
ministerial and patriotic rivals until the end of 1788. Whether because
it was subsidized by ministers—in this case Necker—or by reason of
residual rhetorical inertia, the ministerial pamphlet persisted in
"wanting its monarchism to be pure and absolute" well into 1789.[68]
And whether subsidized or written by real magistrates or not, a chastened but still visibly patriotic response to this accusation of "aristocracy" was tactically to concede a doubled delegation—sometimes
even the vote by head—to the Third Estate, but urgently to call its distracted attention to the ministry's tactic of dividing and conquering, of
"making a fulcrum of the Third Estate and using the nation to subjugate the nation."[69]

The distribution of rhetorical energy did not even change fundamentally during the four months preceding the meeting of the Estates
General in May 1789.[70] While it is true that a species of Third Estate
propaganda gradually detached itself from the ministerial agenda and
became a genre in its own right, and began visibly to distance itself
from French history as an incorrigibly "aristocratic" form of discourse, the Royal Council's deciding the issue of the doubling of the
Third Estate's delegation in the Third's favor on 27 December gave a
further lease on life to the thesis of an historic and ongoing alliance
between the monarchy and the Third Estate.[71] And while it is equally
true that the nobility hardened its stand against the still unresolved
issue of the vote by head or order, gradually conflating any distinctive
patriotic voice—at least on this issue—with that of the nobility *tout
court*, it remains the case that the totality of reforms urged in the
pamphlets on the one side and the other represents the accumulation
of reforms urged against each other by ministry and parlements in the
course of their preceding two-year confrontation.

At the patriotic pole, some pamphlets continued to preach the
Jansenist constitutional verities of the *Maximes du droit public
françois* on the assumption that a still corporately structured nation
would unanimously impose these reforms on the ministry and that
no dissension had arisen between the orders.[72] And at the ministerial
extreme, pamphlets pressed an ambitious and radically egalitarian
civil and social agenda on the assumption that it would be enacted by

commoners in cooperation with the king.[73] If prerevolutionary pamphlets can be taken as indicative, if not of public opinion, at least of the sorts of expectations that deputies brought with them when they gathered at Versailles in the spring of 1789, there is every reason to suppose that had the monarchy resolutely taken one side or the other of the controversy—had either voluntarily relinquished its legislative prerogative in return for fiscal help in cooperation with the "privileged" orders or asserted its reformist will against the "privileged" orders in cooperation with the Third Estate—neither the French Revolution nor its Declaration of Rights as we know them would ever have seen the light of day.

≺ VI ≻

New Events and Old Memories

As it happened, the monarchy took neither of these courses, thereby alienating the good will of all three orders as well as pitting them against each other. Perhaps the deputies of the Third Estate might have been able to endure the many insults they sustained at an anachronistic inaugural ceremonial if, in the estates' first plenary session of 5 May, they had heard an encouraging word from their putative advocate Jacques Necker. Instead they listened to Necker's "astonishing" invitation to the three estates to begin their deliberations separately—to a disavowal, that is, of the implicit promises of his *Rapport* of 27 December and the spirit of the electoral regulations of 24 January. Yet Necker's interminable speech of 5 May also succeeded in alienating noble deputies like d'Antraigues by intimating that the king intended to relinquish none of his authority, that he intended to receive advice but not orders from an Estates General conceived as his Royal Council writ large.[74]

Off to that inauspicious start, the monarchy then did nothing for a crucial three weeks. This inaction first augmented the influence of the rabidly anti-noble Breton delegates and the renegade noble—but pro-royal—comte de Mirabeau, on whose advice the Third Estate refused to verify the credentials of its delegates separately—refused even to constitute itself in any way, until what its spokesmen were already calling the "privileged" orders agreed to the verification of credentials in common. The government remained inactive while the nobility verified its delegates' credentials and on 13 May sent the duc de Praslin at the head of a delegation to announce this noble gospel to the Third Estate.[75] In response, the Third Estate, narrowly rejecting Le Chapelier's peremptory motion to invite the two "privileged corps" to join it in a common verification, instead temporized by accepting Rabaut's motion to accept the clergy's proposal to participate in "conciliatory" conferences with commissioners of the other orders for the purpose of resolving the procedural differences. These conferences proved fruitless, what with Target and Rabaut invoking "reason" and "equity" while the noble commissioner—probably d'Antraigues—appealed to history and the consideration that the division of orders was the best defense against "the progress of ministerial despotism."[76] After the collapse of these conferences the noble delegates clearly "affirmed themselves more and more in their system of aristocracy," in the journalist Le Hodey's words, and on 28 May declared that if their binding mandates obliged them to give up their pecuniary privileges, the same mandates as well as France's historic constitution committed them to the principle of deliberation by separate orders.[77]

Despite the monarchy's inaction, it was the threat of "aristocracy" that thus far preoccupied the Third Estate, leaving the nobility to worry about "ministerial despotism." That began to change when the government finally intervened, demanding on 4 June that the "concilatory" conferences be resumed in the presence of royal commissioners. This belated royal initiative presented the first chance for the Third Estate's own veterans of parlementary constitutionalism to come into their own. Speaking, to believe Le Hodey, with "prodigious force and energy," the Jansenist barrister Armand-Gaston Camus warned his fellow delegates that the king's request represented "a danger even greater than that of the awful privileges of the two orders," seeing that the monarchy was clearly up to its old trick of dividing the orders the better "to renew its blows of authority" and "violate [our] liberty," and he moved to reject the royal request outright.[78] It took all of Mirabeau's power to persuade his colleagues that the Third Estate was still strongest "united with the king" against the "resistances of private interest," and therefore to accept the king's invitation to resume the conciliatory conferences. But he did so at the cost of uttering the word "aristocracy" for the first time and of hardening the Third's stance with the proviso that its commissioners not be allowed to compromise the principle of common verification of credentials. The result of this new round of conferences was another deadlock along the same lines as before, reminding the "commons," as they now called themselves to the king's face, "of that natural alliance of throne and people against diverse aristocracies whose power can establish itself only on the ruins of royal authority and public felicity."[79]

On 4 June the government went further: Necker proposed a complicated compromise which, while preserving the distinction among the three orders, would have given the king the final decision over contested credentials. The clergy accepted it but the nobility rejected it, for the moment sparing the Third Estate the onus of doing the same as well as enabling even the monarchist Mirabeau to see that the ministers' "clearly manifested intention was not to favor aristocracy but rather to establish the most absolute despotism over the totality of citizens."[80] Refusing to discuss or vote on Necker's proposal, the "commons" let the "conciliatory" conferences run their course, whereupon, on 10 June, they revived Le Chapelier's proposal of 13 May and, on Sieyès's motion, voted to summon—amended to "invite"—the "two privileged chambers" to join them for common verification and began a roll call of all the delegates—clergy, nobility, and commoners alike. After crucial defections from the clergy by mainly Jansenist curés, the "commons" felt strong enough on 17 June to abandon the interim label of "commons" and, on Sieyès's motion again, to rename themselves the National Assembly. Although some may have thought with Mirabeau and Rabaut that this measure required the king's sanction, and most may have convinced themselves, with the barrister Nicolas Bergasse, that "it was [the king's] authority itself that you are defending against a religious, military, and judicial aristocracy," Camus made it plain to them that "the king cannot make us not be what we are."[81] Whether they all knew it or not, the deputies of the now National Assembly had burned their bridges to "despotism" as well as to "aristocracy."

That they had inherited the Parlement of Paris's long war of attrition against "despotism" became clearer on the morning of 20 June when, in a scene reminiscent of the "siege" of the Palais de justice on 6 May 1788, they found themselves disbarred from their meeting place by royal troops and so repaired to an indoor tennis court where they swore an oath not to disperse until they had "established and fortified" the constitutional rights of the nation.[82]

The Assembly's break with "despotism" became clearer still when, in the infamous *séance royale* or "royal session"—the same as what the *lit de justice* of 19 November 1787 had been called—the king annulled the Third Estate's assumption of the title of National Assembly, reaffirmed the traditional distinctions among the three orders, and belatedly promulgated his own program of reform. In the wake of the king's exit it was again Camus who made the crucial motion, proposing that the Assembly "persist, without any reservation, in all of our previous decisions."[83] But by this point even Mirabeau, who as recently as 16 June thought "aristocracy" still the Assembly's chief enemy, joined Camus in a posture of defiance, and on 27 June wondered aloud why Louis XVI, "who had the noble courage to convoke the National Assembly, would not listen to its members with at least as much favor as [he had] to the judicial courts, which defended their own interests as often as the people's." Objecting to the peculiarities of royal discourse in the "royal session," the Jansenist deputy Denis Lanjuinais observed the same day that the king had no more right to say "I wish" and "I order" than he previously had had to say "we wish and we order."[84]

This process of equal yet opposite politicization against either "despotism" or "aristocracy" is poignantly visible in the case of two obscure Third-Estate deputies who left accounts of the Estates General's transformation into the National Assembly. Jacques-Antoine Creuzé de La Touche (later Creuzé-Latouche), the lieutenant general of the seneschal court of Châtellerault in Poitou, arrived in Versailles full of respect for royal authority but, despite his noble-sounding name, precociously persuaded of the evils of "aristocracy." The "conciliatory" conferences elicited from him the unconciliatory comment that "it is false that the institution of the nobility is the support of the throne," seeing that "so long as the nobles have been powerful, the throne has always been in shambles, and on the contrary enjoyed no stability except when Louis XI, the cardinal Richelieu, and Louis XIV strengthened it on the ruins of the nobility." If there were no nobility at all, he thought, "virtue, talent, and merit would accede to all positions, and the King would encounter nothing but friends of the monarchy." Such was the effect of noble recalcitrance in these conferences on Creuzé that by the first of June he had concluded that the existence of the nobility could sustain neither the "proofs of history" nor the "examination of *natural justice*," and that monarchy would do very well "without that unreasonable and ambitious caste called *Nobility*."[85]

Creuzé de La Touche's unique preoccupation with the nobility—and his unqualified admiration for Mirabeau—lasted until Necker's compromise plan of 4 June, at which point his journal shows growing respect for Camus. By 25 June and the debate over how to rename the Third Estate he was of the opinion that "the veritable title of the Assembly, for naming it what it is, by no means needs the sanction of the King." Although the events leading to the "Tennis Court Oath" finally prompted him to denounce the "ministerial coups," he still regarded them as "the last resource of the aristocratic cabal." But his first denunciation of the "coups of despotism" followed hard behind, coming on the same page and unaccompanied by any reflections about "aristocracy." The measures unveiled in the "royal session" of 23 June left him little choice except to conclude that their "despotic" dispositions were the king's own, and Camus joined Mirabeau among his heros of that day. Puzzling over the evident contradiction between Necker's *Rapport* of 27 December 1788 and the electoral regulations on the one hand, and the events of 20 and 23 June on the other, he still thought "the abominable manoevres of aristocracy" most to blame, but the "agents of despotism" ran a close second. In reality, he had come to conflate these two villains.[86]

The opposite trajectory is illustrated by the case of Adrien-Cyprien Duquesnoy, an inactive barrister in the Parlement of Nancy in Lorraine, who came as the Third Estate's deputy from that city to Versailles initially convinced that ministerial despotism was the realm's main problem. "Who is really oppressing us, is it the nobility?" he asked himself, even while the conciliatory conferences were proving so fruitless. "No, it is the ministry," was his answer, convinced as he was that it mattered little to "the miserable inhabitants of the country whether there were a hereditary nobility or not, provided that they paid few taxes."[87] To be sure, he noted how manifestly "discontent" was the Third Estate in reaction to the inaugural speech by Necker; but that disappointment was not really his. On the contrary, he was at first most annoyed with Mirabeau—"a ferocious beast, an *enragé*," specializing in "a bad French, fallacious reasoning, contradictions, and bad faith"—and the radical Breton deputies "to whom it mattered little that the nation be free and happy, provided they humiliate the nobility." He much preferred the deputy Victor-Pierre Malouet's advice to negotiate in good faith with the nobility to Mirabeau's tactic of calculated inactivity.[88]

Yet the rest of his journal is a record of his growing irritation with the nobility. Reacting on 15 May to the "audacious and insolent manner" with which the duc de Praslin informed the Third Estate that the nobility had constituted itself, Duquesnoy thought that since the nobility had now thrown "the gauntlet into the arena, it will be necessary to pick it up," and that it was now probable that the Third Estate would "declare that it represents the nation, that it is the nation, and that the other orders are only exceptions"—all of this "thanks to the nobility's arrogance and precipitation." By 9 June Duquesnoy predicted even more confidently that the Third Estate would soon constitute itself, not as such, but "as the National Assembly or at least the Assembly of the Commons of France, taking that word in its largest sense, that is, as envisaging the commons as *the people, the nation,* and the other orders as classes under its protection, under its safeguard, but obliged to obey it."[89]

≺ VII ≻

"The End of History"

Outside the Estates General, new newspapers like Bertrand Barère's *Le point du jour* now joined the pamphlets in amplifying and trying to influence the reactions of the deputies in Versailles. Although some echoed the counsels of compromise and moderation of a Duquesnoy or Pierre-Victor Malouet, most that spoke in the name of the Third Estate amplified Creuzé de La Touche's initial bias in favor of the monarchy and against the "privileged" orders. Despite their show of loyalty to the monarchy, these orders were "most opposed to your desire to do good," an anonymous "non-deputized citizen" told Louis XVI in his pamphlet. If only the king would order the clergy and nobility to verify their credentials in common with the Third Estate "on pain of disobedience and the crime of *lèse-National,*" this citizen promised to "answer for the obedience of your faithful commons." Again, the nobility's insistence on the vote by order would result in "the veritable establishment of an aristocracy of nobles in the midst and name of a monarchy," more peremptorily warned the anonymous *Spectateur*, who also urged Louis XVI to order the nobility to verify its credentials in common in his capacity of "at least provisional legislator."[90]

But surely the *ne plus ultra* of all anti-aristocratic rhetoric to appear in the period of May-June 1789 was the *Le premier coup de vêpres*. "Oh Nobles, Nobles, how I hate you," groaned this anonymous author. "Is it not enough that your sumptuous carriages crush us, that your luxury is our despair, that your insolence vexes us every day; is it not enough that to your exclusive monopoly of graces and honors you add an exemption from all public impositions and the atrocious privilege of ruining us at our expense?" Holding out "no reform to wait for, no regeneration to hope for, so long the Nobility subsists," the author urged the Third Estate to have done with conciliatory negotiations and to declare itself the "nation's only mandatories"—in the certainty, however, that "you will be supported in this by a Prince whose popularity seems to increase daily, and by a Minister whose signal protection will not fail you in that decisive moment." So while the author's diagnosis that France was afflicted by a noble "leprosy spread throughout the body politic" may have been radical, his cure was still a traditional one: the historic alliance between king and commoners.[91]

Some of these self-annointed spokesmen for the Third Estate were already so anti-historical as to suggest that France had no constitution. Yet such polemics were aimed less against history as such than against the particular historical constitution that the nobility claimed to be defending: namely one that gave the "privileged" orders a veto over the decisions of the Third. Like Linguet, therefore, they railed at Montesquieu, the English constitution—any balanced constitution that claimed to derive the general interest or will from the counteraction of corporate particular interests. Quoting Rousseau, one self-styled "plebian" rhetorically asked the comte d'Antraigues whether he was "still so little advanced in politics as to believe in that childish concoction (*enfantillage*) of intermediate counter-weights." If the monarchy had any enemy, he assured d'Antraigues, it was not the people, but surely "the aristocracy of nobles and all privileged intermediary corps."[92]

Another pamphleteer justified the Third Estate's assumption of the title of National Assembly with the argument that no matter how small the number of generally interested citizens in comparison to the number of corporate and therefore particular interests, that number "would nonetheless form an absolute entity, together with all its prerogatives and power to organize its interests as a veritable sovereign." So consistent was this pamphleteer's Rousseauian logic that he did not shrink from the conclusion that even if that number consisted of "a single just citizen [the king?] . . . he would concentrate within himself the entire plenitude of sovereignty." Not surprisingly, he thought that those public spirited nobles and clergymen who wished to be released of their constitutents' binding mandates to vote by order might have recourse to the authority of the king in his "capacity as supreme guardian of the general interest."[93]

None of this, however, was quite tantamout to an outright rejection of French history. Like the Third's deputies in the Estates General, most of these same pamphleteers invoked their own—usually royalist—version of French history against their noble adversaries. France's most pristine historical constitution, thought one, was that of Charlemagne, under whose beneficent rule "I will show you the Nation convoked by him without any distinction of Orders." All agreed that the *example* of French history proved that things had always gone best when "the King and his People" stood together, that the example of all history was that the worst enemy of royal authority was "aristocracy."[94]

To be sure, this radically anti-aristocratic version of the *thèse royale* never entirely monopolized journalistic discourse on the events of May and early June, any more than it did so among the deputies of the Third Estate. In language that recalled judicial Jansenism and the *Maximes du droit public françois*, for example, an anonymous pamphlet addressed "to the three orders" also urged the Third Estate to deliberate no longer and to "reclaim power without delay," not in the first place from the first two orders, but from royal power become too "arbitrary and indefinite." If the "commons" had always been faithful to the monarchy as anti-aristocratic publicists had maintained, explained this pamphleteer, "that is only because it is fully persuaded that it is God who calls princes to the throne and by the people that they are elected . . . and that it is only at the request of the people that they became *his annointed*." The pampleteer went on to cite the Old Testament prophet Samuel and the example of early Frankish history on the popular origin of kings, and to invoke such "maxims" as that "the nation has the right to convoke

itself"—indeed, that "the will of God is best accomplished in convoking it for its own conservation."[95]

But it required the monarchy's "despotic" intervention on the
side of the nobility and *against* the Third Estate to make this language the order of the day, to enable it to make its unique contribution to revolutionary ideology. And that of course is just what the
monarchy did on the days of the Tennis Court Oath of 20 June and
the royal session of 23 June. As in the Estates General in the person
of Camus, it was then for those familiar with the language of patriotic constitutionalism among Third Estate publicists to give meaning to these events. "Let us then open our annals, [and admit] that
our Louis XIs and Louis XIIIs, the Richelieus, Mazarins and Briennes
have attacked, savaged, and oppressed sundry corps and particulars;
but is it possible to believe that twelve-hundred deputies of the nation are subjected to the caprices, to the fickle and momentary
velleities of a despotic ministry?" cried Le Hodey de Saultchevreuil.
Again, "consult the history of France; how many good ministers can
you count since the Capets have occupied the throne? Abbé Suger,
Chancellor l'Hôpital, the duc de Sully, but among the others, good
lord! How many monsters!"[96]

But it took other pamphleteers to call what happened on 23 June
by its proper name. Is it possible, a pamphleteer had the king of England ask Louis XVI, that you thought that "the Nation could be
pushed around like the parlements with *lettres du jussion*? It should
have been easy for you, or so it seems to me, to surmise that that assembly, whose *cahiers* are not remonstrances ... would have acted
toward you with the determination of destiny." What Louis XVI attempted to do to the National Assembly, one recently deceased Paporet patiently explained to Louis XV in the afterworld, was "what in
your time was called a bed of justice [*lit de justice*], even though that
Assembly witnessed neither justice nor a bed."[97]

The events of 20 and 23 June and their interpretation by patriotic
discourse, then, effectively discredited the thesis of a natural alliance
between king and commoners—and with it the reading of French
history as illustrative of that alliance. Royal and ministerial "despotism," it now seemed, was a danger after all. But this new awareness
of the past and present danger of "despotism" did not eliminate the
threat of "aristocracy," nor did it reconvert anybody to the thesis that
French history bore positive witness to the existence of some pristine

\ constitution in need of restoration. Having substantiated, with generous help from events, each other's worst case "despotic" and "aristocratic" scenarios, patriotic and ministerial discourses joined in a
kind of negative alliance that did not entail acceptance of either's
more positive agendas. "Our misfortunes," concluded one pamphleteer, "attest to the non-constitution of the State, which has sometimes degenerated into an insufferable aristocracy, sometimes into a
real despotism: in order to heal these [ills], it is therefore imperative
to fix that constitution."[98]

Momentarily bowing to the Third Estate's *fait accompli*, Louis
XVI ordered the clerical and noble holdouts to join the National Assembly on 27 June, provoking a noble manifesto in defense of the
"constitutional" principles of "the independence of the orders" and
"the form of voting by orders."[99] Alas, this "aristocratic" swan song
was only the prelude to more displays of "despotism." The monarchy's concentration of royal troops around Paris and Versailles in
early July, the dismissal of Necker and the apparently botched attempt at a sort of *coup d'état* on 12 July—these well-known events,
featuring a "despotic" use of royal power in apparent *defense* of an
embattled "aristocracy," cemented the negative conflation of "despotism" and "aristocracy" once and for all. On the day of the storming
of the Bastille on 14 July, and in the National Assembly itself, the
abbé Henri Grégoire set the tone, proclaiming that "a constitutional
despotism is trying . . . to destroy the hopes of a nation," while "aristocrats hope to consummate their crimes with military force."[100] Outside the Assembly, the pamphlets soon followed suit. "It is all over
with it, my dear fellow citizens, despotism has been destroyed forever," exulted the author of *Le tombeau du despotisme ministériel* in
the wake of the storming of the Bastille. If successful, however, the attempted coup would have preceded a "massacre" of the people by
"Aristocrats and their pusillanimous partisans."[101]

While fusing the epithets "despotism" and "aristocracy," the cru-
cible of events of late June and July 1789 also consumed whatever
positive past may have remained to revolutionary "public opinion."
Indeed, the principal factor that distinguishes prerevolutionary from
revolutionary opinion may well be this break with a positive or "usable" past. Even before 16 June, French history had been already hard
put to serve the Third's delegates deadlocked with the nobility in the
conciliatory conferences on the issue of common or separate verification of credentials, reduced at best to urging "how little the authority

of facts is conclusive on the issue," and therefore "inviting Mssrs. of the nobility to please consult the rules of reason."[102]

As it turned out, however, it was less "reason" than new historical "facts"—those of late June and early July—that proved most conclusive against all of French history until that point. To be sure, the still patriotic pamphlet *Aux trois ordres assemblés et non réunis* urged Third Estate deputies to "reclaim" or "take back" power on the assumption that under Charlemagne or Louis XII they had once possessed it. But when the Third Estate acted on this advice, the title of National Assembly that it took was without precedent in French history and flew in the face of Malouet's reminder that "we are not a new people. . . . We are deputies to the Estates General."[103] It is also true that when the deputies found their meeting hall closed to them on 20 June, some of them suggested that they repair to the *Places d'armes*, "that is to say, some said . . . to relive the beautiful days of our history, there where [with our kings] we used to convene on the Fields of March."[104] Yet they gathered instead in an ahistorical indoor tennis court, leaving the Fields of March to the comte d'Antraigues. And when, again, the National Assembly wondered what to do on 12 July in response to the news of the dismissal of Necker, the comte de Lally-Tollendal reminded his colleagues that "if the Parlement of Paris had been within its rights to demand the dismissal of Mazarin, are we not within ours to demand the return of the most virtuous of ministers?" But that advice came from a liberal noble who had already conceded that "it is with principles that France will be saved and it is with [historical] examples that she will be lost."[105] It was perhaps without ironic intent that the bookseller Nyon sent a book to the National Assembly on 2 July, and it was apparently without amusement that the president "received" it on behalf of the Assembly, but the subject of the book, the history of France *before* Clovis, could hardly have been more appropriate to France's situation in July 1789.[106]

≺ VIII ≻

Text and Context

French history continued to have advocates, of course, even after the peasant *jacquerie* in the countryside combined with the National Assembly's famous session of 4 August had in principle destroyed most of the "historically" rooted provincial, corporate, and social privileges and exemptions. For one thing, most noble and clerical delegates joined the National Assembly after 14 July, momentarily reinforcing the ranks of the historically minded. And for another, large swaths of future legislative activity—the liquidation of "feudal rights," for example—lay well beyond the relevance of classical history or the writ of atemporal "reason," forcing deputies to argue their cases in the language of Old-Regime French or ecclesiastical history whether they wanted to or not.[107] Not even the debates over the Declaration of Rights and the new constitution entirely silenced French history, which found a voice in the comte de Sillery's plea for a declaration clearly rooted in a specific time and place, in Lally-Tollendal's similar advocacy of a declaration of factual and empirical rights in the English mode, and in Malouet's and Antoine-François Delandine's arguments against any preliminary declaration of rights at all.

The Assembly's decision on 4 August to promulgate a declaration of rights before "fixing" the French constitution was already to take a stand against French history, if only because, as the comte Stanislas de Clermont-Tonnerre pointed out on 27 July, "the demand for a [preliminary] declaration of the rights of man . . . is . . . the only difference between the *cahiers* that call for a new constitution, and those that call only for the reestablishment of . . . the existing constitution." For one of the strongest arguments against the promulgation of a prefatory declaration in the debates of 1–4 August was that such an abstract preliminary manifesto ran the risk, in Antoine-François Delandine's words, of "breaking a dike maintained by many centuries." Militating against history as well was the Assembly's decision on 4 August not to accompany its declaration of rights with a declaration of duties, seeing that such a declaration, in the opinion of Jean-Baptiste Lubersac, the liberal bishop of Chartres, would have acted as an antidote to the dangers of individual "egotism and pride" and given newly enfranchised citizens a moral ballast that only France's Christian—and specifically Catholic—past could have provided.[108]

But these anti-historical decisions themselves were all but inscribed in the immediate history preceding them. By damning French history as either "despotic" or "aristocratic," the circumstances of the prerevolution had severely impaired the case for an historical declaration and greatly enhanced the chances for one in a universalist and "metaphysical" mode. When both the moderate deputy Adrien Duquesnoy, who had come to Versailles thinking that the three orders should circumscribe royal power within "reasonable bounds," and Rabaut de Saint-Etienne, who had hoped that the king would lead the Third Estate against the privileged corps, could espouse the opinion that the declaration "ought to be invariable amidst revolutions" and "changing circumstances," it is clear that these revolutionary times and circumstances had conspired to efface themselves in favor of a declaration for all times and for all circumstances.[109] Hence, the answer to one of our initial enquiries: why the French Declaration's "metaphysical" cast, which so distinguishes it from its American predecessors?

Yet the fusion of anti-despotic and anti-aristocratic agendas also produced results more positive than the elimination of French history from revolutionary ideology. This same synthesis carried with it the union or coming together of political and individual rights to liberty championed by the patriotic agenda and social rights to equality touted by the ministerial agenda. Kept apart from and opposed to each other so long as patriotic and ministerial programs remained in competition, these two bodies of rights—of participation in legislation in order to protect the freedom of one's person, property, and expression against "despotic" arrest, censorship, and taxation; and of equality under the law and of equal access to all professions and positions against "aristocratic" privilege and exemption—began to coalesce in proportion as circumstances forced patriotic and ministerial agendas together.[110]

Hence the presence of all these rights in the finished Declaration of the Rights of Man and of the Citizen, which acknowledged the political principles of national sovereignty and the constitutional separation of powers (Articles 3, 6, 14–16); the individual's rights to property and resistance to oppression and to the freedom of person, action, and expression (Articles 1–2, 4–5, 7–11, 17); and the rights of commoners to equality under the law and access to all "public dignities, positions and employments" (Articles 1, 6, 12–13). The relatively few articles devoted specifically to equality in comparison to constitutional and individual freedom are semantically reinforced, however, by repeated appeals to the criteria of "utility," "public necessity," the "benefit of all" or the "welfare of all" (Preamble, Articles 1, 12, 17), which had come from the "ministerial" side of the debate and had been deployed by Linguet and others on behalf of social equality. These appeals were balanced on the patriotic side by appeals to "sovereignty" and its source in the "nation," "liberty" or "freedom" in general, and the "natural and imprescriptible rights of man" in particular (Preamble, Articles 2–4, 11–12). Finally, the principle of the "general will" (Article 6), presumed progenitor of the declaration's many appeals to the "law," was perhaps an ambiguous reference, seeing that it had been invoked by both sides of the debate in roughly equal proportions.

Yet the consensus that finally enabled the deputies of the Constituent Assembly to write the Declaration of the Rights of Man and of the Citizen could no more have entirely displaced the conflict that led up to it than the Declaration's universalist or "metaphysical" form could have entirely obscured the history—and "histories"—that produced it. Like two slowly shifting continental plates, two whole histories of France—absolutism and resistance to absolutism—came together in the Declaration of Rights, and they could hardly have joined in 1789 without provoking some monumental clashes and leaving some permanent fault lines.[111]

The clashes are of course the easiest to detect. Most germane to the argument of this chapter is the one that occurred on 21 August apropos of what became Article 6. Formulated by Bishop Talleyrand of Autun, that article employed the expression "general will" in a kind of major premise leading to the conclusions of juridical equality and equal access to public positions. That is to say that, as used in that article, the ambiguous expression "general will" carried ministerial rather than patriotic connotations. As originally proposed by Talleyrand, moreover, the article apparently did *not* contain the words "according to their capacity," which qualified the conclusion of equal access to public position. Was it to dull the article's egalitarian flavor that Jean-Joseph Mounier, a barrister trained in the school of parlementary constitutionalism, proposed to amend the article with the addition of those words? That at least seemed clear to the journalist Le Hodey, according to whom Mounier gave to "capacity" the "broadest meaning possible"—therefore "tending to maintain humiliating distinctions"—as well as to numbers of Mounier's constituent colleagues who, perceiving these implications after the amendment had passed, filled the hall with "cries against aristocracy." Order returned only with the help of Lally-Tollendal's proposed addition of the phrase anticipated in a 1787 pamphlet: "and on the basis of no other distinction than that of their virtues and talents."[112]

Less obvious are the Declaration's many fault lines which allowed deputies coming from either side of the old patriotic-ministerial divide to understand the Declaration in ways more or less consistent with their previous orientations. Thus the expression "general will," which d'Antraigues, who contributed constructively to the debate on the Declaration of Rights, was still free to construe as a concourse of particular if not corporate wills and which Maximilien Robespierre may already have understood as a virtuous preference for the collective interest untainted by particular aims. Thus, too, the "separation of powers," by which a former *parlementaire* like Adrien Duport might have understood a separation of countervailing institutions on the English model, such as some thought had once obtained between Estates General, the Parlement of Paris, and the monarchy; but by which Robespierre certainly conceived a mere separation of functions subordinating an executive monarchy to an all-powerful legislature.[113] Thus also the relation of "representatives" to their electors, which deputies as different as d'Antraigues and the proto-democrat Jérôme Pétion understood as direct and binding, but which others like Mirabeau and Mounier might regard as quite indirect if not autonomous.[114]

Thus, finally, the conception of the rights of man and the citizen themselves, which some persisted in thinking of as inherent in "man," and therefore "natural and imprescriptible" and only acknowledged by "law," and others as pertaining primarily to the "citizen," and therefore dependent on legislation and the Declaration's many references to "law." That is to say that, aside from the Declaration's "metaphysical" form and semantic break with history—arguably a force in favor of radicalism—nothing textually predestined it to the revolutionary year II, the Terror, or to an omnipotent Convention. Implicit in the Declaration was the possibility of a limited and moderate constitutional government scrupulously respectful of individual rights—the kind that Mounier later argued would have made France "free" and that would have been compatible with an emphasis on the fallibility of human nature.[115] "An assembly can err," stated the otherwise quite radical (but Jansenist) abbé Grégoire during the subsequent debate over the royal veto.[116] He was far from alone in worrying about power, in worrying that a subsequent legislature might become as "despotic" as the monarchy and the ministry had ever been.

What tended to thwart this constitutional potential, however, was the same combination of discursive and "real" circumstances that accounts in part for the declaration's "metaphysical" and universalist form. Along with competitive versions of French history, real and still existing institutions had been among the casualties of the prerevolutionary set-to between the monarchy and the parlements, between anti-"aristocracy" and anti-"despotism."

For where precisely were the proponents of a "balanced" constitution to locate institutional restraints on the velleities of the National Assembly and its legislative successors? The monarchy and its proposed veto over legislation, even reformed and acting as the agent of the national will? The subsequent debate over that veto was to show how much the recent events of 20–23 June and 12–14 July had indelibly associated the monarchy with acts of "despotism." The monarchy also meant ministers, and did not the reign of Louis XV present "the most revolting tableau of ministerial power?" asked the marquis de Sillery in his "eloquent" speech of 10 September.[117] A senate or upper house? That connoted an institutional base for the high nobility, and the same debate over the veto was to show how much the recent controversy over the verification of credentials and the vote by head or order had marked the notion of a senate with the stigma of "aristocracy." That stigma stuck even to the idea of a supreme court that would judge the constitutionality of laws, such as Dupont de Nemours urged. To any number of deputies, such a proposal smacked of the Parlement of Paris, mortally tainted since 25 September 1788 for its "aristocratic" ruling in favor of the forms of 1614.[118]

There remained of course the appeal to the "nation," that is to say to the National Assembly's own constituents, as a check on that and subsequent legislative assemblies. Such an appeal was supposed to have been the purpose of the suspensive veto finally given to the king. Yet any possibility of a constitutional, time-consuming appeal to the "nation" had been rendered suspect not only by its connection with a "despotic" veto but by its recent association with the judicial bailiwick or *bailliage* and the binding mandate that noble deputies like d'Antraigues had invoked in defense of the separation of orders and the vote by head. That left the city of Paris, the journalistic deliberations at the *Palais royal*, the threat of "twenty-five million vetos," and the "decree" of 29 August to revoke the powers of "ignorant, corrupt, and suspect deputies"—in short, the revolutionary intervention of the people, who displayed their power as early as 5–6 October 1789.[119]

Far from balancing it, however, the revolutionary appeal to the people tended to reinforce the power of the National Assembly, which alone among institutions remained untarnished by either "despotism" or "aristocracy" and toward which all the nation's business—executive, fiscal, and judicial as well as legislative—now rushed. These circumstances thus tended to validate the strongest and most high-handed readings of "sovereignty," the "general will," and "public necessity," which, coming from the ministerial side of the prerevolutionary debate, now empowered the "nation" in its representative assembly.

Classical liberal historiography—to return to the second of our enquiries—is therefore not entirely off the mark in insisting on the importance of quite palpable circumstances to explain how the Revolution developed as it did. The Declaration of Rights was susceptible of numbers of constitutional interpretations, and contingent circumstances like the royal session of 23 June or the abortive *coup d'état* of 12–14 July were surely decisive in deciding which of these interpretations prevailed. Yet these events did not come with ready-made meanings, and so it took circumstances of a different order, those having to do with a debate about the meaning of French history with roots deep in French history, to give these events the meanings of "despotism," "aristocracy"—and finally both. It thus fell to the French Revolution to take on the burdens of "despotism" and "aristocracy" at the same time, and that, as the prescient abbé Gabriel Bonnet de Mably foresaw as early as 1758, would prove to be too heroic an agenda for any merely "managed revolution."[120]

Betwixt Cattle and Men

Jews, Blacks, and Women, and the Declaration
of the Rights of Man

SHANTI MARIE SINGHAM

M EN ARE BORN AND remain free and equal in rights: thus began the Declaration of the Rights of Man and of the Citizen,
promising freedom and equality to all Frenchmen. But was the Declaration really applicable to *all* Frenchmen? Did its promises extend
to the Jews, confined to a separate existence and subject to numerous
taxes and humiliating obligations in Old Regime France? Was it relevant to the hundreds of thousands of Black African slaves treated
with barbarity in the French West Indies? Did it encompass well over
half the population of France, historically denied civic rights or political consideration, namely women? On the status of these groups,
the Declaration was silent, thus opening the door for vigorous debates concerning the place of Jews, Blacks, and women in the evolving body politic.

Discussion of Jews, Blacks, or women in the French Revolution
still evokes much of the passion and anger elicited by the same debates in the 1790s. Some praise the Revolution for emancipating the
Jews from their medieval shackles; others see it as the first moment
in the long trajectory of modern anti-semitism culminating in the
Holocaust of the twentieth century.[1] Some praise the Revolution for
abolishing slavery and elevating the Black man to the dignity of citizenship; others consider the French abolition of slavery nothing more
than an ex post facto reaction to the Black armed struggle for autonomy, the first successful slave revolution in Western history.[2] As for
women, their fortunes have been almost entirely ignored until the recent wave of feminist historiography, which, for the most part, has
condemned both the liberal and the republican traditions emanating
from the Revolution as inherently and irrevocably sexist.[3]

It is not my intention to avoid these controversies, but rather to treat them within the context of the unfolding of events of the French Revolution. As early as 24 August 1789, the deputy Maximilian Robespierre condemned the attempts of moderates to sully the clause on the freedom of the press in the Declaration with all kinds of restrictions, insisting instead that "free men must not express their rights in an ambiguous fashion."[4] Ambiguity, however, clouded the expression of the rights of Jews, Blacks, and women during the Revolution—in part because the fortunes of these groups were linked to various political causes and practical considerations that complicated the cause of their freedom.

The fate of the Jews was linked to the attack on the Catholic church. Intent on passing the Civil Constitution of the Clergy and afraid of having it denounced as a Jewish and atheist plot against the Church, the Jansenist abbé Henri Grégoire, a clerical deputy from Nancy and one of the Jews' most active defenders, remained silent on Jewish emancipation during his presidency of the National Assembly in the winter of 1790–91. The freedom of Black slaves in Saint Domingue[5] was linked to the economic importance of West Indian sugar to the French economy as well as to the international implications of Anglo-French rivalry in the New World, inducing Robespierre to argue for the preservation of slavery in 1791. The fortunes of women were tied to their important interventions on behalf of the Revolution as well as to their unfortunate coalitions with losing parties, like the Girondins and the Enragés in 1793.[6] Politics, the complicated game of winning, losing, and compromising, played havoc with the implementation of the high-sounding ethical principles of the Declaration.

The interests of the three groups sometimes conflicted with and sometimes complemented one another, depending on the manner in which they became contingently linked. Olympe de Gouges, a leading advocate of women's rights, outspokenly supported slave emancipation and linked the rights of Mulattoes to those of females.[7] In spite of Jewish involvement in the slave and colonial trades, by fighting to deny rights to both Jews and Blacks, the National Assembly encouraged the advocates of one minority to look favorably upon the cause of the other.[8] Speaking of the extension of the rights of citizenship to comedians and actors in December 1789, the Jewish pamphleteer Zalkind Hourwitz angrily remarked that "It is astonishing that the National Assembly has adjourned the business of Jews of all colors and men of color of all religions while it lets the directors and secretaries of gambling-casinos enjoy all the rights of citizenship. To be a citizen and even a legislator in this country of equality and liberty, it suffices to be the owner of a white foreskin and to have just enough honesty to avoid being hanged."[9]

Those revolutionaries in favor of emancipating the Jews, freeing Black slaves, and giving women social and political equality developed similar rhetorical strategies, using slavery as the archetypical model to describe their diverse conditions. The slave motif had become common in parlementary and patriotic publications during the eighteenth century. Comparisons between slavery, Oriental despotism, Bourbon tyranny, and feudalism abound in these works.

Rhetoric was important, for language widened horizons. Thus women attacked the sexism whereby men were "considered, even in everyday grammar, to be the more noble and honorable sex" and demanded the restructuring of French accordingly, foreshadowing current debates.[10] Patriots had earlier argued to cleanse French of words like *master* and *obey*, which encouraged men to behave like slaves.[11] And advocates of Jewish and Protestant rights during the Revolution argued for the abolition of seemingly benign words like *toleration* that implicitly acknowledged the superiority of Catholicism.[12] They steadfastly opposed attempts to call the Catholic church the *dominant* religion of France, pointing to the slave motif in the notion of domination.[13]

The attempt to restructure language was part of the attempt to restructure the entire culture undertaken by the French Revolution. Revolutionaries encapsulated their cultural program in the notion of regeneration. They were determined to regenerate Frenchmen, to change their language, customs, habits, and education, so as to end centuries-old patterns of submission and inculcate instead a republican and revolutionary *esprit*. They strove to create a new identity for the French citizen. As to the distinguishing marks of this citizen, everyone, including Jews, Blacks, and women, had a say, or so it appeared from the oblique language of the Declaration. For implicit in the Declaration was a wide definition of citizenship and mankind, one that conceivably could even be disengendered to refer to women.

At the core of the Declaration, indeed in its very title, stood a host of unanswered questions that it seemed to be asking. What is man? Were all men *naturally*, biologically, the same? Did man refer to *mankind*, thus encompassing women as well? Similarly, the Declaration enlarged the frontiers of the debate concerning citizenship. Who ought to have it? What constituted citizenship? Were cultural similarities necessary in making someone qualify for the title of Frenchman?

The debate on citizenship had implications not only for Jews, Blacks, and women, whose culture and whose physical characteristics tended to disqualify them from being considered true Frenchmen, but also for the vast majority of poor peasants in France.[14] Wealth was to become a major determinant of citizenship in the first revolutionary constitution of 1791, in spite of the efforts of radicals, like the abbé Grégoire, who considered the erection of an "aristocracy of riches" contrary to the meaning and spirit of the Declaration.[15] Yet even after the National Assembly agreed on the monetary qualifications for citizenship, Jews, Mulattoes, and free Blacks meeting these requirements were denied entrance to the body politic. As to women, their claims for political consideration fell on deaf ears throughout the Revolution.

The debates on nature, citizenship, and French identity were carried on amidst the turmoil and the ever-changing events of the French Revolution. Jews, Blacks, and women were to suffer in varying degrees from the militaristic and nationalist aspects of the revolutionaries' experiences beyond France. But the Declaration also held out the promise of fraternity, even sorority, in its ambiguous embrace of mankind, prompting sustained struggles by the advocates of Jews, Blacks, and women for admission to the community of free and equal Frenchmen. It is to these struggles that we now turn our attention.

≺ I ≻

Jews

Even before the Declaration had been agreed upon, the abbé Henri Grégoire encouraged his fellow revolutionaries to take up the Jewish cause. Speaking as a "minister of a religion that regarded all men as brothers," Grégoire evoked Christian humanism in defense of an internationalism that defied religious, ethnic, or racial difference. He demanded that Jews be treated with the equality and respect befitting Frenchmen.[16]

The promulgation of the Declaration in August and the numerous petitions sent from Jews throughout France to the National Assembly in the fall of 1789 gave Grégoire cause to redouble his efforts. Yet, in spite of the universal language of the Declaration, support for the Jewish cause in the Assembly and in the country was marginal. Few shared Grégoire's tolerant and inclusive Christianity, a by-product of his unusual Jansenist upbringing. Instead, traditional clergymen like the bishop de la Fare and the abbé Maury joined hands with the future Jacobin deputy from Alsace, Jean-François Reubell, to put a halt to Grégoire's initiatives.

Through such efforts the Jews were excluded from the provisions granting civic rights to Protestants, actors, and comedians on 24 December 1789. The debates leading to Protestant enfranchisement and Jewish exclusion were passionate, uninformed, and vitriolic. Anti-semites argued that Jewish separatism was self-imposed. Keeping kosher, adhering to a Saturday sabbath, marrying in the sanctity of a Temple under the rabbi's supervision—all were adduced as proofs of the unwillingness of Jews to mix, marry, even eat, with their non-Jewish neighbors. Reubell insisted, contrary to evidence, that the Jews were not even interested in obtaining citizenship. Instead, he insisted, their dream of returning to the Holy Land would keep Jews from making a firm commitment to France or any other nation. The Jews were and would always be foreigners, the prince de Broglie insisted, wandering nomads forever incapable of national allegiance and/or assimilation.[17]

In his *Motion en faveur des Juifs*, published in October 1789, Grégoire insisted that Jewish separatism was a result of government policy, not of Jewish intent. He pointed out that the corporate organization of Jewish communities under the Old Regime, set up by a government anxious to collect special taxes from Jews and subject them to various restrictions and regulations, was the true cause of Jewish separatism. Grégoire squarely laid the blame for Jewish conditions on Christian intolerance, monarchical greed, and popular ignorance. Arguing against the racial and ethnic biases undergirding anti-semitism, Grégoire insisted that Jewish evil was not innate, but circumstantial, as he was later to argue that neither race nor wealth was a legitimate reason to construct political inequalities.[18] Although he admitted that the Jewish people were in need of ethical regeneration, Grégoire went to great length to portray their strengths favorably. He gave historical examples of Jewish military and patriotic service to different nations, underlined the purity of Jewish sexual and familial mores, and denied the relevance of dietary or religious rituals for admission to the body politic. He provocatively demanded that Jews be given the chance to become good men by being welcomed into the expanding fold of French citizenship.

If pro- and anti-semites alike agreed that Jewish separatism was an evil, Jews often had more complicated and mixed feelings.[19] Jewish petitioners were anxious to put an end to the debilitating conditions imposed on them. They sought free access to cities, entry to French universities and professional careers, and an end to special taxes imposed on them as permanent "foreigners" resident in France; and they joined in the clamor for equality and citizenship along the lines of the Declaration. They were not, however, necessarily anxious to see their corporate institutions and practices ended.[20]

Corporate existence under the Old Regime had been the source of both comfort and dismay for Jews in France. On the one hand, Jewish corporations or *Kehillots* were representative bodies that gave form to Jewish community life. They oversaw charity, distributed the Jewish tax burden, collected funds, and supported both rabbis and Jewish schools.[21] On the other hand, Jewish corporate definition enabled local and regional bodies, as well as the national government, to subject Jews as a people to various special taxes and numerous restrictions. Jewish corporate status proved a source of difficulty in the years to come.

Differences between and amongst Jews proved yet another source of difficulty in the debates concerning Jewish rights. Fragmented into local corporate entities reflective of differing histories of migration and/or absorption into the French kingdom, French Jews were split into antagonistic and contending factions with vastly different economic conditions and privileges. Most successful were the Sephardic Jews of Bordeaux, many of whom were rich, well educated, and well integrated in enlightened society. At the other end of the social and geographical spectrum were the Ashkenazic Jews of northeastern France, most of whom were poor, hated by the surrounding peasantry, and subject to numerous humiliating taxes and restrictions. In between these two extremes were small numbers of Jews in various regions such as Avignon, Marseilles, and Paris.

Relations between the Sephardim and Ashkenazim were hardly

cordial.[22] The Sephardim traced their roots to Spanish and Portuguese Jews expelled from those countries in the fifteenth century. They had been admitted to France under the guise of being "New Christians," or *Conversos*, nominally subject to the authority and prerogatives of the Catholic Church. Most of these Spanish and Portuguese immigrants to France had settled in Bordeaux. Keeping their Judaism discreet and inoffensive, the Bordeaux New Christians enjoyed numerous privileges, including the right to trade and the right to move freely throughout their region. They spoke French, were actively involved in the colonial and slave trades, and even participated in the elections to the Estates General in 1789.[23] By contrast, the Ashkenazic Jews of Alsace, Lorraine, and Metz were recent members of the French community who still spoke Yiddish and adhered to a more traditional type of Judaism. Although a handful were wealthy purveyors, responsible for supplying the French army in the Rhineland with horses and grain, most of them were extremely poor. Subject to hated and humiliating taxes, the Ashkenazim were forbidden freedom of movement and relegated to the countryside, alongside an equally poor and resentful peasantry. Yet, since they were forbidden to buy land, they were unable to become farmers. They made their living instead in petty trade, supplying peasants with essentials and loaning them money in hard times.

Jews from other areas in France had varying statuses and rights. Those Avignonese Jews who had settled in France were fairly privileged, tending to specialize in draperies and the silk trade. Parisian Jews, on the other hand, had no legally recognized existence and were merely tolerated.

During the Revolution, French Sephardic Jews insisted on distinguishing themselves from the "mongrel Ashkenazim," whom they despised.[24] In the fall of 1789, when other Jews were scrambling to have the National Assembly recognize their claims to consideration under the Declaration, the Sephardim remained silent. They assumed that they were already encompassed by its decrees. When this proved not to be the case in the course of the debates of 24 December the Sephardic and Avignonese Jews demanded that they be given the rights of citizenship. Writing to the National Assembly on 31 December 1789, the Sephardim argued that, unlike the Ashkenazim, they had been naturalized and recognized Frenchmen for centuries. As proof, they referred to royal letters dating from the sixteenth century.

They drew attention to previous acts of patriotism, claimed to enjoy the status of *bourgeois* in Bordeaux, and proudly noted that they owned and traded in all types of property. They also denied having separate laws, officers, or tribunals and implied that, unlike other Jews in France, they were not organized into corporations.[25]

The Sephardic request of 31 December drew fire from pro- and anti-semites alike. Abbé Grégoire attacked it as a selfish maneuver destined to further isolate and debilitate the poor Ashkenazim, for whom he spoke. Reubell, on the other hand, argued against Sephardic enfranchisement on the grounds that it would set a dangerous precedent for the ever insistent Ashkenazim. The men of the National Assembly, however, were swayed by the persuasive arguments of the Sephardim. On 28 January 1790, the Sephardic and Avignonese Jews were admitted to the ranks of French citizenship providing they fulfilled the requisite financial conditions. In spite of some local opposition, Jews in Bordeaux took the civic oath amongst much public enthusiasm. Although only a handful of rich Jews obtained active citizenship, in accordance with the Constitution, the decree of 28 January nevertheless indicated that the men of the National Assembly were willing to forgo religious and cultural prejudices in the interests of a more universal conception of revolutionary citizenship.

Although numerous disabilities against the Jews were removed by committees of the National Assembly in the next year and a half, Catholic and Alsatian pressure combined to prevent the extension of citizenship to Ashkenazic Jews of northeastern France and Paris. Threats of peasant pogroms and the Church's assault on the Civil Constitution of the Clergy worked against Jewish enfranchisement. In spite of numerous petitions, and the active support of the Commune of Paris for Jewish equality, the cause of the Jews languished until the question was raised on the floor of the Assembly in September 1791.

As the term of the Assembly drew to a close, pro-semitic deputies anxious to resolve the Jewish question before its disbanding focused on removing the last vestiges of Old Regime prejudices and privileges. The Sephardic precedent of January 1790 helped Grégoire and others argue that religious and cultural inequalities were out of spirit with the Declaration. Invoking fraternity, these deputies argued for the extension of citizenship to men of any religion residing in France. Swayed by the emotion of a climactic finale to the constitutional work of France's first revolutionary government, the Assembly extended the rights of citizenship to all Jews. In the same gesture, it also extended the rights of citizenship to men of color, to Mulattoes and Blacks, resident in France. The new nation, these pronouncements indicated, was to be composed of free and equal citizens regardless of race or religion.

The decree, emancipating Jews from centuries of oppressive second-class status, was not without its costs. Furious at the decision, anti-semitic deputies proposed various clarifying restrictions. Using the ever-present threat of peasant pogroms against Alsatian Jews, the prince de Broglie and Reubell persuaded the men of the Assembly to explicitly link Jewish citizenship with a renunciation of corporate privileges and economic regulation. By insisting that all Jews who took the civic oath thereby "renounced all privileges and exceptions previously granted to them," the National Assembly swept away centuries of traditions. It was an abrupt change, taking little account of the peculiar manner in which Jewish religious and civic life had become meshed.

The assault on corporatism had, of course, already affected most Frenchmen in the aftermath of the night of 4 August 1789. Wiping away privileges, exceptions, and institutions, however, meant something different to a beleaguered minority than to other Frenchmen. The Jews were unsure of either the longevity or the good intentions of this new piece of legislation. Since the qualifications for active citizenship made most Jews in the northeast ineligible, and the vast majority of poor Jews were not particularly interested in the machinations of national politics, the Emancipation Decree appears not to have been greeted with the same enthusiasm in Alsace as it had been in Bordeaux. The complicated intermeshing of religious and civil law in Alsatian Jewish communities meant that problems were bound to ensue in the untangling of these two types of authority. What would become of Jewish charities, of collective debt, of cemeteries and burials, of marriages, in the new regime? How would military service affect the observation of a Jewish sabbath? These were some of the questions the Emancipation Decree posed for Alsatian Jews as they took the civic oath and joined the French nation in the fall of 1791.

The answers to these questions would vary in the years to come. Some regimes, particularly the Jacobin one, would opt for a rigorous interpretation of the Emancipation Decree, pursuing policies that appeared anti-Judaic at best, anti-semitic at worst.[26] The Terror combined Enlightenment promise and prejudice, supporting toleration and fraternity while simultaneously decrying the persistence of religious rituals as indicative of superstition and divisive discord. Voltaire, the maverick of the Enlightenment, had attacked Judaism for its religious proximity to Christianity, thinly disguising much anti-semitic sentiment as anti-religious diatribe. During the Terror, local Jacobin anti-semites were to do likewise. Voltaire had earlier argued that "a Jewish philosopher is an impossibility," since any genuine philosopher would leave aside the foolish superstitions of the Jewish religion. In like manner, Jacobins would argue that should Jews wish to join the revolutionary French family, they would have to leave their religious and cultural baggage behind.[27]

Pursuing a joint war against Catholicism and Judaism as part of its de-Christianization campaign, the Jacobin dictatorship in 1793 and 1794 allowed local officials to adopt policies that stretched the limits of the newly formed Jewish commitment to the Revolution. In the northeast, the Terror became associated with closing synagogues, burning Hebrew books, exiling obdurate rabbis; the nationalization, sale, and theft of religious artifacts; forbidding Jews to wear beards or side locks as signs of religious fanaticism; and even forcible intermarriage. Even though the Jacobin government stepped in to defend Jews from peasant pogroms, and although no Jew appears to have lost his life during the Terror because of his religion, the years of the Jacobin regime were not favorably remembered by most Jews.[28] Special taxes and numerous forced loans reminded Jews that they were still treated as a people apart. The threat of using the "regenerating guillotine" against those Jews more loyal to their old religion than to the new religion of the state caused those of more orthodox sensibility to flee France. For many Jews, especially those in the northeast, the new religion of liberty, equality, and fraternity appeared to be hostile to the existence and persistence of cultural and religious difference.

Even more hostile than the anti-corporate sentiments of the Emancipation Decree were its economic provisos. On 28 September 1791, the National Assembly passed additional instructions singling out Jews as moneylenders and subjecting them to economic regulation at the hands of unsympathetic local officials. Reubell, the most vigorous anti-semite in the Assembly, had procured these provisions by appealing to the popular hatred of Jewish moneylenders. He insisted that Alsatian peasants, although worth only three million livres, owed over fifteen million livres to Jews. Since Jews "were not the type of people to lend fifteen million livres to those worth only three million," it was clear, Reubell argued, that the vast majority of this indebtedness was usurious, hence unjust. To satisfy "this numerous and unhappy class living under the oppressive usury of the Jews," he proposed that local officials oversee the immediate repayment of all debts owed to the Jews.[29] Upon presenting themselves for the civic oath, Jews were required to produce detailed lists and information concerning their debtors. With this information, district officials were instructed to establish realistic proposals for repayment.

The lists required of the Jews were never produced. Alsatian peasants appear to have been assuaged by news of these requirements; the pogroms that had been portended did not occur. Peasants interpreted the Decree as releasing them from past obligations owed to the Jews. Those Jews who were moneylenders suffered significant losses. For some, especially for the rich, the attainment of equality and citizenship was worth the price; but others were probably less enthusiastic.[30]

Hatred against the Jews as usurious moneylenders was the driving force behind the Emancipation Decree's qualifications. Jewish pamphleteers pointed out that just as some Christians were moneylenders, not all Jews were moneylenders. The recital of these facts, however, fell on deaf ears. Moneylending was commonly viewed as a peculiarly Jewish vice. Anti-semitic pamphleteers were convinced that Jews extracted interest from non-Jews but lent interest-free to their fellows. Old Testament texts were brought forward as proof.[31] The city of Strasbourg, long an anti-semitic stronghold, went even further, detailing the sordid character of Jewish economic life in order to add force to its demand to keep the Jews out of the city.

What Jews called commerce, the city insisted, was nothing less than brigandage. The spirit of thievery came naturally to them. "If you look at their [Jewish] conduct in what they call commerce," the city's address of April 1790 to the National Assembly noted, "you will notice that they are always watching people's needs carefully, creating needs and presenting false attractions by making them appear necessary by perfidious means, convincing young people and servants to buy their goods, and hounding their victims until cupidity finally leads to their [the buyer's] ruin."[32] The economic evils of capitalism were, by this account, inherently Jewish. Such a selfish and ungenerous ethos, the address concluded, disqualified Jews from citizenship.

The Jewish capitalist ethos brought envy and condemnation from diverse quarters in France. Many abolitionists condemned Jewish involvement in the slave trade and decried Jewish slave-owning as particularly brutal. In fact, there appears to have been only one known Jewish slave-owner in eighteenth-century France, Isaac Mendès France. The strength of anti-semitism, however, gave particular notoriety to this case. Isaac Mendès France had brought two Black slaves, Pampy and Julienne, from Saint Domingue to France in 1775. They accompanied their master to Paris as domestic servants. Shortly thereafter, Pampy and Julienne engaged the services of the abolitionist lawyer Henrion de Pansey to petition for their freedom. Pansey's published memoirs in their defense, avidly read by the Parisian public, combined an eloquent defense of African virtues with a bitter harangue against Jewish vice. Even those of ostensibly liberal bent appeared to share the envy and hatred of Jews characteristic of French peasants in Alsace.[33]

During the Revolution, pro-Jewish advocates exhibited the same fear of Jewish economic dexterity. Stanislas Clermont-Tonnerre, a deputy outspoken in support of Jewish enfranchisement, admitted that popular hatred of the Jews was well justified. Their greedy and rapacious ethos, even if a consequence of Christian oppression, deservedly brought upon the Jews the opprobrium of the masses.[34] Similarly, the abbé Grégoire, although convinced that Jews had become moneylenders because they had been forbidden the honor and luxury of owning land, considered Jewish economic practices evil and unpatriotic.

Contradicting his maxim that history, not innate characteristics, determined a people's character, Grégoire attributed Jewish economic practices partly to native ability, to the Jews' "genius for calculation" that had resulted in the creation of the medieval bill of exchange.[35] Like others, Grégoire had complicated attitudes towards Jewish commercial activities. On the one hand, he believed that Jewish commercial acumen could prove extremely useful, even magically healing, to the French economy, particularly in times of stress. On the other hand, Grégoire was convinced that money was inherently dangerous, moneylending usurious, and land the only honorable and viable source of long-term economic stability. The Jews were thus simultaneously useful and dangerous.

Grégoire shared the economic prejudices of an agrarian society whose most enlightened economic thinking was associated with the Physiocrats. Jansenist strictures against usury contributed to ill-dispose him towards monetary activities. Jews symbolized the dangers of a world economy coming into being. Elsewhere, interest-bearing moneylending was an acceptable practice, overseen by what were to become national banks and considered a vital component of national economic growth. More at home in the open economies of America, the Netherlands, and Great Britain, Jews suffered acutely in France's agrarian economy. Denied land, they were forbidden access to the one respectable form of property. Not surprisingly, a crucial element in Grégoire's program was to transform Jews from moneylenders into land owners. The land, he argued, would attach Jews to France, would give them a basis for patriotism. It would also serve to rid them of the vices associated with money, hence aiding in their ethical regeneration.[36]

The lifting of restrictions against the Jews and the national sale of church lands following the Civil Constitution of the Clergy in 1791 made it possible for Jews, at last, to own land. Although they were never to become the peasant proprietors Grégoire had hoped for, many Jews attempted to benefit from the new availability of church lands. Other Frenchmen, however, were not as anxious as the abbé Grégoire for Jews to become land owners. As economic conditions during the Revolution worsened, rumors that Jews were speculating in the buying and selling of national lands led to peasant pogroms against Alsatian Jews in 1793 and 1794. Combined with the anti-Judaic religious policies of local Jacobin officials, the pogroms caused the flight and exile of many Jews.[37]

Even though technically the Jews were no longer a people apart and their corporate status had been terminated, Jewish debt to the government, assumed during the Old Regime, was recovered through Jewish corporate agencies. In August 1793, Jews from Avignon protested this arrangement. They demanded that their debt, like debt of all other corporations, be nationalized since it, too, had been forcibly incurred during the Old Regime to "underwrite the military costs of an oppressive government." Noting that the Jews had gladly given up their corporate existence in order to enjoy French citizenship, and that they had sacrificed their Temples and other buildings to the national cause, the petition from Avignon pointed out the hypocrisy underlining the government's treatment of the Jewish debt. How was it possible, the petition rhetorically asked, to continue to collect a corporate tax on a people no longer organized as a corporation?[38] Yet revolutionary regimes continued to collect payments as late as 1797, and special taxes and forced loans were periodically levied on Jewish communities throughout the Revolution.

In spite of the anti-corporate and economic provisions qualifying the Decree, emancipation was embraced by Jewish spokesmen during the Revolution.[39] Jewish petitioners hoped for an American solution to the problem of difference, and they evoked the patriotism and particularism of Quakers in America as an example of how a sect could be integrated into a larger and very different body politic. A handful of revolutionaries, including the future leader of the Gironde, Jacques-Pierre Brissot, concurred, endorsing a non-assimilationist program of Jewish integration into French society.[40] To those fearful that emancipation would result in France being besieged by Jewish immigrants, Jewish pamphleteers replied that France should be proud to become an asylum for the oppressed of the world.[41] For many Jews, the Emancipation Decree fulfilled at last the fraternal hopes of the Declaration. They looked forward to positive change in the century to come.

Such a liberal interpretation of emancipation, preserving room for difference, extending brotherhood to Jews near and far, and allowing the Jews to set their own pace for assimilation, was not an impossibility in 1791. Religious freedom seemed secure and civic rights had been assured. To be sure, the details of adapting to the new civic requirements, especially those affecting Jewish religious rituals and customs, would have to be worked out, as would economic matters. But a spirit of optimism and goodwill pervaded the National Assembly as it neared term's end, promising a harmonious and cooperative effort at integration.

As to how the Decree would affect the long-term evolution of Jewish identity, this was still an open question. The anti-Judaic policies of the Terror and Napoleon's forcible reorganization of the Jewish community along assimilationist lines boded ill for a solution respectful of the preservation of Jewish traditions. Grégoire's involvement with Napoleon's project suggests that he too was interested in the Jews becoming as indistinguishable as possible from other Frenchmen. The Zionist historian Arthur Hertzberg has traced Jewish self-hatred, the desire to make oneself as inconspicuous as possible (faites-vous oublier), back to the ideology of men like Grégoire.[42]

Grégoire's vigorous defense of the Jews has been attributed to a millenarian desire to pave the path for their eventual conversion to

Christianity.[43] Grégoire was certainly interested in the elimination of as much difference as possible. His support of reformed Judaism at the turn of the century reveals his decided preference for a more western and Christian form of Judaism. Like many other revolutionaries, he was opposed to the proliferation of differences characteristic of the Old Regime. For Grégoire, differences were a result of the chaotic and anarchical organization of feudal society, resulting in the division of society into competing corps, regions, and classes. In the overthrow of this order, an especially important element was linguistic reform. Grégoire avidly pursued linguistic unification, hoping to eliminate the regional dialects which separated Frenchmen of Breton, Basque, and Yiddish tongues. His antipathy towards Yiddish was no different than his dislike of Breton, but it nonetheless made him appear insensitive to Jewish cultural peculiarities.[44]

Yet in his writings during the debates on the Declaration in 1789–91, the abbé did not mention the goal of eventually converting the Jews to Christianity. Equality for the Jews was fought for along the lines of universal brotherhood and toleration. Prejudices, especially economic ones, against the Jews remained, as did distrust for the separatist character of Jewish life. But Grégoire and his supporters were convinced that separatism was a function of the oppression of the past, and they looked forward to initiating an era in which Jews could become more and more integrated into the mainstream of French society. That the terms of this integration became increasingly assimilationist as time wore on is indicative both of the enduring character of popular prejudices against the Jews and of the fear and hatred of difference in a revolutionary society determined to break with the gridlock of divisiveness associated with the feudal past. Both liberal promise and the Revolution's intolerance towards divisive difference inhered in the Emancipation Decree of September 1791, leaving open multiple paths for the integration of France's Jews into French society. It was a complicated new beginning, carrying with it the seeds of much unfinished business.

≺ II ≻

Mulattoes and Blacks

Admitting Mulattoes, free Blacks, or Black slaves—the colored population of the French West Indies—to the French polity proved to be even more difficult than admitting the Jews. Although anti-semites implied that Jews were racially different, during the Revolution they were still viewed primarily as a religious group. Their identity was, consequently, capable of radical transformation in an act of conversion. Mulattoes and Blacks, on the contrary, were unmistakably different, and as was proved in the vigorous debates in the National Assembly, race was an especially strong divide. The politics of race was a colonial matter, centered in the African slave trade to the New World. Of the French colonies, Saint Domingue was the most important. Its robust population of 30,000 whites, 28,000 free coloreds, and 465,000 Black slaves produced more sugar than all the other West Indian islands. The sugar and slave trades were of inestimable value to the Old Regime economy, transforming Bordeaux and Nantes into flourishing port cities and stimulating the growth of a new mercantile elite. Although white colonists chafed under the mercantilist restrictions imposed on them by the French government, they enjoyed a great degree of local autonomy in the islands, enabling them to construct a society to their liking. A noted feature of colonial life in the eighteenth century was its strict racial hierarchy.

France's slave code, the *Code Noir* of 1685, had made possible the growth of a large and substantial class of free Mulattoes and a smaller group of free Blacks in the colonies. Their representatives were to come to Paris in 1789 demanding equal status with their free white counterparts.[45] Many of them owned plantations and slaves.[46] During the eighteenth century, however, rich and poor whites conspired to subject Mulattoes and free Blacks to legislation undermining their freedom. Forbidden access to various professions, not permitted to sit at the same table as whites, and consigned to segregated companies in the local militia, Mulattoes and free Blacks were constantly reminded of their racial inferiority.[47] As to the Black slaves, their treatment at the hands of French colonists was so severe that they were unable to replenish their stock naturally. On the eve of the French Revolution the vast majority in Saint Domingue had come directly from Africa. Memories of African freedom kept resistance alive and contributed importantly to the upcoming revolution.

Even though most Blacks and Mulattoes lived across the Atlantic, their plight was not unknown in France. Travel literature and scientific treatises were preoccupied with the new races and civilizations Europeans came into contact with during the age of seaborne exploration. Especially important in popularizing knowledge of Africa and

New World slavery in eighteenth century France were the abbé Raynal's *Histoire des Deux Indes* and the comte de Buffon's multi-volume *Natural History*, both of which underwent numerous printings and circulated widely amongst the enlightened elite. These works were critical of the European enslavement of the African. Raynal's impassioned denunciation of the harshness of slavery in the West Indies continued to provoke the ire of white colonists well into the Revolution, as did his exhortation to the slaves to free themselves through armed revolt.[48] Buffon also opposed the slave trade. His pronouncements in this regard, however, were less influential than his scientific reflections on the nature of racial differences.

Buffon was firmly committed to a monogenetic account of the origins of mankind, that is, to the belief that all mankind shared a common ancestor. Since the common ancestor was white, the other races of mankind represented significant deviations from man's original condition. Over centuries, across continents, subjected to differing environmental and climatic conditions, original man degenerated from his pristine European purity. In spite of his contempt for African civilization, however, Buffon was unsympathetic to the flourishing slave trade of the eighteenth century. He thought the Africans unhappy enough in their natural condition and suggested that Europeans leave them alone. As to their ultimate salvation, Buffon was convinced that over centuries, if subjected to the temperate climate of Europe and introduced to French foods and culture, Black men could become white. There was hope, then, for their attainment of equality with white men. But only in the long, long run, and at the expense of abandoning their barbarous culture in favor of assimilation.[49]

As Buffon's work predisposed Frenchmen to look sympathetically on the long-term possibility of assimilating Blacks into French culture, so the rhetoric of the patriotic and parlementary opposition to the king in eighteenth-century France encouraged radicals to condemn the institution of slavery. Especially important was the case of the slaves Pampy and Julienne. The Parlement of Paris declared in their favor, ruling against the validity of the royal declaration of 1738 limiting Negro rights in France. It challenged the declaration on the grounds that it had not been enregistered by the Parlement. By freeing Pampy and Julienne, the Parlement struck a victory, once again, against royal authority. Reaching its decision in the aftermath of the patriotic victory against the Chancellor Maupeou, the Parlement reminded the government that France was to be the home of the free, for Blacks as well as for Frenchmen.[50]

In spite of these precedents and the important anti-slavery motif of patriotic pamphlets in the 1770s and 1780s, the French abolitionist movement on the eve of the French Revolution was small and fairly weak.[51] Indeed, it was not the abolitionists but their adversaries who first raised the colonial issue on the floor of the National Assembly. White colonists eagerly joined in the fray of revolutionary activity in Paris, hoping to secure local autonomy and break the stranglehold of French mercantilist restrictions on their trade. Successfully obtaining the right to a delegation in the Assembly, the colonists proceeded to argue that as they contributed a disproportionate share to France's national income, their delegation should be expanded to include twenty deputies.

This demand stimulated abolitionist sentiment in the Assembly. When the colonists attempted to increase the size of their representation on the basis of the number of slaves they owned, the comte de Mirabeau, a liberal aristocrat and one of the founding members of the *Société des Amis des Noirs*, scoffed at their efforts. Either slaves were men, Mirabeau argued, in which case they were free, or they were beasts. If the latter, they could no more be counted to enlarge one's delegation than could the cows or mules belonging to French farmers.[52] Jean-Louis Lanjuinais, a Jansenist deputy from Brittany, went even further. Noting that his constituents from Brittany had bade him struggle for the abolition of slavery, Lanjuinais argued that masters could not represent the interests of their slaves.[53]

Successfully thwarting the colonists' attempt to increase the size of their delegation, abolitionists appeared to be in a very strong position as the summer of 1789 drew to an end. They did not continue to pursue emancipation at this time, however, and may well have missed the most opportune moment for pushing through an abolitionist agenda.[54] The reasons for missing this opportunity were many, not least amongst which was that the demand for equality by Mulattoes and free Blacks preoccupied Frenchmen for several years.

The Declaration's universal statement of rights was seen by Mulattoes and free Blacks as a direct invitation to reassert their undermined civic equality and to demand enfranchisement. Distinguished Mulattoes, like Julien Raymond and Vincent Ogé, joined the *Société des Colons Américains*, an organization determined to achieve full

equality for all free men of color.[55] Working closely with the abbé
Grégoire, Mulattoes got the Credentials Committee to accept free
colored representation in the Assembly.[56] The vote was a narrow one,
however; and facing concerted opposition, the abolitionists dug in
their heels for what was to become a long fight.[57]

For abolitionists, defending the rights of Mulattoes and free Blacks
instead of slaves proved to be politically expedient. Economic and international political considerations made the attack on slavery unpopular; abolitionists were accused of fomenting slave rebellions to
aid the British, anxious to secure the demise of France's prosperous
colony. The charge of treason induced abolitionists to focus instead
on Mulatto enfranchisement. Mulattoes were an easy group to defend. Of mixed blood, wealthy, propertied, patriotic, and culturally
French, they were, as one deputy put it, "children of the same mother
. . . our brothers, nephews, cousins." He demanded the immediate enfranchisement of these men, related by blood and culture to the mainland.[58]

The cause of the Mulattoes was used by abolitionists to challenge
the "aristocracy of skin color" erected in the West Indies. Yet precisely because Mulattoes were of mixed blood, this cause could be
construed to strengthen, not weaken, the racial organization of colonial society. Many abolitionists argued that the mixing of races inevitably worked in the direction of lightening the stock. Mulatto
rights were argued for on the grounds that they "could be called
white, since they looked white and nature inevitably led to this result
by the third or fourth generation."[59] For abolitionists, racial intermix-
ture appeared to be accelerating a Buffon-like regeneration of Black
men into white men. Like Buffon's paternalistic and culturally racist
natural history, these views simultaneously hindered and helped the
broader cause of African equality.

More detrimental to the cause of African slaves were the economic arguments employed by abolitionists to defend the Mulattoes.
Since many Mulattoes were slaveowners, abolitionists argued that
their enfranchisement would strengthen the institution of slavery:
that Mulattoes and rich whites would work together to preserve property of all sorts, including slaves. Julien Raymond appeared before the
National Assembly to plead the Mulattoes' case. He displayed equal
contempt for poor whites and for slaves, neither of whom had possessions of any worth. Noting that Mulattoes had been responsible for

the pursuit of runaway slaves throughout the century, Raymond assured the deputies that they "loved most whites" and would protect the cause of property.[60] Thoughtful abolitionists warned the Assembly of the possibility of a Mulatto and slave coalition should the legitimate demands of these tax-paying free men be denied. The resulting race war, they intimated, would far exceed the costs of Mulatto enfranchisement and a class alliance of propertied men of all races.[61]

In spite of these admonitions, however, the men of the Assembly failed to enfranchise either the Mulattoes or the free Blacks. Instead, they accepted the white colonists' argument that an intermediary class of racial inferiors was a necessary safeguard for the preservation of slavery. Black slaves could only be kept in their place, so it was argued, if all Blacks and men of color were firmly treated as inferiors. That abolitionists had already quiescently accepted the legitimacy of slavery helped to weaken the cause of the Mulattoes whom they defended. International rivalry with Great Britain and Spain, along with threats of colonial secession should France not heed the will of white colonists, convinced deputies to adopt the decree presented to the Assembly by the Colonial Committee on 8 March 1790.

The decree granted the colonies internal legislative autonomy, promised not to "innovate in any branch of colonial trade," and assured them of their independence in implementing the ambiguous electoral requirements sent along with the decree. Article 4 extended electoral rights to all persons in the colonies fulfilling a residence requirement and either owning property or paying the requisite amount of taxes. Race was not mentioned. Since the electoral assemblies already in existence were given the power to interpret and implement these instructions, Article 4 was widely understood both by Frenchmen and by colonists to exclude Mulattoes and free Blacks.

One of the more radical Mulatto leaders, however, decided otherwise. In Saint Domingue, Vincent Ogé began to mobilize Mulatto support for participation in the upcoming elections. He assured his fellow Mulattoes that they were included in the ambiguous Article 4. But in Saint Domingue, the impenetrable racial barriers of the eighteenth century held fast. Met by staunch resistance on the part of white colonists, Ogé's electoral machinations soon turned into armed conflict. White colonists, rich and poor, banded together to prevent Mulattoes from asserting their political rights. Capturing Ogé in the fall of 1790, the colonists subjected him to a mock trial, whereupon he was brutally lynched by a white mob.[62] Infuriated by news of Ogé's brutal murder and strengthened by the developing class war, the left in France pushed for a revocation of the 8 March decree. Petitions demanding immediate Mulatto enfranchisement were sent to the National Assembly from Jacobin strongholds throughout France.[63] Radical newspapers gave lurid accounts of the armed conflict underway in Saint Domingue. Under pressure, the National Assembly capitulated, issuing a compromise decree on 15 May 1791. This decree enfranchised only those Mulattoes born of free mothers *and* fathers, a tiny proportion of the entire Mulatto community. Hardly satisfying the numerous class of Mulattoes and free Blacks in the islands, the decree was nevertheless stubbornly resisted by colonial whites. A rightward swing in public opinion, coupled with the fearful news of a slave rebellion in August 1791, encouraged the deputies in the National Assembly to abrogate the 15 May decree on 24 September 1791. Once again, they reassured white colonists of their autonomy and promised not to interfere in the racial affairs of Saint Domingue. It was an ignominious conclusion to the work of the National Assembly, standing in sharp contrast to its decrees to emancipate Jews and free those Blacks and Mulattoes resident in France.

Disillusioned and distrustful of French support for their cause, the Mulattoes at last resorted to armed struggle against the white colonists. Some of them allied with slaves, whose massive armed rebellion was a direct response to the empowering use of the Declaration flaunted by Ogé and his followers.[64] The joint uprising of Mulattoes and slaves against the white colonists changed forever the contours of Saint Domingue. Whites either fled, joined counterrevolutionary royalists, or worked with the British and Spanish to secure Saint Domingue's independence. The economy lay in ruins. French troops, sent to Saint Domingue to restore order, were forced to rely on Mulatto and slave support. Mulattoes and slaves worked with the French civil commissioners to push back the British and Spaniards and to resist indigenous counterrevolutionary forces. For their efforts, they were handsomely rewarded. The Girondin-dominated Assembly of 1792 extended equality to all free men of color. It was an ominous precedent, ripe with possibility for the slaves who had also aided the French effort to restore order in Saint Domingue.

That the Mulattoes were finally enfranchised by a Girondin-dominated Assembly in Paris came as no surprise to onlookers. The Girondins were disproportionately represented in the abolitionist movement. Foremost amongst them was Jacques-Pierre Brissot, one of France's most articulate spokesmen for revolutionary fraternity.[65] Brissot was largely responsible for pushing France to declare war against her counterrevolutionary neighbors, especially the Austrian Habsburgs, and he welcomed the international battle that ensued. For Brissot, the war was not merely defensive. Besides serving to protect France from the threat of international counterrevolution, the war promised to spread the enlightened revolutionary gospel near and far, to the citizens of the world. French revolutionary armies would break the bonds of serfdom, slavery, and tyranny wherever they encountered them. Encouraging these trends, Brissot's rhetoric pushed Frenchmen to see the revolution in Saint Domingue as part of this broader movement.

One of Brissot's important supporters, Léon-Félicité Sonthonax, was sent to Saint Domingue as civil commissioner in 1792. Sonthonax worked closely with the unfolding Mulatto and slave revolutions in the colony, allying with Blacks and Mulattoes to overthrow royalists in league with the British and Spaniards. Convinced that only Black aid could keep the colony French, Sonthonax declared slavery abolished in the fall of 1793.[66] Several months later, the Parisian legislature added formal sanction to Sonthonax's decree. Slavery was officially abolished, without compensation, in all French colonies in February 1794.

Sonthonax's emancipation decree was not simply the result of necessity. His abolitionist sentiments preceded his appointment to Saint Domingue. As early as 1790, Sonthonax had advocated that France admit a "frizzy-haired legislator" to the National Assembly.[67] The idealism of men like Brissot and Sonthonax was matched by a wellspring of support for the abolitionist cause in Paris and other urban areas in France.[68] The Emancipation Decree, heralded by Jean-Baptiste Belley-Mars, the first Black deputy to a French legislative assembly, was greeted by the thunderous approval of the Convention. Paris feted the occasion with an enormous public procession to Notre Dame. On their shoulders, Frenchmen carried numerous colored citizens, symbols of the final eclipse of the racial divisions that had hitherto divided revolutionary France.

Cynical commentators point out that antislavery was merely a rhetorical tool used by Parisian radicals to struggle for French freedoms and that they showed little real concern for the condition of Black slaves.[69] Yet it was precisely through rhetoric that Frenchmen came to have compassion for the condition of African slaves. Patriotic discourse in the eighteenth century had stressed the similarities of the conditions of Frenchmen and those of slaves. Arbitrary arrests, *lettres de cachet*, the Bastille, *lits de justice*, and the numerous forcible exiles of resisting *parlementaires* stood as glaring examples of the erosion of French freedoms that threatened to turn Frenchmen into slaves, and French monarchs into Oriental despots. The language of antislavery pervaded the patriotic literature of the Maupeou years, linking the political disenfranchisement of absolutism to the lack of freedom characteristic of slave regimes less hypocritical than the French. As patriotic literature assumed a more social physiognomy during the Revolution, slavery was once again used as a metaphor. This time it conveniently described the inequities of an aristocratic social order.

Especially comparable to slavery was the forced labor tax, the *corvée*, levied on French peasants to build royal highways. Cautious thinkers, like Antoine Nicolas de Condorcet, condemned slave-like conditions in France, but considered the condition of African slaves to be far worse than that of the French peasant or beggar.[70] Others, swept up in the revolutionary frenzy pushing France towards an assault on the aristocracy, were less careful. Especially persuasive were Brissot's pamphlets comparing the white colonists with the *seigneurs*, *émigrés*, and princes under attack by the unfolding social revolution in France. The white colonists, Brissot argued, were aristocrats intent on putting a halt both to the Black and Brown revolutions in Saint Domingue and to the French Revolution on the mainland. "The subordination and pursuit of blacks in the colonies will lead to the subordination and pursuit of whites in France," he warned, "the servitude of one group will lead to the servitude of others."[71]

To accuse the white colonists of social treason against the Revolution in a time of increasing radicalization was strong tonic. That it was effective was proven by the hatred and venom directed against the white colonists, many of whom were to fall early victims to the guillotine under the Terror. Brissot, too, was to fall victim to the Terror, a result, in part, of the vituperative personal attacks on his character launched by his slaveowning enemies.[72] But if the man was sacrificed, his principles were not. Slavery was abolished in France at the most radical moment of the Revolution, during the Terror. Brissot's rhetoric, convincing Frenchmen that they were involved in a global and universal struggle against slavery, had done much to convince Parisians and fellow revolutionaries that their cause and that of the Black slaves in Saint Domingue were the same.

Positive attitudes toward Blacks had also been encouraged by the myth of the noble savage. This myth tempered Buffon's negative portrayal of the Black man as a degenerated white man. The noble savage, like Rousseau's man in the state of nature, was endowed with primitive ethical virtues distinguishing him from his civilized but corrupt European ancestors. Stretching back to the French encounter with Amerindians in the sixteenth century, the myth of the noble savage was appropriated by abolitionists in the eighteenth century to describe the superior virtues of African slaves. "Ah! Black Africans," Brissot noted, "even while enslaved and enchained, they are full of virtues, especially those of kindness, generosity, and loyalty."[73] The abbé Grégoire was particularly impressed by African respect for elders and filial piety, "touching virtues," he noted, "almost unknown in our society."[74] Slaves were even considered superior to their white masters. "Most of these men," an early antislavery tract pointed out, "are capable of commanding their masters. They are abundant in virtue, and carry some virtues to a degree which our weak and corrupted souls could never achieve."[75]

In spite of this complimentary portrait, however, abolitionists were intent on incorporating Blacks into the French polity and introducing them to the intellectual virtues of French culture.[76] They hoped to transform Africans into Frenchmen without disturbing the superior moral equilibrium of men close to the state of nature. An excellent example of this abolitionist ideal is contained in Olympe de Gouges's play *L'Esclavage des noirs, ou l'heureux naufrage*, performed at the Comédie Française in the autumn of 1789.[77] De Gouges's hero, Zamore, was an educated house slave, exposed to the superiorities of French culture and civilization by a beneficent master. Drawing a sharp contrast between colonial whites and enlightened Frenchmen from the mainland, Zamore counselled his fellow slaves to refrain from violently overthrowing slavery and patiently to await French aid. "The French look upon slavery with horror," he had been told, "and when they are themselves free, one day, they will occupy themselves with your [the slaves'] freedom."[78] For de Gouges, the Revolution would prove regenerative of both Frenchmen and slaves, restoring freedom and combining clemency, justice, and enlightenment with the purity of African morals.

Although the emancipation of 1794 did not turn out to be exactly like de Gouges's picture in 1789, there were remarkable similarities between the two. Toussaint L'Ouverture, leader of the slave revolution in Saint Domingue, had much in common with the mythical Zamore. A semi-educated house slave, well treated by a benevolent master, Toussaint remained cautiously committed to France throughout the Revolution. Upon the declaration of emancipation, he took measures to strengthen his alliance with the French, working closely with Sonthonax and instituting policies that would strengthen Saint Domingue's cultural and economic ties with the mainland. Especially important were his attempts to bolster the weakening economy by imposing harsh labor conditions on the ex-slaves. In spite of their desire to flee the plantations and set up independent farms in the mountains, Toussaint forced them to continue working on sugar plantations. Although his power was autocratic, and Saint Domingue enjoyed virtual independence under his rule, Toussaint's policies were geared towards strictly aligning his island with revolutionary France.

Napoleon's rise to power, however, spelled the end of cordial relations between the slave revolution in Saint Domingue and the motherland. Capturing Toussaint by ruse, and imprisoning him in a dungeon in the cold Jura mountains where he was to die in 1803, Napoleon attempted to reinstate slavery in the French West Indies. In Saint Domingue, his efforts met with dismal failure. The ex-slaves replaced Toussaint with a leader of very different sensibilities. Furious at France's treachery, the new leader, Jean Jacques Dessalines, tore the white from France's tricolor flag, declaring the remaining blue and red fragments the flag of a new independent nation, Haiti. Haitian independence destroyed the comfortable illusions of the assimilationist program and defiantly promoted cultural autonomy. In the next century, the new nation would preserve much of its African and Amerindian heritage, promoting a cultural pluralism at odds with the assimilationist ideal. Culture, however, could not rectify the wounds inflicted on this proud nation by a resentful Europe and a fearful America. Subjected to a punitive economic isolation, Haiti was to plunge into the depths of despair and poverty from which she is yet to recover.

Napoleon's restoration of slavery in the remaining French colonies put an end to one of the Revolution's most important accomplishments. If emancipation proved to be short-lived, however, its historical legacy proved of enduring importance to Africans throughout the nineteenth and twentieth centuries. Slavery had been overthrown by armed struggle on the part of Blacks in Saint Domingue, and its overthrow had been embraced by the Convention and the people of Paris. It was a dangerous precedent, especially for the surrounding slave societies of the New World. The abolition of slavery in Saint Domingue proclaimed that revolution and racism were incompatible and that the rights of man and citizen enunciated in the Declaration were truly universal. Universal, that is, so long as man and mankind were understood in a strictly gendered and masculine way.

≺ III ≻

Women

For the men of the revolutionary assemblies, it was clear that the empowering clauses of the Declaration did not apply to women. Political and scientific thought in the eighteenth century had conspired to paint a picture of women as biologically different from and naturally inferior to men.[79] Their proper place, as Jean-Jacques Rousseau so eloquently pointed out in his popular *La Nouvelle Héloise*, was in the home, in the domestic or private sphere. Creatures of feeling, incapable of reasoning, physically weak, and, in any case, debilitated by the chores of childbearing and childraising, women were expected to follow quietly their men's lead in matters of politics or intellect. Men of vastly different political stripes spoke forcefully against the extension of political rights to women on the grounds that it was against their nature and that society would not benefit from such a novelty.

Yet women did not remain quietly confined to the domestic sphere during the tumultuous days of the Revolution. Throughout the eighteenth century, women had played an active role in both the intellectual life of the capital and in opposition politics.[80] During the Revolution, they became even more active.[81] They attended weekly section meetings and pressured male politicians in the galleries of the assemblies and the courtrooms of the revolutionary tribunals. Women formed their own clubs, the most notable of which was the

Society of Revolutionary Republican Women, and they participated in mixed clubs like the *Cercle Social* and the more popular Fraternal Society of Male and Female Patriots, Defenders of the Constitution.[82] They were especially active in some of the more dramatic moments of the Revolution, including moving the king from Versailles to Paris in October 1789.

Of varied class backgrounds and displaying varied political sentiments, women made alliances with several political factions during the Revolution. With their liberal Girondin supporters, they fought for the right to divorce, changes in the inheritance laws, and equitable education for women. With their radical *Enragé* allies, they fought to enforce the *maximum*, price controls on the sale of bread and other essentials, thereby ensuring Parisians of a cheap and plentiful supply of food. Some, albeit very few, even raised the demand for women's right to be full-fledged members of the body politic through voting and holding office.

In the early months of the Revolution, women's voices could be heard in occasional pamphlets and some of the *cahiers* sent to the Estates General. These were almost exclusively concerned with women's economic plight. The promulgation of the Declaration in August 1789 acted as a catalyst for very different types of demands. Outspoken feminists argued that the egalitarian pronouncements of the Declaration entailed the enfranchisement of women. Others used specific articles of the Declaration to argue for the extension of particular rights to women. Demands as diverse as the right to carry arms and the right to divorce were argued for by referring to the provisions of the Declaration. Meaning different things for different people, the Declaration came to represent for women a text of entitlement and empowerment of seemingly endless scope.

The obvious linguistic problems of applying a declaration of the rights of *man* to *women* were dealt with differently by two of the leading feminist theorists of the Revolution, the marquis de Condorcet and Olympe de Gouges. Initiating a tradition still alive today, Condorcet ignored linguistic differences and assumed that man referred to mankind or the entire human race, to which women obviously belonged. In his path-breaking essay of 1790, *On the Admission of Women to the Rights of Citizenship*, he set out to demonstrate that the natural rights of women were "absolutely the same as men," thereby ignoring the supposedly natural differences between men and women.[83] De Gouges, on the other hand, stressed the differences between women and men and argued that it was precisely the superior feminine attributes that entitled women to political and social consideration.

De Gouges drew up a *Declaration of the Rights of Woman*, addressed to a female audience through the persona of the queen. Convinced that women's interests would never be met by male-dominated governments, de Gouges demanded that women constitute a separate national assembly. This, along with the extension of numerous other rights to women, including the right to vote, the right to government employment, the right to public leadership, equal access to wealth, and "especially (the right of) resistance to oppression," would ensure that women's special but socially useful interests were met.[84]

By focusing the debate on nature, natural rights, and the natural differences between men and women, de Gouges courageously took on the medical and political savants of the eighteenth century.[85] She argued that the natural world did not provide evidence of female inferiority. Nature was full, she insisted, not of examples of the "tyrannical empire" of males over females, but rather of cooperative and harmonious intermingling. "Go back to animals," she insisted, "consult the elements, study plants, finally glance at all the modifications of organic nature and surrender to the evidence; search, probe, and distinguish, if you can, the sexes in the administration of nature. Everywhere you will find them mingled; everywhere they cooperate in harmonious togetherness in this immortal masterpiece."[86] For de Gouges, the natural world was proof of diversity, pluralism, and variation, not of hierarchy, subordination, and slavery.

De Gouges saw in the equality and diversity of nature similar assurance for the rights of men of color.[87] But whereas color was a merely physical quality, sexual difference was more substantial. She paid tribute to the peculiar strengths and virtues of womanhood and derived women's rights from this vantage point. She sought to undermine "perpetual male tyranny" by teaching women to free themselves by struggling to regain their natural rights. Foremost amongst these was the right to free speech and political persuasion. "Woman has the right to mount the scaffold," de Gouges boldly declared, so "she must equally have the right to mount the rostrum." Women's right to free speech was argued for in specifically feminine terms, namely the need to openly name and make responsible the fathers of their children, legitimate or illegitimate. In like manner, she demanded that women be given an "equal share, not only of wealth, but also of public administration" and that they be made full owners of the property they inherited or shared with their husbands.[88]

Linking women's domestic suffering to their political disenfranchisement, de Gouges framed women's rights in such a way as to ensure them the social and economic independence necessary for a free and intelligent exercise of political rights. By enfranchising women even while preserving their unique and special attributes, de Gouges expected to transform and revitalize French society in a variegated and pluralistic direction.

Today, amidst the difficulties women face attempting to earn equality by being the same as men, some are apt to look sympathetically on de Gouges's insistence on the empowering differences of women.[89] In the eighteenth century, however, arguments based on difference and nature threatened to weaken women's claims. The plentiful sexist literature of the last three decades of the Old Regime delighted in pointing out just how destructive the involvement of women in the public arena had been. From the attacks on patriotism in the 1770s as a movement led by frivolous women, to the attacks on queens and mistresses culminating in the Diamond Necklace Affair of 1783–86, where the young Queen Marie Antoinette was exposed to public ridicule as an extravagant and unfaithful wife, pamphlets of differing political opinion agreed that women were irrational creatures prone to using their tremendous sexual powers irresponsibly.[90] Even prostitution was considered a peculiarly female vice. As to women's positive virtues, such as gentility, beauty, and charm, these were best confined to the privacy of the domestic sphere in order not to encourage lust, infidelity, and adultery.

It was to combat these negative portrayals of women that Condorcet insisted on underlining the similarities of men and women. Men and women shared the ability to reason and to arrive at moral judgments;[91] as rational creatures, they were essentially and naturally the same. Childbearing was no more or less debilitating for women than the periodic illnesses afflicting any particular man. Condorcet did consider women more gentle and less egoistical, and he expected them to continue performing the lion's share of domestic chores. But these chores were simply a job, like any other job.

They did not legitimate women's political exclusion from the electoral process, he insisted, any more than the duties of farming or artisan work excluded men from participating in the political process.

Condorcet did think that the daily preoccupations of work would make women, and male manual workers, unlikely candidates for political office; but this was no reason, he argued, to exclude them by law. He dismissed men's fear that women would take over the political arena as irrational and short-sighted. It was based on the misconception that "every person admitted to the rights of citizenship immediately thinks of nothing but governing others."[92] As soon as the dust of revolutionary energy settled, he argued, few individuals, male or female, would have the time or interest to place politics in the center of their lives. The newfound interest in power and politics, Condorcet assured his male readers, was merely a temporary aberration.

In the long run, Condorcet believed, both society and individual males would benefit from the enfranchisement of women. Enfranchisement was one of the many ways in which women could receive a political and public education. Condorcet insisted that environment, not nature, determined the important differences between the sexes; and he therefore became an active exponent of women's education. Condorcet did not think, however, that it should be a prerequisite for women's enfranchisement; enfranchisement itself would begin the educational process. By directing women's attentions away from the secretive and seductive means of influencing men and by exposing them to the complexities of public debate and responsible decision-making, enfranchisement would help mold women into better mothers and more attractive spouses.

Condorcet actively supported efforts to improve France's system of education. Although none of the various educational proposals presented to the government in the early years of the Revolution was implemented, they contain much interesting information. Central to these debates were issues of gender. While most of the proposals fervently insisted that women receive a different, less rigorous education than men, Pierre Guyomar, a deputy to the Convention from the Côtes-du-Nord, argued instead that women receive a rigorous training in the sciences and mathematics. Like Condorcet, Guyomar thought that such an educational system would better prepare women for citizenship and for the exacting educational requirements of motherhood. He also agreed with Condorcet that the present lack of such a system should not stand in the way of women's immediate enfranchisement. Women, Guyomar thought, would bring their gentle and pacific characters to bear on matters of state. The attendant politicization of feminine virtues would lead to international peace, an end to the "fatal craft of the soldier," and the demise of destructive and divisive nationalism.[93]

A more common view than Guyomar's of the possible consequences of women's enfranchisement and education was that of the deputy Tallyrand-Périgord. Convinced that "society's happiness" rested on women's exclusion from political life, Tallyrand-Périgord insisted that a handful of exceptions, of educated women, did not disturb the "general plan of nature" whereby women were destined for a domestic and retiring life. Women were to be narrowly instructed in religious, ethical, and domestic affairs befitting their role as wives and mothers.[94] Even more unequivocal was the report of Alexandre Deleyre. Using the historical example of Sparta as a warning, Deleyre revealed deep-seated fears of sexual transgressions. In its lust for military grandeur, Deleyre argued, Sparta had trained women to be patriotic and self-sacrificing citizens. The results were disastrous. Women had been transformed into men. In order to preserve instead women's gentle and feminine attributes, and to ensure that women could properly fulfill their job "to please" men, Deleyre suggested that women be trained in literacy, domestic responsibilities, music, and dance. Not science and mathematics, but "needlepoint," according to Deleyre, was the proper arena of women's expertise.[95]

That Deleyre's view was shared by women is revealed in the *Petition of the Women of the Third Estate to the King*.[96] This petition demanded that women be educated in order to prepare them for stable and secure occupations. Speaking for the poor women of France, it insisted that specific trades be reserved for women, not as an affront to men, but in order to shelter unfortunate women from the ravages of fortune. As to the type of education women ought to receive, the petition considered the subjects of language, religion, and morals proper to inculcate the "virtues of our sex . . . kindness, modesty, patience, and charity." Women ought to be kept away from the study of the sciences, the petition emphatically asserted. For "the study of sciences," the petition argued, "would lead to the opposite result . . . they serve only to inspire us with a stupid pride, lead us to pedantry, go against the desires of nature, make us *mixed beings* who are rarely faithful wives and still more rarely good mothers of families."[97]

Neither de Gouges nor Condorcet was surprised that women were critical of their own liberation. Neither thought that the antifeminist stance of some women thereby legitimized women's oppression; and they hoped that their writings and the fervor of revolutionary activity would help activate dormant womankind and place on the agenda the natural rights of all humankind.

The great majority of women, however, failed to take advantage of the revolutionary excitement to pursue a feminist platform. Even women active in the *Cercle Social* and avid supporters of favorable social legislation for women, like Madame Roland, wife of a prominent Girondin and an important power broker in the early 1790s, refused to endorse women's suffrage. Convinced that the majority of women were ill-prepared for citizenship, Madame Roland considered education a necessary prerequisite for women's enfranchisement. Until women were educated and transformed, she noted, "our superstitions, our bad customs may seem ridiculous to those women who would make something of themselves, and . . . (would) annihilate any advantage which, otherwise, they might be able to get."[98] Ignorance, not nature, stood in the way of women's progress. It was, for Madame Roland, an ignorance peculiar to women, associated with the vice and frivolity characteristic of a group condemned to asserting power sexually in the interstices of the Old Regime.

Popular literature made persistent attacks on women's sexual prowess. Songs, rhyming couplets, epitaphs, and satires depicted women as lustful and decadent agents of the moral corruption of city life, high and low. Prostitutes were a favored target of attack, symbols of the dangerous sexuality of women. Rarely were the male clients of prostitutes considered contributory agents in this debasing institution. In response, thoughtful individuals, like the Jansenist barrister and abbé Henri Jabineau, blamed the evils of prostitution not on female vice but rather on economic misery, and insisted that women be ensured a steady supply of decent work so as to escape the clutches of this abominable profession.[99] *The Petition of the Women of the Third Estate to the King* seconded Jabineau's demand, but it was more critical of the "pretty girl" drawn from the provinces into the den of iniquity. It sought to clearly differentiate its legitimate claims from those of whores. "We would want this class of women to wear a mark of identification," the petition demanded, since "today, when they [prostitutes] go so far as to adopt the modesty of our dress, when they mingle everywhere in all kinds of clothing, we often find ourselves taken for them."[100]

The petition's claim that honest women were often taken for prostitutes was no idle chatter. It reflected a common and purposeful confusion, especially on the part of male pamphleteers anxious to berate women's political and public aspirations. Responding to the organization and activity of women in response to the Declaration, the anonymous anti-feminist *Déclaration des droits des citoyennes du Palais Royale* claimed that if equal rights were to be extended to everyone, "women can visit, eat, and sleep anywhere they please, practicing their trade [prostitution] in every quarter in Paris."[101] The accusation that women out of place, women in politics, were akin to whores was an old one that took on renewed power as women aspired to equality during the Revolution.

The radical feminist Pauline Léon argued for perhaps the greatest transgression of male roles by women, namely that of the assumption of the warrior's calling. She confronted the National Assembly in March 1791 with a petition demanding the right of women to bear arms. Believing that arming women was the best way to "terrorize aristocracy and tyranny" and keep the Revolution safe from counter-revolution, she also evoked more selfish reasons. "We wish only to defend ourselves the same as you," she told the Assembly. "You cannot refuse us," she insisted, "and society cannot deny the right nature gives us, unless you pretend the *Declaration of Rights* does not apply to women."[102]

Léon's petition had been signed by three hundred persons. Its demand was echoed by others. Etta Palm d'Aelders, a Dutch feminist active in the *Cercle Social*, considered the right to military employment an important gain to be acquired by women, as did the anonymous *Requête des dames* and the *Demande des femmes aux États-généraux*.[103] Reinforcing the worst fears of those anxious to prevent a French occurrence of the Spartan phenomenon, the *Requête* arrogantly demanded that women be allowed to wear men's clothes, especially culottes. This would represent a triumph over the demeaning practices of the past, especially those that forced disgraced military personnel to don female apparel as a mark of their humiliation.[104] The

Requête considered genuine emancipation to consist in women adopting as many male attributes as possible.

Women's demand to be armed, to adopt an aggressive stance in the upcoming battle against counterrevolution, found particular resonance within the milieu of Parisian artisans, workers, and craftsmen referred to as the *sans-culottes*. Sans-culottes women had been active in the great popular uprisings of the Revolution. One of them, Marguerite Pinaigre, petitioned the National Assembly for a pension which both she and her husband had earned as a result of their efforts in the storming of the Bastille. This *"citoyenne* wife . . . worked equally hard with all her might . . . resolved to triumph or die. It is she," Marguerite proudly declared "who ran to several wineshops to fill her apron with bottles, both broken and unbroken, which she gave to the authorities to be used as shot in the cannon used to break the chain on the drawbridge of the Bastille."[105]

As France went to war, the role of sans-culottes women increased. Defending the Revolution and feeding their families in the absence of their fathers, husbands, and brothers, women from the popular classes took on the task of revolutionary surveillance. They crowded into the courtrooms of the revolutionary tribunals, demanding vengeance from speculators, hoarders, and other counterrevolutionary traitors.[106] Women attended neighborhood section meetings, as well as the proceedings of the Commune and the Convention, openly displaying their favor or displeasure with policy decisions under discussion. They were especially active in enforcing the Maximum.[107] On the daily bread lines of a hungry Paris in 1793 and 1794, women terrorized bakers, merchants, and others standing in the way of what they considered to be economic justice.

It was from these ranks that Pauline Léon and her colleague Claire Lacombe recruited members for the Society of Revolutionary Republican Women, established in 1793. Closely allied with Jacques Roux and the *Enragés*, these women threatened Jacobin hegemony of the Revolution. Anxious to contain the popular revolution, the Jacobins expressed open antipathy to Léon and her followers in their club and sought a pretext with which to close the Society of Revolutionary Republican Women. An argument between members of the Society and the marketwomen of les Halles provided just such an opportunity. Accusing the women of the Society of forcing them to wear the red bonnet, symbol of patriotic commitment to the Revolution, the marketwomen won from the Convention the right to dress as they pleased.[108] Some of them approached the Convention and asked that the Society be shut down. The men of the Convention readily concurred, closing the Society and outlawing all women's clubs on 30 August 1793. It was the first Jacobin offensive against the *sociétés populaires*, to be followed by restrictions on other popular organizations and clubs.[109]

By closing the Society of Revolutionary Republican Women and forbidding women to attend club meetings of any sort, the Jacobin Convention dealt an important blow both to the *Enragé* movement and to the cause of women's equality. The language employed to denounce Léon and her followers suggests that anti-feminism was as important a motive as anti-*Enragé* sentiment. In the Convention and in the Paris Commune, the Society was denounced as a club of "emancipated women," "female soldiers," "denatured women," "viragos," "impudent women who want to become men."[110] Determined to put women firmly back in their place, the Jacobin deputy André Amar underlined the natural basis of women's inferiority. "Women," he explained to the Convention, "by their constitution are open to an exaltation that would be ominous in public life . . . the interests of the state [should women be allowed to assume a public persona] would soon be sacrificed to all kinds of disruption and disorder that hysteria can produce."[111] By outlawing women's clubs, Amar and his colleagues put an end to the disorderly experiments in female activism made possible by the opening of political and public space during the Revolution. Women would continue to be active in the Revolution periodically, but never again in as organized or as determined a manner.

Although the Jacobins sealed the political fate of feminism, they did not undo the positive social legislation women had gained during the Girondin-dominated legislative assembly in 1791 and 1792. Even though the Girondins had failed to struggle for women's suffrage while in office, they had made good on their promises to reform marital and inheritance laws in a more equitable direction. Many women considered this to be more important than the vote, since only domestic reorganization could give women the economic and legal wherewithal to leave a bad, often abusive, marriage and begin an independent life. The fight for divorce was especially characteristic of the program of the *Cercle Social*, composed of fairly wealthy women able to take advantage of the hoped-for legislation.[112]

The first legislative victory celebrated by women was the repeal of primogeniture in October 1791. A survival of the obsolete feudal order granting the largest share of an estate's patrimony to the eldest son at the expense of all his siblings, primogeniture was opposed in the legislative assembly on the grounds that it perpetuated social inequality instead of equally endowing all heirs with a modest fortune. By establishing the principle of equal inheritance for all children, however, the new ruling extended important property rights to girls. This, along with other reforms, such as making women majors at age twenty-one, enabling them to contract debts, and giving them some say over the administration of their property, began laying the foundation for economic equality within marriage.

No freedom was truly possible, however, without the guarantee of divorce. Moreover, the National Assembly's law on adultery, passed in the summer of 1791, stood as a glaring affront to the principle of equality within marriage. The law stipulated that only men could pursue charges of adultery against unfaithful spouses. In addition, it gave them by way of compensation complete control over their wives' dowry. Etta Palm d'Aelders spoke out forcefully against the new law in the *Cercle Social* and petitioned the National Assembly in the name of French *citoyennes* to repeal this infamous decree. D'Aelders considered this type of discriminatory legislation "a natural consequence of the oppressive regime of the indissolubility of marriage." For d'Aelders, the right to divorce, one of humankind's "natural freedoms," was implicit in the freedoms guaranteed by the Declaration. Likening marriage to a social compact between two "separate but equal" individuals, she insisted that such a compact could only be ensured if either party had the freedom to leave under unbearable circumstances.[113]

The reform of marriage into a compact between equals did not necessarily run counter to the interests of men. Farsighted and liberal individuals prominent in the Girondin faction carried on d'Aelders's struggle for divorce within regular political channels, obtaining a law of divorce in September 1792. The right to divorce represented a victory against both the sacerdotal view of marriage endorsed by the Church and absolute male authority in the household. It was greeted enthusiastically in the Assembly and the *Cercle Social*.[114] It represented a triumph for women, for love, and for friendship, as well as for the power of the State at the expense of the Church.[115]

By making marriage a civic institution, and by ensuring the rights of either partner to leave an intolerable situation, the law of September 1792 proved momentous. Numerous appeals for divorce flooded the civic courts in the following years. Most of these appeals issued from women, almost always on the grounds of physical abuse.[116] Despite its popularity, however, the law on divorce, like the abolition of slavery in 1794, did not prove longstanding. Article 213 of the Napoleonic Code restored man's unlimited power over his wife, noting that "the wife owes obedience to her husband."[117] Much of women's legal equality was undermined by the new code, although the right to divorce was not repealed until shortly after Napoleon's reign during the Restoration.[118] Thus ended the brief reign of marital equality, perhaps the most important feminist victory of the revolutionary years.

Women's public and political activities, severely curtailed by the Jacobin prohibition of female club activity, were subject to continuing attack in the later years of the Revolution. During the years of reaction to the Terror, women's very rights to free speech and assembly were curtailed. On 20 March 1795 women were expressly forbidden from attending the proceedings of the Convention, even as onlookers. Three days later, their right to publicly assemble in groups of five or more was forbidden. "All women are to return to their domiciles until otherwise ordered," the Convention decreed, "those found on the streets in groups of more than five one hour after the posting of this order will be dispersed by force and then held under arrest until public tranquillity is restored in Paris."[119] With this ignominious house arrest the valiant struggles of feminists, men and women alike, to bring about greater equality between the sexes drew to an end. It bore truth to Olympe de Gouges's assertion that men's *esprit de corps* was a long way from changing. "What advantage have you received from the Revolution?" she demanded of women. "A more pronounced scorn, a more marked disdain," she replied.[120]

< IV >

Conclusion

In April 1790, the city of Strasbourg sent a petition to the representatives in the National Assembly asking them to heed public opinion on the Jewish question, as with all other matters. "In fifteen assemblies of the city's commune," the petition noted, "composed of persons of all estates, our representatives have unanimously voted against the admission of Jews to the city. Such a unanimous will," it emphasized, " is a terribly strong argument against the Jews."[121] Public opinion and the will of the people had, indeed, changed. From being the voice of the oppressed under the Old Regime, public opinion had come to speak for the oppressive majority of the Revolution.

The initial hesitancy of the men of the Assembly to extend rights to Jews, Mulattoes, and Blacks was a powerful arsenal in the hands of anti-semites and racists intent on excluding men of different ethnic and cultural backgrounds from the new French community. "By not pronouncing on the Jews," the city of Strasbourg reminded the men of the Assembly, "you already proved that the rights of the *Declaration of Man* were not applicable to all . . . that important considerations could lead to exceptions to the general rule."[122] The Jews were the first exception, the Mulattoes and Blacks the next. In each case, claims of political expediency and economic incentive competed with the more abstract standards of justice and morality evoked by those favorable to the Jews and the men of color. The specter of peasant pogroms in Alsace, slave revolts in Saint Domingue, and colonial secession gave weight to the arguments of exclusion. Balancing the interests of diverse groups and heeding to the pressures of popular prejudice, the men of the National Assembly forestalled the emancipation of Jews, Mulattoes, and Blacks, in spite of the universal language of the Declaration.

Given this powerful vortex of interests, it is quite surprising that the French Revolution finally managed to extend the provisions of the Declaration to these groups. The valiant efforts of a number of committed individuals, especially Jansenists and supporters of the Girondins, as well as the sustained activity of Jews, Mulattoes, and Black slaves to free themselves, were crucial factors in the ultimate success of emancipation. Changes in the Revolution itself, especially the war, the social battle against feudalism and aristocracy, the unraveling of Old Regime corporatism, the attack on the Church, and the leftward drift of political discourse fostered the abandonment of religious, ethnic, and racial stereotypes. And the idealist ideologies of the Enlightenment, coupled with the abstract language of the Declaration, pushed men to think in universal and fraternal terms.

In the expanding fraternity of the 1790s, women were not admitted. Their irreducible biological difference, something which assimilation and acculturation could never eliminate, made them unlikely candidates for admission to the French body politic. French revolutionaries displayed great antipathy towards difference of any sort. Heirs to an absolutist tradition, determined to destroy the plurality of hierarchies and privileges built into the corporate organization of Old Regime society; influenced by Rousseau's distrust of parties, factions, and other sources of political instability; and facing an international war of immense proportions, the revolutionaries of the 1790s set about rebuilding the French nation on grounds that would admit of no division. Such zealous activity, carried to extremes during the Terror, destroyed the possibilities of pluralism, either liberal or reactionary, political or cultural.

Antipathy towards cultural difference played its part in the evolving revolutionary synthesis. Jews, Mulattoes, and Blacks were to prove both beneficiaries and victims of the hostility of the new national identity to differences past and present. They were beneficiaries insofar as the revolutionaries, albeit with much struggle, eliminated the debilitating differences of the Old Regime. They were victims insofar as they were encouraged to eliminate or downplay traces of their original cultural and religious traditions in order to become Frenchmen, to assimilate at the cost of themselves forgetting from whence they came. Race, of course, was the more difficult factor to downplay or ignore. But since Frenchmen in the eighteenth century adhered not to a biological but to a cultural/climatic notion of the origins of racial difference, they were more sympathetic than their nineteenth-century or Anglo-Saxon counterparts to the long-term possibility of African assimilation into the main body of French citizens.[123]

Women's differences, however, were unavoidable and irreducible. In spite of Condorcet's persuasive attempts to the contrary, revolutionaries were more apt to concur with Olympe de Gouges's characterization of the natural differences between men and women. They did not, however, concur with her political conclusions. De Gouges's pluralistic vision of a society composed of varied and different individuals was unique. But it grew out of a world view shaped in the interstices of Old Regime corporatism, of a society composed of different individuals having different rights. So it, too, had to be rejected. Moreover, neither Condorcet nor de Gouges could convince the vast majority of men that it was in their best interest to liberate women. Centuries of male dominance, resulting in inestimable benefits to men of all classes, would not be so easily shaken. On this issue, men of different political persuasion stuck together, displaying a unity sadly lacking at so many other points in the Revolution.

Intolerance to difference proved to be the Revolution's major shortcoming. But if this intolerance had led to disastrous results, especially for women, it had also resulted in unprecedented freedoms. The universal and abstract freedom and equality proclaimed by the Declaration had set afire the ideological foundations of centuries of prejudice and hate. The emancipation of the Jews and the abolition of African slavery were the result. That these results were not enduring is another chapter in French history. The nineteenth century was to witness renewed anti-semitism, the reimposition of slavery in the French West Indies, and the development of new forms of racial and ethnic bigotry on the part of the French populace. For women, too, the nineteenth century represented a considerable setback. In spite of their formal exclusion, however, women continued to look back favorably upon the Declaration and the Revolution, as did Jews, Mulattoes, and Blacks. It was a time of promise, when all things seemed possible and no barrier insurmountable.

The Idea of a Declaration of Rights

KEITH MICHAEL BAKER

THE SEARCH FOR ORIGINS can be hazardous. In the case of the Declaration of the Rights of Man and of the Citizen, its pitfalls have
long been evident in the classic exchange between Georg Jellinek
and Emile Boutmy now a century old. In 1895, Jellinek set out to demolish two prevailing opinions regarding the sources of the Declaration. The first traced the principal inspiration of the text to the philosophy of Rousseau. Jellinek had little difficulty in pointing out that
the essential terms of the social contract, as Rousseau imagined it,
involved the complete transference to the community of all the individual's rights. Nor did he fail to note Rousseau's insistence that,
since the general will emanated from all and applied to all, individual
citizens needed no guarantees against the sovereign they collectively
constituted.[1] This being the case, Jellinek concluded, "the principles
of the *Contrat Social* are accordingly at enmity with every declaration of rights."[2] The idea of a Declaration of Rights had to find its origin elsewhere.

In the opinion providing Jellinek's second target, this origin was
assumed to lie in the American Declaration of Independence. Jellinek, however, deemed the opening paragraph of the latter document
far too general to serve as the model for the French text, which he
found instead in the bills of rights preceding many of the constitutions adopted by the American states between 1776 and 1783. The
French may have packaged their declaration in a more metaphysical
wrapping, flavoring it perhaps with a Gallic hint of Rousseauism. But
Jellinek's comparison of articles and clauses left him convinced that
the essential ingredients of the Parisian product were imported from
Virginia, with embellishments from Massachusetts and Maryland,
North Carolina and New Hampshire, Pennsylvania and Vermont.

The French articles, he concluded, "brought out nothing new, or unknown to the American stipulations."[3]

The prevailing wisdom thus demolished, at least to his own satisfaction, Jellinek went on to trace the American defense of rights to two earlier traditions. First came common law protection of the rights of Englishmen, rights these latter enjoyed not by their very nature as individuals but as members of a common people. Jellinek traced this tradition to the forests of Germany, primal source of that Teutonic conception of the state in which "prince and people form no integral unity, but stand opposed to each other as independent factors."[4] Second came the Reformation, its affirmation of religious individualism issuing in claims for the right to liberty of conscience that lay at the heart of the American experience. In this experience, Jellinek argued, the common rights of Englishmen were gradually infused with higher value as rights endowed upon all individuals by their Creator.

Not surprisingly, such an assertion of the Germanic, protestant sources of the Declaration of the Rights of Man elicited an irritated response from across the Rhine. It came from Emile Boutmy in 1902.[5] Boutmy found no contradiction in the claim that Rousseau's arguments had inspired many of the articles of the Declaration of Rights, whether or not their author had actually made a case for a declaration of this kind. Nor did he see anything to preclude a sovereign people from utilizing this form to promulgate an essentially Rousseauian understanding of the principles of equality and universality as the essence of freedom under the law. Neither the form nor the content of the French Declaration owed much in Boutmy's judgment to the American models. In his analysis, similarities between the American and French documents (when they were not the illusory effect of Jellinek's method of comparison) derived less from any direct influence than from a common matrix of eighteenth-century thought. The differences were in any case more fundamental. They were differences in style, between the crabbed juridical idiom of the American declarations and the vibrant, universalistic tones of the French. And they were differences in substance, between Anglo-Saxon insistence upon the limits upon power and an indisputably Gallic—and transparently Rousseauian—affirmation of freedom through the common exercise of sovereignty.

Not that Boutmy insisted on the influence of the *Social Contract* alone. Behind Rousseau, he descried Locke, Montesquieu, Voltaire, and other exponents of the theory of natural rights. In his view, indeed, the Declaration of the Rights of Man and of the Citizen gave quintessential expression to the thinking of an entire century. Where Jellinek traced the origins of this affirmation of individual rights back to the Reformation, Boutmy saw it as the essential offspring of Enlightenment. Liberty of conscience, he insisted, was not the fruit of the Reformation, which had to the contrary inflamed the sectarian intolerance of religious fervor. Toleration was the child of the Enlightenment, which finally dared in the name of reason to free humanity from the scourge of religious passions. The signature of the Declaration of the Rights of Man was that of "the whole eighteenth century, destroyer of all tradition, creator of natural right."[6]

Who was right, Jellinek or Boutmy? Perhaps both? Perhaps neither? Jellinek was surely justified in insisting upon the fundamental importance of the example the Americans offered in prefacing their state constitutions with explicit declarations of rights. It would now be difficult to deny, in the face of Franco Venturi's research, the passionate interest in these constitutions evoked in France (as elsewhere in Europe) in the years preceding the Revolution.[7] Nor, after the careful recent readings of the debates of the Constituent Assembly by such scholars as Marcel Gauchet and Stéphane Rials, could one dismiss the urgency with which the Constituents sought to define and distinguish, with an eye to the American models, their own views of the meaning of a declaration of rights and its proper relationship to the constitution they had sworn to create.[8] Define *and* distinguish: for it is abundantly clear that the French deputies kept the American example in mind for a variety of purposes, those on the right of the Assembly warning against its dangers no less vociferously than those on the left set out to surpass its limitations.

If Jellinek's insistence on the pertinence of the example of the American bills of rights to the composition of the French declaration seems to have been borne out by subsequent research, however, few scholars would now subscribe to his assertion that all the essential articles of that document came from across the Atlantic. Nor would many deny Boutmy's contention that the French deputies drew on Rousseauian formulations at absolutely crucial points in the composition of their document, in ways that went far beyond the application of Gallic style to Anglo-Saxon truths. Few, moreover, would even wish to dispute Boutmy's more general claim that the Declaration bears the marks not only of Rousseau but of Enlightenment thinking in many of its aspects. Why, indeed, contest a claim that is so general as to be virtually meaningless?

For the fact of the matter is that the Declaration of the Rights of Man and of the Citizen is an immensely complex document. It was also drawn up with enormous difficulty and great urgency, at the cost of bitter argument, inevitable linguistic compromises, and dramatic theoretical tensions, by an assembly profoundly divided over the nature and purpose of the text it was struggling to construct. It seems remarkable, in retrospect, that neither Jellinek nor Boutmy appears to have been in the least interested in the process by which the Declaration of the Rights of Man was actually composed, or the purposes it was intended to serve. Whether there should be a declaration of rights; what it would mean if there were; whether it should be drafted or proclaimed before or after the redaction of a new French constitution; what articles it should contain; how its every clause might be worded: each of these issues was highly contested, within the National Assembly and outside it, in the summer of 1789. Each involved a struggle to define the nature and meaning of the revolutionary situation; each bore on the political choices of language from which the Declaration of the Rights of Man and of the Citizen eventually emerged. Arguments invoked and ideas espoused in the debates doubtless came from many sources; it is important to identify them as precisely as possible. But the study of origins and influences cannot capture the particular significations these arguments and ideas assumed in the context of the assembly's debates, nor can an historical pedigree alone fix the meaning of the text to which the debates ultimately gave rise.

Fortunately, it has been one of the salutary effects of recent scholarship to shift attention precisely from questions of origins and influences to questions of meaning and situation. Before it was a text, Marcel Gauchet has aptly remarked, the Declaration of the Rights of Man was an act.[9] It was a speech act, one might say, that derived its meanings—for they were as multiple as they were contested—less from the historical sources of its particular utterances than from the illocutionary force of these utterances in a particularly tense and complex situation. In what follows I shall first try to sketch the principal competing

understandings, in prerevolutionary discourse, of the act of promul-
gating a declaration of rights; then I shall turn to the process of deliberation which led the National Assembly finally to take such an act.

≺ I ≻

The American Models

An undated, fragmentary note among the papers of the abbé Emmanuel-Joseph Sieyès, the French Revolution's first constitutional
theorist, offers a fascinating comment on the history of declarations
of rights before 1789. Earlier documents of this kind were, in Sieyès's
view, no more than chapters in the history of despotism. Assuming
the form of treaties between masters and their rebellious subjects, he
argued, they were no more than pacts between two contending powers who wished to demarcate the boundaries between their respec-
tive rights and prerogatives. Forced by circumstances to recognize
the subjects' grievances, a despotic ruler would make concessions
that "loosened some links in the chain of general servitude." But by
accepting these concessions rebellious subjects in effect acknowledged their ruler's sovereignty. Declarations of rights were thus
drawn up "the way one reaches a settlement before a notary. The general and common character of all the declarations is always the *implicit recognition* of a seigneur, a suzerain, or a master to whom one
is naturally obligated, and of some oppressions one wishes no longer
to endure. Everything comes down to these words: 'You promise not
to renew this link in your chain.'"[10]

In Sieyès's analysis, the American Revolution was the first to
break with this traditional pattern in that it overthrew the entire
yoke of despotism rather than merely alleviating it. But the break was
not complete. In drawing up their bills of rights, the Americans continued to regard the governments they were establishing in the same
spirit of suspicion with which they had confronted the power they
had overthrown: they wished, above all, to guard themselves against
abusive authority. "They declared their own rights, it appearing that
thus reassured one could go about one's business in peace. The memory of ills suffered, of those most resented, guides the pen of the authors of the *declarations of rights*."[11]

It was a profound mistake, Sieyès thought, for the Americans

thus to persist in conceiving a declaration of rights in the traditional
manner, as a direct response to immediate injuries. Declarations
drawn up on this assumption could only be particular in their articles, as each people recalled its most bitter grievances. But particularistic declarations of this kind, insisted the French theorist, must
ever be the symptom of incomplete revolutions. A people regaining
its complete sovereignty needs only the universal. "It cannot say:
man, the citizen, will not bear such and such a chain. It must break
them all. All that was *different* in the declaration of rights of all the
peoples of the earth cannot enter into its declaration. . . There is only
that which is common to all; that which belongs to man, to the citizen." On this assumption, the entire character of a declaration of
rights must change. "It ceases to be a settlement, a transaction, a
condition of a treaty, a contract, etc., between one authority and another. There is *only one* power, *only one* authority."[12]

Was this characterization of traditional declarations accurate as a
description of the bills of rights adopted in the American state constitutions? Alexander Hamilton, writing in *The Federalist*, certainly
thought so. "It has been several times truly remarked," he argued,
"that bills of rights are in their origin, stipulations between kings and
their subjects, abridgements of prerogative in favor of privilege, reservations of rights not surrendered to the prince . . . It is evident, therefore, that according to their primitive signification, they have no application to constitutions professedly founded upon the power of the
people, and executed by their immediate representatives and servants."[13] But that was in 1787. The bills of rights were much closer in
their assumptions about government to a very different theory, which
Hamilton himself espoused in 1775 when he argued the principle that
"the origin of all civil government, justly established, must be a voluntary compact between the rulers and the ruled."[14] This principle of
compact, it was insisted, required "that certain great first principles
be settled and established, determining and bounding the power and
prerogative of the ruler, ascertaining and securing the rights and liberties of the subjects, as the foundation stamina of the government;
which in all civil states is called the constitution, on the certainty and
permanency of which, the rights of both the ruler and the subjects
depend."[15]

Like the Declaration of Independence, the American bills of rights
bolstered traditional collective claims with new appeals to the rights

of individuals. But their essential concern was the defense of the common law freedoms of the ruled against their rulers. Born of rebellion against the despotism of Crown and Parliament, they extended the same mistrust of power to the magistrates and legislative bodies upon whom authority would be conferred by the new state constitutions. They were intended to ensure the continued exercise of those rights of the people which could never be divested by any compact. Hence the formulation of the "DECLARATION OF RIGHTS made by the Representatives of the good people of VIRGINIA . . . which rights do pertain to them and their posterity, as the basis and foundation of Government." Hence, too, the "Declaration of the Rights of the Inhabitants of the Commonwealth or State of Pennsylvania." These declarations, and others similarly entitled, defended the collective rights of the inhabitants of each state against their magistrates and representatives. The Massachusetts declaration, for example, burst with references to "the people of this Commonwealth"—"the people" whose rights it reserved in order "to prevent those, who are vested with authority, from becoming oppressors."[16] By contrast, the French Declaration of the Rights of Man and of the Citizen refers only once to "the French people," only once to "the nation," and several times, but only in an abstract generic sense, to "society" (or its members). The collectivity from which the document is ultimately held to derive is virtually effaced by the abstract form of its appeals to universality. Part of the task of understanding the Declaration of the Rights of Man and of the Citizen must be to explain this profound difference between the American models the French deputies invoked as they began to discuss their declaration of rights and the text of the document upon which they were finally able to reach agreement.

≺ II ≻

The Uses of a Declaration of Rights

The first French declaration of rights bore all the characteristics of a traditional bill of rights. It was that "declaration of the rights of the nation" proclaimed on 3 May 1788 by the Parlement of Paris in its last-ditch resistance to monarchical policies. This defiant resolution of the king's magistrates against the encroaching despotism of his ministers was perhaps the purest expression of what I have elsewhere called the "discourse of justice" in eighteenth-century French politics. The discourse of justice drew on the conceptual resources of a constitutional tradition with deep roots in French history: a tradition effaced by the growth of absolutism since the sixteenth century but dramatically revived and reworked in the constitutional conflicts of the late eighteenth. As these conflicts escalated, so did the vehemence with which parlementary theorists reasserted the existence of fundamental laws limiting royal sovereignty, falling back upon these laws as the indispensable ramparts of an historical constitution to which both king and nation were party.

Accordingly, the declaration of 3 May sought to avert the despotism of an unconstrained royal will by appealing to a compact between the people and its ruler—a compact the magistrates construed as perpetually renewed by "a general oath, that of the coronation, which unites all of France with its sovereign." It declared that France was a monarchy governed according to fundamental laws fixing the rights of the Crown, on the one hand, those of the nation on the other. These latter included the right of the nation to give its free consent to taxation through the organ of the Estates General, "regularly convoked and constituted"; the irremovability of judicial magistrates and the rights of the courts to register the legal expression of the king's will in accordance with the constitutional laws of each province and the fundamental laws of the state; protection of each citizen from arbitrary arrest by the right to trial, without delay and only by "his natural judges."[17]

The rights of the nation, it was to turn out after 25 September 1788, were also held by many to include the constitutional separation of the three Estates of the realm and their separate representation in the Estates General. The political explosion over that claim transformed the pattern of French political contestation, opening up conflicts over the composition and form of the Estates General that were only to be resolved by the revolutionary creation of the National Assembly on 17 June 1789. It also introduced a profound ambiguity into these conflicts. For after 25 September 1788, French political discourse revolved around two overlapping but quite distinct issues: the issue of liberty, or the need to limit power, specifically the power of the monarch and his administrative agents; the issue of equality, or the need to assert power—initially the power of the king; ultimately the power appropriated by the nation itself—to destroy aristocracy and institute civil equality. This ambiguity ran throughout the debates that occurred, before the Estates General met and in its early weeks, over the existence or non-existence of a French constitution and the necessity to fix one. It ran, similarly, through the many demands or proposals for a declaration of rights that would characterize such a constitution.

In this context, a formal declaration could be seen as a means of reasserting traditional rights of the French people against abuses of power, but it could also be used to reinforce the defense against arbitrary rule (as in the American examples) by appeal to the doctrine of natural rights. This was the syncretic spirit in which *cahiers* could demand "a declaration of national rights," "a reestablishment of the French nation in all the rights of man and of the citizen," "a French charter which will assure for ever the rights of the king and of the nation," a proclamation of the rights that "belong as much to each citizen individually as to the entire nation," or a "fundamental declarative law, enunciating the natural, essential and imprescriptible rights of the nation."[18] In such formulations, historical rights frequently merged with natural rights, those of the nation intermingling with those of the individual. In such demands, too, a declaration of rights frequently seemed synonymous with a constitutional charter. Assuming the power of the monarch, they sought to contain it: they envisaged the limitation of an existing power rather than the institution of a new one.

The same may also be said of more liberal projects for a declaration of rights, written with the American example more explicitly in mind. The marquis de Lafayette's first draft for a declaration of rights in January 1789, for example, assumed that France was and would remain a monarchy in declaring that "Nature has made men equal, and the distinctions between them necessitated by the monarchy are based, and must be measured against, general utility."[19] It insisted that "all sovereignty resides essentially in the nation" (amended in subsequent drafts to read "the source of all sovereignty resides [imprescriptibly] in the nation");[20] but this proposition led directly to a statement of the principle of division of powers, in a grammar that subtly acknowledged the existing authority of the king. The legislative, Lafayette proposed, "*must be* principally exercised by a numerous representative assembly," while the judiciary "*must be* entrusted to courts whose sole function is to keep the repository of the laws," applying them strictly, independently, and impartially. But the executive, he wrote, "*belongs* solely to the king."[21]

In Lafayette's succeeding drafts for a declaration of rights, specific references to the monarch were gradually effaced. His final version of a declaration, presented to the National Assembly in July 1789, offered a far more abstract formulation of the principle of the balance of powers, now justified on the grounds that the common good "requires that the legislative, executive and judiciary powers be distinct and definite; and that their organization assure the free representation of citizens, the responsibility of [administrative] agents, and the impartiality of judges."[22] But Lafayette still explained the necessity of such a declaration as crucial "at the moment when the government takes a certain and determinate modification, such as the monarchy in France."[23]

It was in the same spirit of the modification of existing institutions that Jean-Joseph Mounier, famed for his prerevolutionary leadership of the constitutionalist resistance in Grenoble, drew up his own draft declaration of the rights of man and of the citizen. In Mounier's analysis, presented to the National Assembly in a speech of 9 July on behalf of its first constitutional committee, the deputies had indeed been charged (in the language of the Tennis Court Oath) to "fix the constitution" of France. Yet they had not been charged to begin that task *de novo*. "The French are not a new people that has just left the forests to form an association," Mounier emphasized in a language that was to echo throughout the assembly's early debates, "but a vast society of twenty-four million persons that wishes to tighten the bonds uniting all its parts and to regenerate the realm, a society for whom the principles of true monarchy will always be sacred."[24] Mounier held it to be the deputies' task to build a complete constitutional order upon the basis of fragmentary historical foundations and rudimentary fundamental laws. In his thinking, the tradition of French constitutionalism, eroded by decades of ideological contestation, had indeed been reduced to its barest minimum: the enduring national choice of monarchical government, on the one hand; the principle of consent to taxation, on the other. But the deputies, he nevertheless insisted, had been assembled to regenerate their monarchy, not to inaugurate an entirely new social contract.

Accordingly, when Mounier came at the end of July to prepare a draft declaration of rights for discussion by the National Assembly's second constitutional committee, he offered a text by which the "representatives of the FRENCH NATION, convoked by the king, gathered in a NATIONAL ASSEMBLY," would "declare and establish by the authority of our constituents, as Constitution of the French Empire, the fundamental maxims and rules, and the form of government."[25] Like Lafayette's draft declaration, Mounier's began with the proposition that "nature has made men free and equal in rights. Social distinctions must thus be based on common utility." Like Lafayette's, it insisted that "the source of all sovereignty resides in the nation; no body, no individual can have authority that does not emanate expressly from it." Like Lafayette's, too, its provisions for limiting the monarchical power included a formula for the separation of powers. "To prevent despotism and assure the empire of the law," it proclaimed, "the legislative, executive and judiciary powers must be distinct and cannot be united." Similar formulations recurred in the draft declaration Mounier formally presented to the Assembly on 27 July, this time on behalf of its constitutional committee. But the committee found it particularly important to elaborate upon the case for the separation of powers. "To prevent despotism and assure the empire of the law, the legislative, executive and judiciary powers must be distinct," it now insisted. "Their union in the same hands would put those entrusted with them above all the laws, for which [those so entrusted] would be able to substitute their own wills."[26] For Mounier and his allies on the constitutional committee, this principle would eventually be translated into an argument for constitutional government dividing and balancing powers along the lines of the English model.

Within this constitutionalist discourse of justice, then, there was a close link between the idea of a declaration of rights and the notion of a separation of powers. Each was seen as a fundamental device for limiting an existing monarchical power: the first by establishing the incontrovertible rights of the individual and the nation, the second as an indispensable constitutional guarantee of the preservation of those rights. But there was no necessary logic linking the project of a declaration of rights to specific constitutionalist assumptions regarding the separation of powers. The two could, indeed, be conceived as strictly antithetical. This much is made entirely clear in the extended notes added to the French edition of John Stevens's *Observations on Government* published early in 1789.[27] Stevens's *Observations* had

been written in 1787 to repudiate the conception of a balance of powers elaborated in Delolme's account of the English constitution and
proferred to Americans as the model of political freedom in John
Adams's *Defence of the Constitutions*. In 1789, the French translation of his work became the vehicle for a sustained attack, by the marquis de Condorcet and Pierre-Samuel Dupont de Nemours among
others, on the essential assumptions of balanced government in the
Anglo-American style.

For political rationalists like Condorcet and Dupont de Nemours,
heirs to the physiocratic tradition, the idea of separating and balancing powers was the very epitome of incoherence. Tyranny would be
destroyed not by an artificial and irrational balancing of potentially
arbitrary wills, they argued, but by setting forth the first principles of
social organization in a rational exposition of the rights of man. The
American declarations had been neither systematic nor complete;
but the Americans had had the genius to recognize the need to put
these declarations first, before any merely constitutional provisions.
It was only necessary to reason more systematically from this premise to arrive at a declaration of rights that would be universally applicable. "One can reach such a degree of perfection in this genre that
there could not be two declarations in the entire universe that would
differ from one another by a single word. Where would arbitrary governments be then?"[28]

In the logic of this physiocratic discourse of reason, the very act of
declaring the rights of man was the fundamental antidote to despotism. Publicity itself was the essence of a declaration of rights; publicity itself was the force that would make such a declaration the
measure of all governments and the touchstone of all laws. "Ignorance is the first attribute of savage and isolated man," François
Quesnay had insisted in his *Droit naturel*; "in society it is the most
fatal human infirmity, it is an enormous crime, for ignorance is the
most general cause of the evils of the misfortunes of the human
race."[29] If ignorance was the principal cause of human misfortunes, it
followed that instruction was their principal remedy. Accordingly,
Quesnay, the founder of the physiocratic school, had made it one of
his fundamental maxims of government that *"the nation be instructed in the general laws of the natural order, which evidently
constitute the most perfect government."*[30] Public tranquility and

prosperity were possible only to the degree that knowledge of these laws was made general, he insisted. "The more a nation applies itself to this science, the more the natural order will dominate within it and the more its positive order will be regular. No one would propose an unreasonable law in such a nation, because the government and the citizens would immediately see its absurdity."[31]

In physiocratic theory, then, public knowledge of the rational principles of social order—which is to say, of the natural rights and duties of individuals in society—was the essential remedy for abuses of power. The very self-evidence of these principles, once communicated to an entire nation, would render despotism impossible because absurd—just as it would render constitutionalist notions of checks and balances obsolete because incoherent and dangerous. For decades, accordingly, physiocratic propagandists had argued against political mechanisms for dividing authorities and multiplying countervailing powers. For decades, they had proclaimed that authority should be unitary but rational, transformed from within by the logic of social reason, constrained from without only by the direct and immediate force of enlightened public judgment. Those seeking means to prevent the abuse of wealth and power had invented "a thousand different kinds, all totally useless," insisted another physiocratic propagandist, the abbé Nicolas Baudeau, in his *Introduction à la philosophie économique*. But the only truly efficacious means of achieving this end was public, general, and continual instruction in the (physiocratic) principles of the natural social order. "All the other means, such as republican forms, political counterforces, and the demand for human and positive laws, are insufficient remedies to halt abuses of the predominant force."[32]

Writing in 1771, at the height of the constitutional struggles over the Maupeou Revolution, Baudeau had been anxious above all to defend the principle of unitary authority in the service of enlightened reform. Not surprisingly, then, he had reserved his most emphatic scorn for those remedies against arbitrary power favored in the constitutionalist discourse mobilized in opposition to chancellor Maupeou's attack upon the parlements. In his vocabulary, "fundamental laws" could be reduced to vestiges of arbitrary human wills lacking any foundation in the principles of social order, and hence destructive of the true rights of mankind; an "intermediary power," in its turn, was ultimately no more than a means of preventing what was beneficial to society and ensuring what was harmful to it. As for "countervailing forces," were they really more than "the shock of blind, exclusive, oppressive, usurping passions against other blind, exclusive, oppressive, usurping passions, as celebrated modern writers understand and formally explain?" Could they ever be more than a recipe for social disorder and political confusion? "This continual battle among repositories of authority ceaselessly struggling . . . is evidently a state of war; it is the antithesis of society—in its principle, in its action, in its effects."[33]

Never more baldly stated than by Baudeau, opposition to the constitutionalist program for separating and dividing powers remained a fundamental tenet in physiocratic thinking. Unitary political authority at once sustained and transformed by publicity into the exercise of social reason; ignorance, that most profound source of human ills, eliminated by general knowledge of the true principles of social order; arbitrary government rendered impossible by the immediacy of enlightened public judgment: these were the essential maxims of the physiocratic discourse of reason as it took form in the last decades of the Old Regime. These, too, were the convictions that gave the issue of a declaration of rights its supreme importance to Condorcet and Dupont de Nemours on the eve of the Revolution.

Physiocratic Discourse [margin annotation]

The rationalist case for a Declaration as the essential remedy against arbitrary power was passionately made in Condorcet's *Idées sur le despotisme, à l'usage de ceux qui prononcent ce mot sans l'entendre.* "The sole means of preventing tyranny," he argued, "which is to say the violation of the rights of men, is to bring all these rights together in a declaration, to set them forth there clearly and in great detail, to publish this declaration with solemnity, establishing there that the legislative power, under whatever form it is instituted, can ordain nothing contrary to any of these articles." The more detailed and comprehensive this declaration, Condorcet insisted, "the clearer and more precise it will be; the surer of being protected from any tyranny will be the nation that has recognized it and become attached to it by principle, by opinion. For any tyranny evidently attacking one of these rights would see general opposition arise against it." Liberty would thus be secured at no cost to public tranquility or social progress. For an enlightened nation "armed with this shield would cease to be anxious about every innovation."[34]

Not that Condorcet and Dupont lacked anxiety themselves as they watched the Estates General assemble. Whatever the long-term effects they expected from a declaration of rights in transforming the nature of French politics and society, their insistence on the importance of such a document was also motivated by a more immediate concern: fear of what the Estates General might do once it seized legislative power. Preoccupied for decades by the need to transform royal authority from within rather than limiting it from without, and for that reason unenthusiastic about the convocation of the Estates General, these advocates of enlightened administrative reform now found the risks of despotism augmented rather than diminished by the prospective assertion of popular will.[35] While Condorcet warned of the dangers in his *Idées sur le despotisme*, Dupont reiterated physiocratic doctrine concerning the definition of legislative power in another note added to the *Examen du gouvernement d'Angleterre*. There he insisted that legislative will can never be unlimited; even the people does not have the right to act unjustly. From this it followed necessarily that "legislation in its entirety is contained within a good declaration of rights." And not only legislation, of course, but legislators. This was the obscure wisdom Dupont found locked into the canny linguistic fact that at the origins of societies men had chosen *legislators*, not *legisfactors*: those who would bear the law from the repository of nature rather than making it of their own will. Necessary as a guide to the legislators, a declaration of natural rights would also provide the very touchstone by which their actions would be judged. "Every citizen has the right to subject [them] to the test of this touchstone by a free discussion, communicated as broadly as possible to other citizens. This is why the invention of printing is infinitely helpful; this is why liberty of the press must be placed among the imprescriptible rights of all and of each."[36] Palladium of rationality, the declaration would by its very presence transform political will into public reason.

For Condorcet and Dupont, therefore, a declaration of universal human rights would not only serve as an instrument of social and political transformation. No less important, it would become an immediate safeguard against the potential dangers of revolutionary political will. It is striking, however, that Sieyès, that other heir to physiocratic doctrine, placed quite a different inflection upon physiocratic language in this respect. To be transformed, in his judgment, power had first to be seized. Before it could become an instrument for the rationalization of society, a declaration of rights had to function as a justification for revolutionary legitimacy.

The revolutionary potential of a declaration of rights for such use was made quite explicit by Sieyès in writing, on behalf of the duc d'Orléans, the latter's instructions regarding the *cahiers* to be drawn up in the electoral assemblies of the baillages under his jurisdiction. The very first item appearing in these instructions under the rubric of "most pressing national needs" concerned a Declaration of Rights. Such a document would designate the purpose of the legislative body, Sieyès explained, while also propagating among the people the true principles of social existence. But no sooner had Sieyès enumerated these two general purposes of a declaration of rights than he slipped into a more urgent, unenumerated third, linking the need for a declaration precisely to the exigencies of a revolutionary moment.

"One sees how a declaration of rights is a constitutional need in our present position," the *Instructions* argued; "we are far from directing our conduct only according to the principles of the social order." It followed from this extraordinary situation that, in the forthcoming Estates General, constituent power (in Sieyès's new political language) would necessarily be confused with constituted power, the will of the nation necessarily usurped by its representatives. "It will be necessary to allow this usurpation," Sieyès maintained, "as we would surely allow our friends the initiative to seize our possessions from the hands of a stranger, even without any special charge from us to do so." The essential point was that the deputies make good use of this usurpation "and that in arrogating to themselves the right to give us a constitution, they place therein a principle of reformation fit to be developed, to follow constantly the progress of enlightenment, and to recall it to its true origin."[37] Thus the revolution, Sieyès already announces in effect, will be a revolution of the deputies; entrusted with legislative power, they will seize constituent power on behalf of the nation even in the absence of any explicit charge to do so. In this revolutionary usurpation of power, the gap in legitimacy will be filled by "presenting the peoples with the table of their essential rights, under the title of *Declaration of Rights*."[38]

For Sieyès, then, the most immediate use of a declaration of rights would be to proclaim and legitimate the assertion of a revolutionary political will, breaking with all existing powers. In this manner, his project for a declaration of rights found its justification within a radical discourse of will invoking a language of national sovereignty. But it did not thereby lose its importance within a rationalist discourse of society. Here, as elsewhere in his political theory, Sieyès blended Rousseauian and physiocratic themes.[39] No sooner would the nation recover the exercise of its sovereignty, he anticipated, than it would use its power to institute a new order inaugurated in accordance with the necessary and universal principles governing the social art. Hence the two general purposes of a declaration of rights to which he had earlier adverted. In the first, a declaration "designates for the legislative body the social *goal* for which it is created and organised; it leaves [the legislative body] all the power, all the force to arrive at this goal with a firm step, and at the same time it surrounds it with precautions, such that it possesses neither power nor force the moment it wishes to diverge from the road set out for it."[40] Note the formulation: the declaration designates the goal to be followed by the legislative body, but it leaves this body all the power to reach that goal; at the same time, it functions in such a way that this power is lost immediately the legislative body diverges from the purpose set out for it. Power was not to be checked by countervailing power in Sieyès's imagination. It was to be either exercised or lost—turned on or off, as it were, by some kind of automatic switch governing its flow through the political grid. It would circulate through the political system with the same ease as wealth would circulate through the ideal, unimpeded economy.

What would govern the operation of this switch? Sieyès does not make his answer to this question explicit in this text. But a clue may be found in the second of the general purposes he has earlier attributed to a declaration of rights: to serve as an instrument of enlightenment, "penetrating the generality of the citizens with the principles essential to all legitimate, which is to say *free*, human association."[41] Put these two purposes of a declaration of rights together and the point seems clear. Sieyès's declaration will rationalize power by setting forth for everyone to see the principles underlying all social organization. On this basis, a representative body will be instituted to decide on behalf of the nation, but in accordance with invariable principles; the nation in its turn will be enlightened to such a degree that any act of the legislative body in contravention of its rationally established purposes will automatically and immediately become null and void. Under the aegis of a declaration of rights, power will be exercised rationally, or not at all.

The constitutionalist limitation of power as conceived within a discourse of justice, the revolutionary appropriation of power justified within a discourse of political will, the transmutation of power understood within a discourse of social reason: these were some of the hopes invested in a declaration of rights before the Estates General met. They afforded many competing possibilities as regards the purpose, the form, and the content of a declaration. But transformed into a National Assembly after 17 June 1789, the deputies of the French nation had first to decide whether they wanted a declaration of rights at all.[42]

≺ III ≻

Declaratory Dilemmas

On 27 June, Louis XVI, reluctantly acquiescing for the moment in the National Assembly's existence, ordered that it be joined by those clerical and noble deputies who had continued to meet in their separate assemblies. Bertrand de Barère, writing in *Le Point du jour*, celebrated this reunion of the nation's representatives as finally inaugurating the reign of reason. "Doubtless the assembly's first use of its time and enlightenment will then be given to the declaration of the rights of the nation and the constitution of the state on unshakeable foundations," he declared. "The force of opinion will finally destroy the slavery of abuses; natural justice will bring to an end the tyranny of usages; the courageous and enlightened patriotism that animates all the national representatives will at last achieve the most beautiful revolution accomplished on earth."[43] But this was the rhapsody of a man who thought that the constitution could be sketched out in the work of a day. He was soon to discover otherwise.

The assembly now called upon to establish a declaration of rights labored under immense difficulties. Its size was enormous: a body of some twelve hundred persons could not easily reach agreement regarding the draft of any document. The terms of its composition also remained profoundly ambiguous, consisting as it now did of the deputies of the Third Estate who had declared themselves a National

Assembly on 17 June, the liberal members of the privileged orders who had voluntarily decided to join it before or after that date, and the more recalcitrant clerical and noble deputies who found themselves in this common assembly only on the king's orders. Moreover, it had no established organization and forms of procedure, and no accepted rules for deliberation and voting, all of which remained to be defined. Its conditions of existence remained uncertain: early discussion over a declaration of rights took place as the assembly found itself surrounded by royal troops threatening its dispersal; later debate was interrupted by the crisis of widespread unrest in the provinces. And it faced a constantly escalating series of issues as the deputies were obliged, in response to successive crises, to take on the functions of a legislative and executive body in addition to those of a constituent assembly.

All of these conditions merely served, however, to exacerbate the assembly's most profound problem: the radical uncertainty of its constitutional task. By the Tennis Court Oath, the National Assembly had sworn not to disperse until the constitution of the realm had been "established and strengthened . . . on solid foundations."[44] But what did it mean to "establish" or "strengthen" the constitution? Was there a constitution to be restored—an ancient constitution ravaged by despotism, whose remnants were to be recovered, reassembled on more secure foundations, and reinforced with new protections? Or was there, to the contrary, a constitution to be created —a constitution instituting a true political order where none had previously existed? The division over this matter to be found in the mandates the deputies had brought to Versailles was made clear to the National Assembly by the comte de Clermont-Tonnerre, reporting on behalf of its constitutional committee, on 27 July 1789. "Our constituents want the regeneration of the state," he affirmed. "But some have expected it from the simple reform of abuses and the reestablishment of a constitution that has existed for fourteen centuries . . . Others have regarded the present social order as so vitiated that they have demanded a new constitution, and (excepting monarchical government and its forms, which the hearts of all the French are disposed to cherish and respect) they have given you all the powers necessary to create a constitution."[45]

The question of a declaration of rights lay at the very heart of this dilemma. Indeed, as Clermont-Tonnerre acknowledged, the demand for such a declaration was "the sole difference existing between the *cahiers* desiring a new constitution and those demanding only the reestablishment of what they regard as an existing constitution."[46] Nor was Clermont-Tonnerre simply reporting on the language of the *cahiers* in this respect. He was also recapitulating a fact that had become abundantly clear in the assembly's earliest deliberations. To debate the question of a declaration of rights was necessarily to open up the most profound differences within the assembly regarding the nature of its constitutional task.

Reporting to the assembly on 9 July, on behalf of its first committee on the constitution, Mounier had done his best to efface these differences by defining a common ground upon which all could agree. In his analysis, it was more important to give French government a determinate form than it was to decide whether a new constitution was thereby being instituted or an old one restored or perfected. "Let us fix the constitution of France," he exhorted the deputies. "And when good citizens are satisfied with it, what will it matter that some say it is new and others say it is old, provided that by general consent it assumes a sacred character?"[47] The same spirit of compromise led Mounier to insist at once on the necessity for a declaration of rights and the means of containing its potential dangers. To be good, he reasoned, a constitution had to be founded upon, and clearly protect, the rights of men. This required that "the principles forming the basis of every kind of society" be reiterated in advance, so that each constitutional article might be understood as a consequence of one of these principles. Mounier deemed it essential, however, that the statement of principles take the form of a short, concise preamble to the constitution, rather than becoming a separate document. Otherwise, "arbitrary and philosophical ideas, if they were not accompanied by their consequences, would make it possible to imagine other consequences than those accepted by the Assembly."[48] The declaration of rights should accordingly be considered an integral part of the constitution, to be neither definitively adopted until the constitution itself was completed, nor published separately from it. Only in that way could the dangers of abstract principles be contained by positive constitutional provisions.

What dangers? Chosen to define a middle ground, Mounier's language remained oblique. But the concerns to which he was alluding were quickly made more explicit by the comte de Lally-Tollendal in response to the first actual draft of a declaration of rights presented to the Assembly: that proposed on 11 July, to enthusiastic applause, by Lafayette. Lally-Tollendal did not repudiate the idea of drawing up a declaration of rights as a necessary preliminary to the drafting of the constitution, but he expressed alarm at the possibility that such a document might take on a life of its own before the completion of the constitution. The French, he insisted, were not "an infant people announcing its birth to the universe . . . a colonial people breaking the bonds of a distant government." They were "an ancient and immense people, one of the world's first, which gave itself a form of government for the past fourteen centuries and obeyed the same dynasty for the past eight, which cherished this power when it was tempered by customs and will revere it when it is regulated by laws."[49] Such a society, he feared, could be rapidly thrown into disorder by the spread of metaphysical principles and abstract notions of equality.

Isolated from precise constitutional provisions, Lally-Tollendal warned, a declaration of natural rights would open the Assembly to charges that it was subverting authority and throwing all social order into confusion. It would lead to the possibility that "disturbed imaginations, misunderstanding our principles . . . [or] perverse minds wishing to misunderstand them, would give themselves over to disorders or willfully go to extremes." It would produce problems and delays at a time when "the people suffers and demands real help from us, far more than abstract *definitions*." Ascent to the metaphysical peaks of natural right principles had therefore to be followed by a rapid return to the plain of positive law. "Let us certainly go back to natural law, for it is the source of all the others; but let us pass quickly down the chain of intermediary propositions; and let us hasten to descend again to the positive law which attaches us to monarchical government."[50]

The "incalculable dangers" of metaphysical abstractions in a complex traditional society, and the more compelling need for immediate, practical measures of political and social reform and social relief: these were to become the central themes in the arguments of the many deputies within the assembly who opposed a prior declaration of rights. Clearly sounded by Lally-Tollendal on 11 July, they received overwhelming support. At his suggestion, Lafayette's proposed Declaration of Rights was quickly referred to the thirty *bureaux* into which the assembly had divided itself for regular discussion in smaller groups, a measure that effectively precluded its immediate adoption by the assembly as a whole.

Three days later, on 14 July, surrounded as they were by the royal troops that threatened their very existence as a body, the deputies returned again to the issue raised by Lafayette's motion. "In what circumstances if not when they are violated must we recall the rights of men?" a deputy had demanded. "They would be the enemies of monarchy who said that a declaration of rights is contrary to it."[51] But some deputies wanted a declaration of rights to be placed at the beginning of the constitution, as its foundation; others would only accept a declaration that would appear at the end of the constitution, as its consequence. All that could be agreed, after lengthy debate, was that a declaration of rights should appear somewhere in the constitution. That decision, in its turn, simply raised the question of how the constitution itself would be drawn up. Eventually, the assembly decided upon the appointment of an eight-person constitutional committee drawn from the three orders in proportion to the numbers of their representatives. But even as the deputies debated, a popular uprising was underway in Paris. That evening they received the news of the storming of the Bastille. They were not to hear from their new committee until 27 July.

When it came, the anxiously-awaited committee report was divided into three parts, presented respectively—with obvious symbolism—by a deputy from each of the three Estates that had been so precisely balanced in the committee's composition. The first, offering a general outline of the committee's views, was brought to the assembly with the moral authority of the clergy by Jérôme-Marie Champion de Cicé, archbishop of Bordeaux. The second, the report on the *cahiers* prepared by the comte de Clermont-Tonnerre, carried the weight of tradition. Analyzing the content of the *cahiers*, it divided their constitutional demands into "acknowledged principles" (monarchical government, consent to taxation, the sanctity of property and liberty) and still open questions. But these latter included such issues as the balance of the three Estates within the Estates General, as well as its constitutional relationship to the monarch. Clermont-Tonnerre's vocabulary offered a striking contrast to the language the National Assembly had been forging since 17 June— and with it a powerful reminder of the traditional social claims still to be fully confronted within an assembly where deputies drawn from the three Estates now so ambiguously coexisted. It underlined the fact that the difference Clermont-Tonnerre reported between those *cahiers* demanding the restoration of a traditional constitution and those demanding a new one—the difference he found symbolized in their positions regarding a declaration of rights—necessarily involved the constitution of society as well as of its government.

It was left to a deputy of the Third Estate, Mounier, to present the articles on which the committee had so far agreed. They consisted of a statement of the principles of French monarchical government, preceded by a Declaration of the Rights of Man and of the Citizen. For the constitutional committee had indeed accepted the arguments for a prior declaration of rights as an indispensable means of establishing the principles upon which a new constitution should be based—and judged by the nation as a whole. "This noble idea, conceived in another hemisphere, must preferably be transplanted first among us," proclaimed Champion de Cicé.[52] He was convinced that the deputies wanted the ineffaceable principles of the rights of man constantly before them. They wanted the nation "to be able, at every moment, to relate and compare to [these principles] each article of the constitution it has entrusted to us, to assure itself of our faithful conformity to them, and to recognize the obligation and duty that arise for it to submit to laws that inflexibly maintain its rights." They wanted, in erecting "a continual guarantee for us against our own errors," to ensure that, should any future power seek to impose laws incompatible with the principles so declared, "this original and perpetual model would immediately denounce to all citizens the crime or the error."[53]

But if the National Assembly needed a declaration of rights to secure its own revolutionary legitimacy, it needed also to guard against the dangers of such a document. True to the logic of Lally-Tollendal's earlier warning, the constitutional committee had therefore hastened to move from abstract principles to positive law. Its proposed declaration was to be welded as tightly as possible to the forms of a monarchical constitution. Written by Mounier on the model of Lafayette's earlier draft and his own, the Declaration the committee presented on 27 July was "short, simple, and precise"—as Mounier had earlier insisted it should be. In opting for it, the committee had emphatically set aside the alternative model for a declaration of rights, that of the systematic exposition of the principles of political association presented to it by Sieyès.[54]

Champion de Cicé portrayed this choice as a strategic rather than a philosophical one. He allowed Sieyès's version the virtue of building a systematic and complete exposition upon the first principles of human nature, "following it without distraction in all its developments and in its social combinations." Indeed, he praised it as the work of a genius "as profound as it is rare." But this was only to ask whether there were not disadvantages "perhaps in its very perfection," since its philosophical qualities might place it beyond the comprehension of the universality of citizens. In Mounier's draft, to the contrary, Champion de Cicé found the same principles of human nature enunciated in "formulations that are complete, but detached one from another."[55] The educated, in reading them, could fill in the logical connections; the uneducated could retain them more easily as separate propositions, free from an intimidating philosophical apparatus.

This was a shrewd understatement of the implications of choosing Mounier's draft over Sieyès's. There was more involved than mere form. It was Sieyès's claim that only a systematic exposition of the rights of man could make clear that the deputies were acting not simply to limit an existing authority but to institute an entirely new order through the exercise of an originary constituent power.[56] Behind the choice between Mounier's telegraphic articles and Sieyès's extended, systematic exposition, as the deputies were soon to discover, there still lay the fundamental question of whether the French were reforming a traditional system of government or inaugurating a new society.

≺ IV ≻

Rights or Duties?

Before the National Assembly could decide the issue of a Declaration of Rights, it had first to decide how to decide. It was not until 29 July that it reached agreement on its rules of procedure, including the fundamental one that decisions would be reached by simple majority vote (with no provision for graduated pluralities to protect the rights of privileged minorities). At the same time, it was decided that the deputies would continue to meet daily in the separate *bureaux* for more informal discussion, while assembling for deliberation in general session only twice weekly. This latter arrangement seems to have found little favor among the most fervent advocates of a declaration of rights, particularly those endorsing Sieyès's draft. They detected little prospect of early action as *bureaux* meetings, when not inconclusive, continued simply to reject the draft declarations submitted to them.[57] By the evening of 30 July, Charles-François Bouche was already proposing that the assembly meet daily in plenary session, rather than twice weekly.[58] Compromise with ancient prejudices was all that Bouche expected from intimate assemblies, like the *bureaux*, in which ideological differences were blunted by traditional habits of deference.[59] He looked instead for decisive action from large assemblies in which "spirits are fortified and electrified; names, ranks, and distinctions count for nothing; everyone . . . will regard himself as a portion of the sovereign whose representative he is."[60] Bouche's motion was passed the following day, on 31 July. He was about to have his electrifying general debate.

Thus it was in the uncertain early days of August that the National Assembly, constantly inundated as it was with news of widespread popular disorder throughout the countryside, came finally to debate whether the constitution should actually begin with a declaration of rights. On 1 August, opponents of a prior declaration failed to turn the assembly's discussions immediately and exclusively to the business of the constitution, "such as it must be in a monarchical state, without there being any need for a declaration of rights."[61] No fewer than fifty-six deputies thereupon declared their intention to speak—and began doing so at such length that the first day's debate produced a call (from none other than the impatient Bouche) for a time limit on speeches![62] "The moment has finally arrived when a great revolution in ideas and things is going to transport us, so to say, from the mire of slavery to the land of liberty," rhapsodized the *Journal des Etats-Généraux*. "In the new hemisphere, the brave inhabitants of Philadelphia have given the example of a people seizing back its liberty; France will give it to the rest of the globe."[63] The *Point du jour* was more measured in its assessment. In Barère's judgment, the moment had come for the deputies of the French nation to decide whether the practice of the New World could indeed be naturalized in the Old; whether the examples of nascent republics might be followed in an ancient monarchy; whether there were now greater dangers to be feared from a declaration of the rights of man than from ignorance and contempt for them. "It was in the midst of these doubts and uncertainties," he reported, "that the debates began."[64]

The charge of those opposed to a prior declaration of rights in the current circumstances was led by Jean-Baptiste-Marie Champion de Cicé, bishop of Auxerre. Unlike his brother, the archbishop of Bordeaux, this noble prelate remained among those who mistrusted the transatlantic example of a country inhabited only by "propertyholders, farmers, equal citizens." He deemed it necessary for the French to establish laws to hold society together before announcing indiscriminately the ideal of equality.[65] This reasoning found substantial support. The principles of the rights of man were eternal, Antoine-François Delandine acknowledged; they had been clearly demonstrated by modern philosophers. But since they were easily misunderstood by the people, they were more wisely reserved to legislators capable of recognizing in the postulate of equality "a philosophical fiction that disappears as soon as there is born, alongside a feeble infant, another stronger one whose intellectual faculties will be greater." An abstract declaration would be dangerous, Delandine insisted, precisely because "each individual, interpreting it at will, could give it a terrifying extension."[66]

Pierre-Victor Malouet expounded along similar lines. "They took man in the bosom of nature and presented him to the universe in his original sovereignty," he acknowledged of the Americans. But it was one thing to do this in a society untouched by the legacy of feudalism, among a people already prepared for democracy by its customs, manners, and geography. It was quite another to do so in the midst of a vast mass of propertyless persons long oppressed and ignorant, a multitude desperately seeking subsistence in the midst of luxury and opulence. In such a situation, the bonds of society had first to be tightened, the classes brought together, the roots of luxury attacked, the spirit of family restored, love of the *patrie* consecrated; only then would it be wise to "announce in an absolute manner to suffering men, deprived of knowledge and means, that they are equal in rights to the most powerful and most fortunate." The conclusion was clear. "An explicit declaration of general and absolute principles of liberty and natural equality can destroy necessary bonds. Only the constitution can preserve us from universal disruption."[67]

The most radical response to these arguments was an avowedly (if quirky) Rousseauian one. Jean-Baptiste Crenière, deputy of Vendôme, invoked the *Contrat social* in distinguishing the constitution of a people from the mere form of its government. "Since every association is voluntary," he argued, "only the will of the associates can determine their relations." A people's true constitution was the act of association by which an assemblage of individuals agreed to form a political society; only by virtue of that act did they acquire rights in their relations one to another. Thus a true declaration of rights, enunciating the terms of the contract by which the French constituted themselves as a people, was necessarily prior to the institution of any particular form of government.[68]

Beyond a passing correction from Mounier, Crenière's speech elicited little response from other deputies. None was prepared to follow him so boldly in a reading of Rousseau that reduced rights to the consequences of a political convention.[69] Those favoring a prior declaration of rights preferred instead to find justification for the assembly's actions in principles beyond human will. "The rights of man in society are eternal; no sanction is needed to recognize them," reasoned the young comte de Montmorency-Laval. It followed that a declaration of rights was the essential foundation of the constitutional edifice; it had to be laid before this edifice could be constructed.[70]

In this view, there was greater danger of disorder in preserving ignorance and prejudice than in declaring universal truths. "The truth cannot be dangerous," insisted Guy-Jean-Baptiste Target, author himself of a much-discussed draft declaration. Moreover, any attempt to conceal the truth would be both criminal and useless. "The people does not sleep for ever; it is gathering its forces to overthrow the yoke with which it is burdened; we must direct its efforts with wisdom and prudence."[71] It would be a profound mistake to stress the dangers of a declaration of rights, added the comte de Castellane, particularly in a moment of social unrest "when all the springs of government are broken, and the multitude abandons itself to excesses that inspire fear of even greater ones." To the contrary, the "true means of stopping licence" was "to lay the foundations of liberty."[72] "Philosophical and enlightened peoples are calm," Antoine-Pierre-Joseph-Marie Barnave reassured the assembly; "ignorant peoples act restlessly." It followed necessarily that the constitution be preceded by a simple declaration comprehensible to all, a declaration that would become an indispensable *catéchisme national.*[73]

But there were many more-experienced catechizers in the National Assembly than Barnave, and they were far from imagining his catechism of *rights*. In fact, members of the clergy were conspicuous in the debate during its third day as they insisted that any declaration of rights also comprise a declaration of *duties*. The development was a telling one: it meant that the debate was shifting from the issue of whether there should be a prior declaration to the question of what it should contain. "One of the most interesting spectacles for a philosopher is to observe the rapid progress of truth and reason in the national assembly," reported the *Point du jour* in its account of the assembly's deliberations. "The first day of the debates, it seemed doubtful whether even the idea of a declaration of rights separate from the constitution would be adopted; the second day, the objections raised against all declarations (this example to French liberty given by American liberty) evaporated; finally, the third day, the discussion was only about whether the declaration of duties would be combined with the declaration of rights."[74]

On this third day, over repeated appeals for an immediate vote on the issue of a prior declaration, the assembly suddenly began to hear demands that any exposition of principles preceding the constitution include duties as well as rights. "This was one of the most tumultuous of sessions," reported the *Journal des Etats Généraux*, describing the "hurricane of ideas" that blew as successive speakers persisted in the face of cries "*Aux voix! Aux voix!*"[75] The clash of opinions was fundamental, touching as it did upon the deepest convictions regarding the nature of enduring social bonds. "Let us first establish and fix the duties of man; for to whom shall we give laws when the very natural spirit of independence has excited all minds and broken the bonds that maintain the social pact?" urged Pierre-Charles-François Dupont, one of the deputies of the Third Estate of Bigorre.[76] "If a declaration is necessary," thundered the bishop of Chartres, "there is a pitfall to avoid. There is a risk of awakening egoism and pride. The flattering expression of *rights* must be accompanied by *duties* as a *corrective* . . . It is desirable that there be, at the head of this work, some religious ideas nobly expressed."[77] The abbé Baptiste-Henri Grégoire, future revolutionary bishop, was no less passionate in insisting that a declaration of the rights of man was inseparable from a declaration of the duties necessarily paralleling and limiting them. While some deputies countered with the argument that duties were simply the corollary of rights— and therefore needed no explicit exposition—others now struggled, in refutation, to prove the converse. In the meantime, the Jansenist canon lawyer Armand-Gaston Camus obstinately demanded a formal vote on his amendment to the motion: "Will there, or will there not, be a declaration of the rights and duties of man and of the citizen?"[78] In the shouting match that followed, the clergy demonstrated its passionate conviction of the dangers of any attempt to found a society on purely individualistic principles.

The demand for a declaration of duties was strong enough to dictate a roll-call vote but not to convince a majority of the deputies: the motion was defeated by 570 to 433. Nevertheless, the issue had been a decisive one. In voting against a declaration of duties, the deputies had in effect opted for a declaration of rights.[79] Before closing the morning session of 4 August, the assembly decreed—"almost unanimously"—that the constitution would indeed be preceded by a Declaration of the Rights of Man and of the Citizen.

It is scarcely necessary to describe the events of the evening session of that same day. Acting on the celebrated Night of the Fourth of August to abolish every vestige of the "feudal regime," the National Assembly suddenly swept aside the bonds of a traditional social order opponents of a prior declaration of rights had been so anxious to defend. The writers of Mirabeau's *Courier de Provence* saw a direct— and surprising—connection between this "holocaust of privileges" and the preceding debate. They claimed the emotional abandonment of privileges was sparked by a desperate final maneuver on the part of those still opposed to a prior declaration.[80] This is an unlikely interpretation: the plan to propose an abandonment of privileges seems rather to have come from those favoring a declaration of rights than from those opposing it.[81] Yet there is little doubt that the emotions that swept the National Assembly on the Night of the Fourth of August were charged as much by the frustrations and delays of the preceding debates over a declaration as by the need to restore social order. "A great question agitated us today; the declaration of the rights of man and of the citizen has been deemed necessary," acknowledged one deputy during that night of sacrifices. "The abuse the people makes of these same rights presses you to explain them, and to establish with skillful hand the limits it must not cross." The assembly, this deputy nevertheless insisted, "would have prevented the burning of chateaux" had it been quicker to declare its determination to annihilate "the terrible instruments" of oppression they contained.[82] The deputies had indeed left it very late. Now those who had pressed for a prior declaration of rights rushed to embrace the immediate concrete actions their opponents had long demanded as an alternative. Making dramatic use of the sovereignty to which it had laid claim on behalf of the nation, redefining property rights in the act of upholding them, the National Assembly began to give substance to its notion of the rights of man and of the citizen.

≺ V ≻

"A Difficult Work"

It was to take the deputies a week to translate into legislative form the momentous decisions of the Night of the Fourth of August. Having done so, they returned immediately to the question of the Declaration of Rights—only to be confronted by the dozens of proposed declarations which had by then accumulated. Anxious for a text that would provide a basis for rapid deliberation, the assembly agreed on 12 August to form a Committee of Five to consolidate the various proposals into a working text.[83] Led by the comte de Mirabeau and Jean-Nicolas Démeunier, an authority on American politics and a strong advocate of a declaration of rights, the committee quickly set aside the existing proposals to produce a new version of its own.

This draft appears to have been composed largely in Mirabeau's "workshop" with the help of the Genevan exiles he had assembled to constitute his personal writing-stable and think tank. Mirabeau "had the generosity, as usual, to take the work upon himself and give it to his friends," one of them, Etienne Dumont, later recalled. "There we were, then, with Du Roveray, Clavière and himself, drafting, disputing, adding one word and eliminating four, exhausting ourselves in this ridiculous task, and finally producing our little piece of marquetry, our mosaic of supposedly eternal rights that had never existed."[84] Indeed, Dumont claimed to remember that, feeling all the absurdity of a "puerile fiction" as dangerous as it was fallacious, he became so disenchanted with the entire project that even Mirabeau and the other Genevans were persuaded of its futility.

It is difficult to evaluate these recollections written much later by a man who was to end up editing that classic refutation of the Declaration of the Rights of Man and of the Citizen, Jeremy Bentham's

Anarchical Fallacies. Etienne Clavière and Jacques-Antoine Du Roveray, after all, were political refugees, veterans of a revolutionary democratic movement that had claimed the inspiration of Rousseau, and almost certainly acquainted with the textbook account of natural rights theory propounded by their compatriot, Jean-Jacques Burlamaqui. Indeed, Du Roveray's *Thèses philosophiques sur la patrie*, published in Geneva in 1767, had ended in a political call strikingly similar to a famous phrase of the preamble they now prepared for the Declaration of the Rights of Man: "Our misfortunes must instruct us, we owe all our ills to forgetfulness of these eternal maxims."[85] It seems unlikely, then, that Mirabeau's Genevans were quite as disenchanted with their task as Dumont later suggested.

At the same time, it is undeniable that when Mirabeau offered his committee's work to the National Assembly on 17 August, he did so with striking reservations. "The declaration of the rights of man in society is doubtless only an exposition of some general principles applicable to all forms of government," the great orator began. "From that point of view, one would think a labor of this nature very simple and little susceptible of contestations and doubts." But the committee had not found it so. Indeed, it had "quickly realized that an exposition of this kind, when it is destined for an old and almost failing political body, is necessarily subordinate to many local circumstances and can only ever attain a relative perfection. From this perspective, a declaration of rights is a difficult task." The assignment was all the more arduous, Mirabeau continued, insofar as it involved the composition of a document to serve as preamble to a constitution not yet decided, to be prepared in a few days (as the Assembly had charged) as a digest of many conflicting proposals, and to be cast in a manner appropriate for the use of a people "prepared for liberty by the force of facts and not by reasoning."[86]

The *Courier de Provence* (written for Mirabeau mostly by Dumont and Du Roveray) was even more direct about the difficulties of drawing up a declaration of rights in a revolutionary situation. It found its argument in Rousseau's observation that society is advantageous only insofar as all its members have something and none have too much. "This profound truth contains the cause of the difficulties of making a *declaration of rights* for a people grown old in its prejudices," the journal explained. "Truth commands that everything be said, and wisdom invites temporization; on the one hand, the force of justice propels beyond the timid considerations of prudence; on the other, the fear of exciting a dangerous fermentation alarms those who do not wish to buy posterity's good at the price of the present generation's misfortunes. Oh you, tyrants of the earth, you did not feel half the misgivings, in covering it with evils and ravages, that its benefactors experience in seeking to remedy them!"[87]

Whatever their views regarding the intrinsic logic of a declaration of rights, these veterans of revolution in Geneva were apparently convincing themselves, and Mirabeau, that a declaration might produce a general conflagration in a complex and corrupt society. They acknowledged that a philosopher writing for eternity without thought of addressing the multitude was obliged to be uncompromising in announcing the rights of humanity. But it now seemed that the political actor in an immediate situation had necessarily to be more cautious—especially in regard to the dangers of popular misunderstanding. The people could not be armed with ideological weapons unless it was also taught their use, "for fear that it might abandon itself to fury in a first transport of drunkenness, turn them against itself, then cast them aside with as much remorse as horror."[88]

The Committee of Five had nevertheless produced a draft. And in doing so, Mirabeau explained to the Assembly on 17 August, it had preferred a series of articles in the more direct American style to the "scientific abstraction" favored by Sieyès and his supporters. Like the Americans, it had sought to present "political truths . . . in a form that could easily become that of the people, to whom alone liberty matters, and who alone can maintain it." Like them, it had opted for the language of "everyday life and simple reasonings." Like them, it had aimed to evoke "the sensations that have served to kindle liberty . . . setting aside, as far as possible, all that presents itself under the apparatus of novelty." Nonetheless, Mirabeau acknowledged, the committee had encountered many problems in realizing this form. It had proven difficult to distinguish what was natural to humanity from what was specific to particular societies; to enunciate the principles of liberty without entering into details or drifting into the formulation of laws; to avoid carrying "resentment of the abuses of despotism to the point of composing less a declaration of the rights of man than a declaration of war against tyrants." In brief, the Committee of Five had fallen far short of the ideal declaration of rights that "would contain axioms so simple, evident and fertile in consequences that it would be impossible to diverge from them without being absurd and one would see all Constitutions emanate from them."[89]

A revealing remark this, for it suggests that while Mirabeau and his colleagues had rejected the philosophical style of exposition favored by Sieyès they were still far from abandoning the rationalist ideal to which it was linked. Nothing, indeed, revealed this ideal more clearly than the language of the preamble which Mirabeau now proposed:

> The representatives of the French people constituted as the National Assembly, considering that ignorance, forgetfulness, or contempt for the rights of man are the sole causes of public misfortunes and the corruption of government, have resolved to reestablish, in a solemn declaration, the natural, inalienable and sacred rights of man; in order that this declaration, constantly present to all members of the social body, may ceaselessly remind them of their rights and duties; in order that the acts of the legislative and the executive power, since it will be possible to compare them at each moment to the goal of every political institution, may be the more respected; in order that the demands of the citizens, henceforth founded on simple and incontestable principles, may always be directed towards the maintenance of the Constitution and to the happiness of all.
>
> In consequence, the National Assembly recognizes and declares the following articles.[90]

The language of this preamble is, of course, virtually identical to that ultimately adopted in the final version of the Declaration of the Rights of Man. But it appealed less to the popular experience Mirabeau had been invoking than to the physiocratic ideal of a rationality that would unerringly guide the individual choices driving the entire system of modern society. Nor is this surprising. Mirabeau, that often wayward son of a founding father of physiocracy, had certainly been willing in his earlier *Essai sur le despotisme* to reiterate physiocratic demands for instruction that would allow every act of legislation to be compared directly to the ineffaceable and imprescriptible natural laws establishing the rights of man.[91] And he acknowledged the same inspiration yet again in debating the fate of his committee's recommendations. "Everything is in this principle—so elevated, so liberal, so fertile—that my father and his illustrious friend, M. Quesnay, consecrated thirty years ago, and M. Sieyès has perhaps demonstrated better than any other" he admitted; "and all the rights, all the duties of man derive from it."[92]

In this case, though, the physiocratic vision was rapidly conflated with the Rousseauian ideal of collective freedom achieved by the ex-

ercise of a common political will. For the articles that followed in the
declaration of rights drafted by Mirabeau's committee were strikingly Rousseauian. Having declared that all men are born free and
equal, the draft offered a definition of political association that came
directly from the *Contrat social*: "Every political body receives its
existence from a social contract, express or tacit, by which each individual places his person and his faculties in common under the
supreme direction of the general will, and the body simultaneously
receives each individual as a part." This formulation was followed, in
turn, by an article defining a constitution as the explicit expression of
the will of the nation, subject to change by that will at any moment.
"Since all the powers to which a nation submits itself emanate from
the nation, no body, no individual can have authority that does not
derive expressly from it. Every political association has the inalienable right to establish, to modify or to change the constitution, that is
to say, the form of its government, the distribution and the limits of
the different powers composing it." And, in due course, there appeared the Rousseauian insistence that "the law, being the expression of the general will, must be general in its object, tending always
to assure all citizens of their liberty, property and civil equality."[93]

A draft of this kind, presented with such ambivalence, did little to
lay the basis for consensus among the deputies. In fact, it invited a virtual reprise of the arguments of 1–4 August. The ensuing debate left
the Assembly, on 18 August, in a state of utter indecision. In the absence of support for Mirabeau's draft, it was simply thrown back to
where it had been a week earlier—which is to say, faced with dozens
of competing drafts for a declaration of the rights of man. Its only hope
now seemed to be to choose one of these drafts and discuss it article by
article. But even as the deputies began to vote on this procedure,
Mirabeau suddenly adopted a new tack. Abruptly, he proposed reiterating the decision to make a declaration of rights an integral and inseparable first chapter of the constitution, but postponing the composition of this declaration until other parts of the constitution had been
determined.[94] This meant, in effect, that the Assembly would simply
confess its inability to agree on any draft, quietly retreating from its
earlier decision to begin its constitutional work with a declaration
of rights. Applauded by some, Mirabeau's maneuver was bitterly attacked by others as the arrogance of an orator cynically convinced of
his ability to manipulate the Assembly's decisions. In response, the

report of the Committee of Five was simply referred to the *bureaux*. A day later, it was formally rejected as a basis for further discussion.

At an impasse, the deputies reverted to earlier disagreements over the procedural advantages of continuing the search for a text in a general assembly or referring it again to the *bureaux*. This time, it was Lally-Tollendal's turn to insist that they either decide upon the language of a declaration or abandon the attempt. The Assembly's inability to arrive at a draft seemed in his judgment simply to underline the dangers of such a project. "If the twelve hundred of us have such difficulty in agreeing upon the manner of understanding this declaration," he demanded, "can we believe that it will fix the reasoning of twenty-four million in a uniform manner?" In this view, the assembly should immediately adopt a short, clear declaration, hastening to draw true practical consequences from its principles before others drew false ones. If this was impossible, it should save its time and proceed directly to a constitution—as Mirabeau had suggested. "The people is waiting, wanting, suffering" Lally-Tollendal reminded the deputies; "it is not for its happiness that we leave it any longer prey to the torments of fear, the scourge of anarchy, the very passions devouring it, which it will one day blame on those who have inflamed them. Better that it recover earlier its liberty and tranquillity; let it sooner receive the effects and later know the causes."[95]

Faced with this call either to act or to abandon the entire effort of a declaration, a majority of the deputies decided, finally, to cut the Gordian knot. Agreeing to an immediate choice of a text that would serve as a basis for detailed discussion, the Assembly opted for one of the more laconic draft declarations earlier presented to it, that proposed by its Sixth Bureau.[96] With sudden energy flowing from desperation to complete a task that had proved so unexpectedly problematic, the deputies now began discussing and revising this minimal text clause by clause. Within a week, little of the original wording of its articles was left; much had been sacrificed to language taken from other drafts or hammered out in discussion on the Assembly floor. Few members of the Assembly would probably have wished to claim for the resulting document more than that "relative perfection" Démeunier urged them again to accept.[97] But the representatives of the French nation had nevertheless arrived by 27 August, after so much hesitation and difficulty, at a Declaration of the Rights of Man and of the Citizen.

As passionate as they were profound, the Assembly's discussions of particular articles of the Declaration will be considered as necessary in the following chapters. But it is worth remarking here that the preamble to the draft declaration first proposed so unenthusiastically by the Committee of Five, and then rejected so easily by the National Assembly, suddenly became the basis for the definitive text. Several possible preambles were proposed on 20 August. There was even a call for the Declaration to be preceded by the Decalogue (just as Duquesnoy had suggested earlier that it be preceded by the text of the *Social Contract*).[98] Many deputies expressed the importance of invoking the name of the Supreme Being, which was indeed added to the eventual text. But it was the preamble of the Committee of Five and its Genevan ghostwriters—adroitly presented by Démeunier with minor modifications suggested by the tenor of the preceding debate[99]—that suddenly regained favor during a discussion in which, even "at the last minute, one was far from foreseeing the solution."[100] Of all the passages proposed to the National Assembly in the various versions of a declaration of rights submitted to it, this luminous preamble—with its promise of political transparency—found its way into the final document in a form most remarkably close to its initial formulation.

Even so, the text the Assembly had hammered out by 27 August was not yet definitive; nor was it formally adopted as complete. Instead, discussion of further articles was simply suspended on that date, their consideration now being postponed until "after the constitution."[101] The deputies had arrived at a provisional text adequate for the moment to satisfy the philosophical imperative of a prior declaration; they could no longer defer the practical imperative of fixing the French constitution in the light of its principles. "The order of the day had been to deal with articles to be added to the declaration of rights," reported the *Point du jour;* "but the order of needs was to work on the constitution."[102] Long before that constitution was completed, however, the Declaration of the Rights of Man and of the Citizen had taken on a separate and definitive life of its own.

< VI >

A Problematic Choice

Though it has often been seen as at once the most striking proof and almost inevitable product of a notorious French rationalism, the text of the Declaration of the Rights of Man and of the Citizen—indeed its very appearance—was far from being a foregone conclusion in 1789. To the contrary, the story of its composition is one of profound uncertainty and conflict over the meaning and essential purpose of any declaration of rights; over its necessity or desirability; over its benefits or potential dangers; over the form it should take; over the procedures by which it might be composed; over the precise relationship it would bear to the constitution the National Assembly had committed itself to "fix"; over the relative place within it of rights and duties; over the claims of eternal, universal principles as opposed to particular considerations of time and place. Several times, the project of a declaration of rights seemed destined simply to founder in the face of these difficulties and uncertainties. Remarkably, it survived to be realized in a text composed by an assembly of twelve hundred persons in a final week of passionate public debate.

It is scarcely surprising, then, that the resulting document bore the marks of its difficult birth. Though it rapidly assumed a virtually sacred status, it was left by its authors as a text still provisional and incomplete. Though it appealed to eternal principles, it was shaped by acute conflicts over the exigencies of the political moment. Though it held out the ideal of political transparency, it emerged as a work of textual compromise and conceptual ambiguity. In adopting the language of the Declaration of the Rights of Man and of the Citizen, the deputies had not decisively resolved many of the issues dividing them so much as they had arrived at a series of linguistic compromises upon the basis of which they could now turn to debate the constitution. Many of the provisions of the Declaration remained profoundly ambiguous—their meaning left to be determined in subsequent arguments over the constitutional provisions that would give them effect.

The Declaration nevertheless answered enough of the needs of the particular moment, and satisfied enough of the competing political strategies formulated in response to it, to gain the acceptance of a body that had been so profoundly divided over its production. First and foremost, it gave the National Assembly a statement of universal, eternal, natural principles to legitimate its defiance of an absolute monarch.[103] General truths were held out against the despotism of arbitrary, particular will. Truths valid for all times and places were invoked to end the injustices and vicissitudes of a political order now implicitly emptied of the authority of historical prescription and reduced to a regime of power constantly destabilized by the play of vicious interests. The imprescriptible rights of individuals, the inalienable sovereignty of the nation, the natural order of society: these conceptions justified the deputies in their resistance against a monarchical power hitherto constituted as the sole point of unity within a particularistic regime of orders and Estates, the political vehicle by which the transcendent claims of the divine became the norms of earthly existence.

But this revolution carried out in the name of national sovereignty was not, strictly speaking, a revolution of the nation. More precisely, it was a revolution of deputies acting in the name of the nation. Moreover, it was a revolution of deputies who had initially received powers very different from those they soon found themselves exercising—and from a nation defined very differently from the one they were summoning into existence. Recurring debate over the nature of the "mandates" the deputies had received from their constituents constantly revealed the aporia between representation and national sovereignty in the revolutionary situation. The deputies had to legitimate representation even as they broke with the forms that had constituted them as representatives. They had to justify what Sieyès had so frankly called their "usurpation," a usurpation not only in relation to the monarch but in relation to the nation itself. The principles of publicity, immediacy, and transparency set forth in the preamble to the Declaration of the Rights of Man and of the Citizen offered an essential solution to this problem. This declaration that would be *constantly present* to all members of society promised the closing of the gap between the people and its representatives. It promised a world of instantaneous communication in which the deputies would be directly and immediately linked to the nation they served: a world in which the people could therefore assure itself, *at each moment*, that it was at one with its representatives. The physiocratic circuit of knowledge now closed the gap in the Rousseauian circuit of power.

Enough deputies were therefore convinced of the necessity of a statement of universal, eternal principles—and of a promise of political transparency—to make these indispensable features of the Declaration of the Rights of Man and of the Citizen. But many were also fearful of the dangerous implications that might be drawn from abstract principles in a situation of widespread unrest. They feared that disorder would arise from popular insurrection justified by appeal to the primitive rights of man, that anarchy would result from the dissolution of social bonds in the name of individualistic principles of liberty and equality. They were offered some recognition of these concerns in the preamble's promise that the Declaration would ceaselessly remind all members of the social body of their duties as well as their rights, while constantly ensuring respect for the acts of the legislative and executive bodies. But they sought their principal safeguards against anarchy and disorder in language more immediately controlling the implications of the successive rights the Declaration announced. They wanted rights contained by the positive provisions of the law.

This concern for social order became one of the principal motivations behind the markedly "legicentric" provisions of many articles of the Declaration of the Rights of Man and of the Citizen.[104] Time and again, the more conservative or moderate members of the Assembly insisted on the need to qualify the general statement of a right by immediate reference to the constraints of the law and the needs of civil society. "Each step it takes in the exposition of the rights of man," the *Courier de Provence* observed of the Assembly's final debates over the declaration, "it appears struck by the abuse that the citizen may make of them—abuse that prudence will often even exaggerate. Hence these multiple restrictions, these minute precautions, these conditions laboriously applied to all the articles to follow: restrictions, precautions, conditions which almost everywhere substitute duties for rights, hindrances for liberty, and which, encroaching in more than one respect on the most taxing details of legislation, will present man bound by the civil state and not the free man of nature."[105]

But a convergence was possible here between fear of social disorder and fear of despotism. Fear of social disorder required that the subversive potential implications of rights be limited by the law. Fear of despotism required that rights remain free from abridgment by any arbitrary personal power, which is to say that their exercise be limited *only* by the law. With this *"only,"* the law could be established as the solid reality exorcising the competing specters of disorder and despotism. Liberty could be defined as "being able to do anything that does not injure another," with the limits necessary to fulfill this latter condition safely left to be "determined *only* by law" (Article 4). The law, but only the law, could fix the point at which religious opinion troubled the public order (Article 10); the law, but only the law, could determine the cases in which speech or action constituted an abuse of the right to freedom of expression (Article 11). By way of this *only*, the discourse of justice found its place in the text of the Declaration.

Nevertheless, it did so in a curiously alloyed form. For the law the Declaration invoked was henceforth to be understood as "the expression of the general will" (Article 6), that impersonal collective power emanating from all and applying to all. Understood in this way, the law would have the right "to forbid *only* actions harmful to society" (Article 5), and to "lay down *only* those penalties that are strictly and evidently necessary" (Article 8). But the judgment as to which forbidden actions were or were not harmful to society—and which penalties were or were not necessary for their punishment—could not be left to individuals, even though these latter were held to be endowed with an inalienable right of "resistance to oppression" (Article 2). Since the law was the expression of the general will, it followed that "every citizen summoned or seized by virtue of the law must obey at once; he makes himself guilty by resistance" (Article 7). It followed, in short, that *only* the law could decide the limits of the law. But this meant, in effect, that the law—even if *only* the law —could indeed fix the meanings and limit the exercise of the rights of man and of the citizen. It meant that political will—even if only the general will—could ultimately limit the exercise of rights. It meant legislative sovereignty, the sovereignty of the Rousseauian discourse of will.

By such linguistic compromises and conceptual transpositions, the divided deputies finally reached a measure of agreement on a text for a Declaration of the Rights of Man and of the Citizen. But they did so at the cost of accepting a document that blended competing discourses into a volatile compound, a document producing profound ambiguities that would henceforth drive the revolutionary dynamic. The deputies agreed in adopting Article 16 of the Declaration, for example, that "a society in which the guarantee of rights is not secured, or the separation of powers not clearly established, has no constitution." But in the context of the political languages of 1789, the phrase "separation of powers" was susceptible of two quite different interpretations. Within the discourse of justice, it could be understood as applying to a system of checks and balances on the Anglo-American model favored by Mounier and the

Monarchiens. Within the discourse of will, however, it could be construed according to the Rousseauian distinction between legislative and executive power, the former constituting the formal expression of the general will by the sovereign body of the people, the latter its application to particular persons and cases by the act of government. This distinction entailed a clear separation of powers, but proscribed any system of checks and balances; it operated simply to make the executive clearly subordinate to the general will. The language of Article 16 therefore glossed over the differences between two fundamentally antithetical conceptions of a division of powers. It was as compatible with an English model of government as it was with the Rousseauian notion of the general will.

Much, then, depended on the constitutional application of the language of Article 6 to the effect that "the law is the expression of the general will." Was it to be construed as implying the strong Rousseauian notion of a direct and immediate sovereignty that could ultimately have no limits outside itself, no restrictions other than those inherent in its very generality? Or might it imply some less demanding conception of sovereignty? Once again the Declaration was ambiguous. For, having declared the law to be the general will, Article 6 went on to say that all citizens have the right to participate personally or through their representatives in its formation. How, then, was this article to be understood if it admitted the possibility of representation so emphatically denied by Rousseau on the grounds that it was fundamentally incompatible with the notion of the general will? Little clarification could be found in Article 3 of the Declaration proclaiming that "the source of all sovereignty resides essentially in the nation. No body, no individual can exercise authority that does not explicitly proceed from it." To assert that the nation was the ultimate *source* of all sovereignty was not necessarily to say that the nation must exercise that sovereignty directly and immediately. Indeed, it was the specific virtue of this formulation that it glossed over the considerable difference between a strong Rousseauian version of the principle of national sovereignty (embraced by its more radical members) and the weaker one espoused by the moderates led by Mounier.

The choice between these competing definitions of sovereignty lay at the heart of the arguments that immediately occurred when the deputies finally turned, at the end of August, to debate the issue of the constitution. In the course of these debates, the assembly opted for a Rousseauian gloss on the notion of the separation of powers enunciated in Article 16 of the Declaration. It abandoned and repudiated the idea of checks and balances, favoring instead the idea of a binary separation between the legislative power—exercised by a unitary representative assembly, understood as expressing the general will—and an executive power responsible for applying that will to particular cases. This is to say that the Assembly opted, in effect, for a Rousseauian interpretation of the idea of the general will enunciated in Article 6, as of the principle of national sovereignty proclaimed in Article 3. It thus fell back upon a conception of political right that ultimately found individuals protected by the inherent generality of the general will itself rather than by any external, institutional limitations upon it.

But it was a condition of the generality of the general will, in Rousseau's conception, that it be neither alienated nor represented. How then could the deputies avoid profound contradiction when they found themselves compelled to combine the theory of the general will with the practice of representation unavoidable in a large state? Nothing was to prove more problematic for the revolutionaries —or more volatile in its implications—than this notion of representing the general will, which opened up the constant risk that the will represented might be the particular will of the representative body rather than the general will of the nation. The suspensive royal veto adopted by the National Assembly in September 1789 was seen as a mechanism to close this gap between sovereignty and representation by offering a procedure through which legislative decisions could be appealed to the general will.[106]

In the event, it served to widen that gap and to exacerbate the tension between sovereignty and representation. Against the will of the deputies, the royal veto was swept away on 10 August 1792 (and, with it, the very constitution of which it formed part) by a new revolution justified and carried out in the name of popular sovereignty. With that revolution, the dynamic established by the attempt to combine sovereignty and representation became clear. The problematic relation between the people's two bodies—the insoluble problem of making the will of its representative body consubstantial with the will of its sovereign collective body (or those outside the National Assembly who claimed to express that will)—became the critical center of revolutionary politics. The Terror took form as the "people" and its representatives sought, in turn, to purge and purify one another to secure their unity and mutual identity.

The Terror took form, too, as the revolutionaries continued the struggle to realize, *at each moment,* that impossible transparence of will and understanding between the nation and its representatives that had been promised by the preamble of the Declaration of the Rights of Man and of the Citizen in 1789. The principles of that document had been enunciated in the name of universal reason and a common humanity. But its ambiguities served to inaugurate a radical dynamic that subverted representation in the name of the general will, constitutionalism in the name of political transparence, the rights of individuals in the name of the right of the nation.

PART II
Text

National Sovereignty and the General Will

The Political Program of the Declaration of Rights

J. K. WRIGHT

No ARTICLES OF THE Declaration of Rights have left a more enduring stamp on public memory than 3, 6, and 16. These are the specifically constitutional provisions, whose fundamental principles —national sovereignty, law as the expression of the "general will," and the separation of powers—might well be termed the basic *political program* of the Revolution of 1789. Yet for all of its familiarity, the precise character of this program is far from clear. Indeed, opinion has long tended to divide into two opposed camps: those who view "national sovereignty" and the "general will" as fundamentally *liberal* principles, fully congruent with the Lockean outlook of the Anglo-American political tradition; and those who trace these notions to specifically Gallic sources—ranging from the political weight of absolutist conceptions of sovereignty, to the philosophical mortmain of Cartesian subjectivism, or the ideological spell of Rousseau's cult of "ancient liberty"—which are anything *but* liberal. And political motivations aside, there are in fact good reasons for such a wide divergence of opinion. For as we shall see, Articles 3, 6, and 16 straddled the fundamental line of fracture that had already appeared within the leadership of the Revolution by August 1789: the third came from the right wing of the National Assembly, the sixth from the left, while the sixteenth was given wording vague enough to satisfy both camps. At best, the political program of the Declaration of Rights was the product of a very precarious compromise, which was not destined to survive the work of drafting a constitution that followed in September.

The goal of this chapter is to attempt an explanation of the compromise that produced the political program of Articles 3, 6, and 16. Naturally this must take us well beyond the immediate political conjuncture of July and August 1789. When did the concepts of "national sovereignty," the "general will," and the "separation of powers" first gain their place on the political agenda in France? What was the range of meanings which contemporaries assigned to these ideas? How should we assess the contribution of figures such as Locke, Montesquieu, and Rousseau? What is the explanation for the apparent consensus that the Declaration should be one of "citizens" as well as "men"? We will address these questions in the first instance by looking at the emergence of the ideas of "national sovereignty," the "general will," and the "separation of powers" in the thought-world of the Old Regime. For obvious reasons, our survey of the *origines lointaines* of these ideas can only be cursory and schematic. But even a brief glance at their remoter sources should shed some light on the specific moment of their synthesis in the Declaration of Rights. From there we will turn to a closer look at the process of drafting itself and, in conclusion, consider the meaning of the political program of the Declaration of Rights for the larger history of modern conceptions of freedom.

≺ I ≻

Absolutism and National Sovereignty

Let us begin with what is essentially the background to Article 3. It is here of course that the question of an ideological *longue durée* in France poses itself most insistently. For if the specific terminology of "national sovereignty" had no general currency in French political thought before the second half of the eighteenth century, it is evident that the *concept* had an extremely long prior history, which can be traced along two distinct axes. Firstly, there is a long tradition that sees "sovereignty" itself as in some sense the central concern of the entire French political tradition, from the High Middle Ages onwards —a preoccupation that doubtless owed something to the secular difficulties of state-construction in France, in a polity whose geographic spread and demographic density outstripped those of its rivals at every stage in its development, from early feudal to late absolutist monarchy. Sovereignty posed itself as a *problem* in France, on this account, in a way that it never did in the far more unitary monarchy of medieval England.

The evolution of specifically absolutist conceptions of sovereignty is, in any case, a familiar story. The "new monarchy" of the Renaissance inspired celebrations of the energy and grandeur of royal authority from an early date, as can be seen in Claude de Seyssel's sparkling *La monarchie de France* of 1515. Yet Seyssel, still close to the traditions of medieval constitutionalism, specifically denied that the French monarchy was "absolute," and instead described a complicated schedule of "bridles" on the will of the king.[1] It was the ordeal of the religious wars which prompted the decisive rupture with this world. For it led Jean Bodin to produce the specific concept of "legislative sovereignty" (the "absolute" and "perpetual" power to impose "laws unto the subjects in general, without their consent") as the antidote to social anarchy—an innovation which marked a major turning-point in the history of European political thought. Bodin's theory provided the durable basis for the legitimation of absolute monarchy in France. All that remained for later apologists was to elaborate the cult of royal authority it implied—a process which of course reached its climax in the reign of Louis XIV, when Jacques-Bénigne Bossuet's *La politique tirée des propres paroles de l'Ecriture Sainte* famously suggested a concentration of sovereign power to the point of a near-total identification of the state with the physical body of the monarch.

The embrace of the term "absolute" by Bodin or Bossuet should not deceive, however. For the former's conception of legislative sovereignty had its paradoxical limits. The *legitimacy* of "royal" monarchy as Bodin interpreted it, as opposed to extra-European "despotism" or sheer "tyranny," derived precisely from the fact that European kings were subject both to "divine" and "natural" laws, as well as to certain "fundamental" or constitutional laws; above all, Bodin denied that it was permissible for any earthly power to levy taxes without consent. Writing a century later, after the full maturation of Bourbon absolutism, Bossuet was naturally unwilling to invoke "natural" and "fundamental" laws with quite the same vigor. Yet it is also clear that he had no other means at his disposal for establishing the legitimacy of absolute monarchy. Indeed, if Bossuet's curious attempt to provide a scriptural foundation for absolutism represented an effort to free the monarchy from the constitutional encumbrances featured in the theories of Seyssel and Bodin, it also reflected his inability to embrace the fully contractual theories developed by

Anglo-Dutch contemporaries such as Grotius or Hobbes.[2] The distinction between "royal" monarchy and arbitrary rule remained the centerpiece of absolutist legitimation in France: the Bourbon monarchy was destined to be haunted by Bodin's "natural" and "fundamental" laws down to its dying day.

At the same time, the ideological legacy of absolutism should not be reduced to its conceptions of sovereignty alone. For the second axis along which the pre-history of "national sovereignty" can be traced is that of the *nation* itself. This is a subject whose theoretical problems have generated a series of major statements in the past decade.[3] Of these, perhaps the most useful for our purposes is Anthony Smith's *The Ethnic Origins of Nations*. Without discounting fundamental economic determinations, Smith lays special stress on the symbolic aspects of nation-building, suggesting a process whereby pre-modern ethnic identities, either aristocratic or demotic in character, were slowly fused with civic elements to produce the specifically modern national communities, each equipped with historical mythologies of genealogical continuity (legends of "heroic memory") and territorial fixity (landscapes of "poetic space"). As for France, Smith makes it clear, in a number of acute comments, how long a history this process had there, placing it at the forefront of European development as a whole; above all, he stresses how closely it was related from the start to the *monarchy*, as if the ideological prestige and continuity of the latter provided the necessary husk inside which the proto-national community could develop.[4]

The strength of what Smith terms the "dynastic *mythomoteur*" is massively confirmed, in any case, in Collete Beaune's recent *Naissance de la nation France*, whose focus is the late-medieval period.[5] But again, what was surely decisive in bringing the process of creating the "imagined community" of the French nation to its completion was absolutism itself—particularly in light of the exceptional expanse, stability, and durability of the French variant. It can hardly be an accident that the arrival of the modern usage of the terminology in France—assumption of a basic equation between a single territorial state and a single national community—apparently coincided with the maturity of Bourbon Absolutism, in the later seventeenth century.[6]

As it happens, *La politique tirée des propres paroles de l'Ecriture Sainte* provides a particularly telling example. Having insisted that "to form nations and unite the people, it is necessary to have a government," Bossuet described the authority of the king in these terms: "Thus the sovereign magistrate has in his hands all the strength of the nation, which submits to, and obeys him . . . The people gain by this; for they recover in the person of the supreme magistrate more strength than they yielded him for his authority, since they recover in him all the strength of the nation reunited to assist them."[7] Here, it might be said, the shadow of "national sovereignty" had already fallen across French absolutism, even at the peak of its fortunes.

All of this suggests, then, something of the baroque complexity of the ideological legacy of absolutism, as the seventeenth century passed into the eighteenth. On the one hand, apologists for the Bourbon monarchy had developed an unprecedented cult of "absolute" and "indivisible" royal legislative sovereignty—albeit subject to the uncertain limits of "natural" and "fundamental" laws—in an epoch in which other Western absolutisms fell to decay or revolution. On the other, the monarchy had also permitted, or even promoted, the emergence of a precocious proto-national cultural community, far in advance of much of the rest of Europe—as if in compensation for the strength of the local tradition of absolute political sovereignty.

What remains to be explained is how the divorce of king and "nation" was effected, after so many centuries of intimate co-development—how, in other words, the last great absolute monarchy of the West became the victim of the first revolution of *national* liberation in the modern world. There is no great mystery about the start of this process. It can be dated roughly to the last decade of the reign of Louis XIV, when the limits of Bourbon absolutism as a state-form, both in terms of internal institutional development and external martial success, had been reached; and when France began to be overtaken by what Paul Hazard classically termed the "crisis of the European mind," as the vanguard intellectual culture of Amsterdam and London began to make its way into the heartland of continental absolutism.[8] The general result of these shifts was a slow process of "desacralization" of the monarchy, and the triumph of the modern school of natural rights theory in France by mid-century.[9] But what is most important for our purposes is that these changes were the signal for the resumption of *historical* debate on a grand scale, of the kind that had been suspended or driven underground during the reign of Louis XIV. For the specific arena in which we can trace the emergence

of the notion of "national sovereignty" was the long historical dispute over the "ancient constitution" and the "fundamental laws" of
the monarchy that began around the turn of the century and was
ended only by the Revolution itself.

What was the shape of this debate? We can get a sense of its basic
periodization and dynamic by referring to the explanatory framework
established by Denis Richet in a classic essay.[10] The long-term intellectual origins of the Revolution, Richet argued, should be sought in
sentiments of communal solidarity generated within sections of the
ruling classes, the nobility in the first instance, in reaction against absolutism. The decisive juncture was precisely the end of the reign of
Louis XIV, when a consciousness of autonomy from the monarchy
took the specific form of historical representations of an "ideal elite"
which had enjoyed political self-determination in a remote past. The
first half of the eighteenth century thus saw the major statements of
the *thèse nobiliaire*, as it came to be called, which elicited counter-
statements of a *thèse royale* from royal apologists. Around 1750,
however, a second phase in this process opened up, in the wake of
bitter collisions between monarchy and nobility over fiscal and religious issues: the real drama of the second half of the century concerned the way in which the "ideal elite" was gradually enlarged,
principally through the pressure of natural-law egalitarianism, to include an ever-wider social composition—the ideological expression
of an emergent aristocratic-bourgeois coalition, united in opposition
to absolutism. This progress was resisted, belatedly, only by a fraction
of the nobility itself, whose actions in the crisis of 1787–88 effectively shifted this evolution into a third phase, that of the Revolution
proper.

Now Richet's story is essentially one of the advance of *liberalism*: what held this evolving "ideal elite" together through the process of its recomposition was the "negative" unity resulting from opposition to "despotism"—a term whose renewed fortunes dated precisely from the late seventeenth century, though the idea reached its
definitive expression in Montesquieu's theorization. But it is easy to
see how this framework can be adapted for our purposes. For the positive banner behind which all the opponents of "despotism" could
rally proved, of course, to be that of the "nation." Our story, very
schematically, then becomes one of successive versions of "national
sovereignty," each in a sense wider than the last.

The earliest of these we can expect to find in the period of aristocratic resurgence that started in the last years of Louis XIV and
reached its peak during the Regency, before subsiding under the
regime of Fleury. The key figure here was the enigmatic Henri comte
de Boulainvilliers, whose statement of the *thèse nobiliaire* in a number of widely diffused writings gives us our inaugural version of "national sovereignty."[11] The centerpiece of Boulainvilliers's historiography was of course the scandalous doctrine of the *conquest*: the
founding moment of French history was the capture of Gaul, and en-
serfment of its native population, by the Frankish warriors from
whom the present-day nobility descended. The "feudal government"
they founded was essentially a republican one, in which an egalitarian citizen assembly possessed full sovereign authority, electing
non-hereditary executive magistrates. But the widespread appeal of
this rendering of early French history was inseparable from the precise vocabulary of Boulainvilliers's presentation, whose key term
was in fact that of the *nation*. From their first appearance, the Franks
are described not as the conventional "*nation des Francs*," but as the
"*nation française*"; their sovereign meetings on the Champ de Mars
become the "national assemblies"; and in the history of the unraveling of the "feudal government," it is the "French nation" which is
presented as the central victim, gradually stripped of its "legitimate
rights." No doubt Boulainvilliers's own understanding of the "nation" was narrowly "ethnic-genealogical," in Anthony Smith's sense
of the term. Yet the rhetorical effect of his writing was clearly to invite *all* readers, noble or otherwise, to identify themselves with the
great collective victim—all the more so, since even if the original
"nation" was a narrow oligarchy, the *internal* relations among its
"citizens" were ones of freedom and equality: "At the start, the
French [*les français*] were all free and perfectly equal and independent."[12] For all the brutality of his notion of the "conquest" and his
lingering nostalgia for the "feudal government," the real horizon of
Boulainvilliers's thought was always political, not social: what mattered in the present was not so much the social composition of the
current "French nation," but rather the simple fact of its long captiv-
ity at the hands of "despotism."

If this was our original depiction of an "ideal elite," in Richet's
sense of the term, how was its "enlargement" brought about? A glance
at the royalist writers who responded to Boulainvilliers suggests that

they had their own contribution to make to the process. The most important of these was Jean-Baptiste Dubos, whose chief purpose, in his *Histoire critique de l'établissement de la monarchie française dans les Gaules,* was to demolish the idea of any founding "conquest": the Merovingian kings were simply the legitimate heirs of Roman imperial authority in Gaul; the government of Clovis was no less an absolute monarchy than that of Louis XIV. At the same time, Dubos specifically denied that there was any such thing as a "French nation" at the outset; there was merely a "French monarchy" which comprised a multitude of quite distinct "nations," Frankish, Gallic, and otherwise. There was of course a central problem for any attempt to establish the existence of an absolutist "ancient constitution": how should one account for the medieval period, which could hardly help but figure as a massive interruption in the exercise of absolute sovereignty? Following the lead of earlier royalist historians, Dubos argued that after a stable succession to Roman power, the monarchy gradually—not punctually—fell victim to a rapacious and brutal "aristocracy," which dispersed sovereign political authority among itself, reduced the majority of the population to a state of servitude, and instigated the decline into the anarchy and brigandage of the "feudal" period. The slow resumption of absolute authority by the kings of France—together with the freeing of the towns and the enfranchisement of the serfs—was, for Dubos, merely the restoration of the original and only legitimate constitution of the realm. But it was more than that. For it was only at this point, Dubos argued, that the variety of distinct "nations" which had hitherto made up the "People of the French Monarchy" were at last merged into "one and the same Nation, the French Nation."[13] What this amounted to, of course, was a historicization of Bossuet's claim that nations only came into existence when they were formed by a sovereign government; as such, it had already become a prominent theme in late-seventeenth-century royalist historiography. But it is easy to see the direction in which this was heading, under the pressure of eighteenth-century polemics. For Dubos's conception of the "nation" already contained, in embryo at least, the fundamental opposition between "aristocracy" and "nation"—identification of the latter with the Third Estate—that would loom so large in the revolutionary conception of national sovereignty.

Having admitted the act of creation, the great problem for royal apologists, of course, was that of keeping the "nation" from turning, or being turned, against its creator. Everything suggests that this battle was definitively lost shortly after mid-century. For the great turning-point in these debates was the start of the acrimonious collisions between court and parlements, which stretched intermittently from the crisis over the refusal of sacraments to Jansenists in the early 1750s down to the Maupeou coup of 1771 and beyond. The ideological result of the new disequilibrium of monarchy and magistrature was to unleash a fierce battle for control over the definition of the French "constitution," leading to an unprecedented and ultimately fatal polarization of the ruling political culture. In effect, two rival versions of the "ancient" and therefore legitimate constitution faced off, one the projection of a late-medieval Estates-monarchy into the present, the other the retrojection of the image of absolutism into a distant past. The classic expression of the first came in Adrien-Louis Le Paige's *Lettres historiques, sur les fonctions essentielles du parlement* (1753), which supplies us with our second, *parlementary* version of "national sovereignty." Where Boulainvilliers had described an aristocratic "nation" which had *lost* its political independence to "despotism," the Jansenist Le Paige depicted a dehistoricized and abstract "nation" virtually in continuous possession of political sovereignty—except that this was never exercised directly, but was always mediated through a succession of "representative" institutions, of which the parlements themselves were the modern successors. This historical legitimation of parlementary resistance and obstructionism knew an enormous success in the 1750s and 1760s; by 1764, the Parlement of Rennes could declare bluntly to the king: "It is the consent of the nation, which your parlement represents, that completes the law."[14] The royalist response to these provocations, naturally, was to invest massively in the counter-construction of an absolutist "ancient constitution," a process that reached its climax in the career of the royal propagandist Jacob-Nicolas Moreau.[15] For the most part, later royalist historiography merely followed the tracks laid down by Dubos; what was new was the increased emphasis on the monarchy as the protector of the "nation" from the depredations of the "aristocracy"—again, a theme with ominous implications for the future.

The ideological impasse represented by the face-off of "patriotic" and "ministerial" conceptions of the French "constitution"—as Dale Van Kley terms them in chapter 2—persisted more or less down to the prerevolution itself, when the convocation of the Estates General permitted the emergence of the final version of "national sovereignty," now freed from the debris of ancient constitutionalism. In fact, there were numerous premonitions of the eventual outcome well before the crisis of 1787, especially in the period of ideological drift in the wake of the Maupeou coup of 1771. One of the earliest and most interesting examples is provided by the intellectual career of Gabriel Bonnot de Mably, who started as a royalist historian in the manner of Dubos, but then made a surprising about-face at mid-century, embracing a radical republicanism to which he remained faithful thereafter. By the end of the 1750s Mably had sketched what Keith Baker has aptly termed a "script for a French Revolution," clairvoyantly suggesting that parlementary resistance could provide the lever for a convocation of an Estates General, which could then topple absolutism by remaking itself as a "national assembly."[16] In the 1760s and 1770s, Mably then completed his masterpiece, his *Observations sur l'histoire de France*, which set about to destroy the idea that there had ever been a stable and legitimate constitutional order in France; the final volume, written just after 1771, concludes with a relentless attack on parlementary ancient constitutionalism, fueled by outrage over the evident magisterial capitulation to "despotism." But what is most striking is that Mably's version of French history was essentially a *democratic* rewriting of that of Boulainvilliers—the same tragedy of a slow loss of an "ancient liberty."[17] The difference was that, like Dubos, Mably cancelled the "conquest"—or rather updated it two or three centuries—and instead projected an image of the harmonious existence of a democratic "nation" at the outset, which then became the victim first of "feudal" oppression, then of royal "despotism." To revert to Anthony Smith's terms, Mably had transformed the "ethno-genealogical" nationalism of Boulainvilliers into a "civic-territorial" one, producing something very close to the historical outlook of 1789.

This vision or hope was a fragile one. Mably died in 1785, convinced that the prospects for a *"révolution ménagée"* in France had expired in 1771, leaving an Iberian-style decadence as the probable future of the nation. In fact, all that was needed for a generalization of his earlier outlook was the sudden acceleration of events brought on by the impending bankruptcy of the monarchy in 1786. There is no need to recount the final episode of this story in detail, since the course of the prerevolution is discussed elsewhere in this volume. For what Dale Van Kley describes in chapter 2 is in effect the final great contest between the "patriotic" and "ministerial" camps, exemplified by d'Antraigues and Linguet respectively, whose outcome, as the earlier example of Mably would suggest, can be seen as a kind of dialectical synthesis of the two positions. What *is* worth emphasizing, however, is how precarious the emergent "nationalist" synthesis was, for reasons that cast a retrospective light on the process being described here.

In and of itself, "sovereignty" seems to have posed no difficulty. The declaration of "national sovereignty" in 1789 was founded on a widespread consensus as to the nature and definition of sovereign political authority—a consensus that no doubt was the gift of absolutism, in the last analysis. But no such consensus existed in regard to the definition of the "nation." This can be seen very clearly in the writings of the two leading intellectual and political figures to emerge from the tumult of the prerevolution. In their pamphlets of 1788–89, both Mounier and Sieyès championed the transfer of legislative sovereignty to the "nation," and both looked forward to the establishment of a plutocratic representative regime on this foundation. But Mounier's conception of the "nation" was visibly rooted in the "patriotic" vision of the French past, sustained by a nostalgic ancient constitutionalism that continued to see "despotism" as its central adversary.[18] By the writing of *Qu'est-ce-que le Tiers état?*, on the other hand, Sieyès had developed a conception of the "nation" that mingled natural-rights individualism and physiocratic economic ideas, but whose fundamental historical basis lay in the identification of the "nation" with the Third Estate—manifestly a prolongation of the "ministerial" outlook, for which the "aristocracy" remained the primordial enemy.[19]

The battle for the control of French history was not likely to end in 1789, in other words. For the long process of creating the "imagined community" of the French nation—the slow work of transforming the ethno-genealogical nationalism of a figure such as Boulainvilliers into a more properly civic and modern cultural community—had by no means reached its completion. For nearly a century the contest over the definition of the "ancient constitution" had provided an arena in which competing conceptions of the "nation" as an historical entity gradually took shape. The retirement of Bourbon absolutism brought this contest to an end. But it was also the signal for the start of a far more explicit struggle over the definition of the "nation" itself. The latter remained what it had been from the outset, a quintessentially *historical* concept, in the face of which Rabaut Saint-Etienne's famous declaration that "history is not our code" must appear to have been little more than a pious hope.

≺ II ≻

The General Will

If such was something of the long-term background to "national sovereignty," what were the origins, in turn, of the "general will"? We can perhaps be briefer here, given the central role played in its history by a single thinker. In Judith Shklar's words, "The phrase 'general will' is ineluctably the property of one man, Jean-Jacques Rousseau."[20] Nevertheless, a glance at the most comprehensive investigation into the prehistory of the concept, Patrick Riley's *The General Will before Rousseau*, makes it clear that Rousseau came only at the end of a long evolution.[21] The story Riley tells is essentially that of the "secularization" of an idea which ultimately derived from theological discourse. Remote antecedents of the "general will" can be traced as far back as Paul or Augustine, but its modern usage emerged from arcane disputes within seventeenth-century Jansenism, where Arnauld and Pascal used the term to refer to the Divine Will in regard to human salvation. It was Malebranche, however, who gave the notion its classic formulation, fixing it at the center of a systematic theology: God rules over the cosmos, he repeatedly asserted, by means of simple, uniform *"volontés générales,"* as opposed to the fragmented multiplicity of human *"volontés particulières."* As Riley shows, the claim met with violent resistance from Catholic orthodoxy, from Bossuet above all, who correctly saw that the basic thrust of the idea was to *limit* divine authority, by confining it to the sphere of the "general" alone—the expression, of course, of Malebranche's distinctive Christian Cartesianism.

But Bossuet and other critics of the "general will" recoiled from its political implications as well. These were already evident enough in Pascal or Malebranche: both hinted that the king's actions, like God's, should *not* extend to "particulars"—the core value, no doubt,

being the basic egalitarianism secured when laws were unexception-
ably "general" in their application. The explicit transfer of the idea
to the political sphere, in any case, started with Pierre Bayle, who, in
his "Malebranchian" phase, argued that "there is nothing which
gives us a higher idea of a monarch, than to see that he, having wisely
established a law, maintains it in vigor for all and against all."[22] This
led in turn to the definitive "socialization" of the "general will" in
Montesquieu, who deployed the term in his explication of the English constitution in book 11 of *The Spirit of the Laws*, and whose entire theory of social causation was inspired by Mablebranche's conceptualization of the "general" and the "particular." The story then
culminated with the final politicization of the notion in Rousseau,
who completed the transformation of the "divine" into the "civic"
by making the "general will" the centerpiece of a theory of political
legitimacy; Riley provides a detailed inventory of Rousseau's uses of
the general/particular dichotomy, illuminating virtually every aspect of his writing. To his credit, Riley resists the sort of moral that is
typically drawn from "secularization" narratives—exposure of the
hubris or illegitimacy of the process. On the contrary, he concludes
by arguing that the conceptual couplet of the "general" and the "particular" formed a Gallic variant of the more familiar opposition between the "public" and the "private"; as such, it constituted the
defining theme of modern French political thought, permitting it to
occupy a fruitful middle ground between English particularism and
German universalism.[23]

If such was the genealogy of the "general will" prior to Rousseau,
how did the concept actually fit into the architecture of his political
thought as a whole? There is space here only for a few cursory remarks. Rousseau's preeminence and originality within eighteenth-
century thought, it might be said, was owing to his position at the
crossroads of the two major traditions of political thought of his time:
the "modern" theory of natural rights, which had advanced from its
Anglo-Dutch origins in the seventeenth century to become the dominant political idiom of the age by the mid-eighteenth; and the republican tradition whose roots stretched back to Renaissance Italy but
which had known at least a subterranean implantation all across
early-modern Europe. These languages of political thought, embody-
ing appeals to "rights" and to "virtues" respectively, have often been
seen as incompatible or even antagonistic. But as J.G.A. Pocock has

observed, the notion of a profound ideological gulf between them no longer seems accurate once we pass into the eighteenth century, where we find a great flowering of hybrid combinations of the two.[24]

Rousseau's thought represents by far the greatest of these efforts at synthesis. For there is no doubt that the *dominant* political language in it was that of the post-Grotian natural rights tradition.[25] Like Hume, Smith, or Kant, Rousseau belonged to a generation of thinkers who were transforming the classical inheritance of Grotius, Pufendorf, or Locke in a variety of respects: his first important work, the *Discours sur l'inégalité*, was of course a sustained critique of state-of-nature theory. But this should not allow us to lose sight of the fact that Rousseau's major theoretical statement, *The Social Contract*, aims to found political legitimacy, neither on force nor on appeals to transcendent "divine" or "natural" order, but on conventions among individuals, involving transfers of their subjective "rights"—the classic *démarche* of the rights theorist. Moreover, Rousseau's straightforward declarations of the inalienability of certain of these rights make it clear that he was an heir to the specifically liberal or radical wing of the rights tradition, descending from the Levellers and Locke.[26] At the same time, Rousseau brought to his rights theory a set of themes and values that were plainly those of the alternate civic humanist tradition. His famous historicization of natural law theory in the *Discours sur l'inégalité* can be seen, at least in part, as a Machiavellian rewriting of the transition from natural to civil society; while the positive pole of comparison animating his critique was a republican utopia, inspired not merely by nostalgia for his native Geneva, but also by a profound admiration for the city-states of classical antiquity. The legitimate government generated by the *Contrat social*, the alternate social world sketched in the *Economie politique*, the constitutional proposals for Corsica and Poland—all these stand in profound continuity with the entire classical republican tradition.[27]

All the most characteristic elements of Rousseau's political theory resulted from this attempt to deploy the language of the "state of nature" and the "social contract" for what were essentially republican purposes. One famous crux is the tension between his critique of Grotius and commitment to the notion of "inalienable" natural rights, and what might be termed his neo-Hobbesian conception of the legitimate "social pact" itself, which appears to result precisely from an act of total alienation. But Rousseau's most striking innovation, of course, was his redefinition of sovereign political authority as the "expression of the general will"—a move which effected a durable association of the theological language described by Riley and natural rights theory proper. For all of the notorious paradoxes of Rousseau's own presentation, its essential thrust is not in fact difficult to grasp. Following in the tracks of Pascal, Malebranche, and Bayle, Rousseau's chief purpose was to define a specifically *political* sphere of interaction between citizens, in which the dominant value was that of equality. This meant two things in practice. Firstly, the *objects* of sovereign authority so defined were to remain always and everywhere "general"—which amounted to something like a principle of equality before the law. At the same time, sovereign law was to be "general" in regard to its *sources* as well—a principle of popular sovereignty, in other words. The twist in the theory, of course, comes from Rousseau's famous distinction between the "general will" and the mere will of the majority. Besides making it possible for his thought to be pressed into service on behalf of quite different political projects, the distinction has given rise to the persistent misinterpretations of Rousseau as "organicist," "collectivist," or even "proto-totalitarian." But the distinction was necessary only because Rousseau consistently defined the "general will" in terms of the *common interests* of the individual members of society; these, in turn, contrary to every ill-informed legend about what Rousseau actually wrote, could only be determined through free and egalitarian political deliberation by the individuals involved. The "general will" was the name for the optimum *compromise* which emerged from this collective deliberation. As J.G. Merquior put it in his great comparative study of Rousseau and Weber: "The core of Rousseau's theory of political legitimacy is the idea of *participatory democracy*. The general will is always to be activated by constant individual participation in the politics of sovereignty . . . *his was the only social contract theory to equate legitimate law with the will of the people.*"[28]

Naturally, the equation of "sovereignty" with "will" in this fashion was to have its effects on both of the traditions of thought to which Rousseau was a legatee. If it effected a kind of "republicanization" of natural jurisprudence, it also produced a far more *democratic* republicanism than that of any previous European thinker. This points in fact to a specific issue flowing from Rousseau's theory that was to be of particular importance for the Revolutionary epoch. In book 3 of *The Social Contract*, Rousseau launched a famous attack on "representation": "Sovereignty cannot be represented for the same reason it cannot be alienated. It consists essentially in the general will, and the will does not allow of being represented. It is either itself or something else; there is nothing in between."[29] The immediate object of this critique is not in doubt. "Representation," Rousseau insisted, was unknown to classical antiquity, being a "modern" and "feudal" device: what he was rejecting was the claim that institutions such as the English Parliament "represented" the English people, or closer to home, that the Parlement of Paris "represented" the French—these claims just masked what was really a *usurpation* of sovereignty.

But would Rousseau have thereby condemned everything which posterity has chosen to call "representative government"? The sheer variety of institutions and forms falling under this rubric guarantees that no clear answer to the question can be forthcoming from Rousseau's writings. Indeed, as Richard Fralin has shown, Rousseau's own attitude toward "representation" was by no means stable throughout his career, evolving from a "position of passive acceptance in *Economie politique* to overt hostility in the *Contrat social* to qualified opposition in the *Lettres écrites de la montagne* to qualified acceptance in the *Considérations sur le gouvernement de Pologne.*"[30] Everything suggests a fundamental equivocation in Rousseau's mind in regard to high levels of popular participation in government. On the one hand, his rejection of direct democracy, in the classical sense, is clear and consistent throughout his work, even when discussing polities whose size did not rule it out; on the other hand, the "elective aristocracy" he promoted nevertheless was hedged in by recommendations of frequent elections and notions of binding or revocable mandates. In the end, everything turns on the interpretation of the "general will" itself: if the basic thrust of the theory pointed toward direct, participatory democracy, Rousseau's own distinction between the "general will" and the will of the majority virtually guaranteed that, paradoxically, there would be Rousseauist theories of representation, of the kind sponsored by Sieyès—a subject to which we will return below.

Rousseau was not the only theorist of the "general will" in mideighteenth-century France. Besides Montesquieu's glancing reference to "general" and "particular wills" in book 11 of *The Spirit of the Laws,* there was Diderot's remarkable reformulation of natural law in terms of a quasi-historicist conception of the *"volonté générale"* of the human race in his Encyclopedia article on "Natural Right" of 1755.[31] But there is no doubt that it was Rousseau who definitively politicized the concept, and thus prepared it for the widespread currency it was to enjoy in late-eighteenth-century political discourse. To say this, of course, is to confront one of the central problems in the intellectual history of the Old Regime, that of the reception of Rousseau's political thought in his lifetime and in the quarter-century following his death. For there is a long and tenacious tradition—classically established early in this century in the writings of Daniel Mornet—which holds that Rousseau's political texts, as opposed to *Emile* or *Julie,* had little or no impact in France prior to the Revolution.[32] Here it will suffice to point out that this view, which has long since become a commonplace in the manuals of Old Regime history, has itself been exploded by recent scholarship, which is slowly restoring Rousseau to something like his proper place within Enlightenment political thought.[33] Roger Barny, in particular, has carefully documented the extraordinary *variety* of appeals to Rousseau's political thought in this epoch, which ranged along a wide spectrum of bourgeois and aristocratic opinion. Above all, contrary to conventional expectations, he demonstrates the existence of a specifically *aristocratic* Rousseauism, persisting into the Revolution and beyond. Rousseau's message was not infinitely labile, of course. The one political outlook to which it remained fundamentally inimical, not surprisingly, was that of royal absolutism—which is not to say that there were no attempts to confiscate the "general will" for royalist ends, but merely that these are better seen as desperate signs of the growing prestige of the formula in this period than anything else.

Barny also reveals how very quickly the doctrines of *The Social Contract* made their way into the thick of contemporary political controversy, the earliest Rousseauist interventions appearing in the wake of the Maupeou coup of 1771. Of the writers he discusses, perhaps the most interesting for our purposes is the Bordeaux publicist Guillaume-Joseph Saige, whose anti-Maupeou pamphlet *Catéchisme du citoyen* (1775) was based on an explicit appeal to *The Social Contract* and its theory of the "general will."[34] At the same time, as Keith Baker has argued, Barny's description of Saige's outlook as "bourgeois" *tout court* tends to short-circuit the real complexity of his ideological position.[35] For if Saige was an avowed disciple of Rousseau, both the *Catéchisme du citoyen* and his earlier dialogue *Caton, ou Entretien sur la liberté et les vertues politiques*, were also deeply indebted to the more orthodox classical republicanism of which Mably was perhaps the chief French representative. The result of this criss-crossing of traditions, under the polemical pressure of the Maupeou crisis, was to produce a work which expressly conjoined a Rousseauist theory of the "general will" with an appeal to an historically-based conception of "national sovereignty" of the kind we saw in the previous section. In other words, we seem to find language very close to the political program of the Declaration of Rights already being elaborated in the mid-1770s.

≺ III ≻

The Separation of Powers

In fact, the argument of *Catéchisme du citoyen* makes use of the third of our ideas as well. This brings us to one of the central tokens of early-modern political thought—but also one of the most difficult to account for historically, given the astonishing variety of principles and arguments collected under the rubric of the "separation of powers." Still, the main lines of the story here are perhaps clear enough.[36] Analytical distinctions among governmental institutions and agencies had a complicated prehistory in classical antiquity. But the precondition for the *modern* distinction between legislative, executive, and judicial "powers" was plainly the sixteenth-century theory of "legislative sovereignty," as it was canonically formulated by Bodin. For throughout all of its vicissitudes, the core of the idea of a "separation of powers" remained the conceptualization of political agency in terms of *will* and *action, decision* and *execution*—the first identified, of course, with "legislative" power, the second with "executive." As has often been noted, the notion of a "separation of powers" is full of ambiguity, even on its own terms. For if the analytic itself seems to establish a clear hierarchy among two (or three) "powers"—the principle of *legislative supremacy*, that is—the demand for their "separation" and placement in distinct hands can easily point in another direction, toward the dispersal and thus *limitation* of political authority.

A good deal of the complexity of the resulting history of what Vile calls the "pure" doctrine of the "separation of powers" was owing to this double valency—what we might term respectively the "republican" and the "liberal" uses of the idea. But this complexity was made infinitely greater by the fact that the doctrine of the "separation of powers" appeared in "pure" form only intermittently from the early seventeenth to the late eighteenth centuries. Instead, from its earliest usages, it tended to be intimately associated with another notion which itself had a long classical pedigree before becoming a central device of medieval and early-modern political thought—that of the "mixed-government," for which the best form of polity was held to be a mixture of democratic, aristocratic, and monarchical institutions. The political uses of this concept were also highly variable, depending on which of the three components of the mixture, if any, was highlighted. But the typical result of the superimposition of the modern analytic of "powers" onto the classical grid of forms of government was to push the entire package in a proto-liberal direction, whose ultimate result was the late-eighteenth-century emergence of "checks-and-balances" theory proper.

Not surprisingly, the initial arena for the formulation and synthesis of these ideas was not absolutist France, but rather seventeenth-century England, where they emerged in the context of the revolt *against* Stuart absolutism. On the telling of Vile and Gwyn, the distinction between "executive" and "judicial" functions—and calls for their "separation"—may have been the earliest to see the light of day, traceable as far back as Fortescue. But center stage in England was occupied by the more important distinction between "legislative" and "executive" power, which emerged separately in the later sixteenth century. However, it was the sudden opening of horizons by the Civil War which permitted their earliest major statements, together with the first descriptions of England as a "mixed monarchy" in the classical sense. The Interregnum was subsequently a kind of heyday for the "pure" doctrine of the "separation of powers": for Independents, it was a means for promoting the legislative supremacy of Parliament; for Levellers, it served to render such supremacy accountable, by placing the execution of its decisions in separate hands. With the Restoration, however, the "pure" doctrine receded from view, and the "mixed government" became the dominant legitimating device of the epoch. The result was the evolution of the latter into the more nebulous but ultimately quasi-official notion—consecrated by the Glorious Revolution and its aftermath—of the English

monarchy as a "balanced constitution," which deposited sovereign
authority in the hands of a three-headed "king-in-Parliament." The
"separation of powers" survived as a kind of subordinate plank
within the latter, appeals to its "pure" version being most direct in
the case of a succession of marginalized or opposition voices, including Locke and the major figures of the Commonwealth tradition.

This, very approximately, was the complicated legacy inherited
by Montesquieu, who of course performed the services of fixing the
tripartite schema of "legislative," "executive," and "judicial" powers
and bringing the notion of their necessary "separation" to a far higher
level of publicity than it had ever before enjoyed. What was his own
theory of the "separation of powers"? There is hardly a more contentious issue connected with *The Spirit of the Laws*. The following,
however, can be asserted with some confidence. Firstly, the theory of
"monarchy" which dominates the opening sections of *The Spirit of
the Laws* is itself founded on a certain principle of "separation of
powers." This is made explicit at the beginning of book 11, chapter 6,
where Montesquieu introduces a typology of "powers" which is
rather close to that of Locke ("legislative power, executive power
over the things depending on the right of nations, and executive
power over the things depending on civil right"), and then warns that
"liberty" will be destroyed if all three fall into the same hands—examples of this being furnished by the Ottoman Empire and the "republics of Italy." Happily, however, most of the monarchies of Europe are "moderate," owing to the fact that "the prince, who has the
first two powers, leaves the exercise of the third to his subjects"—
there being little doubt, of course, about the identity of these "subjects."[37] However, when Montesquieu turns to the English constitution itself, he in effect reverts to the simpler distinction of "legislative" and "executive" power—declaring that "that of judging is in
some fashion, null"—but at the same time merges it with what is
plainly a version of the "mixed government" (bearing in mind that
the classical nomenclature itself was abandoned in *The Spirit of the
Laws*): legislative power is divided between "popular" and "aristocratic" assemblies, executive power assigned to a hereditary monarch; these "powers" are in turn linked and overlapped in such a way
as to constitute the very prototype of "checks and balances."[38]

Now all of this is of course a far cry from the "pure" doctrine of
the separation of powers, as can be found in the works of the Lev-

ellers or Milton—which is precisely why a long line of commentators have dismissed the idea that Montesquieu made any contribution whatever to the notion of a separation of powers.[39] This judgment, however, seems excessive. The case of Montesquieu instead reminds us of something like a basic axiom of the history of these ideas. For if it was always possible to advance a doctrine of the "separation of powers" without merging it with theories of "mixed" or "balanced" government, or tempering the supremacy of legislative power with "checks" or "balances"—this is roughly the sense of the "pure" or republican version of it in the seventeenth century—it was not possible to do the reverse. *Every* theory of the "mixed" or "balanced" government, or of "checks and balances" proper, Montesquieu's included, depended to a lesser or greater degree on a prior theory of the "separation" of governmental functions—otherwise, it would be impossible to explain the objective role that *The Spirit of the Laws* undoubtedly played in popularizing the notion of a "separation of powers" for its eighteenth-century audience.

At the same time, it is true that Montesquieu's own model enjoyed a far greater prestige and influence in North America than it ever did in France. In brief, it seems that the colonial period in America was in some sense dominated by the theory and practice of the "mixed" and "balanced" government; that the Revolution and Confederacy, in reaction, saw the re-emergence and triumph of the "pure" or republican version of the "separation of powers," ideologically announced in *Common Sense*, and institutionally established in the constitutions of Pennsylvania and Vermont above all; and that the Constitution of 1787 provided a kind of dialectical resolution to this cycle, in its complicated blending of federalism, the "separation of powers," and "checks and balances." In France, on the other hand, as Vile describes it, "the pure doctrine of the separation of powers took hold of men's minds with an intensity, and a durability, not paralleled in America."[40] The explanation for this will no doubt lead us back to absolutism, with its own commitment to notions of legislative supremacy, and the logic of a revolution against it. Nevertheless, we need to inquire into the ideological preconditions for the victory of the "pure" doctrine in France.

Should we attribute a decisive role here to Rousseau? Not surprisingly, his attitude toward the "separation of powers" was one of considerable complexity. He was of course committed to a strong version of legislative supremacy: Rousseau's insistence on the inalienability and the indivisibility of sovereignty was accompanied by a frontal attack on the notions of "mixed" or "balanced" government. On the other hand, his rejection of direct democracy was made precisely on the grounds that it involved an unwise conflation of legislative and executive power, which ought after all to be separated. Rousseau's solution here was a dramatic but logical one: identifying legislative power with the "will" which determines any "free act," and executive with the "force" which brings it about, he redefined *all* "government" as "executive" in nature, as merely enacting the general will of the sovereign community.[41] This might best be seen as a heterodox, if logically consistent, version of the "pure" doctrine, rewritten in terms of the "general will." At the same time, in regard to the organization of powers *within* "government" thus understood, Rousseau could revert to rather more traditional statements of the doctrine of the separation of powers—as in the recommendation on behalf of "elective aristocracy" in book 3, chapter 5 of *The Social Contract* or in the constitutional proposals sketched in the *Considérations* on Poland. Either way, however, he remained an implacable opponent of any conception of the *division* of sovereign power, along the lines of "mixed" or "balanced" government.

But Rousseau, in any case, was by no means the only source for French thinking on these matters after Montesquieu. A glance at the works of Mably, for example, makes it clear that the "pure" doctrine of the separation of powers had no need of being re-routed through Rousseau, but could have been transmitted directly from English Commonwealth sources themselves, which were translated in ever greater numbers, from the 1750s onward—part of the great "republican ferment," as Franco Venturi described it, which overtook France in the second half of the century.[42] For Mably, whose debt to English thought was explicitly acknowledged, sponsored a thoroughly conventional, if not always consistent, version of the doctrine. He both maintained a "Commonwealth" attitude toward the English constitution itself, always taxing the "prerogative" powers of the Hanoverian kings with being in gross violation of legislative supremacy, which could only be assured through its rigorous "separation" from the executive; and retained enough of the "mixed government" to recoil from the radicalism of the American state constitutions, at the very end of his intellectual career.[43] At the same time, Saige's *Catéchisme du citoyen* suggests that it may be pointless to try to draw too sharp a distinction between the positions of Mably and Rousseau in this regard. For Saige's conception of "national sovereignty," which joined the ancient constitutionalism of the "patriotic" outlook to Rousseau's "general will," also contained a "separation of powers" theory. On Saige's account, the "legislative power" possessed by the original Frankish assemblies of the Merovingian and Carolingian epochs was subsequently usurped by the feudal nobility, but then reclaimed by the late-medieval Estates Generals, who in turn conferred "executive power" on both king and parlements, the latter forming a kind of "senate." To convene a new Estates General, in full possession of sovereign legislative authority, would be merely to re-establish the "separation of powers" proper to the French Constitution.

Last but not least in this line of development, there is the figure of Mounier himself, for whom a not dissimilar doctrine of the "separation of powers" was the very centerpiece of his prerevolutionary interventions. The example of Mounier is particularly illuminating, of course, in light of his subsequent revolutionary career as one of the chief sponsors of the Anglophile or *monarchien* constitutional model, with its bicameral legislature and independent executive—so often seen as an application of the doctrine of *The Spirit of the Laws*. Yet like that of his mentor Jean-Louis De Lolme, Mounier's political position was in fact a good deal closer to that of Rousseau, Mably, and Saige than to that of Montesquieu. In the eyes of the latter, the Bourbon monarchy posed no threat to liberty so long as the king, who possessed both "legislative" and "executive" power, left something like "judicial" power in the hands of an independent (venal) *noblesse de robe*. For Mounier, however, this formula was the very recipe for the "despotism" which had afflicted France ever since the late-medieval heyday of the Estates General. What recommended the Estates of 1483 as a model for 1789 (the main burden of his *Nouvelles Observations sur les Etats généraux* of February 1789) was precisely that it suggested a picture of unicameral legislative supremacy *over* the royal executive. The Estates meetings of the following century, conversely, were rejected by Mounier because they already showed signs of the creeping usurpation of legislative authority by the Crown.

Five months later, when Mounier set forth his own prescriptions for "fixing" the French constitution, his starting-point was to insist that "To prevent tyranny, it is absolutely indispensable not to confuse the power to make laws with that of executing them . . . It is an incontestable truth that the union of powers entirely destroys the authority of laws and forms despotism."[44] It may be too much to assert, as Henri Grange once did in an extended comparison of the thought of Mounier and Necker, that the former's doctrine of the "separation of powers" was virtually identical with that of Target or Sieyès, whose ideas in this respect might well be termed Rousseauist.[45] At no phase in his intellectual career can Mounier be said to have owed much to Rousseau. But there is no doubt that in regard to his doctrine of the "separation of powers," Mounier's thought fell squarely within the larger anti-absolutist and roughly "republican" consensus that had been slowly forming in the final decades of the eighteenth century.

≺ IV ≻

Revolutionary Synthesis

Indeed, the various strands of our argument thus far all point to the period between 1771 and 1786 as the decisive juncture for the consolidation of this "republican" consensus. As we have seen, claims that the Bourbon monarchy had usurped the legislative authority that properly belonged to the French "nation" first emerged from the aristocratic reaction to Louis XIV. Seven decades of polemics over the definition of the "constitution" subsequently pushed all sides in the debates toward a declaration, or at least admission, of "national sovereignty," while conceptions of the "nation" itself gradually evolved from the ethno-aristocratic toward the civic-egalitarian. From its origins in Jansenist theology and Cartesian metaphysics, meanwhile, the "general will" had itself become a tool in the intellectual campaign against absolutism, generality being associated with the sphere of political deliberation and decision proscribed by the latter. By mid-century, Rousseau had permanently linked this tradition with the now-dominant language of natural-rights theory, producing a doctrine of popular sovereignty that laid particular emphasis on egalitarian *participation* in the making of legitimate law. The "separation of powers," finally, originated in the currents of radical constitutional thought that flowed in the wake of the English Revolution. Preserved in a variety of opposition traditions, the notion was publicized in France by Montesquieu, and then restored to its purity in both

Rousseauist and more orthodox republican variants. By the 1770s, it had come to stand for an anti-absolutist program whose minimal goals were the restoration of full legislative sovereignty to a renovated representative assembly and concomitant confinement of royal action to mere "executive" power. As it happens, the fifteen years immediately preceding the Revolution are among the least well-mapped in the history of eighteenth-century political thinking—perhaps not surprisingly, given that long-standing structures of thought now came under what proved to be fatal pressures and strains. But everything suggests that it was in this period of the final de-legitimization of the Bourbon monarchy that a significant current of public opinion began to converge on the formulae of "national sovereignty," the "general will," and the "separation of powers" as an alternative program to that of absolutism.

The notion of such a convergence would seem to be confirmed, in any case, if we turn at last to the actual process of proposing and drafting Articles 3, 6, and 16 in the summer of 1789. For what is striking about even the preliminary activity from mid-1788 onwards —that is, calls for the protection of the various "rights" in the *Cahiers de doléance*, and the earliest proposals for a declaration itself— is the evidently high degree of consensus it reveals in regard to our concerns. Taking "sovereignty" first, although it is possible to find gestures in the direction of "popular" sovereignty here and there, some version of *national* sovereignty was overwhelmingly preferred by the writers of these early documents, which reveal a large degree of uniformity of expression. Indeed, Lafayette, in the course of his three successive proposals, arrived at virtually the definitive wording of Article 3 by early July 1789: "The source of all sovereignty resides in the nation. No body, no individual can possess authority that does not derive from it."[46] At the same time, these declarations of "sovereignty" were virtually always intimately associated with calls for a "separation of powers," as though the one necessarily entailed the other. A classic statement can be found in Mirabeau's "Batavian" proposal of April 1788, whose Articles 10 and 11 read respectively: "In order that laws, and not men, govern, it is necessary that the legislative, executive and judicial departments be totally separated"; "The right to suspend laws, prevent their execution, or even to annul them, can only be exercised by the legislative power."[47] Lafayette's first proposal, meanwhile, was very much in the spirit of Mounier's prerevolutionary interventions: "Government divides into three powers, the Legislative, which must be exercised primarily by a large representative assembly, freely and frequently elected; the Executive, which belongs solely to the King, whose person is sacred and to whom the ministers are responsible; and the Judiciary, which must be conferred on a tribunal whose sole function is to maintain the safekeeping of the laws and to apply them literally in the cases submitted to them."[48]

What of the "general will"? While it does *not* appear in Lafayette, the term is in fact extremely widespread in this preliminary material. Although its use varied a good deal, along a spectrum from straightforward republicanism to intransigent royalism, the majority might well be termed Rousseauist, as in an anonymous proposal for a declaration of June 1789: "It is necessary that there be a general will which would direct the totality of forces toward the common interest; it is necessary that each individual in the association submit to this general will."[49] Then there is Sieyès's contribution to the famous pamphlet *Instruction donnée par S. A. S. Monseigneur le duc d'Orléans*, roughly contemporaneous with *Qu'est-ce-que le Tiers état?*, which combines an appeal to the "common will" of the "nation" with Sieyès's distinctive theory of "representation" (to which we will return in a moment): "Legislative power resides essentially in the National will, and it must be exercised by the Body of the Representatives of the Nation ... Individual wills are the essential elements of the common will, and one sees how, given a large population, this common will can only be formed by means of a Body of Representatives."[50] At the other end of the political spectrum, however, it is worth noting the extent to which even Mounier was willing to invoke the language of the "will," if not quite the term "general will" itself. The premier example was his report on behalf of the *Comité préparatoire* of 9 July, in which he called on his fellow patriots to "fix" the constitution: "When the manner of government does not derive from the clearly expressed will of the people, there is no constitution; there is only a *de facto* government, which varies according to the circumstances ... [However] it cannot be said that in France we have been entirely without the fundamental laws necessary for forming a constitution. For fourteen centuries we have had a king: the scepter was not created by force, but by the will of the nation."[51]

These famous lines are a reminder, of course, that even if all the

elements that went into Articles 3, 6, and 16 were already well represented in these early proposals, the Declaration itself was still a long
way off. The election of the first "Committee of the Constitution"
on 14 July naturally marked a major turning point. Much of the
drama here attaches to the evident division in the membership of the
Committee between a moderate-conservative majority, containing
much of the future *Monarchien* leadership, and an equally eminent
minority leaning to the left—Sieyès, Le Chapelier, and Talleyrand.
This drama was heightened by the fact that first Sieyès, then Mounier produced proposals for a declaration which served as landmarks
for the rest of the process of drafting. What do these reveal? As Keith
Baker argues in chapter 4, what is most striking about Sieyès's proposal was his rejection of the whole idea of a simple, preliminary declaration of the kind urged by Lafayette, which he believed could
only amount to a *compromise* between the sovereign nation and a
pre-existing political authority.[52] His sober grasp of the fact that the
Assembly was necessarily acting as a *pouvoir constituant* should
not, however, lead us to exaggerate the radicalism of his outlook. For
Sieyès never questioned the existence of the "nation" itself, which
was evidently as much a historical datum for him as it was for
Mounier: the explicit contractarianism of his "exposition" did not
extend to the creation of the French nation, but was confined to the
establishment of its government.

Moreover, as with Mounier, government in this sense was essentially a matter for the "will of the people"—though Sieyès's contractarianism naturally brought him far closer to the language of Rousseau: "The law being a common instrument, the work of a common
will, it can have no object other than the common interest . . . All
public powers, without distinction, are an emanation of the general
will; all come from the people, that is to say, the Nation."[53] Or was
this the language of Rousseau? For Article 37 of Sieyès's proposed list
of "rights" runs: "The law can only be the expression of the general
will. In the case of a large country, it must be the work of a body of
representatives chosen for a short time, directly or indirectly by all
the citizens who have both the interest and the capacity for public affairs." An innovative theory of "representation" had of course long
since become the central token of Sieyès's political philosophy: did
this not mark an absolute rupture with the thought of Rousseau? As
we suggested earlier, the distance which this theory put between

Sieyès and Rousseau depends a good deal on how rigidly one chooses to interpret the latter's critique of "representation." At the least, however, Sieyès's own language suggests the plausibility of the view, argued by Carré de Malberg among others, that this was not so much an abandonment of Rousseau's theory, as a reworking of it for ends, and in a context, never envisaged by the latter.[54] That the logic of the "general will" could to some extent survive intact, even as it had a theory of "representation" grafted onto it, was in any case to be made clear in the constitutional debates in September, above all in Sieyès's great speech of 7 September.[55]

Whether it was Rousseauist or not, Sieyès's proposal seems to have prompted the majority on the committee to try to seize the initiative in regard to a declaration, even while continuing to insist that it should not be separated from the drafting of the constitution proper. Mounier produced his own draft, of which a modified version was presented to the Assembly in the name of the committee on 27 July. The core of Mounier's proposal was drawn from Lafayette's third and final draft: Article 3, in fact, was simply lifted word-for-word; while Mounier's Article 9 provided a slightly modified version of Lafayette's "separation of powers": "To prevent despotism and assure the empire of the law, legislative, executive and judicial power must be distinct, and must not be reunited."[56] Most interesting of all, however, was Mounier's Article 6, which started from Lafayette, but added a significant clause: "The Laws cannot be established without the consent of the Citizens or of their freely elected representatives, and it is in this sense that the Law must be the expression of the general will."[57] Whether or not this was a direct response to Sieyès, it certainly was a concession to the widespread prestige enjoyed by the "general will"—which at the same time captured rather well its basic participatory thrust. Indeed, it is worth noting how close this formula was to Article 12 of the draft for a declaration produced by the Assembly's Sixth Bureau—also toward the end of July—which was eventually to provide the basis for the definitive Article 6 of the Declaration.

Again, none of this is intended to overlook the obvious differences in outlook separating Mounier from Sieyès. But it seems clear that much of the foundation for the compromise that produced the final Declaration was laid by this point, even before the basic decisions of early August were taken—that is, the rejection of both the final attempt to prevent the drafting of a preliminary declaration and the attempt to modify it by the addition of "duties." These decisions, together with the abolition of the "feudal regime" on 4 August, unleashed a flood of new proposals for a declaration: at least a score were added to those already circulating by the middle of the month. On the whole, these did little to alter the basic menu of proposals already available: indeed, most simply repeated the earlier projects of Lafayette, Mounier, Sieyès, with little alteration. But the one thing worth noting in the newer proposals is the increased presence of the "general will," which can be found, in some form or another, in virtually all of them; and while much of the characteristic variety of its appeal persisted, its usage seemed to be increasingly concentrated on the notion that generality was only to be achieved by participation in the making of the law—nearly always with the assumption of a basic equivalence between direct and representative democracy.[58]

This brings us down to the period of the final drafting itself, which was of course launched by the selection on 19 August of the draft of the Sixth Bureau as the basis for discussion. As Rials, among others, has argued, the basic merit of this proposal was that while its inspiration seems to have derived from Sieyès, this was moderated just enough—in terms of form and content alike—to serve as a kind of bridge back to the right, after the leftward drift of the previous few weeks. In any case, the actual drafting of our political program suggests precisely a compromise between right and left, in a kind of seesaw progression. Mounier seized the initiative first on 20 August, by taking advantage of the evident lack of enthusiasm for the first six articles of the Sixth Bureau's draft, and proposing what were virtually the definitive versions of Articles 1, 2 and 3. His success at this point owed not a little perhaps to the aesthetic choice of returning to the lapidary simplicity of Lafayette. It was the first article that provoked the greatest opposition, as Mounier collided with the left on his favorite terrain of equality; the second less so, and Article 3 apparently none at all, despite the fact that it was modified by the kind of qualification that was typical of Mounier and his circle, and which left the door open for a rather conservative interpretation of what "national sovereignty" entailed.

The declaration thus launched, the second day of debate, 21 August, saw a shift of momentum back towards the Sixth Bureau's draft, as the left took the initiative. First, Alexandre-Théodore Lameth proposed the consolidation of the Sixth Bureau's Articles 7–10, producing the definitive versions of Articles 4 and 5. The marquis de Beauharnais then proposed a similar act of consolidation with Articles 11–15 of the Sixth Bureau's draft, most of which dealt with issues of equality before the law, in both civil and criminal matters. His initial proposal was in a sense not far from the definitive Article 6, but it omitted the substance of the Sixth Bureau's Article 12, whose reference to the "general will" at first glance did indeed look out of place. But what is impressive then is the way in which the "general will" nevertheless ineluctably made its way to the head of the final Article 6 in the course of debate. First Volney and Pison du Galand proposed simply to place Article 12 *before* Article 11; Martineau suggested four new articles, starting with a definition of law as "the expression of the general will"; and Target suggested his own version. Mounier made an attempt to block this momentum, proposing in essence to set aside the "general will" and restore the accent on "duty" contained in the original Article 11. This went nowhere, however. The march toward the "general will" resumed, with proposals in its favor from a number of deputies.

It was Talleyrand, seconded by Barnave, who at last found the winning formula: "The law is the expression of the general will. All citizens have the right to participate personally, or through their representatives, in its formation. It must be the same for all, whether it protects or punishes." Indeed, his version brought out beautifully the underlying logic of the appeal to the "general will": the principle of equality before civil or criminal laws was truly operative only where the law itself was equal, which could in turn only be the case if it was truly the "expression of the general will"—which itself entailed the participation of all citizens, "personally" or through their "representatives," in its formation. Symptomatically, it was only at this point, when the skirmish over the "general will" was over, that the real fireworks of the day started, as Mounier launched his offensive concerning "capacity." This was surely a sign of desperation as much as anything else. Yet it is worth noting that a kind of compromise had emerged in regard to Article 6. For Talleyrand's version of the "general will" was of the mildest sort possible—not far, in the end, from the gesture toward it included in Mounier's own draft a month earlier.

The fiercest debates of the process of drafting the Declaration still lay ahead, of course: those over Articles 10 and 11, on 23–24 August. As for Article 16, finally, it belonged to the bloc adopted rather hastily on the 26th—what proved to be the last day of debate—for the most part with little changes from the Sixth Bureau's draft. When the Assembly arrived at Article 24 of the latter ("Any society in which the guarantee of rights is not secured, nor the separation of powers determined, has no constitution"[59]), a minor tug-of-war ensued. On the one hand, the sentiment in favor of the inclusion of some version of the separation of powers in the Declaration was strong enough that a series of different proposals were made, from quite varied political horizons, including ones from Lameth, Target, and Mounier himself. On the other hand, an increasing number of deputies protested, logically enough, that to make any specification at all in this area was to trespass on the work of constitution-making itself, to which the Assembly as a whole was anxious to move in any case. At length, it was the *Monarchien* Lally-Tollendal who suggested the reasonable compromise of adopting the Sixth Bureau's version more or less unchanged. This finale was in fact emblematic of the entire process of producing the political program of Articles 3, 6, and 16. For if these three articles clearly came from opposed political camps—Articles 3 and 16 were chiefly the work of moderates or *Monarchiens*, while the provenance of Article 6 was plainly the more radical or left wing of the Assembly—what is nevertheless striking is the *lack* of major disputes over the fundamental principles involved.

≺ V ≻

Conclusions

It would be wrong to suggest that the political program of the Declaration of Rights had passed entirely without opposition. Among others, there was Duquesnoy's famous protest, in regard to Article 16, that the separation of powers was a matter of the rights of "all against each person"—a *constitutional* provision, in other words, which had no place in a document whose true purpose was to establish the "rights of each person against all."[60] The criticism has persisted. Already by 1790 Edmund Burke was warning that the "pretended right" to self-government would "totally destroy" the "real rights of men."[61] Two hundred years later, the same Burkean theme, with accents drawn from Tocqueville, resonates within the revisionist historiography of our own time. For Marcel Gauchet, for example, the defining feature—fatal flaw—of the Declaration of Rights of 1789 was precisely that it confounded the two orders of "rights" distinguished by Duquesnoy: "If there is a particularity in its underlying intellectual economy, it is that of being unable properly to dissociate the private enjoyment from the public exercise of liberty."[62]

The result of viewing the Declaration from this perspective has been to overturn what had been the conventional wisdom about its political program. The historiography of the Republican-Marxist tradition had assumed that its principles were basically a variant of bourgeois liberalism, whose sources lay in an Enlightenment culture common to Atlantic civilization as a whole. Revisionist historians, on the contrary, have stressed the specifically Gallic springs for its ideas and argued, above all, for its authoritarian or absolutist character—far more an expression of the politics of the Old Regime itself than of the modern liberal attempt to replace it. How should we judge these claims? There is no question of the empirical gains represented by the revisionist project as a whole. One of its hallmarks has indeed been a careful reconstruction of the actual political culture of the Old Regime, revealing an unexpected variety and effervescence, and promising a far richer and more accurate portrait of eighteenth-century political thought. At the same time, the brief account attempted here suggests that a certain caution may be in order, at least in regard to the grander claims of ideological continuity that are taken for granted today.

The case for such continuity seems strongest in respect to the notion of "national sovereignty." No doubt there was a profound underlying logic in the fact that the last great absolute monarchy in the West became the victim of the first modern revolution of "national" liberation. As we have seen, the secular preoccupation with "sovereignty" in France served as a kind of bridge across the revolutionary divide, permitting the formal transfer of political authority from king to "nation," from individual to collective sovereign. Even here, however, it is important not to underestimate what was perhaps the major *discontinuity* in the history of French political thought in the eighteenth century—the arrival of modern natural rights and contract theory, which after all formed the basis for the declaration of "national sovereignty" in 1789. This was indeed a foreign import, descending directly from the Anglo-Dutch pioneers of the seventeenth century, with very little in the way of roots in the political culture of Bourbon absolutism. Natural rights theory was of course Gallicized on its arrival: as we have seen, it was in fact merged with a distinctively French discursive tradition, founded on the conceptual couplet of "generality" and "particularity." In this sense, Gauchet is surely correct to insist on the pivotal importance of Rousseau in paving the way for the politics of "national sovereignty" and the "general will." However, if the latter idea *was* specifically French in its origins, it manifestly was *not* a token of absolutist political thought. Bossuet's allergy to the idea of a "general will" is enough to remind us that the notion emerged as an anti-monarchical device, its demand for "generality" conceived as the *antidote* to the illegitimate "particularity" of absolutism. The fundamental thrust of the notion of the "general will," in other words, was to try to create a truly autonomous and egalitarian sphere for politics proper, of the kind absolutism had operated precisely to proscribe. As for the "separation of powers," this too owed nothing to French traditions of absolute royal sovereignty, but instead involved a straightforward embrace of notions worked out in the course of early-modern resistance to absolutism elsewhere in Europe.

Overall, then, the picture is one of a complex process of domestication of non-Gallic ideas, together with the prolongation and transformation of native political themes—which suggests, perhaps, that the revisionist emphasis on continuity in regards to the political program of the Declaration of Rights needs to be tempered with a bit of the older "orthodox" stress on the *discontinuities* involved in the emergence of Revolutionary ideology. This leaves us, however, with the problem of finding the proper description for the political program of Articles 3, 6, and 16. For the critique of Gauchet and others tells here: the assumption of the older historiography that "national sovereignty" and the "general will" were simply Gallic variations on themes belonging to a wider bourgeois liberalism seems manifestly inadequate for capturing their specificity, especially by comparison with Anglo-American political traditions. What other possibilities are there? In fact, a plausible alternative has been suggested by Philippe Reynaud, in what, for all its brevity, is probably the most balanced of recent discussions of the Declaration of 1789.[63] Reynaud does not in fact discount the weight of monarchical tradition in accounting for the document's political outlook: he draws specific attention to the confidence in the benign powers of the state inspired by the program of "enlightened absolutism." Nevertheless, what truly distinguished the Declaration of Rights from its counterparts in the Anglo-American tradition, Reynaud argues, was that its authors attempted to synthesize two distinct conceptions of liberty: the liberal conception embodied in the aspiration to protect the "natural rights" of individuals, and what he terms the "participatory" conception whose expression was precisely the political program of Articles 3, 6, and 16.

Reynaud does not do much to explore the remoter sources of this participatory conception of liberty, but it is easy enough to fill in this blank. For what was the tradition of early-modern political thought that insisted most forcefully on participatory citizenship as a condition for the exercise of negative or individual freedoms? The tradition that saw the "rights of each person against all" and those of "all against each person" not as *competing*, but as *complementary* orders of "rights"? To pose the question is to recall in fact how much the political program of the Declaration of Rights owed, in its deepest sources, to the traditions of early-modern *republicanism*. The notion of "national sovereignty" as it developed from Boulainvilliers and Mably to Mounier and Sieyès; Rousseau's refiguration of natural rights theory in terms of the "general will"; the triumph of the "pure" version of the "separation of powers"—all can be seen precisely as transformations of the entire civic humanist inheritance of post-Renaissance Europe.

At the same time, to suggest that the political program of the Declaration be seen as "republican" in this sense, is not to overlook its internal tensions or the precariousness of the compromise that produced it. On the contrary, a redescription along these lines may well be helpful in approaching precisely those problems. For the politics of "national sovereignty" and the "general will" seem to have been the product of a compromise between two competing republicanisms: on the one hand, the more classical and aristocratic civic humanism of Mounier and the *Monarchiens*, whose ancient constitutionalism and historically-based conception of "national sovereignty" had roots deep in early-modern political thought; and on the other, the more modern outlook of Sieyès and others on the left, whose egalitarian and individualist accents, and physiocratic sympathies, pointed forward to nineteenth-century republicanism proper. The watershed between the two was no doubt that central token of early-modern republicanism, the "mixed government," still sponsored, after a fashion, by the *Monarchiens*, decisively rejected by their opponents. In this sense, the Declaration of Rights might be said to mark a pivotal moment in the evolution of a specifically *modern* French republicanism, as it began to free itself from its classical and early-modern appurtenances—an evolution whose ultimate fruits were to be seen in the political culture of the Third Republic, whose lineages are traced in Claude Nicolet's great study of *L'idée républicaine en France.*[64]

We can thus conclude with the suggestion that the politics of "national sovereignty," the "general will," and the "separation of powers" might better be seen in terms of this transitional republicanism, than as either an abortive French Lockeanism or a democratic mutant of absolutism. A redescription of this kind has the further advantage, it might be added, of rescuing something of the *specificity* of the political outlook of the Revolution of 1789—and perhaps something of its dignity as well. The overwhelming concentration on negative freedom and on civil liberties that characterizes the traditions of Anglo-American liberalism has often made it difficult—never more so than at the present—to make a fair estimation of the French contribution to the variety of modern conceptions of freedom. There is no doubt about the liberal aspirations of the Declaration of Rights, announced in its preamble and embodied in so many of its specific articles. What is distinctive is that side by side with the guarantee of the negative freedoms of classical liberalism, the Declaration promised French citizens another kind of freedom as well—the positive liberty of participation in democratic self-government, established in Articles 3, 6, and 16. It is not unusual to view the attempt to combine these two kinds of freedom as chimerical or confused, involving a dangerous crossing of the barrier separating the public from the private. But it is worth recalling that the greatest liberal thinkers themselves, from Constant to Berlin, have always conceded that it is an impoverished sense of liberty that confines it to its negative or private aspects—as if it were Hobbes and Burke alone who defined the true sphere of modern "freedom," to the exclusion of Rousseau and Jefferson. In this sense, the Declaration of Rights is a salutary reminder of the generosity and breadth of vision of bourgeois political thought in its revolutionary youth.

Safeguarding the Rights of the Accused

Lawyers and Political Trials in France, 1716–1789

DAVID A. BELL

DURING THE TWILIGHT of the Old Regime, few issues provoked as great and uniform a degree of loathing for existing customs as criminal justice. The centuries-old accretion of judicial practices that allowed for arbitrary arrest, indefinite imprisonment without trial, legal torture, and purposefully cruel punishment—"the bloody shoals of criminal legislation," as the magistrate Charles-Marguerite Dupaty memorably put it, came in for almost universal execration.[1] On the booksellers' shelves, dramatic accounts of specific injustices jostled for space with scores of treatises on the subject, notably Cesare Beccaria's hugely successful *Dei delitti e delle pene* ("Of Crimes and Punishments"), popularized in France by Voltaire. By 1789, the scandal had grown so great that of the two dozen or so men best known for advocating judicial reform, eleven gained seats in the Estates General.[2] One of them, the comte de Lally-Tollendal, stood as a living rebuke to the judges of the Old Regime: he had made his reputation fighting for the posthumous rehabilitation of his father, whom the authorities had tried and beheaded for the "crime" of surrendering Pondicherry to the British during the Seven Years War.[3]

The men gathered at Versailles in August 1789 therefore needed little encouragement to include strong guarantees for criminal suspects among the "rights of man and citizen." On 22 August, after less than half a day of discussion, they approved Articles 7, 8, and 9 of the Declaration of Rights, establishing barriers against arbitrary arrest and detention, cruel and unusual punishment, and retroactive legislation. The articles also guaranteed due process of law and the presumption of innocence.[4] Very few disagreements occurred on matters of substance. Some debate might have been expected over Article 7, for in apparent contradiction with the right to resistance set

forth in Article 2, it ended up incorporating a passage orignally written by the abbé Sieyès: "Every citizen summoned or seized by virtue
of the law must obey at once; he makes himself guilty by resistance."[5]
But these lines, inflammatory as they sound to modern ears, won easy
acceptance. In fact, the motion to insert them came not from Sieyès
himself, but from one of his moderate opponents, the future *monarchien* Pierre-Victor Malouet, and (according to recent students of the
Declaration) they testify less to the Assembly's reverence for Rousseau than to its concern for the chaos then engulfing the French countryside. The noble deputy Antoine d'André called for their inclusion
by explaining that they affirmed "the rights of society."[6]

≺ I ≻

Lawyers and the Safeguarding of Rights

The case of rights for criminal defendants in 1789 thus seems emi-
nently straightforward: the simple culmination of what Peter Gay
called the Enlightenment's "liberal crusade" for justice.[7] Or is it?
One, seemingly innocuous passage in Article 7 suggests the story is a
little more complicated. This passage reads: "Those who solicit, expedite, execute, or effect the execution of arbitrary orders must be
punished." Originally proposed in slightly different language by the
prominent Parisian barrister Guy-Jean-Baptiste Target, it was recognized by the deputies as a clear reference to the widely-detested judicial practice of the Old Regime called the *lettre de cachet*—an arbitrary arrest order issued over the king's signature.[8] What makes the
passage unusual is that only here, in the entire Declaration of Rights,
did the deputies go beyond stating the existence of rights to ask how
they should be enforced, and to insist on punishment for agents of
the state who violated them. This singularity did not pass unnoticed
on 22 August. In fact it provoked the only serious debate over the
three articles. The deputy Louis-Simon Martineau argued that matters of enforcement belonged not in the Declaration, but in the forthcoming constitution, and called for the passage's deletion. Its inclusion, he contended, would only weaken the general principle that all
men must obey the law. Other deputies concurred, while also asking
if every agent of the state should be held responsible for following
wrongful orders.[9] Martineau's motion made some progress, only to

run into a deadly volley of rhetoric from the great orator Mirabeau. "Our liberty," he thundered, "demands the responsibility of all the hierarchy of agents . . . from the highest vizir to the lowest myrmi-don." Mirabeau argued that without effective enforcement, the theo-retical existence of a right meant nothing: "The law which holds that no citizen can be arrested except by virtue of the law is recognized everywhere, but it did not prevent the *lettres de cachet.*" In the wake of this outburst, the Assembly put Martineau's proposal to a vote, and solidly rejected it.[10]

This little debate seems rather odd, for Martineau had in fact made a wholly legitimate procedural point. Why did the Assembly *not* leave the matter to the constitution as it did with other ques-tions of implementing the principles of the Declaration? By taking the initiative to warn agents of the state against violating the citizen-ry's freedom from arbitrary arrest and detention, it can be argued, the deputies were implicitly holding those agents responsible not to any future constitutional body, but to the Assembly itself. Certainly, such an arrogation of authority was not inconsistent with other ac-tions it took in the summer of 1789 as the deputies struggled to dis-place the symbolic locus of sovereignty from the king to themselves, as representatives of the nation.[11] Why, however, did they choose to take such a step in a Declaration of Rights, and in relation to the rights of criminal suspects?

One partial answer to this question does suggest itself. Among the deputies elected to the Third Estate, far more came from a single pro-fession—the law—than from any other; and under the Old Regime, lawyers had achieved their greatest prominence trying to establish de-finitive rights for the accused.[12] They did so not primarily in legal trea-tises or philosophical arguments, but in a series of *causes célèbres* fea-turing victims of precisely the sort of "arbitrary orders" condemned in the Declaration, from Jansenist clerics who had run afoul of the papal bull *Unigenitus* to supposedly virtuous noblemen imprisoned by their own family members. These trials (which began long before the final burst of prerevolutionary disgust with the judicial system) received tremendous publicity, thanks above all to the lawyers' unique privi-lege of printing and circulating their trial briefs (*mémoires judiciaires*) without censorship.[13]

The importance of these trials to political life in a monarchy lack-ing a free press and elective institutions had been vast. As Tocqueville observed in *The Old Regime and the French Revolution*: "The practices of the law courts had entered in many ways into the pattern of French life. Thus the courts were largely responsible for the notion that every matter of public or private interest was subject to debate and every decision could be appealed from." He called these ideas "the only part of a free people's education furnished by the old regime." Legal briefs in particular arguably had significant influence on French readers, and helped constitute the abstract figure of "the public" as an entity superior to established authorities.[14] As Roger Chartier has observed, they were the exact inverse of *lettres de cachet*, exposing disputes and placing them before the judgment of the public instead of hiding them away at the arbitrary order of the monarch. Many deputies in the National Assembly had made their reputations writing such briefs, and none more successfully than the author of the crucial, contested passage from Article 7: Guy-Jean-Baptiste Target.[15] If, as Marcel Gauchet suggests, the authors of the Declaration sought not only to found a new order, but to underscore the legitimacy of their own assumption of power, the issue of arbitrary arrest and detention would have seemed the perfect place to drive the point home.[16]

This answer, however, is only a beginning. Louis Martineau had also practiced law under the Old Regime, and also owed his reputation partly to participation in *causes célèbres*.[17] Nonetheless, he reached a different conclusion from Target. Why? The accounts of the discussion are rather telegraphic. Possibly Martineau really had no more than a procedural objection in mind. Yet the history of the *causes célèbres* themselves suggests that something more important may have been at stake. Surveying these cases across the eighteenth century, it is possible to trace a clear shift in the way French lawyers talked about the rights of the accused. The shift concerns not the nature of the rights themselves, but rather the issue to which Mirabeau drew attention: safeguarding and enforcing them. Who, within the French polity, had ultimate authority to *enforce* a "law recognized everywhere"? Opinions differed, and one may perhaps read the Assembly's inclusion of the contested passage as the last word in a long discussion.

How may we best define the terms of this discussion? Recent French "liberal" (that is classical liberal) scholarship suggests that in modern societies, two broad models have evolved for resolving the perennial problem of safeguarding rights: the American and the so-called French Republican.[18] In the first, responsibility for protecting rights falls to an independent judiciary within a system of divided powers. In the second, it belongs wholly to the legislature as the direct and unrestricted voice of national sovereignty. Philippe Raynaud describes this second, less familiar model with lucidity: "The majority of [nineteenth-century] 'republicans' were suspicious of Supreme Courts and of a 'government of the judges' which seemed to them to lead to a denial of the rights of the Legislature and, beyond that, to an arbitrary restriction on the Nation's capacity to decide issues that mattered to it."[19] The French theorists explain the evolution of the different models by reference to the political cultures of the two nations. In America, they argue, a "Calvinist" suspicion of all political authority prevailed, leading the founding fathers to seek to protect citizens from the state. France, meanwhile, suffered from twin burdens: the heritage of absolutism with its Bodinian emphasis on undivided sovereignty, and the French Enlightenment's abandonment of natural law in favor of Hobbesian social contract theories which stressed the need to alienate natural rights in order to found and preserve a community. Even the most liberal-seeming elements of the Revolution—notably the Declaration of Rights itself—could not, in this interpretation, escape from France's absolutist heritage. Even the Declaration had as a principal aim the strengthening, not the weakening of state power.[20]

These models, while attractively clear-cut, unconvincingly portray both French and American political culture as essentially monolithic. In the French case, not only the theoretical inspiration, but also the factual basis seems to come from Tocqueville and his pioneering but one-dimensional view of Old Regime government as a highly-centralized, proto-Napoleonic bureaucracy opposed principally by men of letters engaged in "abstract, literary politics." This model has not fared well in recent years, particularly in the English-speaking world. A substantial body of scholarship now tends to present the Old Regime as a more lively place where a chronically broke and embattled monarchy preferred compromise to conflict, and where pious Jansenists and philosophes, Versailles administators and "Grub Street hacks" all contributed to a bubbling ideological stew. Given that the largest single professional group in the National Assembly—lawyers

—had counted among the most consistent *opponents* of the royal administration in the seventeenth and eighteenth centuries, the idea of an overwhelming "absolutist legacy" seems rather exaggerated.[21]

Nonetheless, the models remain suggestive in some respects, and the comparison between France and America still has its uses. In America, James Madison and the Federalists indeed saw the principal dangers to individual rights coming from the tyranny of the majority, which, in a democracy, would express its will most clearly through the legislature ("If a majority be united by a common interest, the rights of the minority will be insecure" he wrote in the *Federalist Paper*).[22] In the Constitution, they thus sought to establish a powerful, independent judiciary as a check on the legislature. Madison himself first doubted that a bill of rights would prove an effective check on popular government. Thomas Jefferson, however, helped change his mind in a letter of 15 March 1789 which argued, in part, that such a bill would put a "legal check . . . into the hands of the judiciary." The American historian Leonard Levy comments: "Jefferson believed that an independent court could withstand oppressive majority impulses by holding unconstitutional any acts violating a bill of rights." Over the next decades, the Supreme Court indeed became the primary defender of the freedoms enumerated in the Bill of Rights.[23]

In revolutionary France, on the other hand, many deputies (like some American anti-Federalists) saw the principal danger to individual rights coming not from government *per se*, but from self-interested *minorities*, whether the aristocracy or "agents of despotism." From this point of view, the democratic legislature itself, incarnating the nation, and not simply a faction, logically represented the best safeguard of individual rights. Thus the two tendencies detected by the French theorists in the Declaration of Rights—on the one hand the protection of individual rights, on the other the *strengthening* of state authority—did not necessarily contradict each other. The more powerful the state, it could be reasoned, the less chance for any malicious minority to usurp its authority and violate individual freedoms with impunity. This analysis suggests that in general, notions of how to safeguard rights are shaped in great part by perceptions of the relative strengths and dangers posed by majorities and minorities within a given polity, as well as by preconceptions about the natural "corruptibility" of government.

How, then, did such perceptions change in the milieu which produced so many deputies to the National Assembly: the prerevolutionary world of the law? How did such concerns play themselves out in
the *causes cèlèbres* in which these men attempted to defend the rights
of the accused throughout the eighteenth century? The following
pages will examine a series of notable cases, lasting from 1716 to 1787,
within a broad context of social, political, and religious change. The
cases will chart the shifting arguments made by the men who argued
them—mostly, but not exclusively barristers—and relate them both
to the immediate issue of judicial rights, and more broadly to the general question of how the revolutionary assemblies sought to safeguard
the rights set forth in the Declaration of August 1789. The chapter will
therefore examine the question of the rights of the accused as it
evolved *in practice*, in reference to specific cases. It will pay less attention to the theoretical basis of those rights (whether, for instance, they
were "natural" or "legislated") than to the mechanisms that legal
writers saw as appropriate to enforce them.

≺ II ≻

Lawyers in Old Regime France

First, however, a few words of background on the legal profession are
needed. It has become common to observe that in the eighteenth century, as ever-larger quantities of printed matter reached an ever-larger
and ever-more-articulate readership, the somewhat undefined figure
of "public opinion" took on tremendous importance in France.[24] But
what groups benefited most from these changes? Historians have traditionally answered: "Men of letters," yet the same rising tide of print
also drastically altered the fortunes of another group: men of the law.
Under the Old Regime (as today), barristers built careers not only by
winning cases, and not only through patronage, but by garnering plau-
dits from a "public" whose active interests in cases supposedly guaranteed the impartiality of the courts.[25] They appealed to this public not
only in their oral arguments, but also in their trial briefs, which were
frequently printed and sold, and whose circulation rivalled those of
popular books and constituted a distinct genre of eighteenth-century
prose.[26] The vertiginous expansion of the French literary market thus
benefited lawyers very directly. The bar already had a reputation as the

profession in France most open to talent (admission required no capital and few formal qualifications), a profession that welcomed men
from a broad variety of backgrounds and constituted the kingdom's
surest avenue of social mobility. In the eighteenth century, it not only
attracted aspiring jurists, but also competed with the republic of letters as a destination for young men with literary ambitions.[27]

For men interested in making their voices heard on political issues, the bar in fact offered a key advantage over the republic of letters. Since legal briefs did not undergo preliminary censorship, and
since barristers enjoyed considerable institutional protection from
the royal authorities, they could write with a large degree of impunity. For this reason, over the course of the eighteenth century, the
bar became a key center of political pamphleteering. The refractory
sovereign courts, in the long battles against the Crown which dominated prerevolutionary French politics, drew their most important
publicists from among Parisian barristers, and when the Crown finally chose to take on the courts in the battle for "public opinion" it
looked for its own champions in the same small stable.[28] The political influence barristers had gained by the 1770s can be gauged by
these comments from Malesherbes, a keen observer of the changes
wrought by printing and publicity in French political life: "The independence of the Order of Barristers, and their freedom in oral arguments and printed briefs now offers citizens their only salvation, the
weak and oppressed their only recourse against aggression and violence. It is the lone rampart protecting our proprieties."[29]

Barristers had an ability to influence not only immediate political
issues, but also the development of French public law. The reason lies
primarily in the incredible complexity and confusion of Old Regime
jurisprudence, which—just as in modern common-law systems and
unlike the *code Napoléon*—gave legal experts a remarkable degree of
flexibility in interpreting shifting and contradictory statutes and precedents. Moreover, relatively few judges numbered among these experts. Before 1789, the magistrates of sovereign courts owned their offices as a form of property (the custom was called "venality of offices"), and needed to satisfy only minimal requirements before
purchasing or inheriting them (in eighteenth-century Paris, they assumed their judicial duties at an average age of only 23). While a solid
minority did develop real legal expertise, many others did not.[30] Barristers, on the other hand, had to supplement the erratic legal instruction

of the universities with an arduous apprenticeship, and acquired clients only if they possessed the sort of practical legal skills valued in common-law systems: an ability to find just the right precedent, a knack for creative interpretation, a familiarity with many styles of legal argument. Thus they shared in the most serious attempts at codification and legal reform, and wrote most of the textbooks, treatises, and legal dictionaries that guided novices through the tangled underbrush of the law.[31] Voltaire wrote that barristers' decisions "can take the place of formal rulings, and direct those of judges." Montesquieu, in *The Persian Letters*, had a magistrate quip: "We have living books —the barristers: they work for us and take charge of our education."[32]

In short, then, barristers had considerable institutional autonomy and considerable scope for innovation in legal interpretation. This independence left them free to draw on sources that had little obvious connection to traditional French jurisprudence. The *Maximes du droit public françois* ("Maxims of French Public Law"), a massive tome compiled by Parisian barristers in the 1770s, draws massively on such unlikely authorities as Harrington and Locke.[33] Because barristers trolled so widely, the notion of "imprescriptible rights" held no mysteries for them, and featured in their legal cases throughout the eighteenth century. But how could these rights be enforced? On this question, barristers' ideas varied considerably.

≺ III ≻

Jansenist Lawyers and the Struggle for Public Opinion

In the year 1716, six clergymen from Reims presented an appeal to the highest court in France, short of the king's council, the Parlement of Paris. A year earlier, they had attracted the fury of their ambitious duke-archbishop, François de Mailly, for failing to approve the papal bull *Unigenitus*, which the authorities in church and state alike hoped would finally extirpate the Augustinian current in the French church known as Jansenism. Three of them fled the city, but Mailly hauled the others up in front of an ecclesiastical court which suspended them from their functions as priests and teachers in the University. All six clergymen then appealed the case to the Parlement (using a legal procedure known as the *appel comme d'abus*), but King Louis XIV blocked this move by evoking the case to his own council.

A year later, however, Louis was dead and Philippe d'Orléans, regent to his infant successor, allowed the Parlement to hear the case after all.[34]

While Jansenists had brought such cases to the Parlement before, several circumstances combined to make this one a novel experience for the French judiciary. For one thing, the old king's death had led to a relaxation of royal controls over the parlements, the church (for a time, the regent appeared to treat Jansenists benignly), and the press. In addition, the bull *Unigenitus*, coming on the heels of the destruction of Port-Royal by royal dragoons, had greatly envenomed relations between Jansenists and their opponents, and led the former to consider desperate measures to safeguard their existence.[35]

Less well known is the fact that the legal profession had also been undergoing dramatic changes. Until the late seventeenth century, barristers, while sometimes attaining individual prominence, had remained largely subservient to the magistrates of the sovereign courts. They had no independent corporate organization, and no independent voice on political matters. The introduction of venality of offices a century earlier had already strained relations within the Palais de justice of Paris and other major cities, for it blocked the promotion of barristers to the magistracy in all but exceptional cases. Under Louis XIV, as the magistrates increasingly imitated the life style of the nobility while simultaneously knuckling under to the king, the barristers accused them of betraying the parlements' traditional constitutional and religious goals of a tempered, limited monarchy and Gallican, Augustinian Catholicism. Barristers, if anything, defended these goals with increased fervor and determination as their own social status weakened. By 1700 their leaders had fallen into the grip of a zealous, austere Jansenism.[36]

In response to these changes, the barristers gradually removed themselves from the magistrates' tutelage, and brought into being a separate organization known as the Order of Barristers (*ordre des avocats*). Between 1660 and 1710, this organization took control over recruitment, training, and discipline within the bar, and became the barristers' principal representative in the world of the law. While its leaders eschewed the formal status of a *corporation* (they feared that a corporate charter would allow the Crown to restrict their independence), the Order nonetheless came to resemble other corporate groups in certain respects, particularly in a fierce attachment to its privileges, and in its demands of total loyalty from its membership.[37] Thus a professional organization was born, not only to protect the socio-economic interests of its members (as sociological models of "professionalization" would have it) but to serve as an *organisation de combat* for "Jansenist-*parlementaire* constitutionalism."[38] Louis XIV's death gave it a chance to test its muscles.

The three principal barristers in the 1716 case—all Jansenists, all leading members of the Order—had little doubt of a favorable verdict, and saw their real mission as struggling against the bull *Unigenitus* itself.[39] They had little recourse to conventional legal arguments, however, because both the pope and the French Crown had placed their entire authority behind the bull. The barristers thus adopted twin strategies that, in 1716, still seemed quite unconventional. First, they directed their speeches and written briefs less at the judges than at spectators and at readers outside of the courtroom. Secondly, they sought to demonstrate that, at least in the case of the church, sovereign authority only extended to a certain point and no farther, and could only compel subjects to what one barrister termed (echoing Romans 12) "reasonable obedience."[40] Thus at the very beginning of Louis XV's reign, the appeal to some sort of "public opinion" and the assertion that individual members of this public held some sort of "imprescriptible rights" (a phrase that Jansenist barristers would soon begin using in their briefs) were bound closely together. The ecclesiastical context of the cases facilitated this strategy. In the realm of secular government, any speculation that certain "rights" had precedence over the sovereign's decrees was anathema, for it violated the current maxims of political orthodoxy. The murkier domain of church government, however, provided barristers with a back door through which to introduce such notions into French political discussion. As Dale Van Kley has argued, Jansenist writings on the government of the church had temporal echoes throughout the eighteenth century.[41]

In the appeal to public opinion, the barristers used the privileges of their profession to mount a publicity operation of unprecedented dimensions in court cases. Within the space of a year, with perfect legality they published twelve pamphlets portraying their Jansenist clients as exemplars of piety and virtue, and martyrs to a wicked ultramontane conspiracy.[42] In their hurry to publish, the printers did not even wait for clean copies of the scrawled, much-revised drafts from which the barristers spoke, instead publishing reconstructions of the oral arguments based on notes taken by courtroom spectators.[43] Jansenist publicists later claimed that the various documents in the case had a great effect on "enlightened people in the Provinces," particularly because the barristers could publish without censorship.[44]

The need to appeal to this broad public in turn shaped the style and presentation of the oral arguments and briefs. The barristers Louis Chevallier and Claude-Joseph Prévost both began their performances not with legal arguments, but with striking, personal professions of faith (based on the thinking of the medieval École de Paris) in which they asserted that infallibility on spiritual matters belonged to the Universal Church alone, not to the pope. Both barristers warned dramatically that the kingdom faced a trial by fire if the persecutions of Jansenists did not stop.[45] A later observer cited Chevallier's performance in particular as the beginning of a new age in courtroom rhetoric, hailing him as "the father of this free and energetic style of speaking which does not obey the constraints of cold composition."[46]

The barristers' attempt to demonstrate a limit on ecclesiastical authority was no less novel than their style. In order to prove archbishop Mailly's actions against his clerics null and void, Chevallier (again, according to a spectator) asserted that "the particular powers which are in the Church are there only to edify, and not to destroy." This amounted to saying that the authority of the pope and bishops was purely spiritual, and Chevallier underlined the point by adding that ecclesiastical judgments must never contradict the will of the temporal authorities.[47] These statements followed naturally from long-standing Jansenist beliefs about the distance between man and God, and the importance of individual acts of conscience as opposed to clerical mediation. But the 1716 case helped translate these beliefs into explicit statements about the limits of pontifical authority.

But if, as Chevallier put it, Catholics enjoyed certain "liberties" that no act of ecclesiastical authority could infringe, who protected these liberties from the likes of archbishop Mailly? To the barristers, the answer was clear. The laws of France themselves had always prohibited any overstepping of ecclesiastical bounds. Here the briefs cited the "ancient maxims" of the kingdom, the considerable body of jurisprudence concerning the *appel comme d'abus*, and also the ordinances of Louis XIV (which Jansenist barristers had themselves helped to compose).[48] These laws, however, could not be separated from their living embodiment, the magistrates of the high court. Here, as Catherine Maire has suggested, the barristers took the Jansenist idea that certain interpreters of scripture formed a "depository of truth" within the Church, and translated it into secular terms, presenting the Parlement as the depository of the principles of French law. The barrister Prévost described the high court as a "temple," "sanctuary," and "altar" in which "respectable doctrine" was "deposited."[49]

Prévost, described by contemporaries as a hulking, uncouth, and violent man, not only defended the magistrates, but made radical claims for them, claims they were unwilling to make for themselves. Did the king, through the practice of "evocation" of cases to his own council, have the right to override the Parlement's protection of individual liberties? As late as 1731, the magistrates themselves did no more than characterize evocation as distracting from the Royal Council's administrative tasks, and being often contrary to the public interest.[50] Prévost, however, called evocations wholly unconventional, dangerous, "repugnant," and finally, biting the bullet, contrary to France's unwritten constitution:

It is to the *parlement*, which represents, so to speak, all the judicial authority of the Kingdom, that those who have believed it necessary to invoke the power of the State against the wrongful application of spiritual authority have always addressed themselves ... Thus to evoke an *appel comme d'abus* to the King's own person is in a way to destroy the foundation, the very idea of justice which, so to speak, has engendered the *appels*.[51]

This passage clearly assigns the king and the Parlement to different spheres of government. While hardly an argument for divided sovereignty, it does bear a certain resemblance to Jefferson's notion of a supreme court as guardian of constitutional rights.

Prévost himself of course did not justify the Parlement's autonomy by any reference to a Montesquieuian division of powers. Instead, he invoked the late medieval language of "the king's two bodies," which in France distinguished between the physical person of the king, and the larger royal "majesty" which never dies. The Crown itself had repudiated this language more than a century before, but Prévost, who shared the bar's common vision of the Renaissance as a golden age of temperate monarchy, did not hesitate to revive it.[52] Addressing the tricky question of what happens to an evocation if the king dies, he wrote:

the evocation having been made to the late King's own person, and not to a Court, which does not die with the King, it must be presumed to have ended with his life; and things must be supposed to remain in the invariable and perpetual order of the Kingdom, which is independent of the life and death of Kings.[53]

Prévost's repeated references to the "king's own person" served to underline what he considered the intrinsically limited, fallible authority of the physical king, as opposed to the royal majesty. It was a distinction which accorded well with his gloomy Jansenist convictions about the corruption of all humans, royal and otherwise. Meanwhile, he explicitly associated the royal majesty with the Parlement itself.[54]

The Reims affair itself soon came to an end, with the reinstatement of the clergymen by the Parlement, but it served as a model for a large number of similar cases, fought by the same barristers and their protégés. Each one involved Jansenist clergy facing sanctions from a church hierarchy supported (after 1718) by the full resources of the French state.[55] Each one featured an *appel comme d'abus* by these clergy to the Parlement, and in each one, the Jansenist barristers followed the same strategies as before. Knowing that a final verdict depended on political considerations, rather than on the merit of their arguments, they directed their speeches and briefs towards the reading public outside the courtroom. Knowing that they could find few helpful arguments in royal legislation, they sought instead to prove that their clients possessed "imprescriptible rights," guaranteed under the unwritten French constitution, that shielded them from such legislation. Fearing that the king would short-circuit the whole process by evoking the cases to his council, they argued for the Parlement's autonomy in judicial matters.

It should be noted that these were not criminal cases. Under the Old Regime, criminal defendants generally did not have the right to counsel.[56] However, the original proceedings against Jansenist clergymen in ecclesiastical courts amounted to ecclesiastical versions of criminal trials, and the judges had considerable police powers at their disposal, including the use of *lettres de cachet*.[57] Thus the *appels comme d'abus* offered barristers a rare opportunity to discuss the situation of criminal suspects and defendants. In order to discredit the church authorities, they strove to point out as many irregularities and instances of blatant unfairness as possible in the clerical trials, and repeatedly cited Louis XIV's great ordinances on criminal procedure. The barristers did not characterize the authorities' behavior as violations of the defendants' rights. Instead, they presented them as an offense against the law itself, and against its guardians in the Parlement. Still, they were developing standards of due process, and these standards led them to condemn not only technical irregularities, but all use of "arbitrary" authority. Chevallier, in a case from 1715 involving a persecuted Jansenist nun, characterized the very institution of *lettres de cachet* as "odious" because of its arbitrary nature.[58]

While they were prosecuting these cases, the barristers' nascent professional organization grew stronger, and over the next twenty years this strength led them to use increasingly provocative arguments.[59] For instance, whereas Chevallier had said elliptically that the Church had the power to edify, not to destroy, a 1718 *consultation* signed by Prévost and thirteen others spelled out the issue forthrightly. "The power of the Keys is purely spiritual," it maintained. "Jesus Christ granted it without wanting to sanction any means of constraint."[60] In 1727, a brief signed by fifty barristers in defense of the beleagured Jansenist bishop of Senez went even further. Its author, Jacques-Charles Aubry, repeated the earlier definitions of the Church's powers, and linked them explicitly, for the first time, to a notion of rights: "Our liberties consist essentially of obeying legitimate pastors, under cover, nonetheless, of certain imprescriptible rights, and certain immutable principles."[61] Aubry also insisted that the "fundamental constitution of the Church" consisted essentially of the rule of law, and that infallibility belonged only to the Church as a whole, not to the pope. Once again, the setting of these cases in the context of ecclesiastical government allowed the barristers to bring in notions that remained strictly anathema in the realm of secular politics.

Such tactics did have their limits. In 1730, the barrister François de Maraimberg asserted in a brief that "all laws are compacts between those who govern and those who are governed."[62] The sentence caused panic in the ministry, which not only condemned the work, but called on all its signatories to retract or disavow. The entire Order of Barristers rushed to assure the king of their fidelity to Bossuet's maxims: "We will always take glory in being able to profess that the Kingdom of France is a purely Monarchical State, that supreme authority resides wholly in the sole person of the Sovereign, and that Your Majesty holds the place in your Kingdom of God himself, of whom you are the living image."[63]

Still, even when banned by the Royal Council and condemned by numerous bishops, the printed briefs of the late 1720s and early

1730s reached wider audiences and had a greater effect than any of their predecessors. They led the *garde des sceaux* to write despairingly that "the barristers' opinions [are] stronger in the Public than those principles whose observation is prescribed by legitimate authority." Cardinal Fleury, the prime minister, in a 1731 letter to the pope, called the barristers "the absolute masters of the Parlement" on all matters concerning Jansenism. In short, the briefs paved the way for the explosive constitutional debates of the 1750s and 1760s.[64]

≺ IV ≻

The Judicial Model

Thanks to these successes, these legal duels fought out in the early years of Louis XV's reign set an important pattern. Until the very eve of the French Revolution, successive generations of barristers defended successive generations of Jansenist "martyrs" in printed legal briefs which provided the juridical background for the Jansenist-*parlementaire* challenge to absolute monarchy.[65] The direct political importance of the briefs faded in the 1750s, as the Parlement resumed its role as the principal secular defender of Jansenism, and it declined still further after the 1760s when Jansenism ceased to provoke political turmoil. But in the meantime, these cases had become part of the daily life of the Parisian bar (itself by far the largest and most influential in the kingdom). For hundreds of men intent on building careers in the Palais de justice, legal practice did not only mean scheming for the latest lucrative aristocratic inheritance case. It meant trying to overturn what amounted to criminal convictions, protesting violations of due process and the use of "arbitrary" authority, invoking the "imprescriptible rights" of desperate clients, and writing briefs that had more the flavor of political pamphlets than of legal documents. Gambetta, Fernand Labori, and the other nineteenth-century *avocats* who saw political action as a fundamental part of French legal practice would have felt very much at home.[66]

The definitive expression of this legal tradition came in the combative work entitled *Maximes du droit public françois*, compiled by Prévost and Chevallier's successors in the 1770s. Historians have usually treated this rich, rambling compendium of citations as a work of political philosophy, but it came from the pens of practicing barristers

who had spent most of their careers defending Jansenist clergymen in
the manner described above. While concerned with the governance of
the nation, not the governance of the Church, the work drew explicit
comparisons between the two subjects, and in fact recast many of the
standard arguments about the rights of clergymen on a secular plane.[67]
Thus, just as the barristers' briefs had long stressed the limited sovereignty of the Church, the *Maximes* now prescribed only limited sovereignty for the secular power, employing the vocabulary of natural law
theory.[68] Using both natural law theory and historical arguments the
authors devoted a long section to "the liberty of actions and persons,"
inveighing against *lettres de cachet*, and asserting that the constitution of the monarchy guaranteed individuals the full right to due
process in the courts.[69] They did not, however, call for any new legislation to safeguard these rights. The best guarantee came from the laws
themselves, aided by "a corps which ensures the conservation of the
rights of the king's subjects."[70]

While these ideas derived partly from the parlements' medieval
heritage as representative bodies and checks on royal power, the importance of Jansenism in their formulation should not be underesti-
mated. The "arbitrary" authority that provoked such a foul taste in
the lawyers' mouths offended not because it was irrational, but because it was unbridled, and tasted of human corruption. The best
safeguards against such authority lay in giving unquestioning obedience to a body of immutable laws, protected by a body of magistrates.
Furthermore, as Catherine Maire has demonstrated, the very idea of
the Parlement as a "depository" of French law owed much to the
Jansenist portrayal of a select body of interpreters as the depository of
truth within the Church.[71]

The barristers' support for an autonomous judiciary also had
links to the status of Jansenists as an embattled minority. To be sure,
Louis Chevallier and his successors had no fear that a tyrannical majority might exercise its will through any sort of democratic legislature. But Cardinal Fleury and *his* successors attempted to extirpate
Jansenism not only for doctrinal reasons, but because it threatened
the confessional unity of the kingdom and raised the long-buried
specter of religious war. They consistently presented themselves as
the agents of the overwhelming majority of orthodox Catholics, and
the Jansenists as a tiny handful of unpleasant dissidents.[72] Under
these circumstances, Jansenists—who often likened themselves to

disregarded prophets or to the people of Israel in the wilderness—
quite naturally preferred to give the enforcement of rights to a "depository of truth" unresponsive to the currents of opinion.[73]

Overall, the ideas on safeguarding individual rights expressed in
this legal tradition thus come fairly close to the "American" model
described above. Both proceed out of a fundamental Augustinian mistrust of human nature, Calvinist on one side of the Atlantic, Jansenist on the other. Like the authors of the American constitution,
the French lawyers vested responsibility for enforcing the law not
with the sovereign, but with a judiciary, one which acted, if not as a
formal check, then at least as a moral restraint on the executive. It
was not an independent judiciary in the American sense, of course,
for it was hardly independent of the all-encompassing institution of
the monarchy. But it did have a certain autonomy from the physical
person of the monarch: to borrow Prévost's words, it was "independent of the life and death of Kings." An analogy between French
Jansenist lawyers and American statesmen may still seem farfetched,
but there is one obvious connection. Certain elements of the French
tradition had a strong influence on a man the American Continental
Congress would later call "the immortal Montesquieu." In *The Spirit
of the Laws*, this former magistrate in the Parlement of Bordeaux
stressed the need for monarchies to possess "depositories of the law"
if they hoped to preserve individual liberty (Montesquieu, however,
did not identify such bodies with the judiciary, which he defined in a
more narrow and restricted manner).[74]

≺ V ≻

Tensions within the Bar

If a revolution had broken out in 1749, instead of 1789, it is hard to
imagine that a National Assembly drawn heavily from the legal profession would not have included some sort of Parlement among the
institutions of a new government. Despite the fierce constitutional
battles of 1749, however, the Revolution waited for another forty
years. What happened, in the meantime, to the barristers' support for
an autonomous judiciary? Before turning to the question itself, we
must consider two developments: the waning of Jansenism and the
continuing evolution of the legal profession itself.

After the expulsion of the Jansenists' great enemies, the Jesuits, from France in the early 1760s, the issue of Jansenism ceased to have much significance in French politics. To be sure, many of the constitutional ideas developed by Jansenist thinkers remained influential until the very eve of the Revolution. The so-called *parti janséniste*—a tightly organized, cohesive group of men and women—did not fade away but went on to form the nucleus of early "patriotic" resistance to the Crown, particularly during the Maupeou crisis of 1771–74 when the king and his chancellor, Maupeou, tried to overhaul the sovereign courts and replace the magistrates with more pliant men.[75] Yet with the waning of Jansenism itself, three key elements that had determined the movement's temperament disappeared: the automatic Augustinian distaste for unbridled authority; the theological background for the idea of a "depository" of truth or law; and the sense of being an embattled minority. After 1775, the most important political authors in the so-called *parti patriote* no longer necessarily held these intimate convictions.

Meanwhile, the legal profession as a whole was evolving in new directions, as its steadily-growing success in appealing to the new and nebulous force of "public opinion" subjected barristers to new temptations and new pressures. Keith Baker, in *Inventing the French Revolution*, has keenly described these sorts of temptations and pressures in an analysis of Malesherbes's famous *Remonstrances of the Cour des Aides*, a key document of *parlementaire* constitutionalism. Malesherbes, Baker writes, attributed tremendous faith to the operations of a rational, enlightened, universal "public opinion," yet in the same breath he called for the preservation of a particularistic social order dominated by the parlements.[76] By the 1750s similar tensions could be detected within the bar. Pamphlets and legal briefs were implicitly democratic and universalistic forms of communication. They addressed themselves to a socially indistinct "public," and by publicizing the details of trials and political controversies, implied that "public opinion" should have a supervisory role over matters that were traditional royal prerogatives.[77] Yet the Order's Jansenist leaders in fact employed these weapons to defend the traditional social order defended by the noble magistrates of the parlements. Moreover, they ran the bar as a privileged corps and ruthlessly purged it of any men who tried to use the bar's powerful position for political or religious ends of which they disapproved. This state of affairs provoked resentment, dissent, and eventually open division in the bar.

These divisions (which I have described elsewhere) manifested themselves in every area of legal practice, including rhetorical style, courtroom protocol, legal education, and, above all, the organization of the profession itself.[78] Broadly, the traditionalists—largely Jansenist or Jansenist-leaning—conceived of the bar as a free, independent association of private individuals who agreed to undergo a strict process of training and moral purification that qualified them to act as intermediaries between "the public" and the judicial process. Their opponents, by contrast, presented the bar as a quintessentially public profession that should be open to all with only minimal qualifications, their practice subject only to the supervision of the "public authorities." This second view, enunciated most forcefully by the eccentric journalist Simon Linguet (who had a brief, explosive legal career), and disseminated by many organs of "enlightened opinion," ultimately prevailed in the Constituent Assembly's virtual abolition of the legal profession in 1790.[79]

These differences greatly weakened the Order of Barristers and contributed both to its eventual acceptance of the parlement Maupeou in 1771, and also to its meek acceptance of the 1790 decision (in contrast to the vociferous protests of other corporate groups). Sometimes they split the Order itself down the middle. In other cases, individuals found themselves pulled in both directions. The future deputy Guy-Jean-Baptiste Target, for example, toyed with acceptance of the parlement Maupeou before deciding on a position of severe refusal, and fiercely condemned the French people's attachment to their *corporations* while composing an uncompromising defense of the Order's own corporate prerogatives.[80] Throughout, these differences served to fuse larger political debates to immediate professional ones. According to Linguet and his followers, support for the Parlement entailed acceptance of a rigid social hierarchy that relegated barristers to the same inferior positions they held in judicial processions—far behind the noble magistrates. It also entailed acceptance of a rigid corporate organization that placed them under the talons of aged Jansenists who only permitted them to speak out on a narrow range of issues, thereby limiting both their freedom and their prosperity.

In short, the legal profession provided a stage on which many of the great political issues of prerevolutionary and revolutionary France were debated in microcosm. Moreover, far from taking place in an abstract, literary manner, these debates were inescapably linked to specific social, institutional, and personal concerns. From the perspective of this corner of the Palais de justice, unlike that of the capital's salons and coffee-houses, issues such as the limits of sovereign power —or the proper way to safeguard natural rights—had very immediate, practical ramifications. At stake was the future of this profession whose situation had changed so drastically since the beginning of the century. Needless to say, many of the aspiring authors who saw the bar as an alternate means of pursuing a literary career had definite views on the direction they wished the profession to take.

To be sure, the legal profession's perceptions of the larger political issues did not infect French political culture as a whole. The *Maximes du droit public françois*, like Malesherbes's remonstrances, arguably contributed much to the formation of a revolutionary discourse that allowed little sympathy for the parlements. Readers without a *parti pris* could take from these works what they wanted, such as the *Maximes'* powerful arguments for the sovereignty of the nation. Such distinctions would matter little had the legal profession sat on the sidelines in 1789. But of course, they did not sit on the sidelines, so it is worth placing their prerevolutionary experiences in high relief (the young Robespierre, incidentally, had dramatic run-ins with his senior colleagues at the bar of Arras).[81]

◄ VI ►
Lawyers into Publicists

In the 1760s, several barristers composed a series of trial briefs which, while written on behalf of men treated as criminals because of their religious beliefs, differed remarkably from the Jansenist variety. Working at the behest of Voltaire, they sought to challenge the criminal convictions of two French Protestants, Jean Calas (who had been executed) and Pierre-Paul Sirven (who had fled to Geneva). Whereas Jansenist barristers invariably presented the parlements as infallible guardians of the law, these men had the task of discrediting judgments issued by the Parlement of Toulouse. Indeed Jean-Baptiste-Jacques Élie de Beaumont addressed his first brief for Sirven to Louis XV, requesting that *bête noir* of Jansenist-*parlementaire* jurisprudence, an evocation of the case to the Royal Council.[82] Thus he had to argue precisely the opposite case from that made by his Jansenist colleagues: that the parlements *did not* best guard the rights of the accused.

For Élie de Beaumont, a would-be *philosophe* married to a woman of recent Protestant descent, the cases aroused strong personal feelings. Nonetheless, he treaded carefully. He knew that while the Jansenist leaders of the bar themselves labored towards the goal of Protestant emancipation, and did not object to his acceptance of the cases, they still had little sympathy for Voltaire, or for attacks on parlements.[83] Élie, who would flirt with disbarment several times in his career, had no desire to anger them. Voltaire himself, meanwhile, hoped that Élie could persuade his Jansenist colleagues to endorse the briefs.[84] Thus while Élie strongly condemned the Toulouse parlement's judicial decisions, employing a melodramatic style influenced by contemporary fiction, he did not suggest any reform of the parlements in general, or of the laws governing Protestants, or of criminal procedure. Indeed, in the Sirven case he reiterated the usual arguments to the effect that the existing laws of the French kingdom, incarnating a sort of immemorial wisdom, provided all the guarantees that the defendants needed.[85]

Élie, however, was not Sirven's only barrister. As the case dragged on into the 1770s, a young *toulousain* named Pierre Firmin de Lacroix implored Voltaire to let him take part in the defense. Voltaire's correspondence presents Lacroix as a young man hungry to establish a literary reputation, and to outshine Élie's earlier efforts. The brief he published in early 1771 indeed resorted to hyperbole on almost every page, and made Élie's loud denunciations of injustice sound like a hesitant whisper of complaint.[86] But more importantly, Lacroix did not hesitate to attack the law itself, and to call for its reform. Seeking to explain why Sirven had fled to Geneva, rather than remain to face the fate of Calas, he wrote: "Our criminal laws, more worthy of Draco's Code than of that of a gentle and polite nation, will terrify the most virtuous man ... We must live with a secret inquisition, that only treats clever or powerful defendants well." He excoriated the French for "habitually regarding as just whatever is authorized by unjust laws," and warned that "the time will come, and it is surely not far off, when this shocking contrast between our manners and our laws will cease."[87]

How to explain the difference between Élie's and Lacroix's conceptions of the law? Literary rivalry undoubtedly contributed, with Lacroix trying to prove himself the better *philosophe*. But another factor also certainly played a part. According to Voltaire's correspondence, Lacroix finished his brief in May 1770, but then continued revising it for months, and only published it in early 1771.[88] This period, of course, coincided with Chancellor Maupeou's decisive strike against the Parlement of Paris, which ended with the magistrates' exile, and replacement by a new, more pliant body. The provincial parlements survived for a short time longer, but by early 1771 could easily read their own doom as well. This *coup d'autorité* turned the entire French legal world upside down. It destroyed not only the Parlement itself, but a mass of subsidiary institutions, including, at Paris, the Order of Barristers itself, as well as a web of informal, unwritten practices that had grown up with the institutions. Thus it suddenly freed barristers from the constraints the Order had imposed on them to respect religion and traditional French jurisprudence, and to cleave to a strict code of courtroom etiquette. It allowed the impatient new generation of barristers—above all, Linguet—to develop a freewheeling new style of legal practice which highlighted the role of barristers as tribunes of the people, made trial briefs into a far more self-consciously literary form, and transformed some trials into ugly vendettas between counsel. According to contemporary observers, the year 1771 marked the start of a new, sensational era of *causes célèbres* in the French courts.[89]

The so-called Maupeou Revolution also had another effect. By transforming the parlements at will, Louis XV asserted the thesis that few, if any, French laws existed independently of his sovereign will. Laws and institutions emanated not from any separate royal "majesty," but from his own physical person. As long as these principles prevailed, appeals to an immutable body of laws guaranteed by a quasi-independent corps of magistrates had little if any meaning. To Maupeou's supporters, the rights of royal subjects could only be safeguarded by the action of the sovereign himself. To his opponents, on the other hand, the crisis had made clear that the parlements, whatever status they aspired to, did not have the actual power to resist royal incursions, and that the entire polity needed redesigning, ideally by the convocation of the Estates General.[90] Thus they too called for an act of sovereign will, this time by the nation, as the first step in guaranteeing rights.

Maupeou's experiment came to an end barely three years after it had begun, but its effects lingered on for another fifteen. The newly-cohesive "patriotic" opposition welcomed the return of the former magistrates, but it now tended to regard them only as the temporary, best available bulwark against royal despotism, not as a necessary, immutable one. Meanwhile the Order of Barristers itself recaptured little more than titular authority over its erring members, and never managed to reimpose its earlier, Draconian rule. The new style of legal practice pioneered by Linguet continued, as one *cause célèbre* succeeded the next, bringing unprecedented fame and fortune to such barristers as Target and Élie.

≺ VII ≻

The Vanguard of Reform

In short, by 1775, the tradition of litigation that dated from the Reims case of 1716, a tradition that had already been sapped by the fading of Jansenism and the growing divisions in the legal community, was irreparably damaged. To a large segment of opinion in the bar, any notion that the rights of suspects could be guaranteed by an already-existing series of laws, embodied in a quasi-mystical Parlement, seemed little short of ridiculous. Indeed, it seemed positively dangerous, for it implied the permanent relegation of the barristers to an inferior position behind the noble magistrates, and their permanent subjugation to the constraining rule of a narrow-minded Jansenist clique. In the last two decades of the eighteenth century, the idea was advanced most prominently not by barristers, but by the more traditional magistrates themselves, notably Antoine-Louis Séguier, who defended the prerogatives of the high court in the same breath that he condemned the newly uninhibited style of legal practice.[91]

During the last years of the Old Regime, lawyers' briefs and speeches concerning the rights of suspects tended to follow not from the Jansenist tradition of Prévost and Chevallier, but from Lacroix's brief in the Sirven case. They tended to argue that citizens had natural rights to justice, and that the existing body of French law neither recognized nor safeguarded these rights. Therefore, new legislation by an enlightened sovereign was called for to put an end to these "abuses." While the authors continued to address their works primarily to an audience beyond the courtroom, now they gave up on almost any pretense of addressing judges. After all, if they acknowledged that the (unjust) law did not support their clients' case, how could they call for a favorable verdict on legal grounds? As Linguet had written to a client years before: "your judges will be, even without realizing the fact, compelled or restrained by the Public. It is thus the Public we must instruct, convince and win over."[92] Thus the effective venue of the trials subtly shifted, not only to the "tribunal of public opinion," but to Versailles, whence legal reform might one day emerge. Now lawyers, far from posing as the defenders of a hunted and despised minority, presented themselves by contrast as the spokesmen for "public opinion." What is the barrister? asked the aspiring barrister Ambroise Falconnet. "The voice of the nation."[93]

Many barristers exemplified this new form of jurisprudence, but two above all stood out: Guy Target and Pierre-Louis Lacretelle, who together appeared in such sensational trials as the case of the comte de Sanois, the case of the marquise d'Anglure, and above all the Diamond Necklace Affair. Lacretelle, in autobiographical notes written after the Revolution, clearly described the changing shape of the profession:

I resolved to only write on cases of the sort which had particular significance for a jurist who was also a *philosophe* and *littérateur*; to elevate these cases as much as I could to their proper dignity; and, when they bore on reforms to be made in the laws, to examine the law itself even after the case, and thus to amass material for new and better legislation . . . To put things frankly, I was hardly a barrister in anything but name.[94]

Lacretelle put such sentiments into practice in the case of the comte de Sanois, whom relatives had imprisoned by use of *lettre de cachet*. His massive brief not only drew on a wide range of literary motifs to depict his client as a piteous victim deserving of restitution, but also contained a long attack on *lettres de cachet* themselves. "I speak," he proclaimed in the brief, "for the rights of man, and for those of the citizen."[95]

In the 1780s, another development only strengthened this new role for barristers: the growing importance of briefs in the legislative process itself. Under a government which wanted desperately to engineer massive reforms, ministers could not afford to ignore suggestions put forth in such a visible manner, in connection with sensational trials that often seemed to monopolize the attention of French readers. Thus they took the trouble to respond in print to barristers, and also made use of briefs to advance their own legislative projects.

Consider the relationship, for instance, between Lacretelle and two important ministers. In 1786, Lacretelle argued a case before the Parlement against the Compagnie des Indes, at the behest of the abbé Morellet and certain unspecified court factions. The controller general of finances, Calonne, who supported the Compagnie, himself composed a short work in response.[96] The same year, Calonne also penned an anonymous defense of *lettres de cachet* ironically entitled *Lettre d'un avocat à M. de la Cretelle*. In it, he chided the barrister's pretensions: "Instead of remaining within the narrow circle of an ordinary subject, he swoops above the constitutive laws of different governments; he sees only great results; every particular case becomes in his hands the program for a question of State."[97] Nonetheless, unlike even Lacretelle's opponents in the case, Calonne did not describe the barrister's attack on *lettres de cachet* as illegitimate, but rather presented his own reasoned arguments against him.[98] Lacretelle also served for several years as an informal adviser to Malesherbes and drafted pieces of legislation for him. Before publishing his brief in the Sanois case, Lacretelle submitted it to Malesherbes for his approval. In early 1788, Calonne's successor Loménie de Brienne asked both men to draft legislation regulating *lettres de cachet*.[99]

Even more striking than this public correspondence between a simple barrister and a minister of state was Target's role in the restitution of civil status to French Protestants. Target helped compose the Edict of Toleration itself, but Malesherbes, a chief promoter of the project, valued the barrister's literary skills more than his legal expertise.[100] Target could serve the cause best by rousing public concern in trial brief, if possible featuring a sympathetic litigant. Target had the perfect vehicle at hand, in the case of the marquise d'Anglure, whose relatives had challenged the legitimacy of her birth—and thus her inheritance—on the grounds of her father's Protestantism.[101] Malesherbes (who had earlier sponsored Target's admission into the Académie Française) summed up his strategy in a letter to Lacretelle:

I beg you tell M. Target that I beg him please to hurry the printing of the brief for Mme. d'Anglure, because I foresee that this brief will provide the occasion for advancing the general case, and I think this quite necessary because in this country we are so overwhelmed by pressing matters that we are quite slow to make up our minds about objects of legislation.[102]

The newssheet the *Mémoires secrets* agreed with this view of the case: "Me. Target has not flattered himself that he can win for the comtesse d'Anglure a case clearly judged by the Law. His broader and more patriotic object is to abrogate this law, this absurd and barbaric fiction that there are no Protestants in France."[103]

Target soon complied with Malesherbes's request in a massive, masterly brief, which first tried to establish "natural" laws of marriage, and then proceeded to examine the actual laws on Protestant marriage which supposedly made the marquise a bastard. He arrived at a double conclusion, first that the current laws contradicted nature, and second, that they also contradicted basic principles of French jurisprudence (he also stigmatized the officials of Louis XIV for "violating the most important of the rights of man, the right of conscience"). It followed that French civil law had "abandoned" French Protestants, leaving them in a legal vacuum.[104] Target therefore called on the king to intervene in the case, invoke natural law, and rule in the marquise's favor. "This affair ... essentially belongs to the Legislator" he asserted. He furthermore expressed confidence that "in this time of enlightenment, zeal and reform," the king would actually change the law and grant Protestants civil status.[105]

It is possible that when calling on the sovereign in this manner, barristers such as Target did not intend for the monarchy to assume permanent responsibility for enforcing rights. Perhaps they wished for the judiciary to recover its independence once the laws had been reformed. The evidence, however, suggests otherwise. Sarah Maza, in a survey of works on judicial reform, many written by practicing barristers, sees as a principal theme the desire to restrain the power of judges in criminal proceedings.[106] One of the most prominent reformers, the liberal magistrate Michel de Servan, believed judges should function not as an active, autonomous "despository" of law, but rather as automata mechanically applying the laws laid down by a legislator: "The magistrate can, by showing the felon the law, say to him 'I am no longer your judge, it is the law itself which condemns you.'" Target himself accepted this point of view to a certain extent. He wrote in the Anglure case: "Judicial decisions on matters of high importance determine public happiness or unhappiness, and so are necessarily subject to revision by the sovereign."[107]

In such sentences, the Parisian barrister revealed the distance that separated him from his Jansenist predecessors. He no longer looked primarily to a quasi-independent court to safeguard rights, while expressing suspicion of an "arbitrary" sovereign power. It was precisely that sovereign power, acting in an "enlightened" manner for the good of the nation, which would most effectively guarantee the rights of man. The barrister, as a spokesman for the nation, helped defend these rights by serving as auxiliary, not to an autonomous judiciary, but to the sovereign himself, acting as representative of the nation. While certainly still wary of the dangers of "despotism," reformers such as Target now saw enlightened action by the king, not the courts, as the best hope for change.[108]

≺ VIII ≻

The Abandonment of the Judicial Model

When, in 1787, Target called upon the Legislator to act, he could not have imagined that only two years later, he would be a legislator himself. But in the spring of 1789, the electors of Paris chose him as a deputy to the Third Estate, and soon, along with hundreds of other barristers, he had become a member of the National Assembly debating a Declaration of the Rights of Man and drafting a constitution. The ideas he and his colleagues had developed trying cases and defending the rights of the accused could now enter into the public law of the kingdom. The decision to include an implicit reference to *lettres de cachet* in the Declaration of Rights shows just how heavily this legacy weighed on the National Assembly of 1789. As I have suggested, the decision can be read as a rhetorical move by the Assembly to establish its own authority over the agents of the judicial system.

But whom did the deputies see themselves taking this authority from? The king? The history of the eighteenth-century legal profession suggests a different answer: the parlements (which were still in existence in the summer of 1789), and in general, an autonomous judiciary. Well within the living memory of many deputies, the legal profession had insisted with near-unanimity (thanks to the draconian discipline of the Order of Barristers) that the enforcement of rights belonged to an autonomous magistracy. Figures like Séguier had continued to defend this view until the eve of the Revolution. Just five days before the 22 August session, however, the Assembly's Committee on the Constitution had released a report on the judiciary which took the trouble to refute this view at length.[109] Its author, significantly, was Nicolas Bergasse, an aspiring barrister (and leading Mesmerist) who had never gained admission into the Order, but nonetheless became one of the most popular authors of printed legal briefs in the final years of the Old Regime. "Our magistracy was strongly set up to resist despotism," he wrote in the report; "but now that there is no more despotism, if our magistracy kept all its original force, the use of this force could easily become dangerous to liberty." The report called for a judiciary "absolutely different" from what France had known before 1789, and demanded restrictions on magistrates that Louis XV had only dreamed of. In particular, it sought to deny them any sort of review power over legislation, such as the American Supreme Court firmly established for itself in *Marbury vs. Madison*.[110]

This statement clearly expresses the shift in legal thinking that underlay the Declaration of the Rights of Man. Until the middle of the century, the men of the law had fought for a government of the judges, and insisted upon an autonomous judiciary as the guarantor of individual rights. In following decades, however, even as they continued to support the parlements as a bulwark against despotism, they increasingly argued that the best safeguard of rights lay *not* with the judiciary, but with the legislature. That is to say, it lay with an enlightened sovereign power: first the sovereign king, as long as he acted in the interests of the nation, and then, in 1789, the sovereign nation. The passage on *lettres de cachet* in Article 7 may be read as a move to insert this crucial principle into public law as soon as possible, even before the drafting of a constitution. It is significant that Louis-Simon Martineau, who opposed this insertion, was one of the handful of barristers still devoted to Jansenism in 1789. Perhaps Martineau, still attached to this self-consciously "minority" movement and still possessing a deep Augustinian suspicion of all forms of political power, felt uneasy at weakening the power of an autonomous judiciary in the new, revolutionary state.[111] (To be sure, the minority position could still be faintly heard in political debate as late as 1791.)

Why had this shift from judicial to legislative guarantees, with all its implications not just for Articles 7, 8, and 9 but for the general principle of unrestricted legislative sovereignty, taken place? The waning of Jansenism certainly contributed. The Jansenist barristers of the early eighteenth century had an innate suspicion of all political power —in this, at least, they shared a trait with American Calvinists. A well-ordered polity was one which restrained the sovereign power from its own natural excesses. As members of an embattled minority who sometimes seemed to long for martyrdom, they naturally sought to anchor their rights in an autonomous, objective depository of law, rather than in a sovereign swayed by the currents of opinion. By contrast, the barristers who used court cases to promote legislation in the late eighteenth century identified themselves not with a minority, but with the vast majority of French society: "public opinion" or the Third Estate. In fact, they tended to see privileged minorities—such as the nobility of the robe—as the real threat to individual liberties, and therefore turned to the majority as a savior.

A second reason lies in the tensions present in the French legal world during the eighteenth century, which are themselves indicative of the growing stresses on the corporate structure of French society. Under Louis XIV, the parlements were still very much the closed, hierarchical little societies represented in their magnificent *processions judiciaires*. Barristers depended on magistrates for institutional protection and professional advancement. But over the course of the eighteenth century this structure broke down. Barristers forged an independent relationship with the growing reading public and relied on their own professional organization for protection. Ironically, these transformations first occurred because Jansenist barristers feared the magistrates had abandoned their ancient ideals of a temperate monarchy and an Augustinian faith. But once they had constructed their separate platform from which to address "the public," others inevitably clambered up to use it as well (even if the original architects long sought to push them off again, generating considerable bitterness). By the late eighteenth century, some barristers were making careers in spite of the judges, not because of them. More important, the chance to participate indirectly in the making of new legislation now offered barristers dazzling opportunities which the magistrates could not hope to match. The role played by Target, Lacretelle, and others as midwives to reform brought them a greater degree of eminence than any barrister had ever acquired while imploring magistrates to take action.

Over the course of the eighteenth century, in other words, the men of the law had ceased to identify both with their superiors in the judiciary, and with the sort of minority group most likely to seek protection from the judiciary. They discovered that it was far more advantageous to identify with the broad "public," and to entrust the safeguarding of rights to that public's representatives. This development helps explain why the French republican model of enforcing rights emerged out of the political culture of the Old Regime, and why a Jansenist-*parlementaire* model, similar to the American one, ultimately failed.

Religious Toleration and Freedom of Expression

RAYMOND BIRN

F ROM THE MOMENT DISCUSSION began on 22 August 1789, it was
clear that acrimony would dominate the National Assembly debate over a formal declaration of religious rights in France. Fewer
than two years had passed since Louis XVI's edict "concerning those
who do not profess the Catholic religion," and it remained conjec-
tural whether deputies wished to extend the edict's acknowledgment
of Protestant civil status to a comprehensive statement on religious
freedom, including the right of public worship, which carried beyond
the limited intent of the law.[1] The Edict of 1787 itself had interred a
great fiction which dominated public life throughout much of the
eighteenth century—that French Protestants needed no acknowledgment of civil liberties because no Protestants existed in the country. Public acceptance of this fiction during the first half of the eighteenth century helped the monarchy to reassert its proper role as defender of French Catholicism, replacing the more limited one as mere
arbiter among sects, which it had been forced to assume between
1598 and 1685. Following the revocation of the Edict of Nantes, and
especially after 1724, the Crown could legitimately exercise full
power to punish heresy and to award, when it so desired, exceptional
grace to so-called *nouveaux convertis*. By 1787, however, *nouveaux
convertis* were being called Protestants again; and pressure had
mounted upon the regime to protect them juridically.

However much the Edict of 1787 recognized the civil existence of
Protestants by formally acknowledging their right to hold property
and enjoy civil marriage, it stopped short of admitting them to judicial
and municipal office or to the teaching profession. More significantly,
it failed to legitimize non-Catholic public worship or permit the restoration of a Protestant clergy. Therefore, between promulgation of
the edict and the debates of 22–23 August 1789, genuine tension

existed in France over the Protestant question. On the one hand, as-
similationists desired to extend the concept of civil liberties so that
such liberties might incorporate the right of formally acknowledged
free public worship and admission to all professions and public
charges. On the other hand, those with long memories maintained
that "tacit tolerance" of Protestant religious practice actually existed
in France, and the monarchy had an historic obligation to continue asserting itself as protector of the established creed (*le culte public*).
Should he once again become mere mediator among contending
faiths, argued those opponents of comprehensive toleration, the king
would find himself irreparably weakened and would invite civil strife
reminiscent of what had plagued the French countryside in the sixteenth century.

In certain respects the historical issue of freedom of expression intersected with that of religious tolerance. During the sixteenth century the press had been a major vehicle for the spread of Protestantism; later Louis XIV's tightening grip over book licensing and
censorship paralleled his persecution of Calvinists; and early in the
eighteenth century the fiction that no publication might appear in
France unless duly censored and bearing a royal *privilège* accompanied the fiction of a Protestant-free country. Even the regime's use of
exceptional grace had parallels in each instance. Just as the post-1685
monarchy defended the faith while tacitly tolerating *nouveaux convertis*, so too did the Crown assume a repressive public posture regarding the press while awarding it indulgences that bypassed the
privilège-censorship process. Meanwhile Jansenists, philosophes, and
royal administrators—often the same persons who called for Protestant civil rights—took the lead in testing royal censorship procedures
and in arguing to replace them with comprehensive forms of press
freedom. Unlike royal policies concerning Protestants, however, tacit
toleration of the written word within the framework of repressive legislation satisfied enough interested parties during the eighteenth century, so that no juridical attempt to guarantee unrestricted press freedom was made until the debate over what was to become Article 11 of
the Declaration of the Rights of Man and the Citizen.

≺ I ≻

The National Assembly Debates of 22–24 August 1789

As the debate erupted over religious toleration, for some in the Assembly it was imperative that the Edict of 1787 be completed with a declaration guaranteeing freedom of public worship. By 1789 Duc François-Alexandre de La Rochefoucauld d'Enville's edition of the *Constitutions des treize États-Unis de l'Amérique* had gone through four printings in France, its attention focusing significantly upon the pronouncements of religious liberty in Virginia, Pennsylvania, Delaware, Maryland, North Carolina, and Massachusetts.[2] La Rochefoucauld, the marquis de Lafayette, and the other *Américains* in the Assembly formed a vocal and influential bloc which insisted upon a statement in France paralleling those from the New World.[3] Meanwhile Voltairean anti-clericals such as the comte de Mirabeau and emancipated Protestants led by Jean-Paul Rabaut Saint-Étienne joined in the call for a positive declaration. Yet the views of these "progressive" advocates were by no means representative of what passed for French public opinion. Several provincial parlements and Estates had opposed the Edict of 1787. The Parlement of Toulouse specifically refused to acknowledge admission of Protestants to civil office; the Parlements of Besançon, Bordeaux, and Douai would not register the edict at all, and *lits de justice* ordering these courts to do so in May 1788 were rescinded the following October. The provincial Estates of Brittany vigorously protested the edict's terms; and the Parlement of Metz accepted the decree only on condition that Jews be excluded from its benefits.[4] Moreover, the *cahiers de doléances* were of little help. Relatively few *cahiers* addressed religious issues, and the majority which did seemed more concerned about maintaining Roman Catholic monopoly over public worship than arguing for a comprehensive statement of toleration for Protestants and Jews.[5]

By the time the Assembly's debate over religion began, more than three dozen draft declarations of the rights of man and the citizen had been submitted to the chair.[6] Concerning religious liberty, Duc Gaston-Pierre de Lévis and Rabaut Saint-Étienne offered the most ecumenical assertions. Yet even these were cautious, assuring freedom of belief but remaining vague about guarantees of public worship. For Lévis, who prior to 1 August had questioned the need for any declaration of rights at all, "Everyone has the right to a religious opinion, following his conscience, and this principle assumes that of tolerance."[7] Rabaut Saint-Étienne, a guiding spirit behind the Edict of 1787 who had expressed disappointment over its limited scope, went slightly further; but even he stopped short of explicitly calling for guarantees of unrestrained public worship. In his *Projet du préliminaire de la constitution françoise* Rabaut Saint-Étienne would have had the National Assembly declare "that consciences are perfectly free, that no one has the right to restrict them, and that each has the right to profess freely the religion he believes to be best."[8] Interestingly enough, in his *Déclaration des droits de l'homme en société* Abbé Emmanuel-Joseph Sieyès ignored the issue of religious liberty entirely;[9] and his adversary Jean-Joseph Mounier adopted a phraseology consistent with the position of those who did not wish to part dramatically from the limited toleration described in the Edict of 1787. Mounier wrote: "No person should be disturbed for his religious opinions, provided that he conform to the laws, and does not disturb the established creed (*culte public*)."[10]

The most representative draft documents addressing religious toleration adopted the parallelism of "rights and responsibilities" which would dominate the final Declaration. For example, Jérôme Pétion de Villeneuve spoke for the libertarians emphasizing "rights" when he wrote in his draft proposal: "Each person is beholden only to God for his religious beliefs and can embrace the creed defined by his conscience, as long as he does not trouble the public peace."[11] However, it was not Pétion's draft but that of the National Assembly's Sixth Bureau which formed the basis for the debates of 22 and 23 August; and the Sixth Bureau's declaration contained articles which to several deputies appeared even more restrictive than Mounier's, thereby reversing the cause of toleration rather than advancing it.[12]

The Sixth Bureau was one of thirty such committees formed in the National Assembly. These were chance associations of forty deputies each who met in July 1789 to learn the craft of parliamentary procedure.[13] During evenings between 30 July and 2 August, Sixth Bureau members had prepared a draft declaration of rights; and on 19 August the Assembly agreed to debate and vote on the bureau's articles. Three articles concerned religion and very likely were influenced by the bureau's chairman, Anne-Louis-Henri de la La Fare, bishop of Nancy.[14] The articles stated:

XVI. Since secret offenses are not within the purview of the law, religion and morality are to compensate for it. For the well-being of society, it therefore is essential that one and the other be respected.

XVII. The maintenance of religion necessitates an established creed. Respect for the established creed therefore is indispensable.

XVIII. No citizen should be disturbed as long as he does not trouble the established creed.[15]

Once François de Bonal, bishop of Clermont, began the debate of 22 August with the assertion that the French constitution must rest on religious foundations, the young comte Boniface-Louis de Castellane responded that the Sixth Bureau's articles could unwittingly serve to threaten the rights of religious minorities. For example, the overzealous might consider the *very existence* of Protestants and Jews as troubling the *culte public* and thereby find reason to persecute these minorities as social dangers. Asserting that the deputies were making a declaration of religious rights, not a constitutional law concerning religion, Castellane suggested a substitute motion for that of the Sixth Bureau. Succinctly he touched upon two of the issues that would dominate debate: the freedom to *hold* religious beliefs different from those of the majority and the freedom to *express* them publicly. Castellane's substitute motion read: "No one must be disturbed because of his religious opinions, nor troubled in the exercise of his religion."[16]

Supporting Castellane, Charles Laborde, a priest representing the *sénéchaussée* of Condom, emphasized the natural right of each citizen to select one's religion and the obligation of the state to protect one's choice: "The legitimate authority may prevent injury to creeds; but it cannot regulate liberty of conscience."[17] Mirabeau then rose to criticize the very principle of toleration as demeaning. He maintained that religious belief was an inherent right and that diversity of such belief was socially determined. To critics of Castellane's motion fearful of the consequences of religious pluralism, Mirabeau pointed out that countries respecting religious liberty seemed to be thriving, and he caustically added: "The Protestants, inevitably damned in the next world as we all know, are managing well enough in this one, undoubtedly due to the benevolence of the Supreme Being."[18] Then Abbé Jean-François d'Eymar de Walchrétien tried to salvage the Sixth Bureau's draft by proposing that its articles be voted separately; however, pandemonium reigned in the Assembly, and without making a decision the meeting disbanded for the day.

Matters did not improve the next morning and tempers flared immediately. The first issue of contention concerned Articles 16 and 17 of the Sixth Bureau's draft. Should they be part of a declaration of rights, or, at best, was their proper place in the still unwritten constitution? Following rambling debate, the matter was put to a vote. The deputies deferred the articles for discussion during later constitutional debates and took up Article 18.[19]

Now Castellane formally offered his substitute motion. It provoked a near-riot in the chamber. The Assembly president for August, Comte Stanislas-Marie de Clermont-Tonnerre, could not maintain order and twice threatened to resign his post. Following a flurry of proposed amendments to Castellane's motion, Mirabeau and Rabaut Saint-Étienne delivered fervent speeches opposing mention of a *culte public* in a declaration of rights. Mirabeau denied legitimacy to any dominant religion, and Rabaut Saint-Étienne demanded that a statement of individual rights embedded in the concept of complete religious liberty be substituted for the principle of corporate privilege implicit in a *culte public*.[20] Rabaut Saint-Étienne addressed the incompleteness of the Edict of 1787. For non-Catholics, "This law, better-known than just, fixes the form of registering their births, marriages, and deaths; as a consequence it permits them to enjoy their civil property and exercise their professions . . . and that is all."[21]

Rabaut Saint-Étienne next broadened the scope of his *Projet du préliminaire de la constitution françoise* to demand freedom for Protestants to worship publicly as a civic right—"their right as Frenchmen." Following the lead of Mirabeau, he rejected as insufficient the notion of simple tolerance: "I demand, gentlemen, for French Protestants, for all the non-Catholics in the kingdom, what you are asking for yourselves: liberty and equality of rights."[22] Appealing to the idea of an overarching civil cult defined by citizenship, Rabaut Saint-Étienne requested that guarantees of free public worship be extended to Jews. His agenda was assimilationist. Granted the legal right to exercise their religion publicly, in the view of Rabaut Saint-Étienne, Jews inevitably would accept "our manners and our customs," thereby renouncing the culture of the ghetto to which they had been subjected during eighteen centuries of barbaric and humiliating treatment.[23] Finally he addressed a messianic challenge to his fellow deputies, one based upon a French interpretation of uncompromising religious freedom: "You are not made to receive examples, but to give them . . . Europe aspiring to liberty expects great lessons from you, and you are worthy of granting them."[24]

Despite Rabaut Saint-Étienne's impassioned speech, deputies still worried deeply about the consequences of guaranteeing public worship to non-Catholics. Visions of Protestant proselytizing and street fights among competing believers conjured memories of the sixteenth-century civil wars and were a powerful counterpoint to Enlightenment principles of natural rights and the Revolution's advocacy of common citizenship.[25] Although few deputies dredged up doctrinal reasons for denying public worship to non-Catholics, the facts of history remained a major stumbling block. Deputies were comfortable enough awarding limited civil rights to religious minorities—as indeed had been done by the king in 1787—but they shrank from going much further. In hopes that by guaranteeing the sanctity of inner beliefs, toleration of their public expression might be assumed, Castellane agreed to withdraw the second part of his motion—"nor troubled in the exercise of his religion." Unfortunately he was overly sanguine. Adversaries let loose with a barrage of successful amendments that sought to restrict his objective. First, by changing guarantees of "religious opinions" to guarantees of "opinions, even in religious matters," the deputies implied one of two things. Either they were converting protection of religious minorities into a kind of exceptional grace, or else they were underscoring the problematic danger of religious freedom. Then Jean-Baptiste Gobel, bishop of Lydda, won the Assembly's approval for another qualification: "provided their expression does not trouble the public order." Finally, the addition of a prepositional phrase further refined the intent of the original motion. The article as approved ultimately read: "No one must be disturbed because of his opinions, even in religious matters, provided their expression does not trouble the public order *established by law*."[26]

Dismayed, Castellane believed that the heart had been torn from his motion.[27] Freedom of conscience was acknowledged, but freedom of worship was hedged. The *Journal des États-généraux* and *Courier de Provence* considered the amendments to contain the potential for a new inquisition.[28] In his journal of the deliberations of 22–23 August the deputy Adrien Duquesnoy found Article 10 to affirm "the odious right of the stronger" and blamed Mirabeau's arrogant manner for turning the majority away from Castellane's generous proposal.[29] Whether the phrase "the public order established by law" represented a protective screen for the Old Régime's *culte public* (Roman Catholicism) or whether the passionate debate itself initiated something even more sinister, the revolutionary and postrevolutionary crises of church and state, can be left to the debates of historians.[30] For the exhausted deputies of 23 August, Article 10 of the Declaration of the Rights of Man and of the Citizen was a compromise gesture. To be sure, private opinions—"even in religious matters"—would be protected; however, public expression of them remained couched in a participle-laden clause replete with ominous possibilities. For whatever it might be, the "law" establishing public order most definitely was *not* the benevolent *ius naturale* of the eighteenth-century Enlightenment.[31]

Moreover, in the debate of 23 August, of all contributors, it was the Protestant Rabaut Saint-Étienne who suggested that a civil cult, countenancing no deviation, was not only possible but desirable. In any case, it remained an open question whether Article 10 would prove more capable of protecting and expanding minority rights than of providing built-in excuses for restraints based upon the needs of public safety.

Contrasting with the rancor that surrounded the debate over religious liberty, the deputies' mood during the discussion of freedom of expression was almost civil. France's comprehensive press law had remained relatively unchanged since 1723. Everyone in the Assembly knew that, set alone, it was both inappropriately restrictive and unenforceable.[32] However, during most of the eighteenth century authors, journalists, and publishers alike had established lucrative careers evading state censorship controls, while the Royal Council, parlements, and the Catholic church abetted the cause of toleration by undercutting each other's claims to controlling the printed word. More recently, the regime's decision in May 1788 to invite public commentary over the composition of the Estates General had given rise to an explosion of uncensored political pamphleteering, and during the next fifteen months the entire apparatus of state press controls gradually disintegrated.[33] Nevertheless, the regime had not yet announced that liberty of expression was at hand; and occasional outbursts of police repression still claimed victims.[34]

Meanwhile, in their demands for press freedom the *cahiers de doléances* were more vocal and clearsighted than they had been in their much rarer claims for religious toleration. Most *cahiers* dealing with the subject called for unrestrained liberty of expression as long as authors and printers identified themselves and assumed responsibility for their opinions. Another body of *cahier* opinion wanted legal safe-guards against slander. Only a very small minority—virtually all from the clerical Estate—desired maintenance of formal preventive censor-ship controls.[35] With the *cahiers* suggesting that the courts were best equipped to deal with abuses, the Assembly's deputies felt encouraged to address the issue of liberty of expression in a declaration of rights.

Most of the draft proposals of July and early August asserted the parallel need for authorial or publisher responsibility to balance one's freedom to write. The issue at hand seemed to be which element to emphasize, rights or responsibilities. Once again, Mounier repre-sented the moderates. He had written: "Freedom of the press is the firmest support of public freedom. The laws should maintain it and assure the punishment of those who might abuse it in order to cause injury."[36] On the other hand, the article proposed by Mirabeau's "Committee of Five," a group of deputies who had unsuccessfully at-tempted to synthesize several draft declarations, emphasized the lib-erals' position: "Thus, free in his thoughts and even in their expres-sion, the citizen has the right to diffuse them by word of mouth, through writing and print, as long as he does not expressly injure the rights of another; the mails especially should be sacred."[37]

The article of the Sixth Bureau presented for debate assumed the existence of rights while recognizing the principle of responsibili-ties: "The free communication of thoughts being a citizen's right, it should be restrained only when it harms the rights of another."[38] The ducs de Lévis and La Rochefoucauld d'Enville disliked the negative connotations of the article and its failure to recognize the positive contribution of the press in recent years: "*It* is what has destroyed despotism!" exclaimed La Rochefoucauld. "Previously *it* is what de-stroyed fanaticism!" And he suggested a possible substitute motion for the Sixth Bureau's: "The free expression of thoughts and opinions is one of the most precious rights of man; thus every citizen may freely speak, write, and print, subject to accountability for abuse of this freedom in the cases determined by law."[39]

In the spirit of compromise, Pierre-Hubert Anson, a member of the Sixth Bureau, offered to amend the bureau's original motion with "No one should be thwarted in the verbal or written communication of his thoughts as long as he does not harm the rights of another."[40] How-ever, Rabaut Saint-Étienne, seconded by Maximilien Robespierre, rejected all qualifications to absolute freedom of expression. Rabaut Saint-Étienne conjured the image of the influential politician, justly criticized by the press, muzzling his detractors with the cry "Order is troubled, the laws are being violated, the government is attacked!" Robespierre went yet further, maintaining that no tyrant would refuse to approve an article as watered-down as the Sixth Bureau's.[41] Submitted to a vote, the proposal of the Sixth Bureau was defeated.

In its place, La Rochefoucauld offered his substitute motion to the chamber. Jérôme Pétion de Villeneuve maintained that it was prematurely conceived, since no laws defining abuses of press freedom could exist prior to a constitution; and the constitution was yet to be written.[42] Pétion convinced very few deputies. La Rochefoucauld's proposal was adopted and became Article 11 of the Declaration of the Rights of Man and of the Citizen. As was the case with Article 10, deputies accepted yet-to-be written laws as establishing invisible boundaries for civil liberties. A vision of the law as a punitive agency, rather than as a protector of these liberties, illustrated how the institutional power of the Old Regime still held sway over the minds of revolutionaries.

≺ II ≻

*The Course of Liberty of Expression
in the Eighteenth Century*

In several ways the eighteenth-century monarchy's definition of liberty of expression paralleled its conception of liberty of religion. French absolutism sought to control the external aspects of expression and belief, punishing severely when need be, yet reserving the right to show exceptional grace when expedient. With respect to policing one's innermost thoughts the regime's program remained ambiguous, but the royal administration did develop an elaborate program of punitive legislation which sought to control their public utterance. The immediate origins of this legislation lay in the reign of Louis XIV. In August 1686, on the heels of the revocation of the Edict of Nantes, a comprehensive press law regulated preventive censorship and established corporate controls over the book trade in Paris.[43] In February 1723, shortly after Louis XV attained his majority —and just prior to the royal declaration which denied Protestants outside Alsace a civil existence—the ministry of Philippe d'Orléans recapitulated and elaborated upon all previous laws dealing with the printed word. In 1744 the legislation was formally extended over the entire country, and in 1777 its economic features were modified.[44]

The Edict of 1723, hereafter called the *Code de la librairie*, was typically monopolistic and punitive. Divided into 123 articles, it defined the corporate character of the Paris publishing industry, limited the number of printers, established guidelines of quality control, and policed the printed word by virtue of royal publication privileges and self-censorship administered by officers of the Paris Community of Printers and Booksellers. Not a word was said about royal censors, scholarly pension-holders who since the 1620s had been exercising pre-publication repressive authority in the name of the royal chancellor. After 1742 the *Almanach royal* identified the censors. By 1763 their number had reached 122; by the 1780s there were nearly 200.[45] Nor did the *Code de la Librairie* give any indication of the conflicting jurisdictions which fought for increasing their authority over the trade: the Royal Council, parlements, universities, church hierarchy, provincial intendants, governors, and municipal police forces. Time and again during the eighteenth century, their rival political agendas touched the *librairie*, complicating policies of repression and unwittingly assisting the cause of toleration.[46]

Moreover, during the eighteenth century no official document could be expected to define the extra-legal techniques of publishing that punitive jurisprudence failed to reach. Between 1750 and 1789, perhaps one of every two books published in France appeared in violation of the laws of *privilège* (primitive copyright) or censorship. There were several reasons why a publisher might seek to avoid normal channels. The most obvious one was that he doubted whether a manuscript would stand up to a censor's formal scrutiny. Or else an author, publisher, or even director of the government's book trade office might want to bypass the cumbersome procedure which could result in outright rejection of a work for reasons unrelated to its intrinsic qualities. After all, personal literary vendettas were not unknown in the eighteenth century, and a bribed censor might certainly abuse his power. Virtually all the canonized works of the French Enlightenment, including the last eleven volumes of the *Encyclopédie* and the major writings of Voltaire and Rousseau, avoided the normal *privilège*-seeking process.

A tacit permit (*permission tacite*) granted by the state director of the book trade office was the most common extra-legal authorization sought by publishers.[47] At times a censor might be called upon to award qualified approval to a work seeking a *permission tacite*; but, unlike instances of *privilège* grants, he did not need to append his name to the manuscript. Most significant for the book's publisher, and once more unlike the *privilège*, the *permission tacite* did not guarantee the publisher property rights over the volume, even though he might have paid the author a stiff sum for the manuscript. Generally, the government book trade office allowed the publisher a single printing of a tacitly approved volume. In such an instance the *permission tacite* might also be called a *permission simple*. If, after distribution, no scandal or condemnation occurred, other publishers might apply for their *permissions simples*. As competition multiplied, price wars inevitably followed. If the first edition had not yet sold out, it was doomed. Foreign publishers who desired their books to circulate in France generally applied for *permissions tacites* as well. Unquestionably, these permits loosened the rigid monopoly of the *privilège* system; and in quantitative terms their use contributed greatly to the circulation of ideas.[48]

Though semi-clandestine authorizations, *permissions tacites* were nevertheless acknowledged by the book trade office in registers employed in-house.[49] Chrétien-Guillaume Lamoignon de Malesherbes, the royal official in charge of the office between 1750 and 1763, explained their use to the writer J.-H. Samuel Formey: "Our policy is to permit works tacitly, or better to tolerate them, because a foreign edition ultimately will gain entry; and it is more worthwhile for French booksellers and workers to make a profit. But since it is not acceptable to leave vestiges of this tolerance in writing, ordinarily such sorts of permission are accorded verbally."[50] Even fewer records dealt with the circulation of "simply tolerated" books, books protected by highly placed individuals, officially prohibited ones, or pirated editions. Book historians in recent years have concerned themselves with the underground subculture of illicit publishing and the transport of prohibited books across the frontiers of France and into the kingdom's most important provincial cities.[51] Titles have been catalogued and book contents analyzed. Measuring the influence of the illicit commerce is a complex affair and likely to remain so; nevertheless, it does seem clear that the trade in books was not treated comprehensively in the regime's formal registration procedures.

This fact notwithstanding, any interpretation of the development of literary freedom in eighteenth-century France must consider as a fundamental theme the slow erosion of punitive jurisprudence despite sporadic efforts at enforcing it through terror. The official book trade archives contain a numbing collection of repressive judgments —hundreds of *arrêts du Conseil*, parlementary decrees, church *mandements*, and police reports—whose ostensible purpose was to protect society by silencing the written expression of thought.[52] Yet these rulings often contradicted one another; and in face of an illicit trade where not only members of the book industry but also customs agents, judges, tax farmers, and the transport service shared profits, it is tempting to emphasize the futility of eighteenth-century repressive censorship. Still, disturbing questions remain: what Jansenist tract or thesis was not hunted down? What classic of the Enlightenment was not, at the time, considered a prohibited book? Even if the public executioner customarily chose blank pages as his actual victim, what work of cultural significance did not submit to symbolic laceration and burning? As for authors, Diderot languished in Vincennes prison, Rousseau had to flee for his life, Helvétius was brutally humiliated, Beaumarchais paid dozens of visits to the police— and these were but the classic textbook examples of authorial harassment. Surviving police reports record dozens of chilling cases where lesser known writers joined printers, booksellers, and peddlers in prison or the galleys. It is true that punishment was sporadic and selective; these facts precisely were what made it intolerable.[53]

Repressive censorship was one means of policing the written word. Preventive censorship was another. Early in the eighteenth century preventive censorship was viewed not only as a way of protecting public morals but also as a means of influencing more decorous expression of the printed word. Like modern book reviewers, censors in their reports invoked the values of elegant style, good taste, accuracy, and logical argument.[54] Religious works were rejected as much for their unverifiable enthusiasm as for their heretical Jansenism. Censors were on guard against superstitious themes and disordered language. They sought to encourage accuracy and good taste while suppressing credulity and the fantastic. By 1750, however, public tolerance of quality controls exercised by hack appointments and the Paris publishing community was ebbing; and sheer demand for the printed word overwhelmed constraints originally formulated in the seventeenth century. Readers now were consuming as many as 3,500 titles and 150 different periodicals per year.[55] Salons, public libraries, and reading rooms became centers of literate culture; book lending and book renting were commonplace.[56] To escape censorship demands, publishers routinely requested *permissions tacites* and devised ingenious means of escaping pre-publication examination altogether; moreover, as Diderot himself noted, French readers flocked to any proscribed book. Its notoriety alone assured best-seller status.[57]

The 1750s represented the crucial decade in the struggle for freedom of expression in France. Post-publication (or repressive) censorship, previously limited in large measure to theological controversies and involving for the most part Jansenist issues, affected the reading habits of a wider public than ever before. The well-advertised *Encyclopédie* experienced two suppressions and went underground. Helvétius's *De l'Esprit*—a work approved by a royal censor and holding a royal *privilège*—subsequently was condemned by Parlement and pope alike, becoming a *cause célèbre* and embarrassing both the state book trade office and its director, Malesherbes.[58] In the aftermath of Damiens's assassination attempt upon Louis XV, a monstrous royal declaration of 1757 sentenced to death anyone convicted of composing, ordering composed, printing, selling, or distributing "writings tending to attack religion, upset spirits, injure our authority, and trouble the order and tranquility of our state."[59] The numbing yet ineffective suppressions and the unenforceable character of the brutal declaration of 1757 persuaded Malesherbes to draw up, in 1758 and early 1759, five memoranda for the king's son, the dauphin, revising what the director of the book trade office considered to be outmoded restraints upon publishing in France. These were the so-called *Mémoires sur la librairie*.[60]

Attacking the arbitrary nature of pre-publication censorship and post-publication seizures, Malesherbes would have replaced the vague punitive legislation with a limited number of clearcut regulations, including a single register of publication permits and a rationally graded structure of penalties for infractions. Because of their fears of reprisal, according to Malesherbes royal censors were inconsistent defenders of moral order; their scattershot condemnations only resulted in clandestine publishing and futile chases of illicit books. The director therefore would reduce the scope of censors' authority by having them administer the regulations routinely. In most instances, as long as authors requested permission to print, Malesherbes would waive censorship requirements and even allow writers the privilege of selling their works directly. If need be, the courts would decide upon books accused of being libelous or dangerous.[61] Defending authors, Malesherbes wrote in his third memoir: "Each philosopher, each orator, each man of letters, should be considered the advocate of what ought to be heard, even when he avows principles believed to be false. Sometimes it takes centuries to plead causes. The public alone can judge them, and in the end, if sufficiently instructed, it always will have judged well."[62] According to Malesherbes, government officials, the king excepted, ought to be subject to authors' critical examination; yet Malesherbes would not countenance personal attacks. Although he conceded pre-publication censorship of religious books, so-called works dealing with *les moeurs*, and others concerning the source of sovereign authority, Malesherbes pleaded for a wide range of toleration of these books. As for Protestant books, he expressed indifference.[63]

Malesherbes was much less solicitous of printers and booksellers than he was of authors. He considered poor and incompetent printers (especially widows) to be the source of piracies and illicit production and would have closed down shops in small, isolated communities. With police manpower thereby freed, shops in larger towns could be regulated more efficiently; journeymen and shopboys were to be surveilled; itinerant peddlers would be registered with the authorities; royal intendants and special commissioners were to assume the police duties of guild officers. Exasperated with the monopolistic practices of master book merchants, Malesherbes proposed reinvigorating the guilds by permitting married apprentices entry into them and by opening the Paris community of booksellers to qualified masters from the provinces. Anticipating the debates of 1789, Malesherbes sought to establish a balance between the libertarian and the regulatory. Just as public opinion and the law were to define the boundaries of free expression and the voice of the market was to determine sales, a newly efficient central authority would snatch police powers away from guild, church, and parlements.[64]

Except for increasing the use of *permissions tacites*, Malesherbes was unable to put his reforms into practice. In 1763 his father, Chancellor Guillaume de Lamoignon, was disgraced and Malesherbes had to give up the directorship of the book trade office. Over the next fifteen years management of the *librairie* remained relatively unchanged; however, the great affairs of the period—the troubles in

Brittany, church-state conflicts, fiscal and constitutional struggles between parlements and ministries, and finally the Maupeou coup—resulted in waves of illicit pamphleteering followed by frantic attempts at repression.[65] Meanwhile, the top crust of individual authors, led by Voltaire, Diderot, and Rousseau, saw their persecutions transformed into public apotheoses.[66] Mere scribblers, printers, and booksellers were not so lucky. In the 1760s, 35 per cent of those sentenced to the Bastille were connected with the book trade. In the 1770s it was 40 per cent.[67]

Yet reformers continued to criticize a repressive system which was as cumbersome as it appeared irredeemable. In 1776, for example, Marie-Jean de Caritat, marquis de Condorcet, produced a reasoned analysis of why censorship no longer should be tolerated. His argument was familiar. He cited the fluctuating values of the examiners, the public costs of supporting them, their failure to be impartial, and their nefarious influence upon authors forced to write about "safe" subjects. Condorcet reiterated Malesherbes's defense of criticizing public officials, viewing it as a citizen's duty; and he added that a free press was more likely to be a responsible one than a press that was shackled.[68] Thirteen years later, at the very moment the Declaration of the Rights of Man and of the Citizen was being debated, the playwright Marie-Joseph Chénier composed a furious *Dénonciation des inquisiteurs de la pensée*, in which he forsook dispassionate argument altogether, bitterly accusing censors of having sold their thought, reason, and souls to despotism. He mocked the traditional argument that ideas were free in France, as long as they were never expressed—"the Jew enjoys freedom of thought in the midst of the Inquisition's faggots"—and he boldly listed France's seventeen chief oppressors of liberty of expression. No one was exempt from Chénier's wrath—not the Sorbonne's faculty, not the episcopacy, not *parlementaires*, nor even the minister of foreign affairs. It was clear to the playwright that, unless all of the oppressors relinquished authority, the press would never be free.[69]

Just prior to Chénier's diatribe, Malesherbes in retirement composed a *Mémoire sur la liberté de la presse*.[70] The moment was auspicious. The public invitation by chief minister Étienne-Charles de Loménie de Brienne for "expert" opinions to deal with the upcoming Estates General had produced a torrent of uncensored printed advice, and book trade office director Poitevin de Miassemy was complaining about the complete breakdown in authority.[71] When he himself ran the office between 1750 and 1763, Malesherbes had urged wider use of *permissions tacites* and oral approvals as a means of reducing submission to formal aspects of pre-publication censorship. Moreover, for Malesherbes such expressions of royal grace illustrated the benevolent power of the monarchy. In 1788, however, Malesherbes changed position. Now he considered tolerated loopholes in the law as exemplifying bankrupt policies. During the previous quarter century authors had gained closer title to ownership of their literary property than ever before; and a significant number of books, whose publication had been monopolized by the rich sellers of Paris, now were in the public domain. According to Malesherbes, literacy in France had increased significantly and unprecedented numbers of French subjects were thinking for themselves. Yet oppressive legislation was still on the books; and Malesherbes mistrusted the Paris Parlement's recent advocacy of greater press freedom. He thought it veiled invidious intentions for those opposing its political program.[72]

Ever the magistrate, Malesherbes advocated a new comprehensive press law which laid emphasis upon both the rights and the responsibilities of authors. However, in light of the benefits derived by bureaucratic and corporate agencies involved in current procedures, he doubted whether the transformation of administrative censorship controls into those emphasizing a free press restrained by the threat of judicial pursuit, would stand a chance in France. Furthermore, Malesherbes did not trust the parlements which would have the final say in cases involving accusations of libel. Therefore, in keeping with the principles of the edict for non-Catholics which he recently had helped to formulate, Malesherbes offered alternatives which were equally pragmatic and voluntaristic. Writers desirous of heeding their own consciences and taking their chances in the courts might avoid submitting their work to pre-publication censorship; however, the magistrate would leave censorship controls in force for authors desiring guarantees from judicial pursuit.[73] Malesherbes's main purpose seemed to lie in winding down the corrupt system of *permissions tacites* and extra-official verbal tolerances.

In all honesty, Malesherbes seemed as tepid about his proposals for the press as most Protestants were about the Edict of 1787. After all, what he offered was less a ringing statement acknowledging freedom of expression than a modest program implementing what he hoped would represent the possible—in other words, a stopgap measure. While criticizing the outrageousness of punitive legislation, neither the misnamed *Mémoire sur la liberté de la presse* nor the equally mistitled Edict of Toleration broke fully with principles of older jurisprudence. The *Mémoire* hesitated at acknowledging unrestrained freedom of expression while the edict stopped short of recognizing freedom of public worship. As matters evolved, however, no attempt was made to implement Malesherbes' proposal. No new royal law ever replaced the *Code de la librairie*. As a consequence of non-enforcement and public disrespect, the censorship system simply crumbled. In 1789 journalists, paymasters of the royal censors, started withholding their contributions. In their turn censors were resigning their posts and torrents of unexamined pamphlets inundated the country.[74]

Recently Carla Hesse has described the disintegration of the *librairie*'s guild structures in 1789 and 1790.[75] As presses and printshops were established in unprecedented numbers, Article 11 of the Declaration of the Rights of Man and of the Citizen confirmed the failure of the old monarchy to manage the flow of the printed word. In place of an overarching restrictive general law, expanded upon through individual instances of repression, modified by virtue of a complex network of exceptions, and administered by competing jurisdictions and their police, a unitary positive statement was to emerge, appealing to natural rights and notions of common decency, and enforced by public opinion and the courts. The Constitution of 1791 certainly took pains to carve out a comprehensive description of libel.[76] Meanwhile it remained to be seen whether the implied "public safety" clause in the Declaration would protect society or else offer a screen for intolerance at least as menacing as the messy administrative structures of the Bourbon kings.

≺ III ≻

*The Course of Religious Toleration
in the Eighteenth Century*

In revoking the last of the corporate privileges won by Protestants back in 1598, the Edict of Fontainebleau (1685) argued that too few Calvinists remained in France to warrant their continued recognition as a religious community. Therefore, the surviving privileges of this community were to be withdrawn. Temples were ordered demolished, Calvinists were denied access to public worship, their ministers were given two weeks to leave the country, their schools were closed, and they were commanded to have their children baptized by parish priests and given Catholic instruction.[77] On the other hand, in treating the civic lives of individuals, the edict was less severe. Emigration of the Huguenot laity was prohibited, but those who had fled prior to publication of the edict were invited to return to France with the promise of the restoration of their confiscated property. Moreover, while denied a communal religious existence, Calvinists were to be left at peace to continue their commerce and enjoy their goods.[78]

Recognizing that destruction of formal Calvinist religious practice alone was an ineffective means of winning converts to Catholicism, Louis XIV's government after 1685 resorted to chipping away at the civil privileges that Huguenots still shared with Catholic subjects. Royal judges were awarded authority to remove children from suspect parents and give them to others to be reared as Catholics.[79] Public offices and professions were closed to those not possessing priest-granted attestations of Catholicity. Moreover, by creating the fiction that Huguenots were nothing more than lapsed Catholics and that Protestantism no longer existed in France (except for Alsace where it enjoyed special protection), the regime was able to defend itself from foreign accusations that it was conducting a terrible pogrom against Calvinists. Indeed, Huguenots were given the designation of "the newly converted" (nouveaux convertis) and were compelled to learn how to be good Catholics again. Along with other French subjects, their children were to be baptized by a priest, just as they were to be married according to "the solemn ceremonies prescribed by the holy canons, especially those of the last Council, and by our laws."[80]

Early in the reign of Louis XV, Duc Louis-Henri de Bourbon-Condé included a "Declaration concerning religion" (14 May 1724) in his consolidation of various aspects of French jurisprudence enacted piecemeal over the previous generation. The declaration's preamble pleaded consistency with Louis XIV's intentions, while blaming insincere conversions upon lax enforcement of the laws. Therefore, a vigorous statement was called for concerning illicit assemblies, education of children, religious tests for public officials, deathbed abjurations, and marriages.[81]

The declaration of 1724 asserted that Roman Catholicism was the unique religion in France and prohibited public assemblies for any other form of worship. The galleys, imprisonment, even death, were considered appropriate punishments for disobedience. Preachers at non-Catholic religious rallies might be accused of inciting revolt and could be subjected to public execution. Parents were ordered to have their children baptized in parish churches within twenty-four hours of the infant's birth. A national program of schoolteacher recruitment was to get underway, with villages paying instructors' salaries; the teachers would help indoctrinate children in the Catholic religion at least until age fourteen, with special attention paid to offspring of *nouveaux convertis*. Physicians were to make certain that seriously ill *nouveaux convertis* would receive Catholic spiritual consolation; priests visiting the sick were urged to be relentless in their exhortations; and relapsed individuals were to be dealt with mercilessly. Judicial officers, physicians, surgeons, pharmacists, midwives, booksellers, and printers had to present attestations of Catholicity. Finally, regulations on the celebration of Catholic marriages were to be observed by everyone, and parish clergy would continue to serve as quasi-state officials in recording the birth, marriage, and death of all French subjects.[82]

As long as *nouveaux convertis* still considered themselves Protestant, the legislation of 1724 represented the highwater mark of a policy of state-directed religious and civil coercion. Protestant public worship was forbidden, parental rights were cast in doubt, and professions were closed. For couples wishing to marry, the choice was either a union considered illicit by the Crown or acceptance of a Catholic sacrament. If the pair opted for the former ceremony, a Protestant preacher, considered by the regime to be an outlaw, would likely marry the couple at a nocturnal outdoor service "in the wilderness." Such a union, however, was, in the eyes of the law, worse than concubinage; it was felonious. The couple's property would then be at risk; and of course their offspring would be considered illegitimate. If the pair chose a Catholic marriage, they would have to bend to the requirements of the *curé*, who in turn determined the couple's religious sincerity. If the priest consented to marry the couple, some act of public acknowledgment was generally expected of them. Once the marriage was performed, the regime might be content with a fresh statistic of newly registered *nouveaux convertis*. However, what about the couple's consciences? And, as church officials well might worry, what about the conscience of the priest who officiated at the service?

Enforcement of the declaration of May 1724 was sporadic. Before performing a marriage some priests insisted upon lengthy instruction, formal abjurations, and regular attendance at mass; others rushed through the ceremony and glumly acknowledged that they never again would see the couple at church. Governors, intendants, parlements, and provincial Estates in regions with large Protestant populations had understandable difficulty accepting a fiction invented in distant Versailles.[83] As for the Huguenots themselves, although nothing occurred resembling the horrific Camisard guerrilla war of 1703–4, armed resistance against persecution tended to erupt whenever royal armies were occupied fighting enemies abroad. This happened most noticeably in 1744, re-creating for officialdom the image of rebellious Calvinist republicans in league with foreign powers. While it became increasingly clear that the tactics of 1685–1724 would never make France Catholic, what could be done? Lenain, the intendant of Languedoc during the 1740s, described the regime's dilemma:

Tolerance today is as useless as it is dangerous. As long as it has limits, as long as the king does not all at once grant them ministers, temples, and the re-establishment of the Edict of Nantes, Protestants will not be satisfied. To accord them part of their pretensions would not make them content, but rather would increase their audacity. Therefore, if the king does not wish to permit free exercise of the Protestant religion in the realm, it is absolutely necessary to assert firmness. But how to maintain it without forces and without troops?[84]

Following another outbreak of bloodshed during the early 1750s, juridical and philosophical opinion began to re-examine royal policy with an eye towards replacing sporadic repression with some form of limited tolerance. Few genuinely advocated a return to the disastrous seventeenth-century experiment, with Protestants forming armed corporate communities in possession of enumerated privileges. In Dauphiné, Poitou, Languedoc, and Provence, Calvinists were praying unmolested at open air services, in defiance of royal regulations. Local authorities tacitly acknowledged these gatherings. However, the issue with which mid-century reformers felt most comfortable was not freedom of worship but civil toleration. In 1751, for example, Vicomte Jean-Emmanuel de Guignard de Saint-Priest, new intendant for Languedoc, estimated that a hundred thousand souls in his province had preferred "wilderness marriages" conducted by fugitive preachers to negotiating with priests over degrees of outward Catholicity acceptable for a sacramental service. While Versailles might still consider Protestant couples as lapsed Catholics living in sin, a conscientious administrator like Saint-Priest perceived them as subjects mired in an irregular social situation not of their making. The state considered their children to be bastards, incapable of inheriting property. For a modern-minded official such circumstances were administratively inelegant and therefore unacceptable.[85]

Saint-Priest's reports began to find sympathetic ears. Of the juridical reforms proposed during the 1750s, perhaps the most widely discussed at Versailles was that of Guillaume-François Joly de Fleury, former attorney-general for the Parlement of Paris and purported author of the clauses in the declaration of May 1724 presupposing a *France toute catholique*. Writing in 1752, at a time when the Gallican clergy was denying sacraments to Jansenist Catholics, Joly de Fleury wished to accommodate these so-called heretics, as well as Protestants, within an all-embracing church guided by Parlement-inspired laws. According to the magistrate, the villains of the moment were the bishops of Languedoc and their clergy, who were demanding unrealistically rigorous—and, to his mind, illegal—tests of orthodoxy prior to admitting Christians to the sacraments. On several occasions, wrote Joly de Fleury, the Parlement of Toulouse had overruled the bishops and ordered priests to conduct marriages of *nouveaux convertis*. He concluded that denial of a sacrament must be subordinated to the magistrate's authority and the act of marriage itself must be confirmed not by a priestly blessing but by the mutual consent of the partners acting within the confines of both natural and civil law. Concerning the ceremony, the magistrate returned to a solution he claimed to have proposed back in 1728. Priests should conduct two types of marriages: a sacramental one for longstanding Roman Catholics and a non-sacramental blessing for *nouveaux convertis*. Priests should be made to understand that their role in either ceremony was primarily as a state agent. Furthermore, in registering births, priests should be prohibited from writing "bastard" beside the name of a child of *nouveaux convertis*, even if the parents were unable to produce a certificate attesting to a Catholic marriage.[86]

In Joly de Fleury's *Mémoire* the civil status of *nouveaux convertis* was an issue subordinated to a larger agenda. The Jansenist question, church-state relations, and parlementary politics were the magistrate's major concerns. Moreover, Joly de Fleury still accepted the fiction that France was Protestant-free. As had been the case in 1728, his proposals on *nouveau converti* marriage were tabled, and an attempt at reaching an accord between the governor and intendant of Languedoc on the one hand and the bishops of the province on the other broke down.[87]

Civil disturbances notwithstanding, toleration of Protestants as Protestants was nevertheless becoming a discussible issue from the 1750s onward. In this vein Jansenist religious and juridical opinion was important. A traditional Jansenist argument, initially articulated by Antoine Arnauld in 1686, had held that both juridically and theologically the revocation of the Edict of Nantes was justified. Needing to protect himself against accusations of crypto-Protestantism, Arnauld likened Louis XIV to a new Honorius who would eradicate Huguenotism much as the Roman emperor had wiped out Donatism.[88] Between Arnauld's time and the 1750s, however, the status of Jansenism in France altered dramatically. The papal bull *Unigenitus* declared it a heresy; Cardinal André-Hercule de Fleury persecuted Jansenists unmercifully; their writings were seized and suppressed; and they were being denied last rites.[89] Their bitter experiences therefore forced Jansenist thinkers into perceiving Protestant heresy in a new light, akin to the one in which sympathetic parlementary jurists were envisioning the Jansenist cause itself.

Distinct from arguments based on either Voltairean religious indifference or the administrative convenience of royal officials, Jansenist discourse sought to construct a rationale for tolerance upon Christian foundations. Never denying the probability of Protestant damnation, Jansenists nonetheless doubted whether coercion any longer served as an appropriate means of persuading heretics to escape their fate. At the same time mid-eighteenth-century Jansenist thought, emerging from the refusal-of-sacraments controversy, emphasized more than ever both the privatization of religious sentiment and desacralization of royal authority.[90] For example, during the late 1750s, in their *Questions sur la tolérance chrétienne*, the parlementary lawyer Gabriel-Nicolas Maultrot and Jansenist abbé

Jacques Tailhé blamed the revocation of the Edict of Nantes upon Jesuits and courtiers, while appealing for toleration based upon natural law principles, respect for property rights, and a need for the state to reassert itself as honest mediator rather than sacral arm in affairs of faith.[91] Subsequently, over the next two decades Abbé Louis Guidi, an Oratorian contributor to the clandestine Jansenist newspaper, the *Nouvelles ecclésiastiques*, further articulated the position.[92] Arguing that the status quo failed to check heresy, turned *nouveaux convertis* into hypocrites, and accomplished nothing to prevent their damnation, Guidi proposed granting civil marriage to Protestants as well as permitting Protestant parents to supervise the education of their children. Guidi fell short of accepting Protestant public worship, but he implied toleration of private forms. He urged the Catholic clergy to treat heretics benevolently. Their Protestantism might be an imperfect form of Christianity, he wrote; but Christian it was, and as such forged a weapon against the greater evil, philosophic materialism. Most important of all, according to Guidi, a tolerated Protestantism was bound to lose its fervor; its practitioners then would be ripe for conversion and thereby attain salvation.[93]

At least as fervent as Jansenist pamphlets grounded in theological argment were those perceived mainly in juridical terms—for example, the *Mémoire théologique et politique au sujet des mariages clandestins des Protestans de France* (1755), long attributed to Jean-Pierre-François de Ripert de Monclar, attorney general for the Parlement of Aix-en-Provence.[94] Generously estimating the existence of three million Calvinists in the country, the *Mémoire* challenged head-on the government's assertion of a Protestant-free France. It doubted the sincerity of those Protestants opting for Catholic baptism or Catholic marriage, adding that such forced practices worked against the interests of both church and state. Moreover, with priests who doubted the sincerity of so-called *nouveaux convertis* refusing to marry them and "wilderness marriages" considered invalid, Protestant couples were in a hopeless situation. Despite government prohibitions, stated the *Mémoire*, many opted for leaving the country—thirty thousand had parted for North America alone; and it conjured up the horrifying specter of depopulation. Finally, the essay suggested a theme that would later be exploited by others—a skepticism as to whether Louis XIV had ever intended to deny Protestants their civil status in the first place. Article 11 of the Edict of Fontainebleau was interpreted as permitting Protestants to remain in France unmolested; and a law of September 1685 was recovered—apparently never formally abrogated by Fontainebleau—tacitly recognizing marriages conducted by Protestant ministers.[95] The *Mémoire* proposed an unequivocal solution to the marriage question: have the king assume the role of the state's chief political magistrate and turn marriage into a civil affair. Stated the *Mémoire*: "If our kings once were able to have a Protestant minister take the place of a priest, with more reason can they have magistrates do the same today."[96]

Despite a small pamphlet debate engendered by the *Mémoire théologique et politique*, the intransigence of Languedoc's bishops during the 1750s hindered the government from making any major effort at ameliorating Protestant civil or religious status.[97] Nevertheless, during this decade at least the *nouveau converti* fiction was gradually abandoned. Calvinists obtained Protestant spokespersons, such as Paul Rabaut, who communicated openly with sympathizers at Court, like Louis-François de Bourbon, prince de Conti.[98] However, approaching sedition, Conti's plots in favor of the Huguenots came to naught, and during the 1760s a status quo policy punctuated by exemplary acts of repression guided the behavior of the royal minister in charge of Protestant affairs, Comte Louis Phélypeaux de Saint-Florentin.[99] Local authorities took the cue, and the consequences occasionally turned out to be atrocious fiascos. For example, the Parlement of Toulouse's dismal handlings of the Rochette, Grenier, Calas, and Sirven affairs were judicial crimes plain and simple.[100] Furthermore, they made for extraordinary copy in the hands of publicists. Enlightenment writers like Voltaire, Diderot, Jaucourt, and Condorcet seized the opportunity to court opinion with moral condemnations of the parlementary decisions in particular and of intolerance in general.

One must not discount the influence of the philosophes in advocating new policies towards Protestants.[101] Montesquieu's *The Spirit of the Laws* urged civil toleration of established religious minorities, with the state serving as a kind of referee among contending faiths.[102] Diderot's *Encyclopédie* article "Intolérance" was an implicit indictment of French church policies over the past century.[103] Chevalier Louis de Jaucourt's suppressed *Encyclopédie* piece "Tolérance" was a tightly reasoned treatise proving that the admissibility of several religions represented an act of brilliant statecraft.[104] Voltaire's *Traité sur la tolérance* (1763) reviewed the case of Jean Calas and laid the

groundwork for the philosophe's unflagging efforts at rehabilitating
Calas and fighting for Protestant civil rights.[105] Of course, the bases for
philosophe discourse were far different from those of Jansenists or jurists. Their own recent persecution had sensitized Jansenists to the
fate of other Christians. Moreover, they believed that a generous attitude towards Protestantism forged, in the long run, the straightest path
to Catholic conversion. For their part, progressive magistrates,
whether Jansenist or not, no longer wished to tolerate selective applications of unenforceable laws. They were unable to accept the false
premises lying behind the *nouveau converti* fiction, and they shud-
dered at the administrative messiness of law-abiding subjects being accused of irregular unions and denied civil rights. As for the
philosophes, they were anti-clericals pure and simple, fed up with epis-
copal interference in politics and determined to do their part in reducing the formal influence of religion in individuals' lives. That is why
while arguing for Huguenot civil rights, they remained curiously am-
bivalent or silent with respect to guarantees of free public worship.[106]

On the other hand, powerful forces continued to resist any improvement of Protestant civil or religious status. After 1745, Assemblies of
the Clergy regularly called for increasingly rigorous application of the
edicts of 1685 and 1724.[107] During Saint-Florentin's ministry, "wilderness marriages" were routinely de-legitimized and couples forcibly
separated.[108] In popular opinion Calvinism might still represent both
damnable heresy and corporate treachery. And the terms *tolérantisme*
and *philosophisme* were invented to define a supposed philosophe-
Calvinist conspiracy out to destroy both Catholic and royal tradition.[109]

Nevertheless, between 1765 and 1787 the evolution of juridical
opinion forced advocates of the status quo to take up defensive positions. In 1767, a royal councillor identified with Jansenism, Pierre
Gilbert de Voisins, addressed a pair of requested memoirs to Louis
XV.[110] The overriding purpose of the memoirs was to put the royal
conscience at ease in the event of a more tolerant policy towards
Protestants, by showing that such a policy would not contradict the
laws of the king's predecessor. Proving Louis XIV's benevolence towards his Calvinist subjects was indeed a tall order, but the royal adviser attempted it by interpreting the concluding sentence of the
Edict of Fontainebleau as a guarantee of civil existence for Protestants as long as they did not practice their religion outwardly. According to Gilbert de Voisins, the turn for the worse occurred with

the Edict of 1724, during the present king's reign, and the creation of the *nouveau converti* fiction. At the moment, however, in 1767, the councillor found Protestants assembling openly for services in Guienne, Languedoc, and Dauphiné; and they were marrying regularly "in the wilderness." The result was social chaos.

Gilbert de Voisins would correct the untidiness by supporting a traditional Catholic definition of toleration previously espoused in the sixteenth century: sufferance of error—"It is preferable to suffer or tolerate what cannot be prevented without greater inconvenience." He advised continuing the prohibition of outdoor Protestant assemblies, but proposed tolerating family and small group worship; he urged Catholic priests to baptize Protestant infants, but without threats or exhortations; he discouraged Catholic proselytizing of children of Protestant parents and advocated establishing schools for Calvinist youth, where general moral topics would be covered in a manner consistent with their, and with Roman Catholic, belief. Finally, Gilbert de Voisins proposed that Protestants be given a choice of marrying either before a secular magistrate or else before a *curé* who would perform the ceremony not exclusively as a church official, "but as a public official authorized by the state as well as by the church." Moreover, either the magistrate or priest would be entrusted with validating "wilderness marriages" so that offspring from them might be legitimized.[111]

Gilbert de Voisins's thinking was consistent with that of an emerging school of jurisprudence in late-eighteenth-century France.[112] In part it drew upon sixteenth-century traditions. However, it also contained a very modern ingredient. In place of punitive laws negligently enforced, the magistrate was offering a specific set of limited rights moderated by clear responsibilities. In his view the most pressing danger to society stemmed from the nocturnal outdoor religious assemblies of Protestants which could easily degenerate into bloody riots. So as to eliminate such occurrences he would tolerate limited private worship. Though public office and most professions were still to be denied Protestants, Gilbert de Voisins would legitimize their marriages and inheritances. For him Calvinists ought to be assimilated gradually into the citizenry, obeying protective legislation that was well-defined and rigorously enforced.

Because Gilbert de Voisins failed to convince Louis XV that his proposals were consistent with the intentions of the king's great-grandfather, they went unheeded. Following initial signs of hope in both the new reign and Louis XVI's progressive ministry under the physiocratic controller-general Anne-Robert Turgot, the government's failure to convert a Cour des aides remonstrance of 1775 into a general edict of toleration meant that any short-term improvement of Protestants' civil status had to emerge from sources other than royal legislation.[113] Local parlementary decisions and appellate court verdicts over contested inheritances formed the preliminaries to Protestant emancipation. In 1769 the Parlement of Toulouse began validating "wilderness marriages," and in 1778 the Parlement of Grenoble started recognizing Protestant testaments.[114] Defense attorneys such as Guy-Jean-Baptiste Target advertised the positions of their Protestant clients in widely distributed judicial *mémoires* which converted civil suits into public *causes célèbres*, and critics like Turgot and Condorcet joined the chorus of appeals in which claims to natural law took precedence over unenforceable punitive decrees like the Edict of 1724.[115] At the same time the Jansenist *Nouvelles ecclésiastiques* reinvented both St. Augustine and Antoine Arnauld as advocates of toleration, which in turn was seen as the surest means of winning souls back to Catholic truth.[116]

Nevertheless, despite positive parlementary decisions and successful courtroom appeals, no royal act of toleration could appear unless juridical minds were able to identify lines of continuity with earlier legislation. Advisers surrounding young Louis XVI insisted upon this, and magistrates committed to positive theories of jurisprudence were forced to accommodate their views to it. Moreover, practical considerations had to guide any strategy leading to emancipation: key churchmen had to be won over, contact had to be made with Protestant communities, the matter had to be guided carefully through the Royal Council.[117]

During the late 1770s Jansenist religious opinion coalesced with juridical discourse on the issue of Protestant toleration. For example, P.-A. Robert de Saint-Vincent, a veteran of the refusal-of-sacraments affair of the 1750s who eventually would prepare the Parlement of Paris for the Edict of 1787, argued passionately against a situation whereby Protestants were forced to profane the sacraments while being deprived of their natural rights to marriage and property.[118] What ultimately turned the tide in favor of emancipation, however, was a secular-pragmatist discussion of civil liberties, merging philosophe religious indifferentism with lawyerly logic. In this vein the arguments of Malesherbes were absolutely central, and the veteran magistrate's thought ultimately shaped the Edict of 1787.[119]

Malesherbes had shown an interest in the Protestants' cause as early as 1775. Entering Turgot's ministry as the official responsible for what had been known under his predecessors as *nouveau converti* affairs, he collected a full dossier on the Edict of Nantes, its revocation, legislation since 1685, and eighteenth-century criticisms of royal policy. What Malesherbes no longer could accept was what once had been a leading rationale for absolutism—a mercifully selective application of the law, punctuated by the royal grace. Malesherbes now envisioned this grace negatively, as a device for placing honest citizens at the whim of power-hungry administrators. Malesherbes's position on Protestants paralleled his position on authors, subjected as they were to the vagaries of official and would-be censors. Overseeing non-Catholic affairs, Malesherbes refused to enforce the punitive legislation concerning Protestants and tried to establish the groundwork for an emancipatory decree. However, his tenure proved too brief to bring his efforts off; and in May 1776 he once again was outside the government.[120]

While in temporary retirement Malesherbes composed a pair of treatises which he circulated privately. In the first, dated 1776, he argued that the revocation of the Edict of Nantes created precisely what Louis XIV had wished to avoid—namely a "nation" or alien corporate body within France. In order to return to the great king's original intentions, Malesherbes argued, Protestants would have to be integrated into French society; and to accomplish this their marriages had to be legitimized in a way acceptable to their consciences.[121] In his second unpublished memoir, Malesherbes saw no harm in offering Protestants rights of private worship or the liberty to marry before their own ministers. For the secular-minded magistrate, however, the religious aspects of toleration remained secondary. "What is essential," he wrote, "is to render to Protestants their rights as citizens." It was imperative for civil authorities to maintain registers of births, marriages, and deaths. These were to be the primary documents for all civil affairs. The clergy, Catholic and Protestant alike, was to have no role in the matter.[122]

Until 1784 Malesherbes did not get far, and the regime took practically no action with respect to Protestant civil or religious status.

Malesherbes himself remained outside the government. However, several new acquaintances of his—the diplomat Claude-Carloman Rulhière, the lawyer Pierre-Louis Lacretelle, Lafayette, and Rabaut Saint-Étienne—shared his interest in toleration and kept pressing for an emancipatory decree.[123] Malesherbes took up recomposing memoirs. His arguments now had become clearly defined: persecution was contrary to natural law and was depriving the kingdom of useful citizens; involuntary conversions were ineffective; arbitrary applications of the law discredited the state. Most important, Malesherbes worked up the argument that new legislation might be consistent with Louis XIV's principles; for, according to the jurist, the great king had never desired to remove Protestants from the body of the nation.[124]

In 1784 and 1785 Malesherbes wrote the pair of memoirs which, when printed, eventually formed the basis for much of the legislation of November 1787. In arguing his case, Malesherbes appealed to moral necessity and simple pragmatism: a discontented body of subjects was harmful to the state and "neither justice, humanity, nor reason permits condemning entire races to bastardy, so as to punish them for the heresy of their fathers."[125] In recalling the historical background of current Protestant status, the magistrate continued to whitewash Louis XIV. According to Malesherbes, Louis's intention was limited to eliminating Calvinism as a potentially dangerous corporate element in French political life. Subsequently the king received conflicting advice and was persuaded by his clergy to seek ways of ridding the country of heresy. This resulted in a contradictory policy of tolerating Protestant marriages (arrêt of 15 September 1685) while exiling Protestant ministers (Edict of Fontainebleau). The wars of 1685–1713 against the Protestant powers forced further intolerance upon Louis, and the Edict of 1724 was the ultimate source of all present misfortunes. Magistrates at the time liked the edict because, in their view, it forced the Catholic hierarchy to marry Protestants disguised as nouveaux convertis. But the bishops ultimately supported it because it brought Protestants before their tribunal of orthodoxy. By holding secret assemblies and marrying "in the wilderness," Huguenots, however, refused to cooperate; and during the 1750s they became pawns in the complicated religious-political conflicts then plaguing the French state.[126]

In evaluating the situation over the past generation, Malesherbes deplored the practice of sporadically enforced punitive laws against Protestants. For him a reasonable jurisprudence stating rights and responsibilities must replace legislation alternating between tacit tolerance and waves of persecution. While no one any longer believed in the fiction of *nouveaux convertis*, acceptance of it remained the basis of French legislation concerning Protestants. Malesherbes considered Protestant civil status to be a purely secular affair, based upon rights —not necessarily royal graces—common to all. He therefore urged the king to protect these rights, recognizing Protestants as belonging to a sect within the church and not as a party within the state. Malesherbes envisioned French society as an inclusive civil community; he pleaded for Jews and Moslems to be represented in a new edict protecting non-Catholics; and his vision of a multicultural yet assimilating France demanded policies of open, universal immigration.[127] Concerning the immediate problem of Protestant status, he called for a new law recognizing civil marriage; birth certification based either upon Catholic baptism or civil registration; and the gradual reintegration of Protestant pastors as French citizens.[128]

Through Malesherbes's efforts, as well as those of Rabaut Saint-Étienne, Lafayette, Loménie de Brienne, and Baron Louis-Auguste le Tonnelier de Breteuil, on 19 November 1787 Louis XVI granted the so-called Edict of Toleration.[129] As early as the previous February, Robert de Saint-Vincent had worked at neutralizing opposition in the Parlement of Paris, and by the year's end it was clear that the edict would face no difficulty from that quarter.[130] As the culmination of forty years of juridical, religious, and philosophical attacks upon the status quo, the law proved to be a timid affair. Far less encompassing than the articles on religious liberty either in the various American constitutions or in the Habsburg Emperor Joseph II's *Toleranzpatent* of 1781, the edict failed to legitimize non-Catholic public worship or institute civil marriage for all subjects.[131] Calvinist ministers were enjoined from preaching or delivering certificates of marriage and burial (Article 4); and members of their flock were specifically denied access to the teaching profession and to judicial or municipal office (Article 1). This notwithstanding, the edict awarded Protestants a right to civil existence without having to consult Catholic authorities. Protestants might, if they wished, ask the *curé* to marry them. Failing to obtain his consent or displaying an unwillingness to do so, they had recourse to a royal judge.[132]

Between December 1787 and May 1789 there were two sources of dissatisfaction with the edict. On the one hand pamphleteers and churchmen still considered the edict as unnecessary and engaged in a rear guard action to prevent parlementary registration of it; on the other hand supporters of free Protestant public worship criticized the edict for ignoring such a pertinent aspect of religious liberty. To make their point, conservative pamphleteers argued that "tacit tolerance" of Protestant religious practice already existed in France. Indeed, they claimed that Calvinists were worshipping inside their homes; that their marriages and burials—even when presided over by an illegal minister—were no longer challenged; and that the courts were unwilling to deny inheritances to the children of their unions. Therefore, no specific legislation guaranteeing civil marriage was either necessary or desirable. What made matters worse, argued the pamphleteers, the Edict of 1787 desacralized the French monarchy, thereby weakening it irreparably. Instead of protecting a Catholic church with which it was seamlessly linked, the Crown was permitting itself to be maneuvered into the reduced political role of civil mediator. Clearly, wrote one pamphleteer, a "philosophe-republican" plot was behind it all, undermining the traditional position of the monarchy as defender of the *culte public* with the hypocritical claim of offering charity to religious minorities.[133]

Although three parlements refused to register the Edict of 1787 and two more tried to qualify its terms, the government held fast to its principles. It paid little heed to the formulaic remonstrances of the Parlement of Paris or the more substantial ones of the 1788 Assembly of the French Clergy; and it pointedly suppressed a *mandement* of the bishop of La Rochelle urging his priests not to cooperate with the marriage law.[134] However, dissatisfaction with the edict was not confined to traditionalists. Others disliked the fact that the edict still left unresolved the question of freedom of worship. Rabaut Saint-Étienne wrote bitterly: "The law allows us to be jewelers or wig-makers and assures that our children will no longer be bastards. According to the prejudices of the age, that is considerable; but in the long run it isn't very much."[135] As he futilely attempted to restore to the edict a retracted article specifically reintegrating Protestant ministers, on 6 December 1787 Rabaut Saint-Étienne wrote to a correspondant in Breteuil's ministerial office: "If you deny [to Protestants] the object which means most to them, namely a religious liberty ever preferable to civil liberty, you will be informing them that you do not wish to satisfy what touches them most deeply."[136] Failing to obtain what he wanted, Rabaut Saint-Étienne nevertheless remained undaunted. Addressing his co-religionists, he noted that the Edict of 1787 at least did not specifically proscribe their need to worship. Therefore, "it leaves us the freedom to extend ourselves little by little, provided we do it without ostentation and with care."[137] Finally, he urged the pastors of Languedoc, whose very existence was not yet formally acknowledged by the government, to restrain their flock from revealing openly their disappointment with the edict. Instead, the pastors were to persuade worshippers that civil toleration now existed on the firm foundations of the law and not upon "the errors, passions, and caprice of royal ministers, placemen, or their most mediocre toadies." Assuredly stretching the intent of the edict beyond its outer limits, Rabaut Saint-Étienne added that "however much freedom of worship is not formally authorized . . . [articles 4 and 25] presuppose its tacit acceptance, even to the point of noting the existence of pastors, and we have reason to hope that the king's generosity will shortly grant us more specific approvals."[138]

Of course, it was not royal bounty but revolutionary decree that provided Rabaut Saint-Étienne with his wish. Following the Edict of 1787 by nearly two years, the Declaration of the Rights of Man and of the Citizen was the next significant legal document in France that addressed the issue of religious liberty. When all was said and done, Article 10 was eventually interpreted as acknowledging free public expression of religious belief. Still, like their predecessors in the Old Regime, revolutionaries were less comfortable with guarantees of public worship than with the award of other civil rights. In the Assembly during August 1789, freethinkers as well as Catholics shrank at recalling the devotion of "wilderness Protestantism" and hesitated at sanctioning such ardent expressions of faith in a solemn declaration.[139] Indeed, one may justifiably ask the question: how much beyond the Edict of Toleration did Article 10 advance the course of religious liberty? Louis XVI's preamble to his edict had maintained: "We ought not to suffer that our laws punish [non-Catholics] needlessly for the misfortune of their birth by depriving them of rights that nature inexorably advances in their favor."[140] To recapitulate Article 10: "No one must be disturbed because of his opinions, even in religious matters, provided their expression does not trouble the public order established by law."[141] The old monarchy took pains to note the limitations of the law, forever restrained by established rights of nature. For their part revolutionaries also acknowledged rights of nature; however, they did so in a pinched, crabbed manner, preferring to qualify any purely libertarian interpretation of religious freedom with the reminder of the law's absolute responsibility in defining and protecting what it perceived to be the common good.[142]

≺ IV ≻

Conclusion

It seems fairly obvious that in defining "the French idea of freedom" in August 1789, deputies identified the law as both framing and absorbing the rights of man. It would be tempting to see the overexcited and fearful politicians of 1789, as they sought to avoid the precipice, desperately grasp the law they were making as the necessary abstract basis of their authority; and this new abstraction was intended to replace the one they had recently rejected, namely that revealed in the royal will. At any rate, as they debated a statement of rights protecting religious expression and written thought, the deputies seemed to display an atavistic need to qualify any purely libertarian set of principles by referring to the law. Concerning civil liberties, the deputies were aware of the twisted path trodden by the old monarchy during the eighteenth century. During the 1720s the regime had made grandiloquent claims of complete control over one's religious faith and written word. Such control was, in essence, a defining characteristic of French absolutism. From the beginning, however, religious controversialists and heretics alike challenged this control by deed and in print; and the monarchy sought ways of dealing with these individuals while maintaining the front of absolute power. By creating the fiction of *nouveaux convertis* and veiling contraventions of its press code behind the system of *permissions tacites*, the regime tried to advertise its benevolent power through its ability to distribute exceptional grace. As the century evolved, however, royal administrators, jurists, and philosophes interpreted such grace as a sign of weakness, not of strength; conversely, with respect to religion and the press, periodic enforcement of the royal will was increasingly envisioned as tyranny; and by the 1780s the Crown itself was referring to the limitations of its own law, forever restrained by rights of nature. While such discourse may well illustrate in microcosm the fatal decline of French absolutism, revolutionaries in August 1789 indeed were groping for a more compelling expression of the law than the tarnished will of their kings. That they primarily saw the law as punitive is undeniable. Nevertheless, by using it to frame imprescriptible rights, particularly those of religious liberty and freedom of expression, revolutionaries left hope that their law would be more just, as well as more persuasive, than the authority they had recently rejected.

Property, Sovereignty, the Declaration of the Rights of Man, and the Tradition of French Jurisprudence

THOMAS E. KAISER

HISTORIANS OF BOTH the right and the left have argued that the Declaration of the Rights of Man and of the Citizen in particular and the French Revolution in general laid the foundation of modern "bourgeois" property relations. To Hippolyte Taine, the French Revolution, for all its political convulsions, represented essentially a "translation of property," which provided the Revolution with its "inner strength, original motor, and historical direction."[1] In recent years, William Sewell has seen in the Revolution a "revolution in property," going so far as to insist that "'bourgeois property' was not so much unfettered by the French Revolution as it was created."[2] In Sewell's view, the Old Regime engendered a reaction against itself in the form of an Enlightenment critique of feudal property relations; inspired by Locke, the philosophes preached a new concept of proprietary right based on a "natural right" to property acquired by labor, which undermined corporate proprietary right and public claims on individual entitlements. The night of 4 August 1789 and the codification of the Declaration of Rights, writes Sewell, was the "great turning point of the Revolution," the moment when property began to change "from a publicly defined and regulated right that marked its possessor as a member of a particular community into a set of physically palpable possessions that a person had annexed to himself by his labor and was free to use in any way that did not infringe on the liberty of other citizens."[3]

In this chapter I do not intend to challenge the notion of a "revolution in property"; the thorough analyses of property and proprietary right before and after the Revolution made by Marcel Garaud and others can leave no doubt that if ever there was a revolution in French property relations, 1789 was it.[4] Rather, I intend to reconsider the ideological mechanisms of this revolution in property and the relationship of those mechanisms to prerevolutionary notions of proprietary right, paying secondary attention to associated developments in the area of taxation. In my view, the "natural and imprescriptible," "sacred and inviolable" right of property sanctioned by Articles 2 and 17 of the Declaration and implicitly acknowledged in Article 14 had important precedents in Old Regime jurisprudence, which well before the Revolution acknowledged the existence of such a right. Conversely, the process whereby modern property right was established during the Revolution, far from eradicating altogether the prescriptive legal heritage of the Old Regime, time and again required its qualified affirmation. For these reasons, modern French property right is better envisaged as the product of a wider application of certain elements of Old Regime jurisprudence than of a violent Lockean assault from without.[5]

≺ I ≻

Property under the Old Regime

Property right in the Old Regime was primarily governed by the diverse local customary laws regarding possession, disposition, and succession contained in the hundreds of local legal codes that had been drafted, usually under royal sponsorship, during the later Middle Ages or shortly thereafter.[6] Composed of varying admixtures of Roman and Germanic principles of civil law, these codes were subject to revision; but despite some royal initiatives in this direction, they were never superseded by a national civil code until the Revolution. Indeed, in comparison with the monarchy's initiatives in changing the structure of the state, royal efforts to reform and integrate local proprietary law during the early modern period appear very timid, indeed.[7]

Although some of these local law codes allowed for considerable freedom to hold and to dispose of one's property, they often made property disposition a complex procedure because of the many distinctions they made among kinds of property and the different sets of laws governing each kind: noble property was regulated differently from nonnoble property, immovable property from movable property, and inherited property from acquired property.[8] Notwithstanding these rules, jurists and, it appears, the general public perceived in property ownership an undeniable element of volitional liberty. To Pierre-Jean-Jacques-Guillaume Guyot, *avocat* and jurist, a proprietor "can dispose, as it pleases him, of the thing that belongs to him . . . so long as he does not violate the laws or the rights of others."[9] Because property was the "right in something that belongs to us privately, apart from all others," argued the eminent jurist Robert-Joseph Pothier, it was the "essence of this right that two persons cannot each have full possession of the whole of the same thing." Thus, although a good could be owned by more than one person, this meant only that there was more than one right in the good, not that the possession of any one right was itself shared, "because the share that one has in a good is not the share of others, and each has only the right to dispose of his share."[10] In more common usage, property right connoted an even greater sense of volitional discretion on the part of its owner, and non-technical definitions commonly referred to ownership of property as "absolute." Thus, Pierre Richelet, grammarian and barrister, defined property as "the right that belongs privately and absolutely to a person in some good, public function, or office," while Antoine Furetière, academician and linguist, defined it as "the resource, the domain, the seigneury of something of which one is absolute master, that one can sell, engage, or dispose of at one's pleasure" and observed that "fiefs and inheritances are held as full property."[11]

If fiefs were owned "privately and absolutely," who was the owner of a subinfeudated fief—the lord or vassal/tenant? From the thirteenth century until the Revolution, rights in fiefs were divided into two sets: the direct domain held by the lord and the usufructuary domain held by the vassal/tenant.[12] Until the early modern period, property right was generally assigned to holders of the direct domain; even Charles Dumoulin, the towering genius of sixteenth-century French jurisprudence who was in many respects hostile to feudal tenures, maintained this position.[13] By the eighteenth century, however, legal opinion, including that of the feudists, had shifted in favor of the holder of the usufructuary domain. If the direct domain had originally incorporated true proprietary right, argued Pothier, it had lost it through alienation; thus, whereas the usufructuary seigneur was "properly speaking the proprietor," the holder of the direct domain could claim no more than "the right of superiority," that is, "the right to have himself recognized as the suzerain by the proprietors and possessors of the inheritances held from him" and "the right to demand certain duties and payments."[14] Hence even before 1789, the distinction between true ownership and the mere "right of superiority," a distinction critical in the eyes of the revolutionaries, had been well established.

What relation did private claims to property have to rights claimed by the central state? Early modern French historians have often been so taken with the emergence of royal claims to and the use of sovereign rights that they have tended to overlook or to minimize the fairly consistent royal professions of belief in the sanctity of private proprietary right from the late Middle Ages onwards. As has already been noted, the monarchy was reluctant to intervene abruptly in the local laws regarding proprietary right and claimed as its responsibility the protection of existing proprietary claims. In theory, the problem of establishing a sphere of individual property entitlement distinct from the public sphere of the state came down to the problem of disentangling the elements of property right and lordship inherent in the notion of the king as suzerain. If medieval tradition, as expressed in the words of Philippe de Beaumanoir, thirteenth-century jurist and royal official, had viewed kingship, and feudal lordship generally, as based on the principle that "fief and justice is a single whole," it fell to royalists of the early modern period, who sought to attribute to the king the sole origin of "justice," to establish the contrary principle that "fief and justice have nothing in common."[15] Elaborated upon by Charles Loyseau, one of the subtlest and most influential jurists of the early seventeenth century, this principle became the basis of a distinction between "public seigneury" and "private seigneury" that would have a long history in French jurisprudence. In postrevolutionary times it would appear in the attribution made by the jurist Jean-Etienne-Marie Portalis of "property" exclusively to the individual and of "empire" exclusively to the state.[16]

As Loyseau conceived of them, "public seigneury" consisted essentially of a "superiority or authority" exerted by a public official principally upon persons and only indirectly upon goods, whereas "private seigneury" consisted of "the true property and current enjoyment of something" exerted by a private person principally upon goods and only indirectly upon persons. Following Jean Bodin,[17] Loyseau acknowledged the historic existence of so-called seigneurial monarchies, in which rulers disposed of both private and public seigneuries, that is, maintained ownership of all public powers, persons, and goods within the polity. But in Loyseau's view, seigneurial monarchies, subjects of which, having lost their personal freedom and their property, were essentially slaves, had to be considered contrary to nature and to Christian principle;[18] humankind was by nature free, argued Loyseau, and, in monarchies that dealt with them as such—namely, the "royal monarchies" of modern Europe—it was clear that private seigneury belonged exclusively to the people, while public seigneury lay exclusively in the hands of the prince. "Just as private seigneury does not run to public power," wrote Loyseau, "so does public seigneury, which consists of Justice, confer no private seigneury or diminish at all the perfect liberty of the subject or person falling under his jurisdiction, but on the contrary, increases and conserves it."[19] Under royal monarchies, Loyseau contended, holders of private seigneuries, being true property owners, were less restricted in the disposition of their goods than were princes in their use of public power, since the latter were bound by considerations of public utility to use their power with moderation. "Private seigneury is perfect property, which one may use at will, but the use of public seigneury must be regulated by justice and must be directed toward the utility and necessity of the people."[20] The proto-liberal implications of such notions would be repeated throughout the Old Regime. In one notable formulation, Claude Fleury contended that the very liberty of the subject was secure only when "the individual has complete disposition of private right and the sovereign or his officers have complete exercise of public right."[21]

One critical aspect of this distinction between public and private seigneury was its implicit and sometimes explicit anti-feudal implications. Dumoulin's hostility to many aspects of feudal tenures is well known;[22] Loyseau, while he could hardly deny the existence of aristocratic suzerainty, that is, the usurped and prescriptive right of lords to exercise a portion of public seigneury, nonetheless considered such suzerainty "absurd";[23] Claude Fleury, historian and *érudit*, regarded the suzerainty of medieval war lords as having embodied the same confusion of public and private spheres of right characteristic of oriental tyrannies;[24] and the jurist Pierre de Caseneuve, in arguing that the French king was far greater in his role as sovereign than as lord, strongly suggested that under feudalism, which had developed out of violence and usurpation, the underlings of the barons had suffered a subjection scarcely better than slavery: "it is far more glorious for a prince to command free persons than to command slaves," he wrote, "because the Doctors have commonly held that the subjection of Fiefs is a kind of servitude."[25] If the emphasis placed by these authors upon the "usurpation" and "tyranny" standing behind feudal tenures served most directly to delegitimate noble claims to sovereign power, they also had the effect of casting doubt upon the legitimacy of at least some of the "odious" feudal dues traditionally paid to lords by their retainers. In the perspective developed by jurists working in the monarchist tradition, the volitional element of feudal contracts could not help but be thrown into question and the basis of feudal obligation reduced essentially to prescriptive right.

How well did this public/private model account for property/state relations as they actually existed under the Old Regime? Some historians, notably William Church, have contended that the model was sufficiently inexact and the exceptions to it produced by ordinary statecraft so numerous that in the end theorists had to do away with it.[26] I would contend that the longevity and frequent reiteration of the model indicates its continuing influence, but there is no denying its failings in accounting for Old Regime practice.

First, allowances had to be made for the reality of feudal fiefs and venal office-holding, however regrettable they might have appeared to the monarchy. Both fief-holding and venality of office tested the delimitation of public and private spheres of right by bringing into conflict the supposed monopoly of public power of the sovereign and the supposed absolute right to property of the subject. If seigneurial rights of justice were historically usurpations of what had originally been offices revocable at the king's discretion, Loyseau argued, prescription had by now conferred upon these offices the status of true property. As Loyseau put it, seigneurs now "have the property they usurped."[27] To account for such usurpation in his model, Loyseau had to complicate his private/public model by distinguishing between two degrees of public seigneury: "sovereignty," that which belonged to the state, and "suzerainty," the usurped part of public seigneury.[28]

Venality of office posed analogous problems: who owned an office, given that its acquisition involved an original transfer of funds from a prospective buyer to the state, in return for which the state assigned the holder a public function?[29] In the end, Loyseau and succeeding

jurists were again forced to refine the public/private model by attribut-
ing to the office holder a property right that was, to use Loyseau's
terms, "in" an office, not "to" an office: that is, the state retained ownership of the power vested in the office which the office-holder held as
a usufructuary right, while the office-holder held as a matter of proprietary right only the fund invested in the office. In the end, the central
difference between a seigneur and a venal office-holder lay in the fact
that the former, unlike the latter, had usurped his jurisdictional powers and converted an office into a seigneury; "for in effect, there is
no other difference between seigneuries and offices except that seigneuries are property, and venal offices the simple function or exercise
of public power."[30]

A second complicating factor in the public/private seigneury
model was that just as feudal lords, and to a lesser extent venal office
holders, still exercised public powers, the king, in certain respects,
enjoyed a proprietary right to his title and his domain. Although
there had emerged a well-articulated notion of kingship as office during the later Middle Ages, even this juridical discourse of public law,
as Sarah Hanley has noted, borrowed heavily from the language of
the customary private law of inheritance for its conceptualization of
the laws of royal succession.[31] During the seventeenth century, the
notion of kingship as an office distinct from its occupants was partially eclipsed, as Herbert Rowen has shown, by a notion of kingship
as royal property. When subtended by doctrines of blood right, this
proprietary notion appeared to make the kingship inseparable from
the royal person.[32]

The royal domain, a motley complex of proprietary rights in land
and rights to tax, evoked similar analysis. Although some jurists argued for a distinction between the king's private domain and that of
the state, the dominant tendency in the early modern period was to
consider the two inseparable.[33] But if kingship and the royal domain
were to be treated as private property, then what, in effect, would be
left of public seigneury? With kings, nobles, and venal office-holders
all scrambling to make individual proprietary claims on the state,
the state risked becoming little more than a joint property with each
claim to power expressed in terms of a proprietary right.

Finally, there were the complicating issues that surrounded the
notion of sovereignty, whose gradual emergence in the late medieval
and early modern period has driven many historians, like William

Church, to argue for a profound disequilibrium between the spheres of public and private right under the Old Regime.[34] Although royal suzerainty allowed the king to demand of his subjects certain revenues, it was his sovereignty that entitled him to levy the heaviest part of the royal tax burden. Such powers to tax flew in the face of medieval traditions, which had it that the king should live principally off his domain, indeed, that the domain was to be preserved in order that the king not seek to impose "extraordinary" taxes on his people —an argument recapitulated by Bodin and others throughout the early modern period.[35] The problems taxation posed for upholders of the principle that "fief and justice have nothing in common" are well known, particularly in the cases of Bodin and Loyseau. Jurists were clearly at pains to deny that kings could confiscate the property of their subjects at will via their taxing rights, yet as William Church and others have shown, they became decreasingly reticent in assigning to the sovereign taxing authority.[36] Bodin still denied to the king the right to impose extraordinary taxes without the consent of the Estates under normal conditions;[37] Loyseau vacillated, first agreeing with Bodin but later falling in with the swelling ranks of royal jurists who determined that the king could tax without the consent of the Estates.[38] As Gaines Post has demonstrated, the legal basis of this right, namely necessity in the face of emergency, was clearly laid out in the high Middle Ages;[39] but it remained to the early modern jurists to translate the doctrine of public necessity in emergencies into an argument for more or less permanent taxation and to add to this argument the rights of prescription. Although Loyseau characteristically insisted that the right to tax without consent of the Estates did not give the prince private seigneury over the goods of his subjects any more than public seigneury gave him the right to enslave them, he argued in effect that because the French king, like other sovereigns, had so often imposed extraordinary taxes without consent, his right to do so had become part of the king's bundle of sovereign rights.[40] Given the persistence of older arguments opposing the constitutionality of such royal powers of taxation, it is certain that such arguments did not universally persuade, yet they were effective enough to grease the skids of the royal fiscal apparatus for the rest of the Old Regime.

Sovereignty also entailed the authority to grant rights and privileges, most notably to the various *corps* and communities that served a variety of public and communal functions. The juridical status of

such corporate institutions as the guilds rested, like so much else in
the Old Regime, upon a mixture of private claims to proprietary right
and a sovereign acknowledgment of that right. In fact, many corporate bodies had little more than immemorial possession to justify
their rights and monopolies, but in theory only royal sanction in the
form of royal letters could legally establish a *corps*, whose rights had
to be confirmed by each succeeding king at his coronation.[41] Sovereign recognition of the rights of corporate institutions, as Charles de
Lavie put it, was "the breath that makes them live";[42] conversely,
royal suspension of recognition could be the kiss of death. Kings were
entitled to revise or even to revoke royal letters for reasons of public
utility. Occasionally they did so, most prominently when Turgot invoked such a right on behalf of the Crown in his hotly contested edict
suppressing certain guilds in February 1776.[43] Notwithstanding the
acknowledgment of some authorities, like Lavie, that all corporate
institutions "hold their power . . . from the sovereignty under which
they were established,"[44] the Parlement of Paris saw in Turgot's edict
a direct and despotic attack upon property rights and protested
against the loss of guild masterships in terms that echoed Loyseau's
argument against the arbitrary suppression of venal offices as "an oppression and pure injustice."[45]

Adjudication of the legal status of *corps* constituted but one of
many powers bearing on proprietary right that was exercised by the
monarchy as overseer of *la police* under the Old Regime. In addition,
the state imposed a host of production and distribution regulations
intended to maintain and direct the flow of goods for purposes of promoting the general welfare as it was understood by governing elites.
Among the most important of such regulations were those issued to
insure the steady supply of grain to urban markets. As Steven Kaplan
makes clear, the right to dispose freely of one's property was bound
to suffer limitation under the web of constraints imposed by the
monarchy. Yet such constraints, he points out, were not promulgated
in order to undermine liberty—whose advantages from the standpoint of production were well understood by administrators well before the coming of the physiocrats—but rather to prevent liberty
from degenerating into license and prompting social disorder among
the urban populace. Whatever the conflicts between individual rights
and government regulation, neither completely subverted the other
under the Old Regime.[46]

In conclusion, it is clear that the jurists of the Old Regime acknowledged a prescriptive right to private property, but one that was conditioned by local customary right, seigneurial law, and sovereign power. Likewise, it is clear that French jurisprudence in acknowledging the king's sovereignty placed the king in a position to confiscate virtually any property, but that in general the king shrank from making use of such rights, however much some of his actions supported charges that he was acting as a seigneurial monarch. Ultimately, all depended upon royal discretion in the use of sovereign power whose limits were ill-defined. The French clearly considered themselves to be "free" in their understanding of the term, not slaves, and that meant at a minimum that their claims to property would be respected and royal powers used with moderation. In France, wrote Fleury, "all individuals are free. No slaves, liberty of domicile, travel, commerce, marriage, choice of profession, acquisitions, disposition of goods and successions."[47] Property, while surely subject to legal restraints and royal encroachments, was considered in Loyseau's perspective to be freer in its exercise than was sovereignty. And if early modern Frenchmen had lost their right to consent to royal taxation, some people at least could claim individual proprietorship in the state itself.

≺ II ≻

From the Old Regime to the Revolution:
The Language of Conflict

The dialectical model developed by Sewell and other historians, which pits the notion of natural rights to property held by the philosophes and revolutionaries against the prescriptive rights of the Old Regime, would suggest that natural rights argument was alien to Old Regime proprietary juridical discourse. Such, however, no longer appears to be the case. In recent work on guilds, Michael Sonenscher has challenged Sewell's model, noting the repeated instances wherein guildsmen defended their rights within a broader natural rights framework that subtended their prescriptive claims; and he has concluded that in general, combinations of natural and prescriptive right were "basic to the conventions of eighteenth-century French jurisprudence."[48] Appeals to natural right, argues Sonenscher, were more than arguments of last resort, even if in the end positive law modified the implications of such appeals. Such was clear in the Paris Parlement's remonstrance against Turgot's edict of February 1776 abolishing many guilds, in which the Parlement sought to justify the guilds' entitlements not upon historic right but squarely upon right deriving from "nature."[49] For earlier periods, William Church and others have demonstrated how Bodin rooted his defense of private property in natural right; and much the same can be said for Loyseau, who also wrote of a "nature that has made us all free," free both in one's person and in one's property.[50] Throughout the Old Regime and the Revolution, the interplay of natural and prescriptive rights to property would remain complex, sometimes supporting and sometimes opposing one another. It is undoubtedly true that over the course of the eighteenth century appeals to natural property right increased in relation to appeals to property on the basis of privilege; but as we shall see, prescriptive right to property never disappeared, even during the Revolution. The ambiguities implicit in the notion of property right as a natural right to dispose of one's property according to law would be exploited by parties as diverse as the Crown, the nobility, the guildsmen, and the Jacobins.

One particularly compelling precedent for the establishment of natural right that had considerable impact on French Revolutionary jurisprudence was the legal status of allodial land. Allods were territories, mostly found in southern and eastern France, that remained in theory completely and in practice largely free of seigneurial obligations.[51] Widely recognized in French law, allods might well be considered anti-fiefs: whereas fief-holding implied the division of direct and usufructuary rights, the allod owner possessed both direct and usufructuary domains; whereas tenancy in fiefs traditionally involved the subjection of the tenant to the jurisdiction of his lord, the allod was said to be "held from God," and owners of allods therefore free of seigneurial jurisdiction, although its defenders were anxious to point out that they fell under the jurisdiction of the king as sovereign. In this respect, no other form of tenure embodied more perfectly the monarchist notion that "fief and justice have nothing in common." Although many allods in fact had become "noble allods," that is lands that had accrued to local lords who by prescription had acquired the rights of immediate justice over them, allods were the closest approximations to perfectly private seigneuries.

Before the sovereignty of the king was firmly established in France, the chief opponents of allods were the local aristocracy. Local lords considered allods fair prey for incorporation into their seigneury. During the meeting of the Estates General of Blois in 1577 they attempted unsuccessfully to establish the decidedly anti-allodial maxim of "no land without seigneur," already inscribed in some local customs, as a nearly universal principle of the realm. In contrast, the monarchy was generally well disposed toward allods, even if royal jurists of the sixteenth and early seventeenth century were uncertain about the allod's historical origins, sometimes arguing that allods derived from royal concessions and other times from lands held privately before the Frankish conquest and thus outside royal suzerainty. In either version, royal jurists could usually wring from their analyses an indictment against the creeping anti-allodial tendencies of the lords. If the king of France had to respect the property rights of individuals, held Benedictus, "inferior seigneurs are even less entitled than he to pretend to the property and domain of others, which can belong to individuals freely, and allodially, unless they have been proved subject to and charged with services; and the burden of proof lies with those who make the claim."[52] In the work of Louis Chantereau-Lefebvre, seventeenth-century jurist and one-time intendant, the saga of the allod was woven into a long institutional history, whose roots lay deep in the tradition of royal anti-feudalism. In the wake of the Frankish conquest, he argued, land was held either as royal domain or as allods; but the progressive usurpation of royal prerogatives by the avaricious lords, the transformation of lifetime grants of land and powers by the lords into hereditary property, the gradual encroachments of seigneurs on allodial liberty, and the allods' incorporation into fiefs had had the effect of turning the mass of Frenchmen into near chattel. "The French . . . not having owed with regard to their persons or with regard to their property any duty or service but to sovereignty, which is the true and essential mark of liberty unknown in the time in which we live, the use of Fiefs changed us into half-slaves."[53]

Even as he wrote, however, the winds of political change had already begun to alter the politics of the allod. Driven by the need to generate more revenues to finance its military ventures, the Crown in the seventeenth century turned more and more to the exploitation of real and alleged domainial rights. In a series of edicts and administrative maneuvers, the Crown began to claim seigneurial rights over all French territories, including land previously held as allods. Issued in 1629, Article 383 of the Code Michaud stipulated that all lands were henceforth to be considered within the seigneurial jurisdiction of the king, except in cases where clear title was held by another lord; in other words, not only was the principle of "no land without seigneur" now re-affirmed for the whole kingdom, but a royal suzerainty was asserted such that it was now the king, not the lords, who was allowed to bring allodial land under direct domain.[54] As Auguste Galland, administrator of the royal domain, put it in his disquisition on the matter, "the king being universal seigneur and sovereign of all lands . . . they must be presumed to proceed from his predecessors and subject to his rights."[55] In 1692, Louis XIV issued an edict which re-affirmed a universal royal direct right over France; all lands, allods included, were now said to derive from royal concessions over which the king held imprescriptible fiscal rights: thus, those now holding allods were to be charged with back payments of the *franc-fief*, although some exceptions were made for areas with customs stipulating "no seigneur without title."[56]

Studies made of the royal domain and the fate of allods make it clear that royal policies in this direction were part of a campaign to farm the royal domain more efficiently—not so much by making the domain more economically productive, as the physiocrats wanted, but by expanding its claims to include property previously thought to lie outside it. To achieve this end, the monarchy sought to draw up new land registers, to collect arrearages on taxes and rents due on domainial and non-domainial land, and, when such attempts failed, to sell exemptions from these impositions to those who were threatened with them.[57] In many ways, this exploitation of the domain resembled the Crown's exploitation of venal offices: on some shaky pretext, the Crown was able to coerce proprietors of domainial lands to pay for something they might well argue they already owned.[58]

Contemporaries were able to perceive the sort of game the Crown was playing, and they often expressed fears that it portended the onset of "despotism." In the 1770s, the physiocrat Guillaume-François Le Trosne offered an extended analysis of royal domain policies in which he took aim at the long history of royal promises made to lease-holders on royal domains and then broken and of other royal efforts to lay claim to property the king did not own; notable among such efforts was the edict of 1692, which, according to Le Trosne, asserted "the principle that all land held as a noble or non-noble free allod derives from the Crown, even though such a tenure is formally admitted by a number of customs." To Le Trosne, the history of the royal domain was marked by a "succession of arbitrary fiscal laws . . . which show to what lengths a despotic administration lacking all principle can go."[59] Even if he was, as a physiocrat, an advocate of royal initiative, it is hardly surprising that Le Trosne would denounce royal efforts to promote feudal tenancy; what needs emphasis here is that Le Trosne's critique fell within a well-established pro-allodial tradition of French jurisprudence based upon natural property right.

The clearest and probably most influential such defense can be found in the work of the early seventeenth-century jurist Pierre de Caseneuve who was called upon to defend the allodial status of land in Languedoc in the 1640s. According to Caseneuve, the allods of Languedoc had their origin in the most basic and "natural" form of property—namely, the freehold, upon which there rested no seigneurial dues. They were thus unlike fiefs, which did not enjoy "the natural liberty" of allods and consequently constituted only an "imperfect possession."[60] Later, property in Languedoc had come under the domination of Roman law, whose provisions allowed property to be held as its nature dictated, namely "free and clear of all servitudes, particularly those introduced by the right of fiefs."[61] In other words, whatever modifications Roman law had introduced, it had preserved the essential natural qualities of the allod intact. With the coming of the Franks, the newly established kings had been quick to sanction the prevailing Roman law of Languedoc and Aquitaine and their successors repeatedly did so until the end of the Middle Ages. At the same time, however, there arose a threat to the allod in the form of the encroaching feudal lords. Denounced by Caseneuve in the harshest possible terms, the lords stood guilty of imposing feudal laws and seigneurial rights on whatever land they could enfeoff. "The counts and other seigneurs have hated this freedom of inheritances, and spared no sort of violence to destroy the independence of the allods." In Languedoc and Aquitaine, "there was no sort of violence, oppression, and injustice that they would not use to subject the allods under the yoke of feudal domination"; and with the king unable to protect the natural

freedom of allods, small allod holders, terrified by the violent retribu-
tion of the lords that awaited them if they did not do so, transferred
allods into feudal property under the lords' jurisdiction.[62]

Filled with the rhetoric of royalist historiography, Caseneuve's
work came very close to indicting the entire system of feudal tenures.
The product of disorder and usurpation, fiefs were, in Caseneuve's
words, "imperfect property"; indeed, Caseneuve believed that it was
even incorrect to say that fiefs were held "in property" at all.[63] Yet in
the end Caseneuve's purpose was not to cast aspersions on the French
lords or their land holdings, but to modify the policy of the Crown. Returning to the well-rooted distinction between public and private
seigneury, Caseneuve sought to persuade the king that his own glory
and prestige were wrapped up not in his rights of "feudal domination,"
but rather in his rights of "royal domination." Although Caseneuve
admitted that in some parts of France the king did possess rights of
suzerainty and did derive revenue from "feudal domination," he was
at pains to argue that in Languedoc such was not the case. In Languedoc, natural land tenures had at least partially withstood the challenge
of feudal usurpation, and Caseneuve appealed to the king to maintain
this battered tradition by respecting the allodial status of property and
foregoing his own domainial claims. Caseneuve denigrated the prestige conferred by the king's "feudal domination"—after all, the lords
also possessed it—and played up the glory of "royal domination,"
which only the king enjoyed. Once again we hear the refrain that by
forsaking claims to the property of his subjects, the king did not de-
tract from but rather enhanced his glory, "for it is much more glorious
for a Prince to command free people than slaves."[64]

Caseneuve's defense of the allod was echoed in the proclamations
and petitions of later seventeenth-century local officials, who protested the imposition of royal dues in the name of "natural liberty"
and a "natural immunity preserved since the beginning of the centuries."[65] Similar arguments were made against royal domainial policies down to 1789. Even though the amount of land effectively held as
allods probably decreased over the eighteenth century because of royal
encroachments on them, protests against such encroachments and
other policies regarding the domain flourished, effectively transmut-
ing charges of violence and usurpation against the lords into an indictment of royal "despotism." One anti-Maupeou pamphlet of the 1770s
claimed that the domainial policies of the Crown would "destroy the

right of property held by all citizens and leave no other proprietor than the Suzerain," and objected to royal efforts to use claims to a universal direct right as the basis for fresh impositions; according to its author, French law stipulated there could be "no seigneur, no tax, no servitude without express title, or at least without ancient possession and reasonable cause."[66] In a remonstrance of 1775, the *Cour des aides* insisted that "it is in listening to the universal testimony of the public that Your Majesty will learn up to what point financiers have abused their arbitrary power in the administration of all the rights included in the lease of the Farms, under the name of the Domain."[67] And in a highly celebrated case of domainial rights along the riverbanks of the Garonne during the 1780s, the Parlement of Bordeaux, charging the Crown with leading "an attack against public liberty and property," raised the specter that should such an attack succeed, "nothing will be assured,"[68] a sentiment shared by the Parlement of Toulouse, which, according to the *Mémoires secrètes* of Louis Petit de Bachaumont, was now formally on guard against "the extension of the tyrannical system that the Domain raises today."[69] At the same time that monarchists were seeking to undermine *parlementaire* opposition by conjuring up images of an oppressive "aristocracy," the opposition was returning the compliment in kind.

Debated widely in polemical literature, royal domainial rights and their abuse were also the subject of serious juristic scholarship, although rarely was this scholarship not tinged with political interest. In many respects, the basic arguments both for and against the king's policies had already been developed in the seventeenth century.[70] If, like Chantereau-Lefebvre earlier, eighteenth-century royalists acknowledged that some lands had enjoyed allodial status in the past, they insisted that such was no longer the case. "The free allod," declared the jurist Bosquet flatly in the later eighteenth century, "does not exist in France."[71] If allods persisted at all, Bosquet contended, they were not true allods, that is, free of all suzerainty. Royal defenders continued to argue in accordance with the August 1692 edict that the king as seigneur of all seigneurs enjoyed the right of universal direct, a right defended as late as 1787 by Calonne before the Assembly of Notables.[72] Since no land was without a seigneur, ran the argument, allods should be considered merely special kinds of royal concessions drawn from the royal domain, not true freeholds. Arguing from the fundamental law against alienation of the royal

domain, royalists held that the king was in fact legally prevented
from establishing true allods, since doing so would necessarily entail
stripping from the domain rights of suzerainty irrevocably belonging
to it.

Those who fought for the allodial status of land invoked the same
range of rights invoked by Caseneuve. In one learned defense of the
allodial status of land in St. Quentin, the barrister Louis Hordret defended his clients in the "declared war" with royal domainial agents
by offering an extended analysis of the natural right to property acquired by humankind before the establishment of society. "Everyone," he wrote, "freely possessed the resources that had been attributed to him by Providence and that he had made valuable by his care
and labor." Hordret embedded such appeals to natural rights in a
broader argument from Roman and customary law, as well as royal
sanction. Summing up his case, Hordret wrote that "the original and
natural liberty of resources or goods, the erection of St. Quentin as a
commune, with the most formal expression of continued absolute
freedom from all seigneurial rights, numerous confirmed charters of
freedom, an immemorial possession of the most peaceful enjoyment,
the enlightenment of the tribunal . . . all testify on behalf of the city
against the Domain of the King; all join together in favor of the inhabitants and of their free allod."[73]

Other scholars developed the historical scaffolding for such argument, much of which recalled Caseneuve's analysis, but generally
laid charges of usurpation and violence more at the door of the Crown
than at the door of the nobility. The progressive medieval incorporation of allods within feudal tenures was interpreted away as a natural
result of the acquisition of allods by noble fief-holders, so that the
"ideas of nobility that had first passed from vassals to fiefs had to pass
subsequently to allods"; infeudation of allods was explained away as
a right inherent in the allods as a natural freehold. As the jurist François Hervé argued in the 1780s, because the allod is a "free and absolute property, from its nature flows the faculty to dispose of it at
will"; hence the owner of the allod had the right to infeudate his land
and subject it to seigneurial dues. After all, Hervé reasoned, if a vassal
of a lord had the right to subinfeudate his land, all the more should an
allod-holder, possessing both the direct and usufructuary domains,
have the right to infeudate his.[74]

To Hervé, it was not the nobility who had threatened the sacred rights of the allod, but the king, whose unconstitutional assertions of a universal direct since the sixteenth century had meant instituting a "universal feudalism" that "existed only in the imagination or in the wishes of the *traitants* who made the greatest efforts to establish it." If the king could act arbitrarily "each time it is a question of the interest or the rights of his domain," Hervé asked, "what other law could he not also revoke?"[75] Given this argument, it was now possible to defend the allodial status of properties against the seigneurial rights of the king, while protecting seigneurial rights on infeudated vassal/tenants holding land within the allod.[76] By this neat trick, the tyranny that Caseneuve had alleged against the noble lords was now levelled against the king, while the nobility reaped the benefits of seigneurial lordship that Hervé justified on grounds of allodial natural right.

Clever as it was, the defense of the seigneury on the basis of its alleged allodial status had its deficiencies. First, not all, indeed not most seigneurial lands could pretend to allodial status. As Hervé admitted, there were some customs in France in which the principle of "no lord without seigneur" clearly applied and only in a minority of customs was the opposing principle of "no lord without title" clearly stipulated; the majority of customs were silent on the matter, and in the areas governed by them allodial status would have to be decided on a case by case basis.[77] Second, most allod holders did not want to undermine the principles of feudal tenure altogether. Even if they wanted to protect themselves against royal encroachments on their property, allod-holders, as Boutruche has shown in the case of Bordeaux, continued to undermine the allodiality of peasant tenures they wanted to enfeoff.[78] Finally, and in the long term most important, the seigneury, notwithstanding pretensions to allodial status, came under increasing attack for being inherently unjust and economically inefficient.[79] Traditionally, historians like Sewell have identified the philosophes and reform-minded administrators as the source of this critique. But recent work has focused attention on similar attacks arising from the peasantry in the form of lawsuits directed against seigneurial landlords, although it is difficult to determine whether the language of such lawsuits alleging that certain seigneurial rights had been "usurped by violence" and were "consequently odious"—language certainly familiar to royal jurists—was used by the peasants themselves or merely by the bourgeois lawyers who argued their cases.[80]

The Enlightenment critique of seigneurialism, especially in its physiocratic form, is sufficiently well known not to need recapitulation here.[81] Several points, however, should be made. First, although this critique was undoubtedly liberal and individualistic in its tendencies—allowing André Morellet, for example, to argue that the general interest was best served when "each citizen makes the most varied, the most extended, the most unlimited use of his property" consistent with the rights of others[82]—even those, like Diderot, who believed profoundly in private property right generally, retained strong moral reservations regarding the indiscriminate use of property right, particularly when that use ran against public utility. Countering Morellet's argument that grain might be hoarded by its owners even in times of famine, Diderot objected that such a notion was "a principle of Tartarus, of cannibals, and not of a civilized man." "Is the sentiment of humanity," he asked, "not more sacred than the right of property, which is limited in peace, in war, in an infinity of circumstances, and for which M. l'abbé preaches respect to the point of exposing us to being killed, having our throats cut, and dying of hunger?"[83]

Second, although much of the Enlightenment critique of seigneurialism, even in its physiocratic form, rested on a theory of natural right to property, the physiocrats and their allies clearly recognized other elements to property right, including considerations of public utility and even historic prescription.[84] Property right might have originated in pre-social times, but that right was, as a number of physiocrats agreed, virtually unenforceable and economically fruitless unless a power existed to protect it. Once such a power, namely the state, exerted its "tutelary authority," the natural legal basis of property was necessarily altered.[85] For if natural law was the basis of positive law, positive law could at the same time determine the limits of the natural right to dispose of one's property. "The limits of liberty," wrote Le Mercier de la Rivière, "should not be more arbitrary than its extension; it is thus the laws of the nation alone that determines them; it is the common will of the nation that determine the way in which everyone can enjoy and dispose of his properties, without hurting the common interest."[86]

Freedom to hold and dispose of one's property was in the social state counterbalanced by the state's requirements for protecting it and the property of others. To justify the fiscal impositions imposed by the state, the physiocrats developed a theory of co-proprietorship:

a supposedly non-arbitrary portion of all net land revenues were to go to the sovereign as a matter of proprietary right, a right that, in theory, was separable from the right of individuals to the remainder of such revenues. Thus, when a proprietor sold his/her land, what he/she was really selling was only a share in the property, the other share being retained by the king. In theory, because landowners had freely consented to alienation of a portion of their property to the sovereign in return for protection of what they retained, co-proprietorship appeared to preserve the integrity of natural right and to allow the physiocrats to deny that freedom was lost in passing from the natural to the social state. "Far from being opposed to the right of landed proprietors, the institution of the tax is on the contrary a use of their right to property."[87] But it is doubtful that outside the circle of true believers in physiocracy, many others agreed that the king in taxing land revenues was merely taking possession of his property. As one anti-Maupeou tract put it, granting to the king co-proprietorship of all lands was "to attribute to him the lion's share; it is to destroy all obstacles to his will, no matter what they are; it is to make it easy to destitute and destroy the Magistracy, which dared to renew its offensive remonstrances in the face of absolute will."[88]

Finally, even if in theory labor invested in land was the origin of all property, the physiocrats were forced to recognize that in postfeudal France most property did not have clear title based on some original investment of labor; as Turgot put it, almost all properties were originally "founded on usurpation" and enjoyed as their "best title . . . the prescription that it has acquired against the public."[89] Did this mean that such usurped rights were to be voided? Hardly. The marquis de Mirabeau in no uncertain terms proclaimed it as his "political principle . . . to respect public law so much that all title to property, even the most egregiously acquired in the past, be one of assured and peaceful possession; that all agreements, even the most onerous and forced, be considered sacred in society."[90] As Turgot put it in the case of the *banalités*, "this kind of property is surely not very desirable, but I want all the consideration for it that one would show for the most respectable property."[91]

Ideally, thought the physiocrats, most if not all seigneurial rights would be abolished and a more "natural" pattern of landholding instituted; but the central problem here was that these rights had themselves become property and could not merely be cancelled without repayment, or the entire structure of property—which the physiocrats surely did not want to endanger—might be put into jeopardy. Economic imperatives, at least in this respect, clashed with proprietary right.[92] The best way to resolve the contradiction in the physiocrats' view was through voluntary renunciation of seigneurial rights by their owners. The physiocrats hoped to motivate seigneurs to renounce some of these rights by demonstrating the inefficiencies of seigneurialism, especially with regard to their collection. In cases where seigneurialism was undeniably profitable, the preferred physiocratic solution was the repurchase of such rights in accordance with complex schemes of indemnification, schemes that clearly pointed the way to similar ones initiated during the Revolution.

Despite their regard for feudal property, the physiocrats in the end undoubtedly helped to undermine it. Anxious to push the pace of reform, the physiocrats were not above proposing measures that severely strained seigneurial property rights, nor did they shirk from campaigning for these measures in language drawn from the rich tradition of royal anti-seigneurialism. Pierre-François Boncerf, writing on behalf of Turgot, announced that he could show how the feudal law establishing the seigneury "had developed in anarchy, was consolidated by tyranny, and . . . had silenced the laws and legitimate authority it had usurped."[93] Others wrote similarly of feudal law as a product of "tyranny" and "anarchy" and took special aim at the seigneur himself. "The seigneury became a kind of despotism that made the proprietor the absolute master of the full extent of his territory; hence servitude became nearly universal; hence the rights of *main-morte*, which was . . . a modified slavery."[94]

Pressed by the critics of seigneurialism, the feudists of the later eighteenth century launched a counter-attack. The critics of seigneurialism, they argued, had gotten their history and hence their law wrong. "One hears everyday that seigneurial rights are odious," wrote the jurist Joseph Renauldon in the 1760s, "but I say that this language is that of prejudice, of ignorance . . . of ingratitude," for what seemed to critics "odious, is in fact but the slightest sign of a very great liberality." The fact was, Renauldon contended, that the French nobility, far from tyrannizing the population and trying to enslave it in the wake of the Frankish conquest, had generously shared their territorial conquests with the land's inhabitants. The great lord "created no other prison than the full extent of his seigneury; he permitted others to settle on the land, to cultivate it, and to clear it freely"; the only charge was "a small share of the fruits, a few days work during the year in the service of the seigneur, these are principal marks of dependence of a captive, who, burdened with chains everywhere else in the world, would have spent all his life screaming from the bottom of some jail."[95]

To project further the image of a feudalism with a human face, feudists now sought to breathe a fresh legitimacy into feudal obligations by placing renewed stress upon the volitional element that attended their creation. Seigneurial dues were now made to appear as the result of bilateral agreements freely entered into, not the product of acts of usurpation brought about by violent means; as the feudists now held, what legitimated seigneurial dues in the present was not only an increasingly contested prescription, but the sacred vows of contract. The fief, insisted Hervé, was in its origin and essence "a simple voluntary concession made for an indeterminate time in exchange for military service," and thus a "perfectly synallagmatic or bilateral contract"; aside from the juridical rights vested in them, what set fiefs and seigneuries apart from other kinds of property was not the form of such agreements, but simply their terms—land in exchange for the "recognition" due the seigneur.[96]

Obviously intended to blunt the critique of feudal rights as usurpations, the argument made by the eighteenth-century feudists was more touched by the winds of reform than has generally been recognized. Renauldon acknowleged that not all seigneurs had been magnanimous in the past or were so in the present and that if some seigneurial rights were "just and legitimate," there were others that had originated in "usurpation" and "the laws of the strongest." Indeed, most notable in Renauldon's analysis of seigneurial rights are the distinctions he drew among them on the basis of their humanitarian implications and their status as free concessions. Much like the revolutionaries later on, Renauldon differentiated between rights "based on equitable motives, the liberalities of the seigneur, or on the more or less onerous conventions, that were free and voluntarily consented to by its parties," and those bearing "the vestiges of the slavery of our fathers" imposed by "conquerors who dealt with their prisoners in chains."[97]

By returning to the notion of feudal contract as an emanation of the right to dispose freely of one's property, the feudists, without erasing the line between allodial and non-allodial land, made titles to seigneuries appear all the more translatable into the language of natural and Roman law. In his celebration of Charles Dumoulin, the jurist Pierre-Paul Henrion de Pansey was willing to admit that French legislation before the advent of Dumoulin had been a "political monster, the son and father of anarchy," and the product of a time when France was "covered with injustice, violence, crimes, unhappiness, tyranny, and slaves." But like Descartes, Dumoulin had rationalized into a coherent system of natural laws the apparent disorder he confronted. As if a physiocrat, he "returned to the source of all laws in natural right; he distinguished that which flows from it immediately from that which was founded on convention, usurpation or privileges." The result was that from Dumoulin's time onwards, no one was any longer "oppressor or oppressed, tyrant or slave"; all were held together in contracts reinforced by "the sacred ties of nature."[98] The real, it seemed, had become rational.

In preaching feudalism with a human face, the feudists did little to help the king, who in the closing decades of the Old Regime found himself charged again and again with "despotism" and with showing a sovereign disregard for the property rights of his subjects. The increasingly desperate conditions of French government finance pushed the government into taking ever more radical remedies supported by ever broader extensions of sovereign and suzerain right. The response was predictable. One pamphleteer raised the specter of all property becoming a "mere shadow."[99] The Parlement of Paris in remonstrance after remonstrance rose to the protection of individual proprietary right, defending it, like liberty in general, as an extension of both the "constitution of the state" and "nature."[100]

Like the seigneurial lords, the king was not unresponsive to accusations of despotism leveled against him in the matter of property rights. The king's defenders once again tried to lessen the impact of such criticism by charging that it only served to promote the cause of oppressive "aristocracy" and by contending that only in a powerful monarchy could liberty reign. The two "moral powers" of nature—property and government—complemented one another, Jacob-Nicolas Moreau contended, and surely government could not exist where there was no liberty or property.[101] Royal edicts proclaimed the king's devotion to the cause of property right, as for example when the king freed the serfs of his domains and argued that such enfranchisement

constituted a "return to natural law."[102] Standing before the National
Assembly on 23 June 1789, Louis XVI formally promised to respect
all properties, seigneurial rights, and privileges, while inviting proposals regarding disposition of the royal domain and calling for an
end to serfdom through indemnification.[103]

That time was running out on both absolutism and seigneurialism
was obviously due to more than one reason, but from the standpoint
of legal and political argument it can be said that both had, in effect,
failed in the political consciousness of many Frenchmen to preserve
the integrity of private property from the abuses of power. In the case
of absolutism, public seigneury appeared to be undermining private
seigneury, thereby raising fears of seigneurial monarchy, rebaptized
as "despotism." In the case of seigneurialism, much of the property
claimed by the lords had come to appear as products of unjust use of
usurped public powers, vestiges of the past which the Crown was either unable or unwilling to abolish fast enough. Even before the Revolution, as we have seen, apologists for seigneurial property responded
by trying to wrap such property in the sacred mantle of natural right.
The Revolution would test just how far that strategy would succeed,
as revolutionaries struggled with the problems of generating a new
positive law for a new order of humanity.

≺ III ≻

The Revolutionary Moment and
the Declaration of Rights

If there was anything the French appeared to agree upon at the start of
the French Revolution, it was the sanctity of private property and the
need to provide better security for it. Such beliefs were clearly and repeatedly expressed in the *cahiers de doléances* drawn up in the spring
of 1789. Beatrice Hyslop has counted in the hundreds the number of
cahiers among all three estates which stipulated the inviolable, sacred nature of property, the hitherto inadequate protections for it,
and the necessity of providing for the swift and complete compensation of property seized on behalf of the public.[104] A strong consensus
reigned on the need to provide some measure of popular consent to
taxation, and some criticized the Crown's abuse of domainial rights,
including the dispossession of lease-holders on the royal domain and

the harassment of property owners through land surveys and litigation over land titles.[105] While opinions differed on the matter, many *cahiers* called for the simple dissolution of the royal domain, even though such a measure would violate the old fundamental law regarding its inalienability.[106]

With such strong sentiment coming from the provinces, it is scarcely surprising that the defense of property rights in the face of royal despotism was on the minds of many legislators as they made their way to Versailles in the spring of 1789. Hardly had the Estates General reconstituted itself as the National Assembly, when as one of its first acts it moved to protect the property rights most at risk in face of a possible royal bankruptcy, namely those of the state's creditors. On 17 June 1789 the Assembly passed a motion drawn up by Guy-Jean-Baptiste Target and Isaac-René-Guy Le Chapelier assuring the state's debt holders that once the "principles of national regeneration were established," the Assembly would re-examine and consolidate the public debt by immediately "putting the creditors of the state under the honor guard and loyalty of the French nation."[107] By way of reassurances, the Assembly went so far as to declare on 13 July that, given national promises to pay interest on the debt, no person in public office would henceforth be permitted to utter "the infamous word bankruptcy" or in any way fail to fulfill public fiscal guarantees.[108]

But what was this almost universally acclaimed right to property? In most proposals for a declaration of rights, there was a curious homogeneity in answers to this question as well as a common vagueness and brevity. Much language regarding property right recalled that of the *cahiers*: for the duc d'Orléans the right of property was "inviolable," a right "of which one cannot be denied, even for reasons of public interest, unless one is compensated at the highest price and without delay"; for the marquis de Condorcet, "no man can be deprived of his right to the property he enjoys except by virtue of a judgment rendered according to the law, according to the forms it prescribes, and by a tribunal it has instituted"; for Target, property was "a right that belongs to each man to use and dispose exclusively of certain things; the inviolability of this right is guaranteed by the Political Body."[109] Such statements obviously foreshadowed Article 17 of the Declaration, composed by Adrien Duport and ratified by the National Assembly on 26 August. Indeed, Duport might have con-

ceived of the essential content, if not the precise wording, of Article
17 well before 26 August. We know he played a major role during the
previous spring in drafting the general *cahiers* of the Parisian nobility, one of whose provisions—"that property will be sacred, that no
portion can be taken except for public utility and providing that a
complete indemnity be fixed publicly and paid in advance"—closely
resembled Article 17 of the Declaration.[110]

Even if Article 17 did have its origins in a vague pre-existing consensus, it should be noted that its ratification occurred at a time of
considerable disagreement within the "patriot" movement over the
precise implications of the "sacred" right of property and other related issues. The debates of early August had revealed deep cleavages
of opinion regarding the status of seigneurial and ecclesiastical proprietary rights, and it had taken all Duport's efforts at compromise
to cobble together and ratify the historic Article 1 of the 4–11 August
decrees that formally abolished the "feudal regime."[111] Moreover, as
Keith Baker has shown, the legal basis of constitutional right, for
which the Declaration was supposed to be a preface, had not yet been
settled, leaving those like Jean-Joseph Mounier, who favored maintaining some traditional aspects of public law, contending with the
Rousseauists, who argued in favor of a single fresh act of popular
sovereignty.[112]

In light of such divisions, what is striking about the drafting and
passage of Articles 14 (on taxation) and 17 by the National Assembly
is not the controversy they engaged, but the lack of it. Article 14 did
invite some possibly interesting debate (there does not seem to be
any good record of it) over the question of whether taxes should be
stipulated as alienations of private property, and Article 17 did
arouse some discussion of the terms "fair and prior indemnity"; but
settlement was reached fairly quickly in both matters, the Assembly
finding in the latter case that Duport's original language was sufficient proof of its commitment to private property.[113]

That consensus on Articles 14 and 17 was reached quickly might
be attributed to pressures to get on with other business, but a more
compelling explanation is that for the moment conflict was intentionally avoided, in part through the use of vague and abstract language. The Declaration makes no direct reference to the dismantling
of the "feudal regime" or to the controversies it had already engendered, and when during the drafting of Article 14, wording came too

close to deciding between whether property right was natural or social in origin, such wording was either dropped or altered. Indeed,
there is considerable reason to agree with the comte de Clermont-
Tonnerre, who, two years after the Declaration was ratified, criticized
it for, among other things, not defining the word "property." As a result of the confusions that this failure had bred, he argued, usurpation
against property rights had continued. In an age when property rights
were declared sacred and inviolable, "there is not one proprietor sure
of not seeing his harvest taken away by a sophism"; indeed, "every
time one wants to take hold of a possession, it suffices to deny (as has
been done) that it is a property."[114]

What is in any case clear is that Duport sought a compromise between those who argued on behalf of a declaration which emphasized
the natural origins of property and those who wanted to emphasize its
social origins. Duport argued that if rights had to be translated into
positive law, there were nonetheless universal rights whose validity
did not depend on statutory provisions, rights that met the minimal
requirements for a free existence. The role of the Declaration, he contended, was to define this minimum, even if it was perfectly well understood that these minimal rights would be redefined and limited in
the constitution and positive law. "The object of a declaration," he
wrote, "is thus to embrace all kinds of rights. What difference does it
make if they contradict the constitution? The Declaration is there to
establish them, the constitution is there to modify and circumscribe
them."[115]

Property rights in the Declaration were thus "inviolable and sacred," but like other natural rights they were limited by considerations of public utility and the rights of others as determined by law. In
this respect, the program outlined by the marquis de Lally-Tollendal
would be fulfilled. "Let us certainly return to natural right, because it
is the principle of all the others; but let us move quickly through the
chain of intermediary principles, and let us hasten to descend into
positive law."[116] The product of a fragile political consensus, the principles of property right enunciated by the Declaration represented a
distillation of common opinion on the requirements for a legitimate
property code, but the precise provisions of that code remained to be
established. Disputes over that code would tear France apart.

If traditional scholarship has it right that the major battle would be
between defenders of prescriptive and defenders of natural right, it

should be pointed out that the battle lines were a far more confused affair than such a simple division would suggest. For one thing, the left did not rest content with the argument from natural right, but harnessed as well the old royalist argument from public utility to justify its own occasional regulation, expropriation, and redistribution of wealth. If appeals to public utility—behind which lay the Rousseauist claim that property had a social rather than natural origin—proved useful in making the case against hated seigneurial rights, they were problematic in that they threatened to undermine any and all claims to property by making property right dependent upon how the new regime defined public utility. As we shall see, no revolutionary government would risk overturning the entire structure of property holding; and thus in the end the argument from natural right was used by the left not only to undermine "feudalism," but also to reassure property holders—especially purchasers of confiscated public lands—that title to their goods was written indelibly into the code of nature and that it therefore could not be revoked in the name of public utility.

Another complicating factor was the use of the argument for natural right made by defenders of prescriptive property in their own cause. For example, in the debate regarding rights of inheritance, the liberty of individuals to deed their property as they wished became a right defended not by the left, which urged that individuals be required by law to divide their estates equally among children on grounds of equity and "reason," but by the center-right, which saw in the unrestricted right to deed property a means of preserving customary law. To the arguments of the left that in requiring equal sharing of inheritances the state was not violating natural right but only interpreting it, the opposition pointed out that such restrictions contradicted the very principle of property inviolability embraced in the Declaration. "Could one call oneself a proprietor," asked François-Jérome Riffard de Saint-Martin, "if one lacked the free disposition of one's own goods? or if one is forced to leave it completely to persons designated by the law?"[117] In such a debate it was not always clear who was advancing the cause of "bourgeois" property.

The struggle over ecclesiastical lands and rights further muddied ideological waters. Committed to the redemption of the national debt and driven by other fiscal needs, revolutionaries were not long in casting a lean and hungry look at Church properties to provide immediate revenues and collateral for further state loans. What is striking in the ensuing debates is the extent to which the left restated the monarchy's previous case on behalf of the royal domain and the extent to which the right sought shelter in individual natural property right to preserve first estate titles and revenues. Emphasizing the distinction between the status of the individual and that of the clergy, the left pressed the argument that the nation, as heir to the royal domain, had the right to appropriate ecclesiastical lands and revenue on the grounds that the corps of the clergy, as the mere recipient of royal/national *largesse*, did not enjoy the same proprietary entitlements as individuals, not even the usufructuary rights formerly claimed by *engagistes* on the royal domain.[118] Indeed, the left insisted that the revolutionary government should be no less aggressive in pursuing the just proprietary claims of the nation than the king had been in insuring the integrity of the domain; as Jacques-Guillaume Thouret put it, "one of the most efficacious acts of regeneration that the nation can exercize by the authority of the constituent power is to recover all the immovable property that has no real owner," property that it would presumably dispose of as best suited the common interest.[119]

Defenders of ecclesiastical revenues and land titles responded, to be sure, by alleging an array of historic titles and prescriptive rights. But sensing a need to build a political bridge to all landholders anxious about the fate of their property under the new regime, they went well beyond such a defense by attacking the metaphysical distinction between the clergy as a *corps* and the individual and by asserting the universality of property right that both enjoyed. In what respect, argued the abbé Jean-Siffrein Maury, citing Rousseau as he went, could the individual better establish his/her proprietary right than could the clergy? Both were dependent upon the state to preserve if not create their right to property; and if natural right, based on the claim of first occupancy, were the standard, no private person had better claim on lands than the clergy, whose possession pre-dated the existence of the nation.[120] For the state to appropriate church property on the grounds that a corporate body did not enjoy the same proprietary rights as the individual, it was argued, was flatly self-contradictory: for did not the proprietary rights of the nation rest on the premise that corporate bodies shared the natural right to property that common opinion accorded the individual?[121]

Of all the many controversial issues regarding property during the Revolution, none was more important in terms of the amount of property affected nor more revealing of the uses to which the Declaration's property provisions could be put than the issue of seigneurialism. I have already examined this matter for the prerevolutionary period; I now turn to the debate it engendered during the Revolution.[122]

If the conflict over seigneurial rights would seem easily enough understood as a conflict between natural capitalist property right and prescriptive feudal property right, enough has already been said to show that such a simple schematization of the conflict is inadequate. Two factors should be kept in mind.

First, as I stressed earlier, prerevolutionary critics of "feudalism," including the physiocratic school, maintained a healthy regard for the property rights held by seigneurial lords, even though these critics were hostile to seigneurial tenures. It is no secret that the revolutionaries intensified attacks on seigneurial prerogatives, but the critical point is that they wanted to do so without destabilizing the general structure of property right by delegitimating most titles. As Philippe-Antoine Merlin de Douai, speaking on behalf of the Feudal Committee, stated clearly in his February 1790 report to the Assembly, "in destroying the feudal regime, you did not intend to destroy properties, but to change their nature."[123] It is, of course, true that as the Revolution moved leftward until the spring of 1794, pressures to regulate, confiscate, and redistribute property for various financial, political, and ideological reasons increased; it is also true that the government increasingly responded to such pressures by taking more and more radically illiberal actions; and yet it remained the case that most revolutionaries—including most of those who wielded real power—continued to defend the rights of private property enough to resist proposals for its massive redistribution.[124] Robespierre rejected any prospect of adopting a so-called agrarian law that would have led to massive property redistribution, considering such a law to be no more than "an absurd scarecrow presented to stupid men by perverse men," that is to say a bogeyman used by the right to discredit the Revolution, and taken in its own terms, an "equally dangerous, unjust, and impractical project."[125] Barère de Vieuzac, expressing similar fears that the right would use the specter of an agrarian law to discredit the Revolution and to undermine the sale of confiscated national lands, successfully moved before the National Convention on 18 March 1793 a motion that explicitly punished by death "all those who propose or try to establish agrarian laws or all other laws and measures subversive of territorial, commercial or industrial property."[126] If bankruptcy was no longer pronounceable, agrarian laws were no longer debatable.

Second, it was by no means obvious precisely which of the hundreds of seigneurial rights and their local variants were abolished with or without indemnity when the death of the "feudal regime" was pronounced by the Assembly in the decrees of 4–11 August. It was for this reason that the Feudal Committee was established and charged with the task of interpreting and administering the decrees. Later legislation on the same subject was similarly attended by confusion, as the persistent calls for clarification make evident. The comte de Mirabeau, speaking before the Assembly, could still suggest in November 1789 that fiefs had "all the characteristics of the property of simple individuals," and, as "true properties," merited "the full protection of the law"; but only a few months later Merlin stated on behalf of the Feudal Committee that the abolition of the feudal regime meant that "there are no more fiefs."[127] As the Revolution moved leftwards and seigneurial rights were gradually restricted, it was no wonder that the right increasingly, if incorrectly, claimed that the revolutionaries were intent on undermining all rights to property, since the line between legitimate and illegitimate forms of property was not only vague, but also mobile. Much like Clermont-Tonnerre, Antoine-Louis Séguier declared that, not withstanding the enactment of the Declaration of Rights, "the right of property no longer exists in France. A mass of decrees have directly attacked the right of property . . . Your assemblies resemble a brigand who imposes on himself the rule to steal only half of what passers-by have in their pockets."[128]

What were the revolutionary assemblies and their feudal committees doing in proposing and executing their schemes to "change the nature" of property right? There can be no doubt that behind these schemes lay the goal of achieving a certain moral equity and liberty frequently, though by no means always, associated with natural right. Above all, those property arrangements, most especially serfdom, that required the subjection of one person to another were to be proscribed in the name of equality. Merlin's Feudal Committee report of 10 February 1790 stipulated the abolition without indemnity of "all honorific distinctions of superiority or of power resulting from the feudal regime," to include among other rights "seigneurial justice, personal *mainmorte*, real or mixed, as well as servitudes of origin, personal and corporal servitudes"—in other words, the sort of services that had been excoriated in the *cahier* of one village because they "make a slave of man born to be free and make each day of his existence odious by the bonds that enchain him."[129] Feudal tenures could no longer continue just because, as previous feudists had made clear, their essential element was an exchange of land rights for a "recognition" of superiority.

Beyond the abolition of personal inequalities arising out of land tenures, the revolutionaries clearly attempted to make property more easily disposable and commercially exploitable, although new restrictions, such as those regarding inheritances, were also imposed. Bitterly resented laws requiring tenants to present detailed listings of properties held from landlords were abolished, as were the special rights of lords to first right of refusal on the sale of lands alienated from their domains. In superseding the local customary laws, national property legislation not only standardized property disposition, but also simplified it by eliminating distinctions between noble and non-noble, inherited and acquired property. But the further the revolutionaries went in trying to distinguish "natural" from "non-natural" properties, the murkier things got. In the question of *mainmorte*, "do you free from servitude the person and the land," wondered the Feudal Committee, "or do you keep on the land the payments that have nothing servile connected to them?"[130] How were rights declared repurchasable to be evaluated? And according to what schedule would they be repaid?

Although the revolutionaries were certainly wary of sliding back too far into the language, principles, and precedents of Old Regime law, it is clear that in trying to answer these and many other difficult questions they were unable to extricate themselves entirely from them—indeed, they found themselves again and again referring back to the civil law of the supposedly unregenerated past. The very way in which Merlin expressed the basic problem they confronted brought them back to the language of the Old Regime controversy regarding the relationship of allodial and seigneurial property: to change the nature of properties meant, to use Merlin's words, "that they have stopped being fiefs and have become veritable allods."[131] In using such language, Merlin was echoing a number of *cahiers* that had called for making the free allod "general" upon indemnification of cancelled seigneurial rights and for abolishing the principle of "no land without seigneur."[132] Duport, similarly, in the midst of the debates over the

4–11 August decrees compared the proceedings whereby certain feudal rights were being abolished to the ordinary jurisprudence of Old Regime tribunals, some of which had ruled against some seigneurial claims upon appeal by the peasants.[133]

What would drive revolutionaries back to the civil law of the Old Regime were in part practical considerations. Revolutionary legislation could hardly replace all at once the intricate property laws of the Old Regime. Yet equity considerations bulked large as well. When reporting to the National Assembly for the Feudal Committee, the jurist François-Denis Tronchet, while clearly reluctant to thwart the intentions behind the legislation of 4–11 August, acknowledged that a fair, rational, and universal scheme of indemnification of legitimate seigneurial property required not the total disregard of the various customary proprietary laws and precedents, but a thorough analysis of their particular advantages and disadvantages. According to Tronchet, it would be necessary to examine "the different established traditions regarding the indemnification of *mainmorte*, to traverse the entire surface of the kingdom to open archives of all the sovereign courts and try to penetrate to the reasoning behind the variety of different traditions."[134] In the face of stubborn peasant refusal to pay traditional seigneurial dues still recognized as legitimate by the revolutionary government, successive revolutionary assemblies until the late summer of 1792 sought to protect these rights by issuing decree after decree reaffirming the status of such rights as property and reconfirming the traditional customary laws governing them. Thus, for example, Title 3 Article 1 of the laws of 15–28 March 1790 stipulated that all rights and duties which were the result of an original contract would continue to be paid and that in the case of contested rights decisions would be made "according to proofs authorized by the statutes, customs, and rules observed until the present."[135] Article 3 of the decree of 18–23 June 1791 proclaimed that "no one on litigious grounds can refuse payment of the *dîme*, traditionally paid, nor of *champarts*, *terrages*, *agiers*, *complants*, or other dues of this kind traditionally paid"; and when later provoked by the peasants' misuse of this decree to justify their refusal to meet their legal obligations, the Assembly explicated this law by declaring that "traditionally paid" meant following "the general maxims established over the centuries."[136]

If the general rules of revolutionary legislation still bore vestiges of feudal law, even more so did judgments made in applying these rules. The Feudal Committee, charged with the adjudication of a long series of particular cases, reverted again and again to the precedents and principles of Old Regime civil law. One prime example was a case the Committee decided on 28 January 1791 regarding the fate of *corvées* in Poitou under the decree of 15 March 1790. Proclaiming that "the disposition of the customs of Poitou is of great consideration in the decision on this question," the Committee argued that its first consideration, in line with revolutionary legislation, was to determine whether these obligations were the result of an explicit original contract; if so they were abolished only upon payment of an indemnity. But inasmuch as there appeared in this case to be no original contract to draw upon, the next step was to return to the legal traditions of the place in which the contracts were conceived. Given that Poitou was a land in which the rule "no land without seigneur" had prevailed and *corvées* had been sanctioned by local laws, the Committee ruled that it must be presupposed that these obligations were included in the original seigneurial contract, that they were therefore property, that "for want of a conventional title, the disposition of customs requires it to conserve the right of the seigneur, when he joins to his own individual title a constant possession of forty years."[137] As this case—one of many—demonstrates, customary law even under the Revolution could have great impact upon the administration of revolutionary decrees, which themselves acknowledged the legitimacy of many Old Regime titles.

There can be no doubt that as the Revolution proceeded and the assemblies abolished more and more rights without indemnity, recourse to customary law declined. As Michael Fitzsimmons has shown, assemblies of the early Revolution became increasingly impatient with traditional legal principles and procedures; and once measures to reduce the amount of civil litigation took effect, the number of civil cases involving seigneurial rights decreased.[138] Near the end of the Terror, Georges Couthon, a former barrister and a leading member of the Committee of Public Safety, could denounce the entire judiciary as "a sort of sacerdocy based on error," and traditional justice as "a false religion that consists entirely of dogmas, rites and mysteries" at odds with the ethics of the Revolution.[139]

In the matter of seigneurial rights, the government not only decided on 25 August 1792 to abolish without indemnity all rights protected by the maxim "no land without seigneur," all "statutes,

customs, rules . . . that stem from feudalism," as well as all arrearages on these rights, but proceeded to suspend all litigation among
notaries, other public officials, feudists, etc. who were "specially employed by former seigneurs of fiefs for the recognition or recovery of
their pretended rights." On 12 February 1793, the Convention released from prosecution or jail all those charged with or already
found guilty of insurrection in protest against payment of seigneurial
dues. And in what was probably its greatest act of defiance of history,
on 17 July 1793 the Convention decreed that all feudal titles, registers, judgments, and decisions regarding rights suppressed by the
Convention be turned over to local agents within three months to be
burned, failing which the holder of such titles could be imprisoned
for five years.[140]

Against these dramatic developments, two points deserve stress.
First, if one examines the *terms* rather than the *outcome* of the debates regarding seigneurial rights, one finds that it was the left more
than the right who had recourse to history in arguing for its position.
Why was this? Essentially because, as we have already seen, it was
the intent of the left not to delegitimate most property titles, but
rather to distinguish the valid ones from the invalid ones. In establishing as its "natural" measure of legitimacy whether a given right
had proceeded from some original, voluntary concession free from
seigneurial duress, the left in effect forced itself to return to history in
order to release peasants from history's burdens. In the face of right-
wing arguments that seigneurial rights represented property protected by the Declaration of Rights, the left felt obliged to reexamine
the past so that, to use the terms of one book claiming to do so, "the
mystery of feudal rights" would be "unveiled."[141] And what was this
"mystery"? Essentially the same one revealed by Caseneuve and
other jurists well over a century earlier—that seigneurial rights derived in large part from usurpations of allodial land. In pamphlet and
speech, Clovis and his minions once again entered a Gaul full of freeholds, whose integrity was maintained until many centuries later,
when feudal lords imposed the principle of "no land without seigneur" through tyranny and violence on the hapless owners of allodial
property, namely the people.[142] Against the presumption that seigneurial rights were protected property, the left wanted to establish its
opposite—namely, that seigneurial rights were usurpations which
prescription had not legitimated unless they were "clearly proved to

be the price of a primitive concession of resources."[143] The greatest mistake of the Constituent Assembly, argued Antoine-Jean-François Lautour-Duchatelet, was that it had placed the burden of proof upon those who were appealing against seigneurial dues, a burden that few could bear especially in areas where the "no land without seigneur" provision had obtained.[144]

What is striking about this general argument is not only its unoriginality but also its reliance upon the findings of legal scholars of the Old Regime and historical scholarship generally. Although wary of falling prey to the errors and prejudices of the *parlementaires*—the running dogs of the rapacious seigneurial lords—the left showed considerable respect for feudists like Hervé, whose work C. Michallet regarded as "the most thorough on the subject"; even Montesquieu was occasionally cited, notwithstanding his suspect status.[145] And beyond the scholars stood the documents themselves, which the left looked to to provide vital evidence for their position—"the ancient charters of the communes . . . the monuments of our history . . . the capitularies, where there is often mention of the oppressors of the people . . . the vicious old titles, titles taken from the dust of the cloisters."[146]

In the face of this argument what could the opposition say? To some extent it tried to construct counter-histories that strengthened seigneurial claims, but a number of deputies in the Assembly preferred to blunt the left's critique by arguing that appeals to history were in certain respects irrelevant and even dangerous. Auguste-Antoine-Joseph Prouveur, for example, contended that history was a poor basis upon which to settle detailed matters of property right since the facts were so often uncertain.[147] Sixte-François-Joseph Deusy, after laying out a weak counter-history of his own, took the offensive by focusing on the weak point of the left's whole position. Reiterating a theme dear to the right from virtually the beginning of the Revolution, Deusy warned that an attack on certain rights to property on the basis of origin would inevitably destabilize the entire structure of property right, since, as Turgot and the physiocrats had previously acknowledged, the vast majority of French property titles were suspect and could hardly stand close scrutiny. "Is one not struck by the danger of shaking . . . the peaceful structure of property? In effect few people can establish their titles for more than a hundred years. I maintain that a quarter of the patrimony of the citizens of the kingdom would survive contestation." Contestation, in other words, would have the

effect of an agrarian law. "Constituted society would publicly pro-
nounce its own dissolution, and in reforming itself in all its parts, it
would assign to each a new share of all goods and determine the manner of enjoying and disposing of it."[148]

A second point regards the limits of revolutionary anti-seigneurial
measures. As Albert Soboul and others have pointed out, even the
most extreme revolutionary legislation intended to eliminate the last
vestiges of seigneurialism in fact allowed some seigneurial dues to survive in more "bourgeois" forms well into the nineteenth century.[149]
Moreover, the provisions for burning property titles as a method for
canceling remaining seigneurial dues proved unworkable, largely because most property titles were laden with references to seigneurial
rights. Confusion reigned as to precisely which titles were to be
burned, while many objected to the law on the grounds that the only
extant title to much property was of the forbidden "feudal" variety. As
one *procureur-général* put it with regard to the condemned titles of
former payers of the *cens*, "when this title no longer exists, how will
they defend their property in certain cases?"[150] Less than three months
after the title-burning decree was passed, the Convention modified it
by extending the deadline for disposing of titles to six months and by
trying to clarify the distinction between valid and invalid titles; but by
January 1794, it more or less gave up the struggle by suspending title
burning altogether.[151] Although the Convention continued to disallow
legal language that "recalls in any direct or indirect manner the noble
or royal feudal regime,"[152] the tide had begun to turn. From January
1794 onwards, some civil suits regarding former seigneurial rights
were legalized, "considering that the action enters into the ordinary
actions of society."[153] The Jacobins, too, had begun to acknowledge implicitly that the burden of the feudal past would continue to weigh
upon property right.

Although succeeding revolutionary regimes refused to alter in
any significant way the provisions of the Convention on the elimination of seigneurial dues, their greater tolerance for "normal" civil litigation and their less overtly political use of law in general allowed
for greater leeway in reconstituting proprietary claims on the basis of
prescriptive right.[154] Napoleonic courts made use of Old Regime titles, and courts as late as the 1840s still respected distinctions between allodial and non-allodial lands in determining whether lands
held from prerevolutionary times were subject to certain rents.[155]

The Napoleonic Code itself, as André-Jean Arnaud has shown,

was a product of both prerevolutionary and revolutionary traditions.[156] One of its chief architects, Portalis, held, like so many before
him, that private property was a natural right, but he also saw it as a
constant part of the social order, denying that it had ever been entirely
eliminated from human affairs. To prove his case, he returned to that
perennial fixture of French jurisprudence, the allod, which even the
grasping medieval lords could not entirely subdue; its survival in face
of seigneurial aggrandizement underscored the notion that "the domains of individuals are sacred properties that must be respected
even by the sovereign himself."[157] Revolutionary legislation, he argued, had been necessary to rescue private property from the remaining bonds of feudal tenure. But it had tended, because of its "revolutionary spirit," to "sacrifice all rights for a political goal and to admit
no consideration but that of a mysterious and invariable interest of
the state." With the return of peace and the security provided by Napoleon's new political order, Portalis wrote, it was now possible to return once more to the ordinary business of humanity within a new
legal structure. In building that structure neither prerevolutionary
nor revolutionary principles would be slavishly followed, for if, "in
matters of laws and institutions the centuries of ignorance are the
theaters of abuses, the centuries of philosophy and enlightenment are
but too often the theater of excesses." Now that the time for excesses
was clearly over, Portalis observed, it was time to re-evaluate the
legal traditions of the past, and he strongly urged that his nation profit
from, not turn its back on, "that tradition of good sense, of rules, of
maxims that has lasted until our time, and forms the spirit of the nation." For if among traditional customs there were those which "bear
the imprint of our original barbarity," there were also those that "do
honor to the wisdom of our fathers, which has formed our national
character, and which are worthy of the greatest ages."[158]

◄ IV ►

Conclusion

The revolutionary moment—especially the laws of 4–11 August and
the Declaration—clearly heralded a major tranformation of French
proprietary right: in the name of natural right subtended by considerations of social utility, property not only changed hands, it also
changed forms. If I have not dwelled on these changes, I do not deny

them; works such as Garaud's have established them beyond any reasonable doubt. Nor would I deny the existence of important changes in the juridical foundation of property. The language of natural right replaced the language of seigneurial right as the pre-eminent means of expressing the complex interrelations of things to people. If natural law served as a buttress to the traditional civil law under the Old Regime, civil law under the new order would be conceived as "nothing but natural law modified,"[159] thereby conferring metaphysical sanction upon existing property claims. What I have tried to show is that this shift in the language of property right took place within a tradition of juridical argument dating back at least to the sixteenth century, when the king and the aristocracy looked to natural right as one means for delineating and reinforcing their spheres of entitlement. With the rise of the centralized state and the progressive dismemberment of what Dumoulin called the *complexum feodale* into "justice" and "fief," the basis was laid for the modern liberal notion of property right as a more or less absolute entitlement to dispose of a thing. In this sense, the rise of the modern state, at least in the European context, and the rise of modern proprietary right devolved from the same process. The Old Regime was certainly shot through with restraints on the use of property, as is, it is well to remember, our own modern "liberal" society. And yet the Old Regime did maintain a tradition of natural property right, which intersected in many curious ways with notions of prescriptive right, as the battle of the allod shows. It did not take the Enlightenment or the French Revolution to invent the idea that the sovereign has no natural right to confiscate the property of his subjects.

When the monarchy no longer abided by traditional counsel to use its discretionary taxing powers with moderation, and when for a variety of reasons, as yet imperfectly understood by historians, the property arrangements of the Old Regime fell under increasing disfavor, critics of absolutism and seigneurialism tried to appropriate the language of natural right and utility to press their case for liberalization. But in embracing so warmly the notion of "natural" proprietorship, they could hardly delegitimate the vast amount of property without clear "natural" titles. Defenders of seigneurial property struggled to show that their rights, too, were "natural" and worthy of protection under the newly emerging proprietary laws. The property provisions of the Declaration of the Rights of Man and of the Citizen did have their radical implications: they did, for example, stipulate a democratic mechanism for imposing public claims on private property in the form of taxes. Yet in being so brief, abstract, and vague, these provisions left undecided a variety of crucial questions regarding the status and disposition of certain properties, from ecclesiastical lands to seigneurial tenures, which would have to be resolved over the course of the Revolution.

In these debates, natural right was certainly harnessed for radical purposes. But just as appeals to history failed in 1789 to settle the fundamental issue of sovereignty in the new order (see chapter 2 above), so did appeals to natural right fail at least in the short run to settle questions of proprietorship, and this for at least two reasons: first, because the revolutionaries' own program did not in reality entail canceling all prescriptive rights to property, and second because the nearly universal subscription to the notion of natural right allowed opponents of the left to make as nearly effective use of it—through appeals to the Declaration—as did the left itself. In the end, translating seigneurial right into the language of natural right required looking back at the historical record in ways that drew directly on the tradition of Old Regime civil jurisprudence. Jean-Jacques de Cambacérès was right to argue that it was more difficult to restore civil rights than it was to restore political rights.[160] After the Terror had passed, Old Regime laws, precedents, and titles—considerably pruned back to be sure—would regain a certain respectablity and even legality. If the above argument is right, it adds strength to Tocqueville's contention that the origins of modern France lay within the political, institutional, and legal logic of the Old Regime.

REFERENCE MATTER

Glossary

Absolutism. Term used by historians to designate the hereditary monarchies of early-modern Europe, whose rulers were typically seen as possessing sovereign authority free from any legal constraint (*legibus absolutus*, in other words). The precise definition and periodization of French absolutism are controversial, but one standard view is to see absolute monarchy as emerging in France toward the end of the fifteenth century, reaching its institutional climax during the reign of Louis XIV in the late seventeenth, and undergoing a slow decline until its overthrow in 1789.

Allod. Territory free of seigneurial obligations, but subject to royal jurisdiction and hence potentially taxable by the Crown. The allod owner possessed both direct and usufructuary domain over his/her property.

Amerindians. Referred to the Native Indians of the Americas, including the Caribbean islands.

Appel comme d'abus. Legal procedure by which legal cases could be appealed from ecclesiastical courts to secular ones. Formally introduced in the sixteenth century, in the eighteenth it was used extensively by Jansenists, under attack from the church hierarchy, who hoped to have their cases heard in the more favorable precincts of the parlements.

Arrêt. A judicial sentence or administrative decree pronounced after deliberation by a parlement or subaltern royal law court or by one of the king's various councils, which also functioned in a judicial capacity. In an Old-Regime state that did not clearly distinguish between justice, administration, and legislation, *arrêts* were often tantamount to legislation; when pronounced by a parlement, they sometimes challenged the king's monopoly of laying down law.

Ashkenazim. The German Jewish community which, from a relatively compact area of settlement in northwestern Europe on the banks of the Rhine, migrated as far as Poland and Lithuania to the northeast and France, the Netherlands, and England to the west.

Assembly of Notables. An *ad hoc* group of hand-picked "notable" personages from the clergy, nobility, and office-owning commoners, convened in principle by the king to give him counsel but in fact to create favorable publicity for measures decided upon in advance. Controller General Calonne convened one in 1787, touching off the prerevolutionary controversy; the last time any such assembly had met was in 1626 under Louis XIII.

Avocat (roughly, barrister). Lawyer charged with advising his clients on points of jurisprudence, and with making oral and written arguments on these points to a court of law. In comparison with modern lawyers, avocats had very limited practices, procedural matters being handled largely by *notaires* (notaries) and *procureurs* (roughly, solicitors). Barristers, who eschewed the more "mechanical" aspects of legal practice, considered their profession a "noble" one. In the eighteenth century, barristers had considerable liberty to speak and write on political issues, and as a result, the profession became one of the principal forums in which new political ideas were debated.

Bailliage (bailiwick). A judicial district endowed with a subaltern royal court presided by a bailiff (*bailli*) and judging under the appellate jurisdiction of one of the "sovereign" courts or parlements. In the event of a meeting of the Estates General, the *bailliage* became the basic electoral district as well.

Banalités. Seigneurial rights owed by tenants to the lord for the right to use the lord's grain mills, ovens, and fruit presses. Frequently attacked in the *cahiers.*

Bastille. The royal fortress in Paris stormed and captured by the revolutionary crowd on 14 July 1789. In the last decades of the Old Regime, the Bastille had come to epitomize the evils of arbitrary power; its capture and destruction became the symbol of the triumph of liberty.

Binding mandate. A means of constraining the freedom of action exercised by deputies to the Estates General, a binding mandate prevented representatives from going beyond the explicitly declared will of their constituents. Traditionally favored by constituents as a defense against royal pressure, it was set aside as an impediment to revolutionary action after the creation of the National Assembly.

Bureau de la librairie. Under the Old Regime, an administrative office reporting to the Keeper of the Seals which organized the book guilds and supervised inspection and censorship procedures throughout France.

Cahier de doléance. A gravamen or written statement of grievances traditionally drawn up by electors to guide the deliberations and voting of their deputies to the Estates General. Formulated separately in clerical, noble, and commoner electoral assemblies in the winter and spring of 1789, these *cahiers* are one of the principal windows on the electorate's state of mind on the eve of the Estates General of that year, and of course of the French Revolution.

Causes Célèbres. Sensational legal cases which, in Old-Regime France, frequently became forums for highlighting defects in the law and government.

Cens. A duty owed to the seigneur by land tenants. Although the *cens* was usually not financially burdensome, payment of it was one of the surest signs of subjection to a lord.

Cercle Social. A political grouping in the early years of the Revolution combining features of a club, a literary salon, a masonic lodge, and a publishing house. Led by its founders Nicolas de Bonneville and Claude Fouchet, the *Cercle Social* functioned as the literary arm of the Girondins and, like many Girondin deputies, favored female emancipation. The *Cercle Social* did not survive the political proscription of the Gironde in 1793.

Chambre syndicale de la librairie et imprimerie de Paris. The Community of booksellers and printers of Paris. Under the Old Regime, a self-regulated corporation which, by virtue of royal privilege, held the exclusive monopoly to produce and distribute printed matter in the French capital.

Champ de Mars. Literally, the Fields of March, where the whole Frankish "nation" had supposedly met annually in military units under the Merovingian and Carolingian kings in order to judge cases, pass laws, and prepare for war. In the pamphlets of the prerevolutionary period, this largely legendary history was invoked to prove the legislative sovereignty, or at least co-sovereignty, of the French "nation" vis-à-vis the king.

Chancellor (Chancelier). Chief officer of the royal judicial system. The most energetic chancellors (L'Hôpital in the sixteenth century, Séguier in the seventeenth, d'Aguesseau in the eighteenth) had tremendous influence on the development of French jurisprudence and royal policies alike. In the late eighteenth century, Chancellors Maupeou and Lamoignon served as point-men for the execution of draconian royal attempts to reform the parlements.

Civic Humanism. See "classical republicanism."

Civil Constitution of the Clergy. That part of the Revolution's first constitution that integrated the French (or Gallican) clergy into the new order. Voted by the National or Constituent Assembly in June 1790, the Civil Constitution of the Clergy redrew France's ecclesiastical map to correspond with the new administrative one, transformed a hitherto quasi-autonomous clergy into salaried agents of the state, subjected both bishops and priests to the vagaries of popular election, and reduced the ties between the Gallican Church and the papacy. About half of the Gallican Clergy refused to swear loyalty to these provisions, creating a counter-revolutionary contingent of non-juring or refractory priests.

Classical Republicanism. Or "civic humanism"—term used by historians to designate a specific tradition of early-modern European political thought, whose career extended from the Italian Renaissance to the epoch of the American and French Revolutions. Self-consciously inspired by the political thought of Graeco-Roman antiquity, early-modern republicanism typically involved a preoccupation with the role of class struggle in politics and the promotion of the "mixed government" as the best regime, a sponsorship of cyclical theories of history and concern over the place of fortune in social life, anxiety over political corruption and an advocacy of the politics of virtue as its antidote.

Code Noir. France's slave code, or "black code," promulgated in 1688 under Louis XIV. By this early decree, free people of color were given the same rights as other colonists. As plantation agriculture progressed, however, these rights were quickly undermined.

Colonial Committee. Set up by the National Assembly in October 1789, this twelve-member body, elected by simply majority vote of the whole Assembly, contained no supporters of the *Sociétés des Amis des Noirs* (Friends of the Blacks). It clearly represented colonial interests and worked against the abolitionist interests of the *Amis des Noirs.*

Committee of Five. A committee established by the National Assembly on 12 August 1789 to fashion a single text for discussion from the many proposals for a Declaration of Rights it had now received. Dominated by Mirabeau, the committee submitted a new draft declaration on 17 August, only to see it rejected by the Assembly two days later.

Committee of Thirty. An informal political club consisting of liberal nobles, barristers, and publicists that formed in the wake of the Parlement of Paris's controversial ruling of 25 September 1788 in favor of the "forms of 1614" for the upcoming meeting of the Estates General. Standing for the doubling of the Third Estate's delegation and the vote by individual delegate in the Estates General, the committee circulated model petitions and *cahiers* and sponsored the publication of pamphlets.

Commons. An obvious reference to the House of Commons in the British constitution, this term was appropriated by the Third Estate to designate its delegation in the early meetings of the Estates General until it christened itself the National Assembly on 16 June 1789.

Compagnie des Indes. The French East India Company, possessing a monopoly on trade between France and wide areas of Asia.

Constitution (concept of). Although demands that the constitution be fixed and respected became the keynote of French politics early in 1789, the notion of a constitution was still ambiguous. Some thought of the constitution as a traditional order of things (social or political) which had to be reaffirmed, recovered or strengthened; others thought of it as the regular form of government the nation had never enjoyed and now needed to give itself by an explicit political act enshrined in a written document. In the course of the revolutionary debates, this latter conception became the dominant one.

Constitutional committee (first). A committee established by the National Assembly on 6 July to consider how the Assembly should proceed with the task of establishing the French constitution. The committee's report was presented by Jean-Joseph Mounier on 9 July.

Constitutional committee (second). A committee established by the National Assembly on 14 July to prepare a draft constitution. The committee of eight, drawn proportionately from the three orders, presented its preliminary report on 27 July. Within the committee, the more moderate view of Jean-Joseph Mounier was preferred to the more radical proposals of the abbé Sieyès.

Consultation. A form of *mémoire judicaire*, generally offered as an outside opinion on a case by a committee of avocats.

Contrôleur général des finances (Controller General of Finances). Royal minister responsible for state finances. Controllers with the ear of the king had potentially vast influence over the development of the French economy. In the eighteenth century, however, a number of controllers with great ambitions (Law, Turgot, Necker) foundered on the shoals of court politics, the vested interests of the privileged, and the decrepit, archaic state of government finances.

Convention. That revolutionary legislative and constituent body which took the place of the Legislative Assembly after the storming of the Tuileries Palace and the fall of the monarchy on 10 August 1792. Convening on 20 September 1792, the Convention declared France a republic, tried and executed Louis XVI, prosecuted the war against monarchical Europe abroad, presided over the Terror at home, and drafted two constitutions before giving way to the directorial regime in 1795. It governed by means of committees of which the most famous is the Committee of Public Safety.

Corporation. Word generally used to describe bodies which held the exclusive right to practice most urban trades and professions. Corporations were generally considered "legal persons" and were assumed to speak with a single voice. In the seventeenth century, royal ministers engineered the creation of hundreds of corporations, making them a central feature of the French economy. In the sphere of French government, corporations were particularly important as financial mediators between the holders of venal officer and the state, and served as an important source of cheap credit for the Crown.

Corps. Any body of incorporated "subjects" recognized as such by the king, who typically approved the corps's statutes and granted them privileges such as ennoblement or exemption from taxation in return for the supposed services they performed. Ranging from the Catholic clergy meeting in its general assemblies on the one side to the pettiest guilds on the other, these *corps* multiplied and metamorphosed into vehicles for royal credit in the course of the late seventeenth and eighteenth centuries in France.

Corvée. Labor service customarily owed to a seigneur. The Crown formally established a royal *corvée* early in the reign of Louis XV that required peasants to work without wages on royal roads a certain number of days a year.

Coup d'autorité. A use of direct royal commands in defiance of customary practices and the traditional rights of subordinate institutions of government such as the parlements. Examples (at least, in the eyes of the patriot party) were the 1753–54 exile of the Parlement of Paris, the dissolution of the parlements by Chancellor Maupeou in 1771, and the even more drastic attempt to reconfigure the legal system by force launched by Louis XVI, Loménie de Brienne, and Chancellor Lamoignon in the "May Edicts" of 1788.

Cour des aides. Sovereign court in Paris, with twelve provincial tribunals, having civil and criminal jurisdiction over many, but not all fiscal duties owed to the king. It was also responsible for registering fiscal edicts and titles of nobility.

Culte public. Literally, the public cult. Under the Old Regime, only the French Catholic church possessed the right to celebrate the religious services publicly.

De-Christianization. A revolutionary movement to rout out Christianity from France. Beginning in October 1793 with the promulgation of the revolutionary calendar, the movement flourished in the cities and larger towns during the Terror with the encouragement of representatives *en mission* like Fouché. It typically closed and pillaged churches and tried to force priests to defrock themselves and marry. Because the movement tended to alienate the peasantry from the Revolution the Convention tried to contain this movement in 1794, although later outbreaks of de-Christianization were to occur in the years to follow.

Décime. An internal tax imposed by the Gallican church on its own clergy, mainly in order to finance debts incurred by granting money to the king. The *décime* should not be confused with the *dîme*, or tithe, a tax in kind imposed by the church on lay landowners for the support of its clergy and eventually abolished without compensation by the National Assembly in the legislation following the famous session of 4 August 1789.

Declaration of 1738. Strengthening the Decree of 1716, this edict aimed at restricting the coming of Black slaves to France with their masters for fear that, once in France, the slaves would demand their freedom. The declaration forbade intermarriage between slaves in France and French subjects, limited the purposes for which they could be brought to France, and attempted to hasten their return to the colonies.

Despotism. A pejorative term originating toward the end of the seventeenth century in the literature of the Huguenot diaspora against Louis XIV and making its fortune in the works of Henri de Boulainvilliers and the baron Montesquieu in the eighteenth century. Unlike its cousin "tyranny" whose meaning focused on the person of the "tyrant," the term "despotism" designated a whole system of government. The term was omnipresent in political discourse on the eve of the French Revolution, especially on the side of the Parlement of Paris.

Diamond Necklace Affair. Complicated scandal in which, in the mid-1780s, two adventurers gulled the cardinal de Rohan, a prominent courtier, into giving them a priceless necklace he thought destined for the queen. It helped the court of Louis XVI and Marie Antoinette gain a reputation for favoritism, corruption, and sexual intrigue.

Dîme. A tax originally owed to the Church on all lands within the kingdom (including the royal domain). Laymen sometimes acquired title to the *dîme* as a result of purchase, exchange, infeudation, and/or usurpation, although lay acquisition of the *dîme* was frequently contested in court. In the eighteenth century, the monarchy acquired revenue by confirming lay rights to the *dîme* in return for a fee.

Domain. A property in a thing, normally a seigneury. From the late Middle Ages on, jurists usually distinguished between "direct domain" (*domaine directe*), meaning supreme ownership of a seigneury that conferred various legal rights to its lord, and "usufructuary domain" (*domaine utile*), meaning the right to cultivate land and dispose of its fruits within the seigneury. The royal domain was composed of a complex of territorial and fiscal rights.

École de Paris. School of theologians at the University of Paris in the late Middle Ages, known for their writings on the powers of church councils, and the superiority of these councils to the pope. Their ideas served as an important source for the development of Gallicanism and of *parlementaire* ideology.

Edict of Nantes. A royal edict bringing closure to the sixteenth-century civil wars of religion whereby Henry IV granted the right of public worship to French Protestants, or Huguenots, who also remained in possession of fortified places and had access to separate courts. This privileged civil and military status was a casualty of Protestant defeat at the hands of Cardinal Richelieu in 1629; the surviving religious toleration fell victim to the Catholic zeal of Louis XIV, who revoked the Edict of Nantes by the Edict of Fontainebleau in 1685.

Emancipation Decree. Although the revolutionary commissioner in Saint Domingue, Sonthonax, decreed slavery abolished in August 1793 during the turmoil of internal civil war, the French revolutionary Convention only ratified his decision and formally promulgated the Emancipation Decree in February 1794. By its terms, slavery was abolished in the French colonies, making France the first European nation to end the enslavement of Africans.

Émigrés. Those who fled France during the Revolution, especially nobles and refractory priests who, sometimes collaborating with powers at war with France, became the symbols of counter-revolution in the 1790s.

Engagiste. A person who enjoyed temporary usufructuary rights—usually for a fee—over a property held within another's domain. Much of the land held within the king's domain was "engaged" by the eighteenth century.

Enragés. A group of extremist revolutionary leaders, including Jacques Roux and Varlet, who were preoccupied with issues such as the price of bread, anxious to feed France's hungry urban populations, and committed to the revolutionary war; they pushed the Jacobins to pass the Maximum in September 1793, but they too were to fall victim to the Terror as Robespierre attempted to reassert control over the Parisian popular movement in the fall of 1793.

Estates General. A primarily consultative assembly of the whole French realm consisting of delegates from the three "orders" of the clergy, the nobility, and the commoners or Third Estate and convoked at the pleasure of the king. Called into existence by Philip the Fair in the fourteenth century, its sole real power, that of consenting to or refusing the king's request for "extraordinary" subsidies, grew less important after the direct tax called the *taille* became permanent in the fifteenth century. It met only four times during the sixteenth century and for the penultimate time in 1614.

Evocation. Removal of a case from one court of law to another. In the eighteenth century, the Crown frequently used this measure to remove contentious cases from the parlements, where they offered plaintiffs and defendants a highly visible public forum in which to criticize royal policies —particularly on religious issues. In turn, some of the bolder publicists for the "patriot party" questioned the legality of evocations, although without much effect.

Feudal Committee. Committee established by the National Assembly on 12 August 1789 to implement the decrees of 4–11 August intended to dismantle the "feudal regime."

Franc-fief. Duty owed to the king by non-noble owners of noble fiefs. Highly unpopular, it was a relatively burdensome charge, typically one year's revenue from the fief every twenty years, plus another year's revenue at time of sale.

Fronde. A series of uncoordinated uprisings by parlements, princes, and the nobility supported by segments of the peasantry and urban plebs against the regency government of Ann of Austria and Cardinal Mazarin, lasting from 1648 to 1653. Whereas the French Revolution was in part a conflict about who would control the national state, the Fronde still represented a challenge to the existence of the state, or at least to the extension of its fiscal and bureaucratic presence into largely autonomous activites and provinces.

Fundamental Law. Term roughly synonymous with "constitutional law." In Old Regime historiography, the "fundamental laws" of the realm referred to a set of usages and traditions, written and unwritten, governing the operation of French monarchy.

Gages. Sums paid annually by the government to purchasers of many venal offices, as a kind of interest on their capital. The *gages*, set higher in edicts creating offices to sell, eroded over long periods as a result of government bankruptcies. From time to time the government did increase the *gages* paid to certain officers (*augmentations de gages*). The purpose was not to restore the interest on old funds, but to extract fresh capital on which the new *gages* were to be the interest. *Augmentations de gages* was a forced loan that expanded the capital in existing offices.

Gallicanism. A French tradition which, in clerical form, insisted on the French Catholic church's right to its own canonical and liturgical usages as well as the universal church's superiority to the papacy in the definition of faith and morals; and which, in political form, insisted upon the independence of the French monarchy from the papacy in "temporal" affairs and tended to subject the Church to the power of the French state, especially the royal courts. Taking shape in the later Middle Ages, the tradition received its most "modern" formulation in the Declaration of the Gallican Liberties by the General Assembly of the Gallican church in 1682.

Garde des Sceaux. Literally, the keeper of the royal seats, this royal minister was responsible, in conjunction with the chancellor, for administering the judicial system.

General Will (volonté générale). The term emerged from seventeenth-century theological discourse, where it was used to distinguish between the general will of God and particular wills of human beings. But its transformation into a political concept seems chiefly to have been the work of Rousseau, who identified the "general will" with the collective will of the citizenry in a legitimately constituted government, as opposed to the "particular" wills of individuals. This was the idea later enshrined in Article 6 of the Declaration of Rights: "The law is the expression of the general will."

Girondins. A loose grouping of men of similar political orientation during the early years of the Revolution, some of whom came from the department of the Gironde near Bordeaux. Originally the most leftist members of the Legislative Assembly, they captured and briefly dominated the ministry in 1792. Its leaders, Roland, Dumouriez, Brissot, Condorcet, and Isnard, were to be proscribed by the Jacobins during the Terror as moderates.

Grande Chancellerie (grand chancellory). This was the largest chancellory, with 300 secretaries of the king. Their designated task was to oversee the writing, signing, and transmitting of a vast official correspondence conducted in the king's name, and further, to affix the royal seal to, and record each item transmitted. In fact, the work was done mainly by clerks. (See "secretaries of the king.")

Greffiers. Officials in the parlements charged with the recording of depositions and interrogations, with drawing up deliberations and final judgments (*arrêts*), and with the keeping and safeguarding of the judicial records.

Intermediate bodies (corps intermédiaires). An expression and concept made famous by the baron Montesquieu's *Spirit of the Laws* referring to corporate bodies like parlements, the church, municipal governments, guilds, etc., that stood between the monarch on the one hand and individual subjects on the other. The idea was that these quasi-independent corporations tempered and moderated the exercise of royal authority before it reached individual subjects, thereby facilitating their obedience and preventing the monarchy from becoming a "despotism."

Jacobins. The most important political club during the French Revolution. Originally an outgrowth of the caucus of the Breton deputies to the Estates General and then the National Assembly, the club took its name from a secularized Dominican or "Jacobin" monastery in the rue Saint-Honoré, where the club met. In Paris, the club functioned as a political caucus for the Revolution's more radical deputies and their sounding board for proposed legislation; in the provinces, where the Paris club eventually corresponded with thousands of affiliates, the clubs acted as exemplars of revolutionary "virtue" and unelected executors of revolutionary legislation. By extension, the term came to designate all fervent adherents to the cause of the Revolution, especially its mixed terrorist and democratic phases in 1793–94.

Jansenism. A movement of doctrinally Augustinian and morally rigoristic reform within French and Flemish Catholicism that stood opposed to supposedly neo-Pelagian tendencies on the part of the Jesuits. Taking its name from Cornelius Jansen, author of a posthumous book about Saint Augustine and bishop of Ypres at his death in 1640, Jansenism continued to define itself as Catholic despite repeated papal condemnations and coalesced with radical clerical Gallicanism and the Parlement's constitutionalism in ever more political form in the course of the eighteenth century.

Jansenist Party (parti janséniste). The very political form that French Jansenism took in the eighteenth century, whereby a cohesive group of magistrates and barristers in the Parlement of Paris and some other parlements, allied with second-order priests and publicists, organized a spirited resistance to the ecclesiastical policies of both the episcopacy and the monarchy. Born in the wake of the formal appeal of the bull *Unigenitus* to a general council in 1717, this *parti janséniste*'s chief mouthpiece was the clandestinely published weekly called the *Nouvelles ecclésiastiques* and its chief accomplishment was perhaps the dissolution of the Society of Jesus, or Jesuits, in France in 1761–64.

Kebillot. These were the Jewish corporate bodies that regulated internal Jewish affairs. They collected taxes, distributed charity, supported a rabbi and ecclesiastical court, had jurisdiction over marriage, and oversaw the minute affairs of the Jewish local communities. In Bordeaux, the Kehilla was dominated by a few wealthy families.

King's Council. Body of advisers to the king, one section of which acted, theoretically under his supervision, as France's highest court of appeals.

League (Ligue). A shorthand for the *Sainte Union*, or Catholic League, a popular ultra-Catholic and anti-Protestant para-military organization that seized control of Paris and numbers of other French cities and defied the authority of the monarchy toward the end of the sixteenth-century wars of religion, from about 1588 to 1594. The League remained a politically charged reference point in the pamphlet literature of the prerevolution.

Legislative Assembly (Corps législatif). That revolutionary legislative body that convened in September 1791 and legislated under the provisions of the Constitution of 1791. The Legislative Assembly declared war on Prussia and Austria, stepped up the offensive against *émigré* nobles and refractory priests, and gave rise to the political division between Girondins and the Mountain. It did not survive the assault of the Tuileries Palace which, by ending the monarchy, ended the constitution by which this assembly had legislated.

Lèse-nation. An expression appearing very early in the Revolution—even in the prerevolution—designating a treasonable act against the "majesty" of the French "nation." The phrase represented a revolutionary appropriation of the Old Regime crime of *"lèse-majesté,"* a treasonous and sacriligious act such as a revolt or an attempted assassination committed against the quasi-sacred person and majesty of the king.

Les Halles. Lively area in the center of Paris, site of numerous stalls selling diverse merchandise including fish, wine, and food.

Lettre de cachet. Literally, a "sealed letter" signed by the king containing orders to be executed immediately and without publicity. It was used most notoriously to imprison people without trial. Although most often seen as a tool of royal repression, letters were also issued on the request of private individuals, often to secure the imprisonment of insane or delinquent relatives.

Lettres du jussion. Royal orders mandating immediate obedience by a parlement in the event of its continuing refusal to register an edict or declaration, even after presenting its remonstrances to the king and receiving his response to them.

L'infâme. Term, meaning "the infamous thing," used by Voltaire for the Catholic church, and sometimes for organized religion in general. Its usage in this sense reveals both the philosophes' visceral hatred of organized religion and their keen sense of how to achieve maximum shock value in their writings.

Lit de justice (bed of justice). A term originally designating the paraphernalia—pillows, canopy, etc.—used to mark off royal space when the king visted his Parlement of Paris, and later a special kind of parlementary session by which the king consulted with his parlement about constitutional matters. By the eighteenth century, however, the expression had come to mean a session in which the king personally forced the Parlement to register hitherto contested measures.

Longue Durée. "Long-term"—phrase typically used to refer to historical structures, whether institutions or traditions of thought, which persist over a very long period. As originally used by the historian Fernand Braudel, the term designated slow geographical and climatic change.

Main-morte. A seigneurial right to seize the goods and rights of a tenant who departed from a fief. Those subject to it were considered virtual serfs.

Mandement, or mandamus. A published address by a bishop to his diocesans. In contrast to a pastoral instruction (*instruction pastorale*), a *mandement* contained orders entailing canonical penalties in the case of disobedience.

Maupeou coup or constitutional revolution. A shorthand for Chancellor René-Nicolas-Charles-Augustin de Maupeou's attempt in 1771 to reform and purge the French parlements, beginning with the Parlement of Paris, so as to make justice cheaper and more accessible—and to break parlementary resistance to royal authority. Maupeou's coup was undone in 1774 when the new king, Louis XVI, dispensed with Maupeou's services and recalled the old parlements.

Maximum. A rate beyond which it was illegal to sell basic commodities, especially grain. The Convention established a Maximum on grain in May 1793, followed by a general Maximum on all necessities and wages in September 1793. The Maximum represented the fruition of efforts of the Parisian *sans-culottes* to lower and stabilize the price of grain in order to make bread affordable for the urban poor.

Mémoires judicaires. Legal briefs, commonly printed and circulated in important trials. In Old-Regime France, lawyers had the right to publish them without preliminary censorship. As they were almost the only sort of documents which had this status, they were frequently used for political purposes. In the first half of the eighteenth century, Jansenist lawyers in particular first publicized many of their most provocative constitutional ideas through this medium.

Mercantilism. An economic policy variously pursued by European states in the seventeenth and much of the eighteenth centuries designed to achieve agricultural self-sufficiency and encourage the export of manufactured goods with a view toward accumulating enough bullion to pay for their expanding military machines, partly on the assumption that the total sum of wealth was a fixed quantity, and that one state's gain was necessarily another state's loss. Rival "mercantilisms" might sometimes themselves be the occasions for military deployment, as in the case of the Dutch-English wars of the mid-seventeenth century and the Dutch-French wars of the end of that century. In France, the coming of physiocracy, with its belief in the creation of agricultural wealth and its advocacy of free trade, represented a departure from mercantilistic thought.

Mesmerism. Pseudo-scientific fad of the 1780s, premised on a belief in "animal magnetism," and drawing heavily on Rousseauian sentimentality. Its tremendous, if brief, success testified both to the growing penetration of Rousseauian ideas, and also to the agitated, unrestrained character of French intellectual life in the decade preceding the Revolution.

Mixed Government. The doctrine that the best form of government consists of a mixture of two or more pure forms of government—typically, of a blend of monarchy, aristocracy, and democracy. The roots of the idea can be traced to ancient Greek political thought; its tripartite version formed a central pillar of early modern republicanism in Europe.

Molinism. A theological tendency named after the late sixteenth-century Spanish Jesuit theologian Luis Molina, whose *Concordia liberi arbitrii cum gratiae donis* (1588) tried to reconcile divine providence with human free will by means of the "science" of God's foreknowledge of what people would freely do under any set of hypothetical circumstances. In the pejorative parlance of Jansenist critics of the Jesuits, Molinism connoted a semi-Pelagian theology of salvation that minimized the agency of divine grace to the benefit of "fallen" human nature and its unaided free will.

Monarchiens. Term used (chiefly by their opponents) for the moderate wing of the Patriot movement, whose ranks included Mounier, Lally-Tollendal, Clermont-Tonnerre, Bergasse, and Malouet, and which emerged as a distinct faction in July 1789. The *monarchiens* were advocates of an English-style constitution, with a strong royal executive and a bicameral assembly. The Constituent Assembly's rejection of their proposals for a separate upper chamber and an absolute royal veto in September 1789 is often seen as a decisive juncture in the radicalization of the Revolution.

Monarchomachs. A term designating the (mainly) sixteenth-century Calvinist authors of political treatises which conceived of the French monarchy in contractual terms, such that it was constitutionally limited by princes of the blood, the Estates General, or municipal "inferior magistrates"; and that armed resistance to it was justified under certain conditions. Among such monarchomach treatises, François Hotman's *Francogallia* (1572) was still frequently cited on the eve of the French Revolution.

Mulattoes. People of mixed blood—French and African—in the New World. Referred to as "people of color," most Mulattoes were free under the terms of the *Code Noir,* although they had been increasingly subjected to restrictions and harassment during the eighteenth century. In Saint Domingue on the eve of the Revolution there were over 28,000 free men of color, some of whom were rich plantation owners.

National Assembly (Assemblée nationale). Also called the Constituent Assembly (*Assemblée constituante*), this is what the Third Estate's delegation to the Estates General decided to call itself when, on 16 June 1789, it proclaimed itself the sole legitimate representative of the French nation. The name stuck when, after a failed attempt to undo this clear usurpation of royal authority, Louis XVI ordered the noble and clerical delegations to join this National Assembly on 27 June.

National Party (parti national). A term used in this volume to designate those individuals and that body of opinion that, beginning in the autumn of 1788, combined the thesis of the nation's sovereignty with the notion of the "nation" as composed essentially of commoners. Although some contemporaries used the term "National Party" in that sense, most continued to use the name of "Patriot Party" that had hitherto designated defenders of the parlements.

National Property (biens nationaux). Former ecclesiastical property, placed at "the disposition of the nation" on 2 November 1789 for the purpose of financing the royal (now national) debt. The National Assembly issued paper currency, called *assignats,* on the security of these *biens nationaux.*

Natural rights tradition. The philosophical tradition that sought to derive principles of political order from the postulate that individuals are endowed with rights inhering in their very nature as human persons. Natural rights arguments were developed in the seventeenth century by such thinkers as Grotius, Hobbes, Pufendorf, and Locke and elaborated in the eighteenth century by Burlamaqui, Vattel, and Rousseau. In combination with appropriate variations upon the theme of an original contract, they could be (and were) used to justify absolute monarchy or popular sovereignty, on the one hand, or to define the essential limits protecting individuals from abuses of sovereign power, on the other.

Night of the Fourth of August. The dramatic evening session of 4 August 1789, when the National Assembly voted to destroy the "feudal regime" in its entirety. Acting in response to widespread rural violence directed against seigneurial rights and dues, the Assembly found itself caught up in a profoundly emotional experience in which successive speakers vied to denounce and abandon the traditional privileges of those they represented. By the end of the session, the entire corporate social order of the Old Regime had been, in principle, dismantled. The decisions were codified by the Assembly in a decree of 11 August.

Nouveau converti. A legally fictive term used to identify French Calvinists after the revocation of the Edict of Nantes in 1685 on the erroneous supposition that they had all been newly converted to Roman Catholicism.

Octrois. A due or levy imposed by towns and cities on goods entering or leaving their boundaries. An octrois may be conveniently thought of as a form of indirect royal taxation, since in the eighteenth century towns usually levied it with royal authorization in order to finance municipal debts incurred by lending to the king.

Officiers ministériels (ministerial officers). Unlike magistrates and a number of other officers, these received no *gages* or interest from the government on the capital they placed in their offices. Their income from office came exclusively from fees paid by clients requiring their services. Among the *officiers ministériels* were auctioneers of movable and immovable goods, receivers of court-ordered payments, *procureurs*, notaries, wigmakers, and (at most times) stockbrokers.

Old Regime (ancien régime). First appearing in the pamphlet literature of the prerevolution, this term was used by revolutionaries to designate the particularistic and privilege-ridden order that they set out to destroy, especially in the National Assembly's legislative holocaust of "feudalism" on 4 August 1789. As loosely used by historians, however, the Old Regime means the French monarchy and society from the reign of Francis I to the French Revolution.

Order of Barristers (bar association). Although the history of an organized French legal profession goes back to the thirteenth century, it was only in the seventeenth that independent Orders of Barristers began to emerge, starting in Paris. These associations soon acquired considerable cohesion and autonomy, allowing the legal profession to become a hotbed of political activity, and a valuable ally to the parlements in their struggles with the Crown.

Origines Lointaines. Long-term or remote origins.

Palais de justice. Central courts building. The Palais de justice in Paris, originally built in the Middle Ages as a royal palace and later greatly modified, was the seat of the Parlement.

Palais royal (royal palace). The residence and other apartments in Paris belonging to the duc Louis-Philippe d'Orléans, prince of the blood and the king's cousin, and to the Orléans family generally. Opened to the public in the eighteenth century, the arcades and piazzas of the *Palais royal* served as focal point for pamphleteers, politicians, and crowds in the early stages of the French Revolution.

Paris Commune. The revolutionary municipal government of Paris from 1789 to 1795. Set up by the electors of the Third Estate in Paris, the Commune generally sponsored the Revolution's leftward thrust including the proscription of the Girondins in the National Convention in May and June 1793, the establishment of the Maximum in September 1793, and the movement of de-Christianization in the months that followed.

Parlement. Not a "parliament" in the British sense, but rather a court of law, possessing final appellate authority (subject only to the king) within its jurisdiction, which in the case of the Parlement of Paris covered a third of the kingdom. The fifteen or so parlements (the number varied over time) were among the most important institutions of government in Old-Regime France, with their activities stretching far beyond what we would now consider the realm of the judiciary. In France, legislation, although promulgated by the king, had to be "registered" on the books of a parlement before taking effect in its jurisdiction. Although the parlements did not have the right to block registration of laws, they insisted on their right to "remonstrate"—sometimes interminably—with the king before acceding to his will on issues where they opposed him. Based on this tradition, the parlements claimed to act as a restraint upon royal authority.

Patriot Party (parti patriote). A label first used to describe the clandestine but organized opposition to Chancellor Maupeou and his attempt to reform and purge the French parlements in 1771–74, then to designate the opposition to the chief minister Loménie de Brienne and his actions against the parlements in 1787–88. The label survived to designate radical revolutionaries as opposed to perceived compromisers and counterrevolutionaries in the early stages of the French Revolution.

Permission tacite. Under the Old Regime, a quasi-legal police authorization to publish books unable to secure a royal privilege because of content or origin of publication.

Physiocracy. A doctrine developed by François Quesnay and the marquis de Mirabeau in the late 1750s and early 1760s. Combining notions of natural rights, laissez-faire economics, and administrative reform, physiocracy ("rule by nature") offered a model of a society in which arbitrary political will would yield to the rule of reason. It exercised considerable influence among the administrative and intellectual elite of the Old Regime.

Plenary Court (Cour plénière). A term with medieval and feudal origins which Louis XVI's chief minister Loménie de Brienne revived to designate the constitutional body with which he proposed to replace the Parlement of Paris for all "public" or legislative purposes in his controversial May 1788 edicts. Forcibly registered by the Parlement of Paris in a siege-like *lit de justice* assembly on 8 May 1788, this measure among others provoked a national resistance which eventually led to Brienne's downfall and the convocation of the Estates General.

Prerevolution. A term now used to designate the period immediately prior to the outbreak of the French Revolution, from the calling of the first Assembly of Notables in February 1787 to the transformation of the Estates General into the National Assembly in June 1789. Coined by the French historian Jean Egret, this label has largely taken the place of the "aristocratic revolution" that had been used to designate the same events earlier.

Pouvoir Constituant. A distinction between the "constituent power" which establishes basic constitutional law and the ordinary functioning of "legislative power" was a distinctive feature of the political theory of Sieyès, among others.

Primogeniture. System whereby the eldest son inherited his parents' entire estate. Revolutionary legislation abolished primogeniture and established equal inheritance for all heirs, male and female, thereby expanding the number of property owners in France.

Privilège en librairie. Under the Old Regime, a royal authorization to publish a book.

Procureur. An officer who handled legal procedures for clients and steered their cases through the courts. The task of the *procureur* (attorney) is to be distinguished from that of the *avocat* (barrister) who drew up written pleadings, developed the legal reasoning, and generally argued the case. The distinction between the two functions, existing then in England, was unknown in America. The *procureur*, unlike the *avocat*, owned an office in addition to his practice, and belonged to a corps.

Procureur général. An untranslatable term referring to one of the "king's men" (*gens du roi*) who, along with the *avocat général*, functioned in principle as a defender of the king's—hence the public—interest in the sovereign courts of the realm. A non-venal officer directly appointed by the king, the *procureur général* along with the *avocat général* presented royal legislation to the parlements and "required" its registration, as it was he who "required" the prosecution of royal cases, proposing a sentence (called "conclusions") which the court might or might not follow.

Remontrance (Remonstrance). Formal complaint issued by a sovereign court concerning royal legislation. Although these documents possessed no legal status, the Crown, by tradition, had to take them seriously. In the eighteenth-century conflicts between the Crown and the parlements, remonstrances were frequently published and served as a principal means of rallying public opinion behind the courts.

Rousseauian. Following the ideas of Jean-Jacques Rousseau, author of the *Social Contract.* Rousseau based his political philosophy on a theory of individual rights and the principle of social contract as the origin of all legitimate government. But he saw political freedom as depending upon the existence of a general will emanating from all citizens and applying to each. Individuals thus found their freedom, in his analysis, through their participation in the exercise of a collective sovereignty rather than in the existence of external checks upon it.

Royal Session (Séance royale). Used in the late Middle Ages to describe sessions of the Parlement of Paris graced with the presence of the king, this term was curiously revived by Louis XVI's ministers Lomenie de Brienne and Chrétien-François de Lamoignon to cloak a forced registration of contested measures—in effect, a *lit de justice* assembly, as that term was then understood—on 19 November 1787. Its further use by Louis XVI to impose his will on the Third Estate on 23 June 1789 backfired badly, enabling it to make good its new identity as National Assembly.

Secrétaires du roi (Secretaries of the king). Owners of some 835 offices in the Grande Chancellerie (Paris) and twenty-one smaller chancelleries attached to the parlements and other sovereign courts in the provinces. The offices, which required no work, were expensive but attractive because they conferred nobility on their holders.

Seigneury. In broad usage, superiority or authority over persons and/or goods; in a narrower sense, a territory in which the lord exercised authority over both lands and people. Loyseau distinguished between "public seigneury," which denoted authority principally over persons, and "private seigneury," which denoted authority principally over goods.

Sénéchaussée (seneschal district). A judicial district which was the seat of a subaltern royal court, comparable to a *bailliage* and presided over by a *sénéchal*, under the appellate jurisdiction of a parlement. The *sénéchaussée* like the *bailliage* functioned as an electoral district for the Estates General.

Separation of Powers. The doctrine that specific governmental functions—legislative, executive, and judicial, in the canonical version—should be distributed among distinct political organs. The doctrine, whose roots can be traced in antique political thought and which received influential modern statements in Locke and Montesquieu, is related both to early-modern conceptions of the "mixed government" as well as to notions of "checks and balances" deriving from English constitutionalism.

Sephardim. Descendants of Jews who lived in Spain and Portugal before their expulsion in 1492.

Sindic (syndic). A member of a corps elected to administer its affairs during a term of one or two years. The *sindic*, with the advice of other senior members, oversaw the corps's internal affairs, and it was he who conducted its business outside—protecting its rights in courts of law and negotiating with royal administrators over collective payments and loans demanded by the government.

Sixth Bureau. The sixth of the thirty subcommittees into which the National Assembly had divided itself to facilitate discussion. The Sixth Bureau was the only one of these subcommittees actually to propose its own draft declaration of rights, which was a modified version of that proposed by the abbé Sieyès. This draft became the basis for the National Assembly's final discussions of a declaration of rights after 19 August 1789.

Société des amis des noirs (Society of the Friends of Blacks). Founded in 1788 in Paris by Brissot and others, the *Société*, modeled on its English counterpart, was determined to abolish slavery but focused primarily on the eradication of the slave trade. The *Société* was actively involved in France's abolitionist movement during the Revolution.

Société des colons américains (Society of American Colonists). An organization established in September 1793 in France by thirty to fifty "citizens of color" determined to fight for the full equality of all free non-whites and for the freedom of mulatto slaves in the New World.

Sociétés populaires. The multitude of popular local political clubs or societies created in Paris and provincial cities on the model of the major Parisian clubs, especially the Jacobins. Centers of *sans-culotte* sociability and popular "vigilance," these societies functioned as important agents of denunciation and Terror.

Society of Revolutionary Republican Women. This was the most famous women's club during the Revolution. Established by Pauline Léon and Claire Lecombe in the spring of 1793, the club helped suppress the Girondins but later drifted away from the Jacobins toward more radical groups.

Suspensive veto. A provision of the first French constitution allowing the king to veto any decision of the National Assembly for the duration of two legislatures (four years). The National Assembly opted for this form of royal veto (as opposed to an absolute veto, or no veto at all) on 11 September, in one of its earliest constitutional decisions. Louis XVI's exercise of his veto power after the constitution went into effect in 1791 became the focus of the political resistance that eventually brought about the destruction of the constitutional monarchy in August 1792.

Suzerainty. Lordship exercised on the basis of feudal obligation. Royal jurists acknowledged that through prescription the lords had acquired the right to act as suzerains in certain capacities, such as providers of seigneurial justice. They also asserted the king's rights as suzerain in order to reinforce the monarchy's taxing authority. However, they tended to treat suzerainty as a bastardized form of sovereignty, since they believed the lords had acquired it through usurpation of regalian rights.

Taille. The principal form of direct royal taxation, based on estimates of personal wealth, before the French Revolution. Becoming permanent in 1439 toward the conclusion of the Hundred Years War, the *taille* fell almost exclusively on the peasantry except for non-noble land owned by the nobility in southern France and, in effect, for land rented out by the nobility to entrepreneurial peasants there and elsewhere.

Tennis Court Oath. The oath of 20 June 1789 by which all the Third-Estate deputies except one and some deserters from the other orders, who now called themselves the National Assembly, swore not to separate until they had "fixed" or given form to the French constitution. The oath is called as it is because, barred by soldiers and workmen from using the *Salle des menus plaisirs* where they had been meeting until then, the deputies repaired to an indoor tennis court in order to hold their session.

Terror (the). The most extreme phase of the French Revolution, perhaps best dated from the purging of the National Assembly (National Convention) by popular action at the beginning of June 1793 until the overthrow of Robespierre (by other deputies) at the end of July 1794. The Terror was characterized, *inter alia*, by the suspension of the constitution; the radical centralization of power in the name of emergency government; a broadening definition of the crimes for which suspected persons might be arrested and a loosening of the procedures by which they were tried; mass mobilization in defense of the Revolution and the escalation of violence against its enemies.

Thèse Nobiliare and Thèse Royale. Early-modern French historiography, from the sixteenth to the eighteenth century, was dominated by two competing conceptions of the "ancient constitution" or "fundamental laws" of the realm. According to the *thèse royale*, the French monarchy had been an absolutist one from the outset, in continuity with Roman conceptions of sovereign political authority; the feudal period saw the usurpation of royal power by the nobility, but the arrival of the "new monarchy" of the Renaissance had signaled the return of the sole legitimate constitution of France. For the *thèse nobiliare*, the "ancient constitution" of France instead embodied the "Germanic" liberty of the Frankish nobility, whose institutional expression was the succession of "representative" bodies which placed limits on royal authority—noble assemblies of the Middle Ages, the Estates Generals and parlementary law-courts of the early modern period—which were in turn threatened by the rise of absolutist "despotism."

Third Estate (Tiers état). Originating as the third and most humble of the three groups into which the clerical elite mentally divided early medieval society, namely priests (*oratores*), knights (*bellatores*), and the majority who worked (*laboratores* or *humiliores*), the Third Estate took juridical form as such when the monarchy created it for the purposes of separate representation in the Estates General in the fourteenth century. On the eve of the French Revolution the Third Estate comprised at least 98 percent of the French population although entitled to no more votes or delegates than either the clergy or the nobility, enabling the abbé Sieyès to say that the Third Estate was juridically nothing while in fact it was everything.

Traitant. Financier who, in exchange for payment of a lump sum, acquired the right to collect and to keep taxes or to sell state offices for profit. *Traitants* were widely despised.

Unigenitus. A papal bull, or "constitution" as it was more frequently called at the time, which condemned 101 propostions taken from the Jansenist Oratorian priest Pasquier Quesnel's devotional book entitled *Réflexions morales sur le nouveau testament*. Fulminated by Pope Clement XI in 1713, this bull was the last and most definitive papal condemnation of French Jansenism, since, unlike the earlier condemnation of Jansen's *Augustinus*, there was no doubt in this case that the anathematized propositions indeed came from the book in question.

Universal direct. The king's claim to seigneurial jurisdiction over all lands in the kingdom, including lands long regarded as allodial property, based on the notion that all territories were held as concessions from the king. Asserted chiefly to generate more income for the monarchy.

Wilderness. A metaphor referring to the outdoor worship services whereby French Protestants defied the prohibition of public worship entailed by the revocation of the Edict of Nantes in 1685. By extension, the term has also come to serve as shorthand for the juridical limbo in which Protestants lived in France between 1685 and the Edict of Toleration promulgated in 1788.

≺ ≻

Abbreviations

AHR	*American Historical Review*
AHRF	*Annales historiques de la Révolution francaise*
AP	*Archives parlementaires*
AN	Archives nationales
Annales	*Annales: économies, économies, sociétés, civilisations*
BN	Bibliothèque nationale
BSHPF	*Bulletin de la Société de l'Histoire du Protestantisme français*
BSP-LP	Bibliothèque de la Société de Port-Royal, Collection Le Paige
D'Antraigues	Emmanuel-Louis-Henri de Launay, comte d'Antraigues, *Memoire sur les Etats-généraux, leurs droits et la manière de les convoquer* (n.p., 1788)
De Baecque	Antoine de Baecque, Wolfgang Schmale, and Michelle Vonelle, *L'an 1 des droits de l'homme* (Paris, 1989)
FHS	*French Historical Studies*
FRH	Hayden French Revolutionary Pamphlets
Gauchet	Marcel Gauchet, *La révolution des droits de l'homme* (Paris, 1989)
Isambert et al.	François-André Isambert et al., eds., *Recueil général des anciennes lois francaises depuis l'an 420 jusqu'à la Révolution de 1789*, 529 vols. (Paris, 1822–33)
JF	Joly de Fleury
JHI	*Journal of the History of Ideas*
JMH	*Journal of Modern History*
LFRADE	*La Révolution Francaise et l'Abolition de l'Esclavage*, 12 vols. (Paris, 1968)
LRFEDJ	*La Révolution Francaise de l'Emancipation des Juifs* (Paris, 1968), 8 vols.
NL	Newberry Library

OC	Alexis de Tocqueville, *Oeuvres complètes*, ed. J.-P. Mayer (Paris, 1951–1991)
Rials	Stéphane Rials, *La Déclaration des droits de l'homme et du citoyen* (Paris, 1988)

≺ ≻

Notes

INTRODUCTION

1. Amos J. Peaslee, *Constitutions of Nations*, 4 vols. in 8 pts., 3d ed. (The Hague, 1965), 1:928–42; 3:*passim*.

2. François VI, duc de La Rochefoucauld, *Réflexions ou sentences et maximes morales*, no. 218, in *Oeuvres de La Rochefoucauld*, ed. M.D.L. Gilbert and J. Gourdauld, 3 vols. (Paris, 1868–83), 1:117.

3. Keith M. Baker, *Inventing the French Revolution: Essays on French Political Culture in the Eighteenth-Century* (Cambridge, 1990), 203–23 but also, in general, all of pt. 3.

4. The quotations are from Jean-Nicolas Desmeuniers in *AP* (3 Aug. 1789), 8:334; and Rabaut Saint-Étienne, ibid. (23 Aug. 1789), 479.

5. Jacques Godechot, "L'expansion de la Déclaration des droits de l'homme de 1789 dans le monde," *AHRF* 232 (Apr.-June 1978): 200. The article was first delivered by its author as a paper to the International Congress of Historical Sciences in San Francisco in 1975.

6. Sweeping generalization though this is, it emerges from a careful perusal of Amos J. Peaslee's compilation of constitutions.

7. "First Drafts of Human Rights Bill Completed," *United Nations Bulletin: A Concise Account of the Work of the United Nations and its Related Agencies* 4 (15 Jan. 1948): 74–78. For the completed text, see ibid. 6 (1 Jan. 1949): 6–8.

8. *AP* (18 Aug. 1789), 8:454.

9. Antoine de Baecque, "'Le choc des opinions': Le débat des droits de l'homme, juillet-août 1789" in de Baecque, 7–35.

10. François Furet, *Penser la Révolution française* (Paris, 1978), *passim*.

11. Gauchet, 19–28, 38, 75–93, 107–10.

12. Blandine Barret-Kriegel, *Les droits de l'homme et le droit naturel* (Paris, 1989), *passim*.

13. Philippe Raynaud, "La Déclaration des droits de l'homme," in *The Political Culture of the French Revolution*, vol. 2 of *The French Revolution and the Creation of Modern Political Culture*, ed. Colin Lucas (Oxford and New York, 1988), 139–49. For another example of the same tendency, see Marcel Thomann's "Origines et sources doctrinales de la Déclaration des droits," in *Droits: Revue française de théorie juridique* 8 (1988): 55–70, which concludes that Lockean positivists prevailed over the proponents of natural rights in August 1789.

14. Stéphane Rials, "L'esprit de la Déclaration" in Rials, 396–98. Compare this assessment with the same author's "Des droits de l'homme aux lois de l'homme," *Commentaire* 34 (1986): 281 ff.

15. Gauchet, 36–37.

16. Le Hodey de Sachevreuil, *Journal des Etats-généraux* (20 Aug. 1789), 3:22–23; *AP* (21 Aug. 1789), 8:463–65.

17. Article 6 of the Declaration seems to have been taken from parts of Articles 18 and 26 of Sieyès's first project or 17, 21, and 28 of his second one; Articles 19, 22, and 25 from Thouret's project; and Article 22 from the Sixth Bureau's project. See the pertinent texts in Rials, 604–5, 618–19, 622, 638–39.

18. *AP* (14 July 1789), 8:231.

19. *OC* 12: *Souvenirs*, ed. Luc Monnier, 83.

20. Leonard Krieger, *The German Idea of Freedom* (Boston, 1957).

21. I am indebted for parts of this paragraph to Paul Cohen's "The Revolutionary Moment of Freedom from Rousseau to Foucault: A Trope in Modern French Thought," which he kindly lent me in manuscript. Cohen in turn derives much from while taking issue with Michel Crozier's *La société bloquée* (Paris, 1970).

22. *OC* 2.1: *L'ancien régime et la Révolution*, 249.

CHAPTER I

Colleagues too numerous to mention (at meetings in Saint Louis, in my department's colloquium, and at the Western Society for French Historical Studies meeting in December 1992) helped by their questions. For providing specific references and observations useful for illustrating or extending the analysis, however, I should thank in particular David Bell, Gail Bossenga, Marvin Cox, Laura Lee Downs, Steven L. Kaplan, Alison Patrick, Jacob M. Price, and of course Richard Davis and Dale Van Kley.

1. Nothing in this brief discussion will surprise readers of Marc Bloch. See his *La société féodale. La formation des liens de dépendance* (Paris, 1939–40) (in English, *Feudal Society* [London, 1961], vol. 1, *The Growth of Ties of Dependence*). For what follows on later feudalism and the state it is no doubt useless to cite all the helpful older works of legal-institutional historians. I should mention, however, a particular debt to the writings of Joseph R. Strayer and, as will be obvious to those who knew it, to the teaching of Charles H. Taylor.

2. The best analysis is by Ladislas Konopczynski who studied why the majority principle failed to develop in Poland. His ideas are outlined in "Une antithèse du principe majoritaire en droit polonais," in *Essays in Legal History*, ed. Paul Vinogradoff (London, 1913), 336–47; the ideas are developed and applied in Konopczynski, *Le liberum véto: étude sur le développement du principe majoritaire* (Paris, 1930).

3. Michael Roberts, "The Military Revolution, 1560–1660," in id., *Essays in Swedish History* (London, 1967), 195–225. Roberts's article has helped to generate an expanding literature, but see in particular Geoffrey Parker, "The 'Military Revolution,' 1560–1660—a Myth?" *JMH* 48 (June 1976):

195–214. Parker opened a friendly debate that left the larger part of Roberts's argument standing.

4. P. G. M. Dickson, *The Financial Revolution in England. A Study in the Development of Public Credit, 1688–1756* (London, 1967). For this and the following discussion of British financial matters, see chaps. 1–5, 9, 10, 19.

5. The interest rates are presented conveniently in T. S. Ashton, *Economic Fluctuations in England, 1700–1800* (Oxford, 1959), 187.

6. Dickson, *Financial Revolution*, 39–50.

7. Philip A. Knachel, *England and the Fronde. The Impact of the English Civil War and Revolution on France* (Ithaca, NY, 1967), 27–28, 36–45, 63–64, 80–90, 108–10, 136.

8. For a fuller discussion of the part of the "system" tied to venal offices, see D. Bien, "Offices, Corps, and a System of State Credit: The Uses of Privilege under the Ancien Régime," in *The Political Culture of the Old Regime*, vol. 1 of *The French Revolution and the Creation of Modern Political Culture*, ed. Keith Michael Baker (Oxford, 1987), 89–114.

9. BN, MSS fr. 14084, "Mémoire sur l'état actuel des offices tant casuels qu'à survivance," 1–21.

10. Norman Sykes, *Church and State in England in the XVIIIth Century* (Cambridge, 1934), 297–315; id., *From Sheldon to Secker. Aspects of English Church History, 1660–1768* (Cambridge, 1959), 36–67. And see Norman Ravitch, *Sword and Mitre. Government and Episcopate in France and England in the Age of Aristocracy* (The Hague, 1966), 194–213, for England and for the comparison with France.

11. AN, P3917, register of receipts for payments by *communautés d'arts et métiers* relative to *édit* of Feb. 1745.

12. The sample comes in part from the AN and BN, but also from the rich pamphlet collection of the Newberry Library in Chicago.

13. AN, D^{XVII}2, doss. 24, no. 8, "Mémoire pour la communauté des procureurs postulans en la cour des comptes, aides, et finances, et au bureau des présidens trésoriers généraux de France de la ville d'Aix. Adressé à l'Assemblée Nationale" [before Aug. 1790].

14. AN, D^{XVII}2, doss. 24, no. 2, "Mémoire pour la communauté des procureurs au parlement de Provence adressé à l'Assemblée Nationale" (printed copy in BN, Lf^{42}48, Aix 1790).

15. AN, AD^{XI}58, *Pétition des agens de change de Lyon à l'Assemblée Nationale* (Paris, 1791), 3, 10–11.

16. NL, Case folio FRC 10176, *Réclamation de la Communauté des Maîtres Perruquiers de la Ville de Dijon, Département de la Côte d'Or, à l'Assemblée Nationale*, 2.

17. AN, AD$_{XI}$58, *Pétition des agens de change de Lyon*, 1–2, D^{XVII}2, doss. 24, no. 2, "Mémoire au parlement de Provence."

18. AN, AD$_{XI}$58, *Mémoire à l'Assemblée Nationale pour les Agens de change de la ville de Paris* (Paris, 1790), 5. Fuller documentation and discussion of the episode are in D. Bien, "Property in Office under the Old Regime: The Case of the Stockbrokers," in John Brewer and Susan Staves, eds., *Early Modern Conceptions of Property* (London, forthcoming).

19. AN, H¹1456, no. 156, "Au Roi, et à nos seigneurs de son conseil." For Turpin, see J. F. Bosher, *French Finances, 1770–1795. From Business to Bureaucracy* (Cambridge, 1970), 115, 242; Michel Bruguière, *Gestionnaires et profiteurs de la Révolution. L'administration des finances françaises de Louis XVI à Bonaparte* (Paris, 1986), 288–89.

20. NL, Case FRC307, *Adresse des ci-devant Procureurs au Parlement de Provence. À l'Assemblée Nationale. Sur le Projet du Comité de Judicature pour le remboursement des Offices ministériels* (Aix, 1790), 9; AN, AD^{IX}540, *Mémoire contenant des observations de localité, Pour les Procureurs au Présidial de Riom*, 6–7; NL, Case folio FRC 10262, *Secondes, et respectueuses Remontrances des Lieutenant et Syndics de la Communauté des Maîtres Perruquiers de la ville de Paris, d'après le voeu des Assemblées tenues en leur Bureau, aux termes de leurs Statuts et Reglemens, à l'Assemblée Nationale* (Paris, n.d.), 4.

21. AN, P4232, *Trésorier des revenus casuels*, register of receipts for payments by *secrétaires du roi*, 1743.

22. AN, P3917, *Trésorier des revenus casuels*, receipts for payments by guilds; *AP* (30 Jan. 1793), 58:53.

23. The random choices for annual reimbursement by identification numbers for the individual contracts permits calculating the approximate number of investors in each of eleven loans of the Estates of Languedoc. See AN, H¹748^{138}, no. 7, *Loteries tirées en présence de Nosseigneurs les Commissaires du Roi et de l'Assemblée des Etats-Généraux . . . de Languedoc . . . du 9 février 1786* (Montpellier, 1786). In 1789 the clergy's loans were made up of 21,628 "parties" or contracts. See tables in AN, D^{VI}11, "Recherches sur l'origine des differentes parties de rentes qui ont été acquittées jusques et compris l'année 1789 à la Recette Générale du Clergé."

24. AN, D^{XI}1, "À Messieurs les Representants de la Nation française" (marked "reçu le 3 octobre, Les Ardennes").

25. NL, Case FRC122, *Adresse à l'Assemblée Nationale par les Procureurs au Chatelet de Paris* (Paris, 1790), 2–10; Case FRC6802, *Pétition des Procureurs au Châtelet de Paris, à l'Assemblée Nationale* (Paris, Oct. 1790), 2 n.1; AN, Y6608–6609, "Registre[s] des délibérations de la communauté des procureurs au Châtelet de Paris" (13 Mar. 1768–12 Oct. 1783).

26. AN, V²55, *mémoire* on finances, Grande Chancellerie, included with minutes of meeting of 16 Nov. 1790; D^{VI}10, "Pétition des cent vingt huissiers priseurs de Paris à l'Assemblée Nationale" (Mar. 1791) and J.A. Lemoine, *Rapport et projet de décret . . . sur le mode de liquidation des offices des huissiers priseurs de la Commune de Paris* (repr. in AP [22 Oct. 1793], 77:392–97); D^{XVII}2, doss. 24, no. 1, "Mémoire pour les procureurs à la Cour des Comptes Aides et Finances et au Bureau des Finances de la Généralité de Provence"; D^{XI}1, "À Messieurs les Representants de la Nation française" (from wigmakers of Sedan).

27. AN, V²72, Registre des délibérations de la Compagnie de Messieurs les conseillers secrétaires du Roy (6 May 1755–1767); V²54, Délibérations [of *secrétaires du roi*], 1769–71; D^{XI}1, "Mémoire relatif aux arrérages arriérés des rentes duës par la sénéchaussée de Grasse"; D^{XVII}6, doss. 85, no. 16, "Raport

pour les officiers de la Sénéchaussée et Siège Présidial d'Armagnac Séant à Lectoure"; BN, JF 2151, fols. 92–105 (papers concerning jurés-priseurs at Châtelet of Paris).

28. AN, AD$_{XI}$58, *Pétition des agens de change de Lyon*, 4–6; Y6609, "Registre des délibérations de la communauté des procureurs au Châtelet de Paris." (Sept. 1776–Oct. 1783), fols. 67–69, 79–81, 86–90; D^{XVII}6, doss. 84, no. 11, letter, no date, Moussu to "Ministre de la justice, garde du sçeau de l'état."

29. AN, Y6608, 6609, délibérations, procureurs au Châtelet de Paris (Mar. 1768–Oct. 1783); D^{XVII}6, doss. 87, no. 4, "Pétition de Mr de Montleveaud, père, Maître des Comptes, au comité de judicature, ou à l'Assemblée Nationale" (n.d.).

30. AN, V^{2}55, 12 June 1782, Guénard to *compagnie des secrétaires du roi*. For *procureurs* at Bourg-en-Bresse, F^{1A}401, *À l'Assemblée Nationale. Pétition des Procureurs du Présidial de Bourg, chef-lieu du département de l'Ain* (Bourg, 13 Nov. 1790), 4; for Parisian wigmakers, D^{XI}1, letter "à Messieurs du Comité de Judicature" (marked "reçu le 20 août 1791").

31. AN, D^{XVII}2, doss. 24, no. 1, "Mémoire pour les procureurs à la Cour des Comptes Aides et Finances et au Bureau des Finances de la Généralité de Provence."

32. Quotations from BN, JF 1728, "Observations sur deux propositions des Arts et Mestiers, Pour connoistre celle dont de Roy peut tirer plus de finance," fols. 55–56. In addition, see fols. 1–201 for other relevant documents.

33. The narrative in this paragraph is derived from the reports on meetings of officers and members of the Grande Chancellerie in 1770–71. The reports are in AN, V^{2}54. All quotations of remarks by the *sindic* and others in the succeeding two paragraphs come from the same reports and can be located from the dates of meetings indicated in the text.

34. Steven L. Kaplan, "The Character and Implications of Strife among the Masters inside the Guilds of Eighteenth-Century Paris," *Journal of Social History* 19 (Summer 1986): 631–47.

35. AN, V^{2}54, minutes of meetings, 6 and 8 May 1769.

36. Bibliothèque de l'Arsenal, MS. de la Bastille 12245, quoted by Kaplan, "The Character and Implications of Strife," 636.

37. NL, Case folio FRC suppl. 152, *Mémoire pour MM. les privilégiés de la communauté des maîtres perruquiers* (at Versailles), 1–4; Case folio FRC 10107, *Pétition des perruquiers-locataires, au Conseil Général de la Commune de Paris* (n.d.). See also Michael Sonenscher, "Journeymen, the Courts and the French Trades, 1781–1791," *Past and Present* 114 (Feb. 1987): 77–109. This article is interesting for suggesting how the settled journeymen, who worked for wages, nonetheless formed communities that were almost mirror images of the corps of masters. The journeymen possessed legally enforceable rights, hired lawyers, commonly entered the courts to defend their interests by lawsuits rather than the strike, and when summoned to do so chose representatives to speak for them.

38. On the breakdown of the old order, see Gail Bossenga, "From Corps to Citizenship: the *Bureaux des Finances* before the French Revolution," *JMH*

58 (Sept. 1986): 610–42; and id., *The Politics of Privilege: Old Regime and Revolution at Lille* (Cambridge, 1991).

Chapter 2

1. Edmund Burke, *Reflections on the Revolution in France* (Indianapolis, 1955), 36–40, 66–70.

2. Adolphe Hippolyte Taine, *Les origines de la France contemporaine*, 35th ed., 12 vols. (Paris, 1904–6), 3:229–30; 4:40–42, 44.

3. François Furet, "The Revolution is Over," in id., *Interpreting the French Revolution*, trans. Elborg Forster (Cambridge, 1981), 1–79.

4. Gauchet, 13–35. See also Rials, 355–72; and Philippe Raynaud, "La déclaration des droits de l'homme" in *The Political Culture of the French Revolution*, vol. 2 of *The French Revolution and the Creation of Modern Political Culture*, ed. Colin Lucas (Oxford, 1988), 139–49.

5. F. A. Mignet, *History of the French Revolution, from 1789 to 1814*, trans. anonymous (London, 1891), 61–62.

6. Alphonse Aulard, *The French Revolution: A Political History*, trans. Bernard Miall, 4 vols. (New York, 1915), 1:155–56. See also Marie-Joseph-Louis-Adolph Thiers, *History of the French Revolution*, trans. Frederick Shiberl, 4 vols. (New York, 1882), 1:86.

7. Georges Lefebvre, *The Coming of the French Revolution*, Robert R. Palmer, trans. (Princeton, NJ, 1947), 173.

8. For example, Article 4 from Pennsylvania's declaration states that "all power being originally being inherent in, and consequently derived from, the people; therefore all officers of government, whether legislative or executive are . . . accountable to them." See Francis Newton Thorpe, *The Federal and State Constitutions, Colonial Charters, and Other Organic Laws of the States, Territories, and Colonies Now or Hereafter Forming the United States of America*, 7 vols. (Washington DC, 1909), 5:3082. See also Articles 2 and 4 from the declarations or bills of rights from the states of Virginia and Maryland in ibid. 7:3813 and 3:1687 respectively.

9. For example, Article 5 in New Hampshire's bill to the effect that "every individual has a natural and inalienable right to worship God according to the dictates of his own conscience, and reason . . . provided he doth not disturb the public peace, or disturb others, in their religious worship" in ibid. 4:2454. See also Articles 2 and 3 of the declaration of Massachusetts in ibid. 3:1891.

10. On the common law of England, see the Maryland declaration, Article 3 (ibid. 3:1686–87); on trial by jury, see the North Carolina declaration, Article 14 (ibid. 5:2788); and on general warrants, see Virginia's bill, Article 11 (ibid. 7:3814).

11. For warnings against a "metaphysical exposition" and advice in favor of an English bill, see the remarkable speeches by Pierre-Victor Malouet and Trophime-Gérard, marquis de Lally-Tollendal, in *AP* (1 and 19 Aug. 1789), 8:822–23, 458–59. For an example of a draft closely modeled after the American ones, see Boislandry's in *AP* (21 Aug. 1789), 8:468–70. On the Sieyèsian

derivation of the draft by the National Assembly's Sixth Bureau, see Ph. Dawson, "Le 6e bureau de l'Assemblée nationale et son projet de déclaration des droits de l'homme, juillet 1789," in *AHRF* 232 (Apr.–June 1978):161–79. That draft can be found in the *AP* (12 Aug. 1789), 8:431–32.

12. For Pétion's comment, see *AP* (23 Aug. 1789), 8:475; and for Rabaut Saint-Etienne's speech, ibid., 479.

13. The best work on the prerevolutionary period 1787–89 remains Jean Egret's *La Pré-Révolution française* (Paris, 1962). More recently William Doyle's *The Origins of the French Revolution*, 2d ed. (Oxford, 1988) and Bailey Stone's *The French Parlements and the Crisis of the Old Regime* (Chapel Hill, NC, 1986), have recounted this period with less emphasis on "aristocratic reaction." Kenneth Margerison first underscored the importance of historical argumentation in the pamphlet literature of the period in "History, Representative Institutions, and Political Rights in the French Pre-Revolution (1787–1789)," *FHS* 15 (1987): 68–98; in so doing, he was following up certain leads in Furet, "The Revolution is Over," 33–36.

14. *Objets proposés à l'Assemblée des notables par de zélés citoyens* (Paris, 1787), 5–7. On the principles of national legislative sovereignty and the separation of legislative and executive powers, see *Recherches curieuses et instructions sur les Etats-généraux* (Amsterdam, 1788), 2; and on the antiquity of national assemblies, *Instructions sur les assemblées nationales, tant générales que particulières, depuis le commencement de la monarchie, jusqu'à nos jours; avec le détail du cérémonial, observé dans celle d'aujourd'hui* (Paris, 1787), 179–82.

15. *Lettre d'un anglois à Paris* (London, 1787), 7–8, 17. For other appeals to the principles of equality, utility, and the general good, see [Jean Baptiste Gerbier's] "avertissement" in *Collections des mémoires présentés à l'assemblée des notables* (Lyon, 1787), vii; and *Le bon citoyen* (n.p., 1787), 17.

16. Antoine-Pierre-Joseph-Marie Barnave, *Esprit des édits enregistrés militairement au parlement de Grenoble, le 10 mai 1788* (n.p., n.d.).

17. For a particularly arresting example of an older species of parlementary constitutionalism which saw the Parlement of Paris instead of the Estates General as the true successor of France's ancient national assemblies, see the anonymous *La nouvelle conférence entre un ministre d'Etat et un conseiller au parlement* (n.p., n.d.), 21, 25-26.

18. For a theologically informed attack on the whole notion of divine right, see Gabriel-Nicolas Maultrot, *Origines et justes bornes de la puissance royale*, 3 vols. (n.p., 1789), 1:1–35; and for an expression of preference for republican government, see Pierre-Jean Agier, *Le jurisconsulte national, ou principes sur les droits les plus importants de la nation*, 3 pts. (n.p., 1788), 3:155–56.

19. D'Antraigues. On its author and number of editions, see Guy-Chaussinand Nogaret, *La noblesse au XVIIIe siècle: De la féodalité aux lumières* (Paris, 1976), 34–36.

20. D'Antraigues, 7, 18, 46.

21. Ibid., 47; see also 20–21, 55–56.

22. On binding mandate, ibid., 19; on medieval declaration of rights, see 103; on medieval parlements, 100–101, 112–13; on recent oppression of parlements, 14–15, 222–23.

23. Ibid., 34–35.

24. On Charles VII and Louis XI, ibid., 132–33, 137; on Louis XII and Henry IV, see 34–35, 150, 191; on Richelieu, Mazarin, and "ministerial despotism," 40, 210–12; and on divine right, 106.

25. Ibid., 7.

26. The Rousseauian lines are in ibid., 8, 17; for some examples of his use of the expression *"volonté générale,"* see 25–29, 127, 234.

27. For citations from Boulainvilliers's *Histoire de l'ancien gouvernement de France,* ibid., 104, 132, 211, 236; and from Montesquieu's *Esprit des loix,* 47, 77. For expressions of sympathy for parlementary magistrates, see 14–15 and 222–23, which mention the imprisoned Duval d'Eprémesnil by name; for condemnations of nobility and feudalism, see 61, 81-82, 85-86, 92-93.

28. *Maximes du droit public françois, tirées des capitulaires, des ordonnances du royaume, et des autres monuments de l'histoire de France,* 2 vols., 2d ed. (Amsterdam, 1775). The work is explicitly cited in d'Antriagues, 163 and 200.

29. D'Antraigues: on grace and divine right, see 61, 106, 160–61; on the right to convoke the Estates General, 189–90; on *lit de justice,* 120–21; on Loyseu, 157–58; on passive obedience, 62–63, 171.

30. Ibid., 106.

31. Ibid., 171. Hotman is cited on 10–11.

32. For the phrase "political Augustinianism" I am indebted to H.-X. Arquillière, *L'augustinisme politique: Essai sur la formulation des théories politiques du moyen âge* (Paris, 1955).

33. D'Antraigues: on the binding mandate, bailliages, and the importance of "antique forms," see 16, 19–20, 112, 122–31, 173–74, 188–89, 191, 226-47; and on the conception of laws as sacred "verities," see 25–26, 173–74.

34. By "general will" d'Antraigues meant, in his own words, "that point where the difference [in interests] ceases . . . [and] which rallies all interests as a single one" (ibid., 29). That definition seems to point, not to the annihilation of particular interest and its replacement by the general will, but to those areas where particular interests overlap or coincide.

35. Ibid., 32.

36. Ibid., 92–93, 246–47. For like-minded compliments proferred to the Third Estate, see 198–99. For judgment of feudalism as "dangerous," see 85.

37. For evidence that some pamphlets were in fact subsidized by the ministry, see for example Siméon-Prosper Hardy, "Mes loisirs, ou journal d'événemens tels qu'ils parviennent à ma connoissance," in MSS Fr 6686, 473 (7 June 1788).

38. *Réclamation du Tiers-état au roi* (n.p., 1788), 3–5; *Délibération à prendre par le Tiers-état, dans toutes les municipalités du royaume de France* (n.p., n.d.), 1, 6.

39. [Michel-Ange Mangourit], *Le tribun du peuple au peuple* (Paris, 1788), 6–7.

40. *La tête leur tourne* (n.p., 1788), 17–18.

41. *Le Tiers-état éclairé, ou ses droits justifiés* (n.p., 1788), 10. Louis XI, in the original text, "met les Rois hors du paye." The expression "hors du paye" is difficult to translate, but clearly means that Louis XI made the monarchy financially independent of the Estates General or of French subjects' right to consent to taxes.

42. *Je m'en rapporte à tout le monde, ou réflexions impartiales sur les affaires actuelles* (London, 1788), 3.

43. For an example of an appeal to an anti-"aristocratic" Rousseau, see the anonymous *De profundis de la noblesse et du clergé* (n.p., 1789), 19. For appeals to the royalist Voltaire, see *Arrêté de la France, pour les Etats-généraux de l'année 1789* (Paris, 1789), 11. On Voltaire's political thought, see Peter Gay, *Voltaire's Politics: The Poet as Realist* (Princeton, 1959); and Durand Echeverria, *The Maupeou Revolution: a Study in the History of Libertarianism* (Baton Rouge, LA, 1985), 147–68.

44. Jean-Marie-Antoine-Nicolas Caritat, marquis de Condorcet, *Sentiments d'un républicain, sur les assemblées provinciales et les Etats-généraux. Suite des lettres d'un citoyen des Etats-Unis à un Français, sur les affaires présentes* (Philadelphia, 1788), 25, 20-21. On physiocratic political thought, see chaps. 4 and 8 below.

45. Nicolas Simon-Henri Linguet, *Annales politiques, civiles et littéraires du dix-huitième siècle*. On Linguet, see Darlene Gay Levy, *The Ideas and Careers of Simon-Nicolas-Henri Linguet* (Urbana, 1980); and Hans-Ulrich Thämer, *Revolution und Reaktion in der Französische Sozialkritik des 18. Jahrhunderts: Linguet, Mably, Babeuf* (Frankfurt, 1973).

46. Nicolas-Simon-Henri Linguet, *Réflexions sur la résistance opposée à l'exécution des ordonnances promulgués le 8 mai; suivi de la différence entre la révolution passagère de 1771, et la réforme de 1788, dans l'ordre judiciare en France* (Brussels, 1788), 90–91.

47. Linguet, *La France plus qu'angloise, ou comparaison entre la procédure entamée à Paris le 25 septembre 1788 contre les ministres du roi de France, et le procès intenté à Londres en 1640, au comte de Strafford, principale ministre de Charles premier, roi d'Angleterre. Avec des réflexions sur le danger imminent dont les entreprises de la robe menacent la nation, et les particuliers* (Brussels, 1788), 111.

48. Quotes from ibid., 82–87.

49. Quotations from [Linguet], *La tête leur tourne* (n.p., n.d.), 8–9.

50. Linguet, *Quelle est l'origine des Etats-générux* (n.p., 1788), 5–6. On "coalition" between the robe, clergy, and nobility, see Linguet, *Onguent pour le brûlure, ou observations sur un réquisitoire imprimé en tête de l'arrêt du parlement de Paris, du 27 septembre 1788, rendu contre les Annales de M. Linguet* (London, 1788), 8–9.

51. Quotations from Linguet, *La France plus qu'angloise*, 123–24.

52. Levy, *Ideas and Careers of Linguet*, 123. For a particularly clear statement of the incompatibility between the general will and particular corps in Jean-Jacques Rousseau's thought, see his *Considérations sur le gouvernement de Pologne* in V. D. Musset-Pathay, ed., *Oeuvres complètes de J.-J. Rousseau*, 25 vols. (Paris, 1823–25), 5:297.

53. Linguet, *Avis aux Parisiens. Appel de toutes conventions d'Etats-généraux où les députés du troisième ordre ne seroient pas supérieurs aux deux autres* (n.p., n.d.), 1–2, 6, 10–11.

54. Four of these are *Réflections d'un citoyen sur l'édit de décembre 1770* (n.p., n.d.); *Nouvelles réflexions d'un citoyen sur l'édit de décembre 1770* (n.p., n.d.); *Remontrances d'un citoyen aux parlemens de France* (n.p., n.d.); and *Réponse au citoyen qui a publié ses réflexions* (n.p., n.d.). The attribution of them to Linguet is Louis-Adrien Le Paige's in Bibliothèque de Port-Royal, Collection Le Paige, ms. 804, nos. 8–11. If, as is here assumed, Linguet was the veritable author of the anonymous *La tête leur tourne*, then he would have quite literally quoted himself in 1788, since that pamphlet had originally been published in defense of Maupeou in 1771.

55. René-Louis de Voyer de Paulmy, marquis d'Argenson, *Considérations sur le gouvernment ancien et présent de la France* (Amsterdam, 1765), 123–24. On the anti-aristocratic and anti-feudal bias of royalist historiography, see Harold Ellis, *Boulainvilliers and the French Monarchy: Aristocratic Politics in Early Eighteenth-Century France* (Ithaca, NY, 1988), 31–39; and J.Q.C. Mackrell, *The Attack on Feudalism in Eighteenth-Century France* (London and Toronto, 1988), 17–47.

56. On medieval justifications, see Gaines Post, "*Ratio Publicae Utilitatis, Ratio Statis,* and 'Reason of State'," in id., *Studies in Medieval Legal Thought: Public Law and the State, 1100–1302* (Princeton, NJ, 1964), 241–309; on appeals to utility and necessity, see also William Farr Church, *Richelieu and Reason of State* (Princeton, 1972), as well as his earlier *Constitutional Thought in Sixteenth-Century France* (Cambridge, MA, 1941), *passim*; and on physiocracy, see Léon Cheinisse, *Les idées politiques des physiocrates* (Paris, 1914).

57. [Linguet], *La tête leur tourne*, 12. On "aristocratic" coalition, see Linguet, *Onguent pour le brûlure*, 8–9; and for more on the "despotism of these supposed [*parlementaire*] enemies of ministerial despotism," see id., *La France plus qu'Angloise*, 8.

58. *Le roi et ses ministres, dialogues* (n.p., n.d.), 3–4.

59. On the probable intentions behind the Parlement's *arrêt* of 25 September 1788, see Dale Van Kley, "The Estates General as Ecumenical Council: The Constitutionalism of Corporte Consensus and the Parlement's Ruling of September 25, 1788," *JMH* 61 (Mar. 1989): 1–52.

60. Assemblée des notables, *Motifs des douze notables, au bureau de monsieur; pour adopter, contre l'avis des treize, l'avis qui a prévalu dans les cinq autres bureaux* (n.p., n.d.), 4, 6-7.

61. Jean-Baptiste Target: on despotism and aristocracy, *Suite de l'écrit intitulé: Les Etats-généraux convoqués par Louis XVI* (n.p., n.d.), 36–37; on en-

larging the delegation of the Third Estate, see *Les Etats-généraux convoqués par Louis XVI* (n.p., n.d.), 48–49, 53, 63. Even his *IIe Suite* (n.p., n.d.), 14, continued to defend the purity of the Parlement of Paris's intentions on 25 September 1788.

62. Abbé Emmanuel-Joseph Sieyès, *Qu'est-ce que le Tiers état,* ed. Edme Champion (Paris, 1982), 36, 54.

63. Joseph-Antoine Cérutti, *Mémoire pour le peuple français* (n.p., 1788), 37; Jean-Paul Rabaut de Saint-Etienne, *Considérations sur les intérêts du Tiers-état, adressées au peuple des provinces, par un propriétaire foncier* (Paris, 1788), 13; Jean-Nicolas Desmeuniers, *Des conditions nécessaires à la légalité des Etats-généraux* (n.p., 1788); Pierre-Louis Lacretelle, *De la convocation de la prochaine tenue des Etats-généraux en France* (Paris, 1788), 8; and d'Antraigues, 17–18.

64. Sieyès's first two pamphlets are *Vues sur les moyens d'exécution dont les représantants de la France pourront disposer en 1789* (n.p., 1789); and *Essai sur les privilèges* (Paris, 1788). My account of the progression of these pamphlets is dependent on Murray Forsyth, *Reason and Revolution: The Political Thought of the Abbé Sieyès* (New York, 1987), 16–17.

65. Sieyès, *Qu-est-ce que le Tiers-état*: on utility, 28–30; on necessity, 34, 56, 82, 85, 87, 90; on nation as master of positive law, 70, 74; on nation and natural law, 68; on political and civil rights, 31, 39, 41, 44, 85; on will and the general will (also called "general interest" and "common interest"), *passim* but esp. 44.

66. Jean-Nicolas Desmeuniers, *Des conditions nécessaires* (n.p., 1788), 16, 24, 32.

67. Rabaut de Saint-Étienne, *Considérations sur les intérêts du Tiers-état,* 35, 38, 57, 64.

68. *L'anti-moteur, ou réponse à la motion de Monseigneur le prince de Conty, du 28 novembre 1788* (n.p., n.d.), 4–5, 6.

69. *Français, prenez y garde à vous* (n.p., 1788), 7, 9, 14.

70. This assertion is more amply documented by Jeremy Popkin and myself in "The Pre-Revolutionary Debate/Le débat pré-révolutionnaire" in Colin Lucas, ed., *The Pre-Revolutionary Debate*: section 5 of *The French Revolution Research Collection* (Oxford, 1990), 1–40. That essay in turn rests on an examination of more than thirty thousand pages of prerevolutionary pamphlets published in microfiche form by Pergamon Press.

71. On the "democracy" implicit not only in this ruling, but also in the electoral regulations of 24 January 1789, see François Furet, "La monarchie et le règlement électoral de 1789," in *The Political Culture of the Old Regime,* vol. 1 of *The French Revolution and the Creation of Modern Political Culture,* ed. Keith M. Baker, (Oxford, 1987), 375–86.

72. *Aux Etats-généraux, sur les réforme à faire* (n.d., 1789); Charles-Pierre Bosguillon, *Code national, dédié aux Etats-généraux* (Geneva, 1788); *Discours à la nation, sur les principaux objets dont elle doit s'occuper dans sa prochaine assemblée, pour la régénération de l'état, par un Français* (n.p., 1789).

73. For example, *Bréviaire des députés aux Etats-généraux* (n.p., 1789); F.-M. Martinet, *Résultat des Etat-généraux prédit par Minerve* (n.p., 1789); and *Réflexions toutes naturelles d'un Normand, qui ne prétend rien aux honneurs ni à la fortune, qui, par cette raison, écrit ce qu'il pense* (n.p., 1789).

74. *AP* (5 May 1789), 8:16, 23–24. The term "astonishing" is Jacques-Antoine Creuzé de La Touche's in *Journal des Etats-généraux et du début de l'assemblée nationale, 18 mai-29 juillet 1789*, ed. Jean Marchand (Paris, 1946), 9–11.

75. *AP* (13 May 1789), 8:36, and in general, 32–36.

76. Ibid. (25 May 1789), 47, and in general, 36–47.

77. Le Hodey de Saultchevreuil, *Journal des Etats-généraux* (28 May 1789), 1:65; and *AP* (28 May 1789), 8:52–55.

78. *Journal des Etats-généraux* (28 May 1789), 1:73–74. See also *AP* (28 May 1789), 8:58–59.

79. *AP* (6 June 1789), 8:75.

80. Ibid. (5 June 1789), 70.

81. For Bergasse's comment, see *Journal des Etats-généraux* (15 June 1789), 1:95; for Rabaut de Saint-Étienne's, Mirabeau's, and Camus's opinions on the need for the king's sanction, see *AP* (15–16 June 1789), 8:113, 118, 121.

82. *AP* (20 June 1789), 8:138–39.

83. Ibid. (23 June 1789), 146; and *Journal des Etats-généraux* (23 June 1789), 1:205–6. Bertrand Barère's *Le point du jour* (25 June 1789), 1:41–42, maintains that Camus was the first to speak.

84. For Mirabeau's comments, *AP* (16 and 27 June 1789), 8:124, 165–66; for Lanjuinais's, ibid., 163.

85. Creuzé de La Touche, *Journal des Etats-généraux*, 9, 11, 14–15, 38–39.

86. Ibid: on Mirabeau, 30; on Camus, 32; on Necker's plan, 86–90; on National Assembly and royal sanction, 113; on day of Tennis Court Oath, 132; on "royal session," 139–42.

87. Adrien-Cyprien Duquesnoy, *Journal d'Adrien Duquesnoy, député du Tiers état de Bar-Le-Duc sur l'Assemblée constituante, 3 mai 1789–3 avril 1790*, ed. Robert Crevecoeur, 2 vols. (Paris, 1894), 1:38.

88. Ibid., 6–10.

89. Ibid: on duc de Praslin and nobility, 18–19; on the Third's constituting itself as National Assembly, 78; on fearful reaction to Tennis Court Oath, 112–13; on "royal session," 121.

90. *Nouvelle adresse des communes au roi par un citoyen non député* (n.p., 1789), 6–7; *Le spectateur des Etats-généraux* (n.p., 1789), 23–24; see also *Le reveil d'un grand roi, 8 juin 1789* (n.p., 1789), 3, 6.

91. *Le premier coup de vêpres: avis à la chambre des communes, sur la retraite des privilégiés* (n.p., 1789), 7–9, 15–16.

92. *Un plébien, à M. le comte d'Antraigues, sur son apostasie, sur le schisme de la noblesse, et sur son arrêté inconstitutionel, le 28 mai 1789* (n.p., 1789), 7, 21, 27.

93. *Exposé des principes de droit public, qui démontrent que les députés*

*du Tiers-état se sont légalement constitués comme représentant la nation;
par l'auteur des Quatre mots, adressés au journaliste des Etats-généraux*
(n.p., 1789), 1–3, 12.

94. For appeal to Charlemagne's constitution, see *Le reveil d'un grand
roi*, 3; for the argument from the Parlement of Paris, see *Nouvelle adresse
des communes au roi*, 6. For two appeals to the example of the historical alliance between the king and "commons," see *Un plébien à M. le comte
d'Antraigues*, 27; and *La toison d'or, ou tout est dit; à messieurs de la chambre des communes de Versailles* (n.p., n.d.), 7–8.

95. *Aux trois ordres assemblés et non réunis*, 2d ed. (n.p., 1789), 9–15.

96. *Journal des Etats-généraux* (20–22 June 1789), 1:163, 184.

97. *Lettre du roi d'Angleterre au roi de France, sur les Etats-généraux*
(Paris, 1789), 6–7; and *Dialogue entre M. Paporet et Louis XV, ou Réflexions
sur la séance royale du 23 juin 1789* (n.p., 1789), 5.

98. *Lettre adressée à l'ordre du clergé et de la noblesse, par un patriote,
membre du Tiers-état* (n.p., n.d.), 8.

99. *Déclaration de l'ordre de la noblesse aux Etats-généraux. Du 3 juillet
1789* (n.p., 1789), 1.

100. *AP* (14 July 1789), 8:232.

101. *Le tombeau du despotisme ministériel, ou l'aurore du bonheur*
(Paris, 1789), 3; for a few other examples, see Claude Fauchet, *Discours sur la
liberté française* (n.p., 1789), 2; and *Avis au peuple, ou les ministres dévoilés*
(n.p., 1789), 15.

102. *AP* (23 May 1789), 8:46. See also ibid. (30 May 1789), 61.

103. Ibid. (15 June 1789), 119.

104. *Journal des Etats-généraux* (20 June 1789), 1:164.

105. Ibid. (12 July 1789), 2:17; and *AP* (15 June 1789), 8:107.

106. *AP* (2 July 1789), 8:181. The volume was entitled *Histoire de France
avant Clovis*.

107. For some examples of how they did so, see chap. 8 below.

108. For Stanislas de Clermont-Tonnerre's report, see *AP* (27 July 1789),
8:283; for Antoine-François Delandine's speech, ibid. (1 Aug. 1789), 323–25;
and for Jean-Baptiste Lubersac, bishop of Chartres's speech, ibid. (4 Aug.
1789), 341. On these debates, see chap. 4 below.

109. Duquesnoy, *Journal*, 38; and *AP* (20 Aug. 1789), 8:462; for Rabaut
Saint-Etienne's declaration of rights, see ibid. (Aug. 12, 1789), 406–7; and for
his speech, ibid. (23 Aug. 1789), 479.

110. This process of amalgamation of hitherto competitive rights is also
visible in the proposals for declarations that began to appear as parts of
cahiers in the late winter and spring of 1789. See the ones published by Rials,
550–67.

111. On the degree of consensus and calculated ambiguity in the Declaration of Rights, see also chaps. 4 and 5.

112. The *AP* makes the phrase "according to their capacity" part of Talleyrand's original motion (21 Aug. 1789), 8:465–66, but why in that case
would Mounier have proposed the addition of that phrase? The best account

of the incident is Le Hodey's in *Journal des Etats-généraux* (21 Aug. 1789), 3:33–40; but see also Duquesnoy's *Journal* 1:308.

113. *Journal des Etats-généraux* (26 Aug. 1789), 3:385.

114. Ran Halévi, "Les ambiguités de la révolution constituante," in *The Political Culture of the French Revolution*, vol. 2 of *The French Revolution and the Creation of Modern Political Culture*, ed. Colin Lucas (Oxford, 1988), 69–83.

115. Jean-Joseph Mounier, *Recherches sur les causes qui ont empêché les françois de devenir libres, et sur les moyens qui leur restent pour acquérir la liberté*, 2 vols. (Geneva, 1792), 1:266.

116. Henri-Baptiste Grégoire, *Opinion de M. Grégoire, curé d'Emberville et député de Nanci, sur la sanction royale. A la séance du 4 septembre* (n.p., n.d.), 10.

117. *Le point du jour* (10 Sept. 1789), 3:331–32.

118. Pierre-Samuel Dupont de Nemours, *Projet d'articles relatifs à la constitution de l'Assemblée nationale, à la forme de son travail, à la proposition, à la préparation et à la sanction des loix. Remis sur le bureau de l'Assemblée nationale, dans la séance du vendrédi 4 septembre; par M. Dupont, député de Nemours* (Paris, 1789). On the idea of a supreme court as "aristocratic," see the vicomte de Mirabeau's speech in *Le point du jour* (5 Sept. 1789), 3:305–6.

119. *Journal des Etats-généraux* (29 Aug. 1789), 3:193–94.

120. Abbé Gabriel Bonnet de Mably, *Les droits et les devoirs du citoyen*, in *Oeuvres complètes de l'abbé de Mably*, 19 vols. (Nimes and Toulouse, 1791), 17:191, 205-11. On this essay which, though written in 1758 was published only in 1789, see Keith M. Baker, "A Script for a French Revolution: The Political Consciousness of the abbé Mably" in id., *Inventing the French Revolution: Essays on French Political Culture in the Eighteenth Century* (Cambridge, 1990), 86–106.

CHAPTER 3

1. The two positions are best represented by Arthur Hertzberg, who sees the Revolution as feeding into the creation of modern anti-semitism; and Robert Badinter, who, as a French Jew, forcefully defends the Revolution's support and defense of his ancestors. See Hertzberg, *The French Enlightenment and the Jews* (New York, 1968), and Badinter, *Libres et Egaux . . . L'émancipation des Juifs (1789–1791)* (Paris, 1989). An interesting discussion of Hertzberg's position is contained in Gary Kates, "Jews into Frenchmen: Nationality and Representation in Revolutionary France," in Ferenc Fehér, ed., *The French Revolution and the Birth of Modernity* (Berkeley, 1990), 105–8.

2. Although he underlined the strength of French support for the slave revolt, C.L.R. James, in his classic *The Black Jacobins* (rev. ed. New York, 1973), argues for the autonomy of slave insurrection in Saint Domingue. A

more recent work stressing the autonomy and importance of slave activity in Saint Domingue is Carolyn Fick, *The Making of Haiti. The Saint Domingue Revolution from Below* (Knoxville, TN, 1990).

3. This is forcefully argued by Joan Landes in her *Women and the Public Sphere* (Ithaca, NY, 1988) and by Carole Pateman in *The Sexual Contract* (Stanford, 1988).

4. *AP* (24 Aug. 1789), 8:483.

5. Presently the island of Hispaniola encompassing Haiti and Santo Domingo.

6. On women and the Girondins, see Gary Kates, "'The Powers of Husband and Wife Must be Equal and Separate': The Cercle Social and the Rights of Women, 1790-91," in Harriet Bronson Applewhite and Darline Gay Levy, eds., *Women and Politics in the Age of Democratic Revolution* (Ann Arbor, 1990); on women and the *Enragés*, see Olwen Hufton, *Women and the Limits of Citizenship* (Toronto, 1992), 3-50.

7. See Olympe de Gouges's play *L'Esclavage des noirs, ou l'heureux naufrage* (Paris, 1989). Some of her other works are contained in *Women in Revolutionary Paris 1789-1795*, ed. Darline Gay Levy, Harriet Branson Applewhite, and Mary Durham Johnson (Urbana, IL, 1979). Other feminist treatises linking the cause of Blacks to that of women include *Requête des dames à l'Assemblée nationale* (n.p., 1790), from FRH, #2593, 2; and Pierre Guyomar's educational treatise, *AP* (29 Apr. 1793), 63:592.

8. On Jewish involvement in the slave trade, see Zosa Szajkowski, "Relations Among Sephardim, Ashkenazim, and Avignonese Jews in France from the 16th to the 20th Centuries," in id., *Jews and the French Revolutions of 1789, 1830 and 1848* (New York, 1970), 255. Deputies in the National Assembly linked the non-freedom of Mulattoes and Black slaves with the condition of the Jews: see *AP* (12 May 1791), 26:7-11 and *AP* (27 Sept. 1791), 31:442. Widespread belief that the Jews were from Asia inclined people to look at them as racially or ethnically different. See *AP* (23 Aug. 1789), 8:479, for a sympathetic look at them as Asian peoples. The insistence that Jews were not a religious group, but a nation, also bordered on defining them in ethnic terms. See *AP* (23 Dec. 1789), 10:756. Jews from Metz compared their situation unfavorably with that of Blacks and Indians. See *AP* (16 Sept. 1789), 9:448. Abolitionists also sought to link these causes. See Marie-Jean-Antoine-Nicolas Caritat, marquis de Condorcet, *Réflexions sur l'esclavage des nègres*, in *Oeuvres complètes de Condorcet*, ed. D.J. Garat and P.J.G. Cabanis (Paris, 1804), 11:163-65, for an innovative suggestion as to how the conditions of slaves and Jews could be simultaneously improved by granting Jews land in the New World on the condition that they slowly emancipate the slaves. See also the abbé Henri Grégoire, *A Report on Behalf of the Colored People of Saint Domingue and other French Islands in America, addressed to the National Assembly*, and his *Motion in Favor of the Jews*, in *Two Rebel Priests of the French Revolution*, trans. and ed. Raymond L. Carol (San Francisco, 1975), 36 and 29-31 respectively.

9. Quoted from Frances Malino, "The Right to be Equal: Zalkind Hourwitz and the Revolution of 1789," in *From East and West. Jews in a Changing Europe, 1750–1870*, Frances Malino and David Sorkin, eds. (Cambridge, 1990), 100.

10. *Requête des dames à l'Assemblée nationale*, 12.

11. See Shanti Singham, "A Conspiracy of Twenty Million Frenchmen: Public Opinion, Patriotism, and the Assault on Absolutism, 1770–1775" (Ph.D. diss., Princeton, 1991), 86–87, 117–18. One of the more popular pamphlets during the period spoke of the need to purify the French language of expressions like "the King my master," since terms like this were reminiscent of slavery. See *Le Parlement justifié par l'Impératrice Reine de Hongroie et le Roi de Prusse*, in *Les Efforts de la Liberté* (London, 1772–75), 4:234.

12. *AP* (23 Aug. 1789), 8:479.

13. Ibid., 477.

14. Eugen Weber makes this argument in *Peasants into Frenchmen* (Stanford, 1976), and discusses its relationship to the Jewish question in "Reflection on the Jews in France," in *The Jews in Modern France*, ed. Frances Malino and Bernard Wasserstein (London, 1985), 8–27. Following this line of reasoning, he makes the unusual claim that the Jewish question was of interest primarily to a handful of Jews and their local opponents during the Revolution. Ibid., 17.

15. *AP* (22 Oct. 1789), 9:478.

16. Ibid. (3 Aug. 1789), 8:336.

17. Ibid. (24 Dec. 1789), 10:780.

18. Grégoire, *Motion in Favor of the Jews*, 24.

19. The Jewish voice is best captured in the numerous petitions, letters, and petitions sent by Jews to the National Assembly. See *Adresses, Mémoires et Pétitions des Juifs, 1789–1794*, *LRFEDJ* 5. Of course, these were written by literate, French-speaking representatives and do not necessarily reflect the attitudes of the vast majority of poor and Judaeo-French-speaking Jews in Alsace. The best modern appraisal of Jewish responses to emancipation, especially of the Sephardim, can be found in Frances Malino's *The Sephardic Jews of Bordeaux: Assimilation and Emancipation in Revolutionary and Napoleonic France* (University, AL, 1978), especially 40–64.

20. The *Adresse présentée à l'Assemblée Nationale le 31 Aout 1789*, *LRFEDJ* 5:14, specifically asked to retain corporate institutions and officers. Later petitions dropped this request. See, for example, *Pétition des Juifs Établis en France adressé à l'Assemblée Nationale, le 28 janvier 1790, sur l'ajournement du 24 décembre 1789*, in *LRFEDJ* 5. See also Zosa Szajkowski, "Jewish Autonomy Debated and Attacked during the French Revolution," in id., *Jews and the French Revolutions*, 579–82.

21. Although representative, the *Kehillots* were not democratic. Szajkowski charts opposition to the dictates of the Sephardic communal organization on the part of poor Jews. See his "Internal Conflicts Within the Eighteenth Century Sephardic Communities in France," in id., *Jews and the French Revolutions*, 267–80.

22. For a detailed description of the differences between and amongst the Jews, see Szajkowski, "Relations Among Sephardim, Ashkenazim and Avignonese Jews in France," 235–66.

23. Jewish involvement in the colonial trades could prove problematic, given the express command of the *Code Noir*, the French slave code, that Jews could not live in New World colonies. In the eighteenth century, these restrictions were relaxed, although Jews in the New World continued to be subject to special taxes as foreigners there. See Szajkowski, "The Jewish Status in Eighteenth Century France and the 'Droit d'Aubaine,'" in id., *Jews and the French Revolutions*, 227–28.

24. Ibid., 250–53.

25. *Adresse à l'Assemblée Nationale, 31 Décembre 1789, LRFEDJ* 5; *AP* (28 Jan. 1790), 11:364. On the complications ensuing from the Sephardic insistence that they had never been communally organized, especially as relates to the fate of the Jewish cemetery in Bordeaux during the Revolution, see Malino, *The Sephardic Jews of France*, 62–64.

26. The point about the degree of rigor differing regimes used in interpreting the Decree is François Delpech's. See his "L'Histoire des Juifs en France de 1780 à 1840. État des questions et directions de recherche," in B. Blumenkranz and A. Soboul, eds., *Les Juifs et la Révolution Française* (Paris, 1989), 13–46.

27. On Voltaire and the Jews, see Richard H. Popkin, "The Philosophical Basis of Eighteenth-Century Racism," in *Studies in Eighteenth Century Culture* 3 (1973): 250. See also Hertzberg, *The French Enlightenment and the Jews*.

28. On the Terror and the Jews, see Szajkowski, "The Attitude of French Jacobins Toward Jewish Religion," in id., *Jews and the French Revolutions*, 399–412.

29. *AP* (28 Sept. 1791), 31:442.

30. See Ruth Necheles, "The Abbé Grégoire and the Jews," *Jewish Social Studies* 33 (1971): 134–35. See also Kates, "Jews into Frenchmen," 110–12, for an important discussion of the manner in which constitutional distinctions between active and passive citizenship affected the Jews.

31. The charge centered on two verses from Deuteronomy. Jewish petitioners claimed that the charge was based on a mistranslation of the Hebrew word *interest* for usury. See the *Pétition des Juifs Établis en France, LRFEDJ* 5:553–54.

32. *AP* (13 Apr. 1790), 12:711–14.

33. For an excellent discussion of this case, see Pierre Pluchon, *Nègres et Juifs au XVIIIe Siècle. Le racisme au siècle des Lumières* (Paris, 1984).

34. *AP* (28 Sept. 1789), 9.

35. This somewhat contradicts his strong statements against innate characteristics, revealing him to be not entirely above society's prejudices. See Grégoire, *Motion in Favor of the Jews*, 26.

36. Ibid., 27–29.

37. Necheles, "The Abbé Grégoire and the Jews," 134–35. She also attrib-

utes Jewish flight to revolutionary legislation of 1793 which specifically abolished Jewish corporations.

38. *Observations pour les Juifs d'Avignon, 15 Aout 1793, LRFEDJ* 5:8–13. The petition went on to note that by continuing to subject Jews to special and extraordinary taxation, "one treats Jews today as before, as citizens in matters of taxation, but as foreigners in matters of rights."

39. See Michael Burns, *Dreyfus. A Family Affair. From the French Revolution to the Holocaust* (New York, 1991), 3–26, for an excellent discussion of the way French Jews continued to remember the Revolution well into the nineteenth century.

40. See Leonore Loft, "J.-P. Brissot and the Problem of Jewish Emancipation," *Studies on Voltaire and the Eighteenth Century* 278 (1990): 465–75.

41. *AP* (13 Apr. 1790), 12:720–33. The Abbé Grégoire had argued, on the contrary, that strict immigration policing should be established to ensure that Jews from the rest of Europe not inundate France. See his *Motion in Favor of the Jews*, 26.

42. Hertzberg, *French Enlightenment*, 361–67.

43. Ruth Necheles, *The Abbé Grégoire. 1787–1831. The Odyssey of an Egalitarian* (Westport, CT, 1971), 11–14, 44. For disagreement with this position, see Bernard Plongeron's comments in "Discussion," in Blumenkranz and Soboul, eds., *Les Juifs et la Révolution Française*, 214.

44. On Grégoire's linguistic crusade, see Tim Parke, "The Abbé Grégoire and the Mother-Tongue debate, 1789–1794," *Modern and Contemporary France* 38 (1989): 26–33.

45. For the *Code Noir*, see Isambert et al. 19:494–504. Discussions of comparative slave systems in the West Indies are contained in Robin Blackburn, *The Overthrow of Colonial Slavery 1776–1848* (London, 1988); and David Brion Davis, *The Problem of Slavery in Western Culture* (Ithaca, NY, 1966) and *The Problem of Slavery in the Age of Revolution 1776–1823* (Ithaca, NY, 1975).

46. They owned about one-quarter of the land and one-third of the slaves in Saint Domingue. See Valerie Quinney, "The Problem of Civil Rights for Free Men of Color in the Early French Revolution," *FHS* 7 (Fall, 1972): 550.

47. For an account of these restrictions, see Pierre Boulle, "In Defense of Slavery: Eighteenth Century Opposition to Abolition and the Origins of a Racist Ideology in France," in *History from Below. Studies in Popular Protest and Popular Ideology*, ed. Frederick Krantz (Oxford, 1988), 219–46.

48. *AP* (28 Mar. 1790), 12:382. On Toussaint L'Ouverture and Raynal, see Blackburn, *Overthrow of Colonial Slavery*, 219, 243.

49. See especially comte de Buffon, "Variétés dans l'espèce humaine," in *Oeuvres Complètes de Buffon*, ed. J.L. de Lanessan (Paris, 1884), 11:128–222. On anti-slavery, 189; on the superiority of the French, 220; on the eventual disappearance of racial difference, 222. Excellent discussions of Buffon's views are contained in Popkin, "The Philosophical Basis of Eighteenth-Century Racism"; Philip D. Curtin, *The Image of Africa. British Ideas and Action, 1780–1850* (Madison, WI, 1964), 60–100; and William B. Cohen, *The French Encounter with the African* (Bloomington, IN, 1980), 67–86.

50. See Pluchon, *Nègres et Juifs*, 33, 256–58.

51. On the relationship between slavery and the French Revolution see David Geggus, "Racial Equality, Slavery, and Colonial Secession During the Constituent Assembly," *AHR* 94b (1989): 1290–1308. Blackburn, *Overthrow of Colonial Slavery*, 161–265, also is useful. On French abolitionism, see Daniel P. Resnick, "The *Société des Amis des Noirs* and the Abolition of Slavery," *FHS* 7 (Fall, 1972): 558–69; Serge Daget, "A Model of the French Abolitionist Movement and its Variations" in *Anti-Slavery, Religion, and Reform: Essays in Memory of Roger Anstey*, ed. Christine Bolt and Seymour Drescher (Folkstone, 1980), 43–63; and Seymour Drescher, "Two Variants of Anti-Slavery: Religious Organization and Social Mobilization in Britain and France, 1780–1870," *Anti-Slavery, Religion, and Reform*, ed. Bolt and Drescher, 64–79.

52. *AP* (3 July 1789), 8:186.

53. Ibid. (27 June 1789), 8:165.

54. This is argued by Bénot and Geggus. See Geggus, "Racial Equality, Slavery, and Colonial Secession," 1294.

55. See *A l'Assemblée nationale. Supplique et pétition des citoyens de couleur des isles et colonies françaises* (n.p., 1789), FRH #2757. Free Blacks and Mulattoes were originally hostile to one another. Free Blacks insisted that as a pure race they were superior to a race of mixed breeds. See *AP* (28 Nov. 1789), 10:329. Geggus has an excellent analysis of the racial complexities of their arguments. Geggus, "Racial Equality, Slavery, and Colonial Secession," 1296–1300.

56. On Grégoire's abolitionist efforts, see Ruth Necheles, "Grégoire and the Egalitarian Movement," *Studies in Eighteenth Century Culture* 3 (1973): 355–68.

57. Geggus, "Racial Equality, Slavery, and Colonial Secession," 1300.

58. *AP* (12 May 1791), 26:5.

59. Abbé Antoine de Cournand, *Réponse aux observations d'un habitant des colonies* (Paris, 1789), 19.

60. *AP* (14 May 1791), 26:68–69.

61. Ibid. (12 May 1791), 8. Especially clairvoyant was the deputy Robespierre.

62. For the influence of Ogé's movement on stirring up slave rebellion, see Carolyn Fick, *The Making of Haiti*, 76–91.

63. Michael Kennedy, *The Jacobin Clubs and the French Revolution* (Princeton, NJ, 1982), esp. 204–9.

64. On Mulattoes and slaves working together against white colonists, see Geggus, "Racial Equality, Slavery, and Colonial Secession," 1300. See also the debates in the National Assembly: *AP* (14 May 1791), 26:70 and *AP* (14 June 1791), 27:234.

65. Unlike many of his other colleagues in the *Société des Amis des Noirs*, Brissot was in favor of immediate emancipation. Grégoire, on the other hand, called the abrupt emancipation edict of 1794 a "disastrous measure" and Condorcet suggested that emancipation take place over a seventy-year period. See Cohen, *French Encounter*, 153, and Condorcet, *Réflexions sur l'esclavage*

des nègres, 108. On the impact of Brissot's American travels on his absolutist sentiment, see Brissot, *Mémoire sur les noirs de l'Amérique Septentrionale*, *LRFADE* 7, and Blackburn, *Overthrow of Colonial Slavery*, 171–72.

66. See Blackburn, *Overthrow of Colonial Slavery*, 217. A good treatment of Sonthonax's activities in Saint Domingue is Robert Louis Stein, *Léger Félicité Sonthonax. The Lost Sentinel of the Republic* (London, 1985).

67. Geggus, "Racial Equality, Slavery, and Colonial Secession," 1305; Yves Bénot, *La Révolution Française et la fin des colonies* (Paris, 1988), 130.

68. Bénot, *Révolution Française*, 75, 86–87, 200-204, 217; Blackburn, *Overthrow of Colonial Slavery*, 161–264.

69. Geggus discusses these types of interpretation in "Racial Equality, Slavery, and Colonial Secession," 1291–1304. The West Indian Marxists C. L. R. James and Aimé Césaire, along with Haitians associated with the *noiriste* school of interpretation, have insisted on the autonomous growth of resistance in Saint Domingue and have argued that these events radicalized the French Revolution rather than vice versa.

70. Condorcet, *Réflexions sur l'esclavage des nègres*, 173.

71. J.-P. Brissot, *Réplique de J.P. Brissot à la première et derniere lettre de Louis-Marthe Gouy* (Paris, 1791), 17,20.

72. Personal attacks between Brissot and the white colonists centered on the charge of treason. Colonists accused Brissot of being a British spy; he retorted that he had no links with the government and/or administration, other than when he was held as a prisoner in the Bastille during the Old Regime. See his *Réplique*, 42. See also his *Discours sur un projet de décret relatif à la révolte des noirs* (Paris, 1789), 2–7. Robert Darnton's "A Spy in Grub Street" in Darnton, *The Literary Underground of the Old Regime* (Cambridge, 1982), 41–70, discusses the personal attacks on Brissot during the Revolution. Colonists also accused the abolitionist Grégoire, besides being a Jew-lover, of having a colored sister-in-law even though he was an only child; and they accused the entire abolitionist movement of being led by a woman due to Olympe de Gouges's abolitionist writings. See Henri Grégoire, *Lettre aux philanthropes, sur les malheurs, les droits et les réclamations des gens de couleur de Saint Domingue et des autres îles françoises de l'Amerique* (Paris, 1790), 19–20, and Olympe de Gouges, *Réponse au champion américain*, *LRFADE* 4:2–3.

73. Brissot, *Réplique*, 10.

74. Henri Grégoire, *Mémoire en faveur des gens de couleur*, *LRFADE* 1:18–19.

75. Henrion de Pansey, *Mémoire pour un nègre qui réclame sa liberté*, *LRFADE* 1:13.

76. On abolitionism as yet another form of cultural imperialism, see Howard Temperley, "Anti-Slavery as a Form of Cultural Imperialism," in *Anti-Slavery, Religion, and Reform*, ed. Bolt and Drescher, 335–50.

77. On reception to Olympe de Gouges's play, see Geggus, "Racial Equality, Slavery, and Colonial Secession," 1295–96.

78. De Gouges, *L'esclavage des noirs*, 56.

79. The best discussion of these views of women is Joan Landes, *Women and the Public Sphere*. Interesting supporting evidence is given by Thomas Laqueur in his "Orgasm, Generation, and the Politics of Reproductive Biology," in Catherine Gallagher and Thomas Laqueur, eds., *The Making of the Modern Body* (Berkeley, 1987). On Rousseau's sexual attitudes, see Joel Schwartz, *The Sexual Politics of Jean Jacques Rousseau* (Chicago, 1984); and Carol Blum, *Rousseau and the Republic of Virtue: The Language of Politics in the French Revolution* (Ithaca, NY, 1984).

80. For a positive appraisal of women's activity in the eighteenth century, see Nina Gelbart, *Feminine and Opposition Journalism in Old Regime France: Le Journal des dames* (Berkeley, 1988), and Singham, "A Conspiracy of Twenty Million Frenchmen," 190–98, 301–17. My dissertation underlines the central importance of Jansenism in the political empowerment of women in the 1770s. It disagrees with David Bell's contention—"The 'Public Sphere,' the State, and the World of Law in Eighteenth-Century France," *FHS* 17 (1992): 912–34, especially 930—that Jansenism merely afforded women religious, hence private and domestic, liberty, and uncovers instead much self-conscious political activity on the party of Jansenist women imprisoned for supporting the opposition to absolutism. For other views concerning women and eighteenth century political intellectual life, see Daniel Gordon, "Philosophy, Sociology, and Gender in the Enlightenment Conception of Public Order"; and Sarah Maza, "Women, the Bourgeoisie, and the Public Sphere: Response to Daniel Gordon and David Bell," *FHS* 17 (1992): 882–911, 935–50 respectively.

81. Important treatments of women's activity during the Revolution are Dominique Godineau, *Citoyennes Tricoteuses: Les femmes du peuple à Paris pendant la Révolution française* (Aix-en-Provence, 1988); Paule-Marie Duhet, *Les femmes et la Révolution 1789–1794* (Paris, 1971); Harriet B. Applewhite and Darline Gay Levy, "Women, Democracy, and Revolution in Paris, 1789–1794," in *French Women in the Age of the Enlightenment*, ed. I. Spencer (Bloomington, IN, 1984); Applewhite and Levy, "Women, Radicalization and the Fall of the French Monarchy," in Applewhite and Levy, eds., *Women and Politics in the Age of Democratic Revolution*, 81–108; and Jane Abray, "Feminism and the French Revolution," *AHR* 80, no. 1 (Feb. 1975): 43–62.

82. On the *Cercle Social*, see Gary Kates, *The Cercle Social, the Girondins, and the French Revolution* (Princeton, NJ, 1985).

83. Condorcet, *On the Admission of Women to the Rights of Citizenship*, in *Condorcet. Selected Writings*, ed. Keith Baker (Indianapolis, 1976), 98.

84. Olympe de Gouges, *Declaration of the Rights of Woman*, in *Women in Revolutionary Paris 1789–1795*, ed. Levy, Applewhite, and Johnson, 87–96.

85. Much of the following discussion has been informed by Joan Scott's "French Feminists Claim the Rights of 'Man'. Olympe de Gouges in the French Revolution," (paper delivered in St. Louis, MO, Apr. 1991), 1–20.

86. De Gouges, *Declaration of the Rights of Woman*, 89.

87. "Man's color is nuanced, as with all animals nature has produced, as well as plants and minerals . . . . everything is varied, and that is the beauty of nature. Why, thus, destroy its work (i.e. by slave trade)?", Olympe de Gouges declared in opposition to slavery. See Scott, "French Feminists Claim the Rights of 'Man,'" 13.

88. De Gouges, *Declaration of the Rights of Woman*, 90–92.

89. Modern advocates of "difference feminism" include Nancy Chodorow, *The Reproduction of Mothering* (Berkeley, 1978); Carol Gilligan, *In a Different Voice* (Cambridge, 1982); and Deborah Tannen, *You Just Don't Understand* (New York, 1990). For response, see Carol Tavris, *The Mismeasure of Woman* (New York, 1992) and Katha Pollitt, "Are Women Morally Superior to Men?" *Nation*, 28 Dec. 1992, 799-807. A different approach is pursued by Elizabeth Fox-Genovese, *Feminism Without Illusions: A Critique of Individualism* (Chapel Hill, NC, 1991).

90. On the attack on patriotism as a movement dominated by women, see my discussion of the series of pamphlets between "the master wigmaker" and his wife in the 1770s, in Singham, "Conspiracy," 301–16; see also Jeffrey Merrick, "Sexual Politics and Public Order in Late Eighteenth-Century France: The *Mémoires secrets* and the *Correspondance secrète*," *Journal of the History of Sexuality* 1 (1990): 68–84; and Sarah Maza, "The Diamond Necklace Affair Revisited (1785–1786): the Case of the Missing Queen," in *Eroticism and the Body Politic*, ed. Lynn Hunt (Baltimore, 1991), 63–89.

91. Although he does imply that women have not "made any important discovery in the sciences" nor have they shown signs of genius. Condorcet, *On the Admission of Women to the Rights of Citizenship*, 98.

92. Ibid., 102.

93. *AP* (29 Apr. 1793), 63:593–94. In an especially unusual vein, Guyomar noted that women were merely men's "unpaid servants" for the domestic chores they undertook, and he insisted that either the French abolish the word *citoyennes*, or make it a living reality by enfranchising women. Ibid., 595.

94. *AP* (10 Sept. 1791), 30:478.

95. Ibid., (3 Jul. 1793), 68:193.

96. An alternative women's view on education is contained in the *Requête des femmes, pour leur admission aux États-Généraux* (n.p. [1788]), FRH #1156, 9.

97. *Petition of the Women of the Third Estate to the King*, in *Women in Revolutionary Paris*, ed. Levy, Applewhite, and Johnson, 20.

98. Kates, "Powers of Husband and Wife," 171.

99. For Jabineau's ideas on prostitution, see Abray, "Feminism and the French Revolution," 47. A contrasting harsh view is contained in [Laurent Pierre Bérenger], *De la prostitution. Cahier et doléances d'un ami des moeurs adressés spécialement aux députés de l'ordre du tiers-état de Paris* (Paris, 1789), FRH #115.

100. *Petition of the Women of the Third Estate to the King*, 20.

101. *Déclaration des droits des citoyennes du Palais Royale*, in de Baecque,

44–45. Another satire against women's demands is contained in *Homage aux plus jolies et vertueuses femmes de Paris. Ou Nomenclature de la classe la moins nombreuse* (n.p., [1789]), FRH #579.

102. *Petition to the National Assembly on Women's Rights to Bear Arms,* in *Women in Revolutionary Paris,* ed. Levy, Applewhite, and Johnson, 73.

103. See Applewhite and Levy, "Women, Democracy, and Revolution," 66. On the demand for women's admission to the ranks of the military, see *Demande des femmes aux États-Généraux; par l'auteur des Femmes comme il convient de les voir* (n.p., 1789), FRH #349, 1–4, 7–8, 11; and *Requête des dames à l'Assemblée nationale,* 12–13.

104. *Requête des dames à l'Assemblée nationale,* 12–13. That wearing men's clothing was no joking matter was proven by the angry assertions of the journalist of the *Révolutions de Paris* who, after women had been silenced in October 1793, asserted "True patriotism consists of . . . valuing . . . rights appropriate to each according to sex and age, and not wearing the [liberty] cap and pantaloons and not carrying pike and pistol. Leave those to men who are born to protect you and make you happy. Wear clothing suitable to your morals and occupations." Quoted in Applewhite and Levy, "Women, Democracy, and Revolution," 75.

105. *A Woman Recounts her Role in the Conquest of the Bastille,* in *Women in Revolutionary Paris,* ed. Levy, Applewhite, and Johnson, 29–30.

106. On women's important role in escalating terror, see Dominique Godineau, "Masculine and Feminine Political Practice during the French Revolution, 1793-Year III," in Applewhite and Levy, eds., *Women and Politics in the Age of the Democratic Revolution,* 61–80.

107. Olwen Hufton, "Women in the Revolution," *Past and Present* 53 (1971): 90–108.

108. *AP* (29 Oct. 1793), 78:20.

109. Olwen Hufton argues that the Jacobin closure of the Society of Revolutionary Republican Women was importantly linked to their offensive against the *Enragés.* See her *Women and the Limits of Citizenship,* 25–38.

110. *AP* (29 Oct. 1793), 78:21. See also Lynn Hunt "The Many Bodies of Marie Antoinette," 124–25.

111. Abray, "Feminism and the French Revolution," 57.

112. See Kates, "Powers of Husband and Wife," 173, on the bourgeois focus of the *Cercle Social.*

113. Etta Palm d'Aelders, *Address of French Citoyennes to the National Assembly* in *Women in Revolutionary Paris,* ed. Levy, Applewhite, and Johnson, 75–77. See also *AP* (1 Apr. 1792), 41:63. On women's support for divorce, see *AP* (13 Feb. 1792), 38:466.

114. *AP* (30 Aug. 1792), 49:117–18.

115. Kates discusses the manner in which *Cercle Social* activists considered egalitarian families to lay the basis for democratic politics. Central to the family was love. On their philosophy of love, see Kates, "Powers of Husband and Wife," 175. On just how radical the divorce law was, see Therese

McBride, "Public Authority and Private Lives. Divorce after the French Revolution," *FHS* 17 (1992): 747–68.

116. Kates, "Powers of Husband and Wife," 167.

117. Abray, "Feminism and the French Revolution," 59.

118. Applewhite and Levy, "Women, Democracy, and Revolution," 66.

119. Abray, "Feminism and the French Revolution," 58.

120. De Gouges, *Declaration of the Rights of Woman*, 92. Even though she made this argument in 1791, she would have found it even more appropriate, had she lived, as an assessment of the situation of women in 1795.

121. *AP* (13 Apr. 1790), 12:711–12.

122. Ibid., 712.

123. On Anglo-Saxon racism in the nineteenth century, see Stephen Gould, *The Mismeasure of Man* (New York, 1981), and Curtin, *The Image of Africa*.

CHAPTER 4

1. Georg Jellinek, *The Declaration of the Rights of Man and of the Citizen. A Contribution to Modern Constitutional History*, trans. Max Ferrand (New York, 1901), 11.

2. Ibid.

3. Ibid., 44.

4. Ibid., 50.

5. Emile Boutmy, "La *Déclaration des droits de l'homme et du citoyen* et M. Jellinek," *Annales des sciences politiques* 17 (1902): 415–43, at 416. Jellinek replied, quoting copiously in support of his position from an impeccably French Aulard. See Jellinek, "La *Déclaration des droits de l'homme et du citoyen*," *Revue du droit public et de la science politique en France et à l'étranger* 18 (1902): 385–400.

6. Ibid., 443.

7. Franco Venturi, *The End of the Old Regime in Europe, 1776–1789. I. The Great States of the West*, trans. R. Burr Litchfield (Princeton, NJ, 1991), 3–143. See also Claude Fohlen, "La filiation américaine de la Déclaration des droits de l'homme," in Claude-Albert Colliard, et al., *La Déclaration des droits de l'homme et du citoyen de 1789: ses origines—sa pérennité* (Paris, 1990), 21–29.

8. Gauchet; Rials. The bicentennial of the French Revolution was particularly fertile for study of the Declaration of the Rights of Man. Other valuable works include de Baecque; Christine Fauré, *Les Déclarations des droits de l'homme* (Paris, 1988); Denis Lacorne, *L'Invention de la République. Le modèle américain* (Paris, 1991). Rials, de Baecque, and Fauré reprint substantial collections of documents relating to the composition of the Declaration.

9. Gauchet, 107.

10. Sieyès, "Manuscrit inédit sur les Déclarations des droits de l'homme," in Fauré, *Les Déclarations*, 321. The date of this note is uncertain, though

Fauré plausibly ascribes it to the Year III. Unless indicated otherwise, translations from the French are my own.

11. Ibid.

12. Ibid., 322.

13. *Federalist* no. 84, as printed in Philip B. Kurland and Ralph Lerner, eds., *The Founders' Constitution*, 5 vols. (Chicago, 1987), 5:10.

14. [Alexander Hamilton], *Farmer Refuted*, as quoted in Gordon S. Wood, *The Creation of the American Republic* (Chapel Hill, NC, 1969), 271.

15. [Moses Mather], *America's Appeal*, as quoted in Wood, *American Republic*, 271.

16. *Founders' Constitution* 5:7–9.

17. Declaration of the Parlement of Paris, 3 May 1788, as printed from Flammermont, *Remontrances du parlement de Paris*, in Rials, 522–28. Rials offers a particularly convenient compendium of French versions of, and drafts for, a declaration of rights.

18. Rials, 275–76, 277.

19. Lafayette, first draft for a declaration of rights (Jan. 1789), as reprinted in Rials, 528.

20. Ibid. Compare Lafayette's second draft (June 1789) and the version finally presented to the National Assembly (11 July 1789), ibid., 567, 591. The composition of Lafayette's successive drafts, composed in consultation with Thomas Jefferson, is thoroughly discussed in Louis Gottschalk and Margaret Maddox, *Lafayette in the French Revolution: Through the October Days* (Chicago, 1969).

21. Rials, 528. Emphases added.   22. Ibid., 591.

23. *AP* (11 July 1789), 8:221.   24. Ibid., (9 July 1789), 8:215.

25. Mounier, *Déclaration des droits de l'homme et du citoyen* (Versailles, s.d.), as reprinted in Rials, 606.

26. Rials, 613–14.

27. [John Stevens], *Examen du gouvernement d'Angleterre, comparé aux constitutions des Etats-Unis. Où l'on réfute quelques assertions contenus dans l'ouvrage de M. Adams, intitulé: Apologie des constitutions des Etats-Unis d'Amérique, et dans celui de M. Delolme, intitulé, De la constitution d'Angleterre. Par un cultivateur de New Jersey* (London, 1789).

28. Ibid., 201.

29. Eugène Daire, ed., *Physiocrates*, 2 vols. (Paris, 1846), 1:54. Dupont had set this essay at the head of the collection of Quesnay's writings he published in 1767 as an introduction to *Physiocratie, ou constitution naturelle du gouvernement le plus avantageux au genre humain*, 2 vols. (Leyden and Paris, 1767–68). The physiocratic origins of the Declaration of the Rights of Man and of the Citizen are brought out particularly in V. Marcaggi, *Les Origines de la Déclaration des droits de l'homme et du citoyen de 1789*, 2d ed. (Paris, 1912).

30. *Maximes générales du gouvernement économique d'un royaume agricole*, in Daire, *Physiocrates* 1:81; italics in original.

31. *Droit naturel*, in ibid. 1:54.

32. Baudeau, *Introduction à la philosophie économique*, in ibid. 2:777.

33. Ibid. 1:795.

34. *Oeuvres de Condorcet*, ed. A. Condorcet-O'Connor and F. Arago, 12 vols. (Paris, 1847–49), 9:165, 172.

35. Condorcet's reservations regarding the calling of the Estates General are discussed in my *Condorcet. From Natural Philosophy to Social Mathematics* (Chicago, 1975), 250–52, 264–65.

36. *Examen du gouvernement d'Angleterre*, 180.

37. Rials, 538.

38. Ibid. On the importance of this function of the Declaration of the Rights of Man in filling the National Assembly's need for legitimacy, see especially Gauchet.

39. On this feature of Sieyés's thinking, see my "Sieyès," in François Furet and Mona Ozouf, eds., *Critical Dictionary of the French Revolution*, trans. Arthur Goldhammer (Cambridge, MA, 1989), 313–23.

40. Rials, 538.

41. Ibid.

42. In what follows, I have drawn on, developed, and occasionally corrected the discussion of the National Assembly's constitutional debates in my *Inventing the French Revolution* (Cambridge, 1990), 252–305.

43. [Barère,] *Le Point du jour, ou Résultat de ce qui s'est passé aux Etats Généraux* 1(2):71–72 (27 June 1789).

44. *AP* (20 June 1789), 8:138.

45. Ibid. (27 July 1789), 283.

46. Ibid.

47. Ibid. (9 July 1789), 215.

48. Ibid., 216.

49. Ibid. (11 July 1789), 222. Barère's response was acid. "Must consideration for ancient prejudices make us forget the imprescriptible rights of man?" he demanded. "Must fear of damaging ideas established till now ever compromise the eternal rights of humanity?" *Le Point du jour* (12 July 1789), 1(2):174–75.

50. *AP* (11 July 1789), 8:222.

51. *Le Point du jour* (14 July 1789), 1(2):187.

52. *AP* (27 July 1789), 8:281. But this praise of the New World prompted a vigorous defense of the originality of the Old—and particularly of Rousseau—in Mirabeau's *Courier de Provence*: "Let us observe that before the independence of English America the *Contrat social* had appeared . . . No, one must never speak of liberty without paying a tribute of homage to this immortal avenger of human nature," *Le Courier de Provence*, no. 20 (24-27 July 1789).

53. *AP* (27 July 1789), 8:281.

54. See Sieyès, *Préliminaire de la constitution. Reconnaissance et exposition raisonnée des droits de l'homme et du citoyen. Lu les 20 et 21 juillet 1789, au comité de constitution*, in Rials, 591–606.

55. *AP* (27 July 1789), 8:282.

56. As Champion de Cicé makes clear, Sieyès had added a summary list of rights to his "systematic exposition" only when pressed to do so by the constitutional committee.

57. [Le Hodey de Sault Chevreuil,] *Journal des Etats Généraux* (30 July 1789), 2:270.

58. Adrien Duquesnoy, for one, was convinced that this motion was the scheme of those who, "seeing that the abbé de Sieyès's constitutional project is not finding favor in the *bureaux,* where it is being coldly examined, wish to carry it into full battle in the Assembly, which is fatigued by long discussion." See Robert de Crèvecoeur, ed., *Journal d'Adrien Duquesnoy, député du tiers-état de Bar-le-Duc, sur l'Assemblée constituante (3 mai 1789–3 avril 1790),* 2 vols. (Paris, 1894), 1:257.

59. The reasoning behind his motion was frankly reported in the *Journal des Etats Généraux* edited by Le Hodey de Sault Chevreuil. "The military, ecclesiastical, and judicial aristocrats craftily develop their ideas in these meetings; they would have kept their silence in an assembly of twelve hundred. They speak boldly before thirty, half of whom encourage them. The good patriots find themselves isolated . . . the obligation of certain kinds of respect, the habit of an ancient deference, regain their empire proportionately, the closer one approaches a bishop or a noble; the latter perorates and the other [the good patriot] falls silent." *Journal des Etats Généraux* (30 July 1789), 2:277–78.

60. *AP* (30 July 1789), 8:307.

61. Ibid. (1 Aug. 1789), 315.

62. Anxious to move the debate to a conclusion, and claiming that at least 200 deputies wanted to present their views, Bouche proposed a five-minute limit on the second day of the debate (3 August). The proposal was rejected in response to vigorous claims for unrestrained deliberation as the essence of liberty. The assembly agreed only that speeches would be given alternately in favor of the motion and against it. For a passionate report on this debate, see *Le Point du jour* (4 August 1789), 2:9–13.

63. *Journal des Etats Généraux* (1 Aug. 1789), 2:306–7.

64. *Le Point du jour* (2 Aug. 1789), 1(2):377.

65. *AP* (1 Aug. 1789), 8:322.   66. Ibid., 324.

67. Ibid., 323.   68. Ibid., 319.

69. However, the comte d'Antraigues did indeed invoke Rousseau in demonstrating that a declaration of rights would sustain rather than subvert respect for property—on the grounds that "in the state of nature, man has the right to all that force can procure for him. In the state of society, man has the right only to what he possesses." *AP* (3 Aug. 1789), 8:335.

70. Ibid. (1 Aug. 1789), 320.

71. Ibid.

72. Ibid., 321.

73. *Le Point du jour* (3 Aug. 1789), 2:6; *AP* (1 Aug. 1789), 8:322.

74. *Le Point du jour* (4 Aug. 1789), 2:20.

75. *Journal des Etats Généraux* (4 Aug. 1789), 2:352–60.

76. *AP* (4 Aug. 1789), 8:340.

77. *Le Point du jour* (4 Aug. 1789), 2:22.

78. "He stubbornly insisted on deliberation on this motion," Duquesnoy

recalled. "It was rejected, but this pigheadedness caused an immense loss of time, and it was noticed with sorrow that M. Camus maintained with a kind of furious determination a proposition upon which the clergy seemed to set so much importance," *Journal d'Adrien Duquesnoy* 1:264.

79. On this point, see de Baecque, 20.

80. *Le Courier de Provence*, no. 23 (3–5 Aug. 1789).

81. See Patrick Kessel, *La Nuit du 4 août 1789* (Paris, 1969), 127–33.

82. *AP* (4 Aug. 1789), 8:345.

83. Ibid. (12 Aug. 1789), 399, 434. The committee, composed of deputies who had not submitted a draft declaration to the assembly, included the comte de Mirabeau, Jean-Nicolas Démeunier, François-Denis Tronchet, Claude Rhédon, and the bishop of Langres, César-Guillaume de La Luzerne.

84. Etienne Dumont, *Souvenirs sur Mirabeau et sur les deux premières assemblées législatives*, ed. J. Bénétruy (Paris, 1951), 97. On Mirabeau's "workshop" more generally, see Bénétruy, *L'Atelier de Mirabeau. Quatre proscrits genevois dans la tourmente révolutionnaire* (Paris, 1962).

85. On these points, see Marcel Thomann, "Le 'Préambule' de la Déclaration des droits de l'homme (1789)," *Tijdschrift voor Rechtsgeschiedenis* 55 (1987): 375–82; "Origines et sources doctrinales de la Déclaration des droits," *Droits* 8 (1988): 55–69.

86. *AP* (17 Aug. 1789), 8:438.

87. *Le Courier de Provence*, no. 28 (17–18 Aug. 1789). On the composition of the journal, see Dumont, *Souvenirs*, 89–93.

88. *Le Courier de Provence*, no. 28 (17–18 Aug. 1789).

89. *AP* (17 Aug. 1789), 8:438.

90. Ibid.

91. The point is made by Marcaggi, *Les Origines de la Déclaration des droits*, 167–68.

92. *AP* (18 Aug. 1789), 8:453.   93. Ibid. (17 Aug. 1789), 438–39.

94. Ibid. (18 Aug. 1789), 454.   95. Ibid. (19 Aug. 1789), 458–59.

96. For the text of this draft, see Rials, 621–24. Its character and origins are well described in Philip Dawson, "Le 6ᵉ bureau de l'Assemblée nationale et son projet de Déclaration des droits de l'homme," *AHRF* 50 (1978): 161–79.

97. *AP* (20 Aug. 1789), 8:462.

98. *Journal d'Adrien Duquesnoy*: 303.

99. *AP* (20 Aug. 1789), 8:463.

100. *Journal des Etats Généraux* (20 Aug. 1789), 3:19.

101. *AP* (27 Aug. 1789), 8:492.

102. *Le Point du jour* (28 Aug. 1789), 2:222–23.

103. This point has been forcefully made by Gauchet.

104. On this point, see particularly Rials, 236, 369–73, 396–403.

105. *Le Courier de Provence*, no. 31 (22–23 Aug. 1789).

106. For an analysis of the arguments over the suspensive veto, see my *Inventing the French Revolution*, 281–305.

CHAPTER 5

1. Specifically, Seyssel described three such "bridles" (*freins*): *la religion*, which provided moral regulation for both sovereign and subject; *la justice*, the domain of civil and criminal law, under the watchful guardianship of the parlements; and *la police*, a more fluid category which included at least two unalterable "fundamental laws" of the realm (inalienability of the royal domain and the Salic Law of male succession), an injunction always to "seek counsel" in decisions, rather than acting by "discordant and sudden will," and an obligation to preserve and protect the basic social hierarchy of the nation. See Claude de Seyssel, *The Monarchy of France*, trans. J.H. Hexter (New Haven, 1981).

2. There is a widespread belief that *La Politique tirée des paroles de l'Ecriture Sainte* betrays the influence of Hobbes's slightly earlier defense of absolutism, or even that the doctrines of the two writers are nearly identical. In fact, what is surely striking is how *little* Bossuet owed to the arguments of *De Cive* or *Leviathan*, despite his evident knowledge of these texts. There are some hesitant steps in this direction, particularly in the first part of *La Politique*—a resacralized caricature of contract theory is presented in its first book, and a few gestures toward it are scattered elsewhere in the text. But these never acquire a central role in Bossuet's argument, nor does the fundamental conceptual category of natural *rights* ever make an appearance in the text. Bossuet's main themes—the "essential characteristics" of "royal" monarchy—are utterly remote from the concerns of Hobbes, if very close to those of James I and VI or of Robert Filmer, who are of course his nearest English analogues.

3. See John Breuilly, *Nationalism and the State* (Manchester, 1982); Ernest Gellner, *Nations and Nationalism* (Oxford, 1983); Benedict Anderson, *Imagined Communities: Reflections on the Origin and Spread of Nationalism* (London, 1983); Eric Hobsbawm, *Nations and Nationalism since 1780: Programme, Myth, Reality* (Cambridge, 1990); Liah Greenfeld, *Nationalism: Five Roads to Modernity* (Cambridge, MA, 1992).

4. Anthony Smith, *The Ethnic Origins of Nations* (Oxford, 1986), 59–60, 90–91, 147–49.

5. Collette Beaune, *Naissance de la nation France* (Paris, 1985).

6. For a specific discussion of the "rise and fall" of a "crown-centered version of French patriotism during the Age of Absolutism," see William F. Church, "France," in Orest Ranum, ed., *National Consciousness, History, and Political Culture in Early-Modern Europe* (Baltimore, 1975), 43–66.

7. Jacques-Bénigne Bossuet, *Politics Drawn from the Very Words of Holy Scripture*, trans. Patrick Riley (Cambridge, 1990), 16–17.

8. Paul Hazard, *La crise de la conscience européene* (Paris, 1935).

9. For a recent description of the first of these results, see Jeffrey W. Merrick, *The Desacralization of the French Monarchy in the Eighteenth Century* (Baton Rouge, LA, 1990); for a general discussion of the post-Grotian

natural rights tradition, see Richard Tuck, "The 'modern' theory of natural law," in Anthony Pagden, ed., *The Languages of Political Theory in Early-Modern Europe* (Cambridge, 1987), 99–119.

10. Denis Richet, "Autour des origines idéologiques lointaines de la Révolution française: élites et despotisme," *Annales* 24 (1969): 1–23.

11. The major recent study of Boulainvilliers, which emphasizes his debt to classical republican traditions, is Harold Ellis, *Boulainvilliers and the French Monarchy: Aristocratic Politics in Early Eighteenth-Century France* (Ithaca, NY, 1988).

12. Henri de Boulainvilliers, *Histoire de l'ancien gouvernement de la France, avec XIV lettres historiques sur les Parlemens ou Etats-Généraux* (The Hague and Amsterdam, 1727), 1:26.

13. Jean-Baptiste Dubos, *Histoire critique de l'établissement de la Monarchie française dans les Gaules* (Amsterdam, 1735), 3:16.

14. Remonstrances of 12 Jan. 1764; cited in Roger Bickart, *Les parlements et la notion de souveraineté nationale au XVIIIe siècle* (Paris, 1932), 11.

15. On Moreau, see Keith M. Baker, *Inventing the French Revolution: Essays on French Political Culture in the Eighteenth Century* (Cambridge, 1990), 59–85.

16. Ibid., 86–106.

17. See François Furet and Mona Ozouf, "Deux légitimations historiques de la société française au XVIIIe siècle: Mably et Boulainvilliers," *Annales* 34 (1979): 438–50.

18. See Mounier's major prerevolutionary statement, *Nouvelles observations sur les Etats-généraux de France* (Paris, 1789), which takes the Estates of 1483 as the the proper point of departure for reconstructing the French "constitution"; for a discussion of Mounier's outlook, see Raymond Birn, "The pamphlet press and the Estates-General of 1789," *Studies on Voltaire and the Eighteenth Century* 287 (1991): 63–65.

19. For a lucid discussion of Sieyes's conception of the "nation," see Murray Forsyth, *Reason and Revolution: the Political Thought of the Abbé Sieyes* (New York, 1987).

20. Judith N. Shklar, "General Will," in *Dictionary of the History of Ideas*, ed. Philip P. Wiener (New York, 1973), 2:275.

21. Patrick Riley, *The General Will before Rousseau: the Transformation of the Divine into the Civic* (Princeton, NJ, 1986).

22. Cited in ibid., 82.

23. Ibid., 251–60.

24. See J. G. A. Pocock, "Virtues, Rights and Manners: A Model for Historians of Political Thought," in id., *Virtue, Commerce and History* (Cambridge, 1985), 37–50; and id., "Cambridge Paradigms and Scotch Philosophers," in Istvan Hont and Michael Ignatieff, eds., *Wealth and Virtue* (Cambridge, 1983), 235–52.

25. This case was established long ago in Robert Derathé's classic study, *Jean-Jacques Rousseau et la science politique de son temps* (Paris, 1950).

26. The distinction between conservative and radical wings of the seventeenth-century rights tradition, over the issue of alienability in particular, follows that established by Richard Tuck, *Natural Rights Theories: their Origin and Development* (Cambridge, 1979).

27. The work establishing Rousseau's classical republican credentials, surprisingly or not, has been of fairly recent vintage; but see Judith N. Shklar, *Men and Citizens: A Study of Rousseau's Social Theory* (Cambridge, 1969), and her "Montesquieu and the New Republicanism," in Gisela Bok, Quentin Skinner, and Marizio Viroli, eds., *Machiavelli and Republicanism* (Cambridge, 1990), 265–79; and Marizio Viroli, *Jean-Jacques Rousseau and the 'Well-Ordered Society,'* trans. Derek Hanson (Cambridge, 1988).

28. J. G. Merquior, *Rousseau and Weber: Two Studies in the Theory of Legitimacy* (London, 1980), 57, 62.

29. Jean-Jacques Rousseau, *The Basic Political Writings*, trans. Donald A. Cress (Indianapolis, 1987), 198.

30. Richard Fralin, *Rousseau and Representation: a Study of the Development of his Concept of Political Institutions* (New York, 1978), 196.

31. *Encyclopédie, ou dictionnaire raisonné des sciences, des arts et des métiers* (Lausanne and Berne, 1779), 11:369–73.

32. The view was first introduced in Mornet's bibliographical study "Les Enseignements des bibliothèques privées (1750–1780)," *Revue d'histoire littéraire de la France* (1910); it worked into Mornet's interpretation of the course of eighteenth-century intellectual history as a whole in his *Les origines intellectuelles de la Révolution française (1715–1787)* (Paris, 1933) and then reached something like its popular apotheosis in Joan Macdonald, *Rousseau and the French Revolution* (London, 1965).

33. At the bibliographical level, the greatest service here has been performed by R.A. Leigh, who has established the widespread diffusion of Rousseau's political writings in the quarter century before the Revolution, the *Contrat social* not excluded; see R.A. Leigh, *Unsolved problems in the Bibliography of J.-J. Rousseau* (Cambridge, 1990). As for the actual pattern of Rousseau's intellectual influence, the major recent work has been Roger Barny's five-volume thèse, *Jean-Jacques Rousseau dans la Révolution française (1787–1791): Contribution à l'analyse de l'idéologie révolutionnaire bourgeoise* (Paris, 1977). Published portions of the work include Roger Barny, *Prélude idéologique à la Révolution française: le Rousseauisme avant 1789* (Paris, 1985); *J.-J. Rousseau dans la Révolution: L'image de l'homme et le début du Culte* (Oxford, 1986); and *L'éclatement révolutionnaire du Rousseauisme* (Paris, 1988).

34. See Barny, *Prélude idéologique à la Révolution française*, 103–10.

35. See Baker's review of *Prélude idéologique à la Révolution française* in *Eighteenth-Century Studies* 20 (1987): 488–91; and his "A Classical Republican in Eighteenth-Century Bordeau: Guillaume-Joseph Saige," in Baker, ed., *Inventing the French Revolution*, 128–52.

36. The major surveys in English remain W.B. Gwyn, *The Meaning of the*

Separation of Powers (New Orleans, 1965), and M.J.C. Vile, *Constitutionalism and the Separation of Powers* (Oxford, 1967); for classical antecedents
of the idea, see Kurt von Friz, *The Theory of the Mixed Constitution in
Antiquity* (New York, 1954); the major recent discussion of the modern
French tradition is Michel Troper, *La séparation des pouvoirs et l'histoire
constitutionnelle française* (Paris, 1980).

37. Montesquieu, *The Spirit of the Laws*, trans. Anne Cohler, Basia
Miller, Harold Stone (Cambridge, 1989), 156–57.

38. "Here, therefore, is the fundamental constitution of the goverment of
which we are speaking. As its legislative body is composed of two parts, the
one will be chained to the other by their reciprocal faculty of vetoing. The
two will be bound by the executive power, which will itself be bound by the
legislative power." Ibid., 164.

39. See Charles Eisenmann, "L'Esprit des Lois et la séparation des pouvoirs," *Mélanges Carré de Malberg* (Paris, 1933), 163–92; Eisenman's views
were in turn taken up in Althusser's great essay on Montesquieu: Louis Althusser, *Montesquieu, Rousseau, Marx: Politics and History*, trans. Ben
Brewster (London, 1972), 87–95.

40. Vile, *Constitutionalism and the Separation of Powers*, 177.

41. For these arguments, see Rousseau, *The Social Contract*, bk. 2, chap.
2; bk. 3, chap. 4; and bk. 3, chap. 1, respectively.

42. Franco Venturi, *Utopia and Reform in the Enlightenment* (Cambridge, 1971), 73.

43. For an example of the former attitude, see Gabriel Bonnot de Mably,
Des droits et des devoirs du citoyen, ed. Jean-Louis Lecercle (Paris, 1972),
44–45; for the latter, see Mably's *Observations sur le gouvernement et les
loix des Etats-Unis d'Amérique* (Paris, 1784).

44. *AP* (12 Aug. 1789), 8:409.

45. Henri Grange, "Necker et Mounier devant le problème politique,"
Annales historiques de la Révolution française 41 (1969): 583–605.

46. For Lafayette's proposals of Jan., June, and 11 July 1789, see Rials,
528–29, 567–68, 590–91.

47. Mirabeau, *Aux Bataves sur le Stathoudérat* (n. p., 1788), Articles 10
and 11. See Rials, 520.

48. See Rials, 528.

49. [Anonymous], *Élémens de droit public, à l'usage de Messieurs les
Députés aux Etats-Généraux de France* (Paris, 1789); see Rials, 582.

50. [Laclos and Sieyes], *Instruction donnée par S. A. S. Monseigneur le
Duc d'Orléans à ses représentans aux bailliages. Suivie des Délibérations à
prendre dans les Assemblées* (Paris, 1789); Rials, 536–37.

51. *AP* (9 July 1789), 8:214.

52. "The general character common to all these declarations," Sieyes
wrote in an unpublished note, referring to the Anglo-American models in
general, "is always the implicit recognition of a seigneur, or suzerain, or
master towards whom one is naturally obliged, and of certain oppressions
which one is no longer prepared to tolerate in the future" (cited in Forsyth,

Reason and Revolution, 110). But no such political authority existed in France, on his account: no "fundamental laws," no elements of a constitution to be "fixed," as in Mounier's speech of 9 July—to create one was precisely the work of the National Assembly.

53. *Instruction donnée par S. A. S. Monseigneur le Duc d'Orléans;* Rials, 537–38.

54. For a comprehensive presentation of Sieyès's theory of representation, see Forsyth, *Reason and Revolution,* chap. 7; for a suggestive discussion of Sieyès's relation to the doctrine of the general will along these lines, see Luc Ferry and Alain Renaut, *Philosophie politique 3: Des droits de l'homme à l'idée républicaine* (Paris, 1985), 91–96.

55. See the discussion of this speech in Forsyth, *Reason and Revolution,* 135–40.

56. *Déclaration des droits de l'homme et du citoyen, par M. Mounier* (Versailles, n. d.); Rials, 606–8. The committee's final version added a further twist: "Their union in the same hands would put those who possessed them above the Laws, permitting the substitution of their own wills for [the laws]"; *Projet des premiers articles de la Constitution, lu dans la séance du 29 juillet 1789 par M. Mounier* (Paris, 1789); Rials, 612–14.

57. This too became slightly more emphatic in the committee's version (Article 11): "Citizens can be subjected only to those laws to which they have consented themselves or by their representatives; and it is in this sense that the law is the expression of the general will."

58. See, among others, the proposals of Thouret (Articles 4 and 25), Sinety (Article 8), and Rabaut Saint-Étienne (Article 5), in Rials, 637, 639, 653, 683. A certain diffuse Rousseauism also characterized the proposal which Mirabeau presented on 17 August on behalf of his Committee of Five: "Every Political Body receives its existence from an express or tacit social contract," ran Article 2, "by which each individual places his person and his faculties under the supreme direction of the general will"; and Article 5 supplied the inevitable: "The law being the expression of the general will, it must be general in its object, and tend always to assure, for every Citizen, liberty, property and civil equality." See *Projet de déclaration des droits de l'homme en société.* Présenté par MM. du Comité chargé de l'examen des Déclarations des droits (Versailles, n. d.); Rials, 747–49.

59. *Projet de déclaration des droits de l'homme et du citoyen, discuté dans le sixième Bureau de l'Assemblée nationale* (Versailles, n. d.); Rials, 747–49.

60. Cited in de Baecque, 192.

61. Edmund Burke, *Reflections on the Revolution in France,* ed. Conor Cruise O'Brien (Harmondsworth, 1969), 149–50.

62. Marcel Gauchet, *La Revolution des droits de l'homme* (Paris, 1989), 201.

63. Philippe Reynaud, "La déclaration des droits de l'homme," in *The Political Culture of the French Revolution,* vol. 2 of *The French Revolution and the Creation of Modern Political Culture,* ed. Colin Lucas (Oxford, 1988), 139–49.

64. Claude Nicolet, *L'idée républicaine en France (1789–1924). Essai d'histoire critique* (Paris, 1982).

Chapter 6

1. Charles-Marguerite Dupaty, *Mémoire justificative pour trois hommes condamnés à la roue* (Paris, 1786), 240.

2. For an introduction to this subject, see Peter Gay, *The Enlightenment: An Interpretation* vol. 2: *The Science of Freedom* (New York, 1977), 423–47; Sarah Maza, "'Innocent Blood Avenged': Emplotting Judicial Reform, 1785–1786," in id., *Private Lives and Public Affairs: The Causes Célèbres of Pre-Revolutionary France* (Berkeley, 1993); and John A. Carey, *Judicial Reform in France before the Revolution of 1789* (Cambridge, MA, 1981). The figures on the advocates of reform come from David Jacobson, "The Politics of Criminal Law Reform in Late Eighteenth-Century France" (Ph.D. diss., Brown University, 1976), 104.

3. See Edna Hindie Lemay, ed., *Dictionnaire des Constituants, 1789–1791*, 2 vols. (Paris, 1991), 2:504–6.

4. The debates are contained in *AP* (22 Aug. 1789), 8:472–74, and in the *Journal des États-Généraux* (22 Aug. 1789), 3:49–56.

5. Rials, 141. Sieyès included the lines in the draft of a comprehensive declaration of rights that he circulated in early July (the text is reproduced in Rials, 591–606).

6. Rials, 235–36; *AP* (22 Aug. 1789), 8:472.

7. Gay, *The Enlightenment* 2:423.

8. *AP* (22 Aug. 1789), 8:470–71. Target presented two draft articles, which, together with the basis of two others proposed by the magistrate Adrien-Jean-François Duport, became the basis for Articles 7, 8, and 9. The original draft read: "All arbitrary orders against liberty must be punished. Those who have solicited, expedited, executed and effected the execution of them must be punished." Stéphane Rials points out (340–41), that this is only one point where the Declaration specifically criticizes aspects of the Old Regime.

9. AP (22 Aug. 1789), 8:471–72.

10. Ibid., 471–72. The *Journal des États-Généraux* (22 Aug. 1789), 3:49–56 gives a slightly different, and in this case seemingly garbled, version of the debate.

11. See Gauchet, and chap. 4 above.

12. Edna Hindie Lemay, "La composition de l'assemblée nationale-constituante," *Revue d'histoire moderne et contemporaine* 24 (1977): 345; Maza, *Private Lives*, passim.

13. On this point see Sarah Maza, "Le tribunal de la nation: Les mémoires judiciaires et l'opinion publique à la fin de l'ancien régime," *Annales* 42, no. 1 (1987): 73–90.

14. Alexis de Tocqueville, *The Old Regime and the French Revolution*, Stuart Gilbert, trans. (Garden City, NY, 1955), 117. The argument on legal

briefs is made in Maza, *Private Lives*, and in David A. Bell, "Lawyers and Politics in Eighteenth-Century Paris (1700–1790)" (Ph.D. diss., Princeton, 1991).

15. Roger Chartier, *The Cultural Origins of the French Revolution* (Durham, NC, 1991), 35. The most complete source of information on Target remains Joseph Hudault, "Guy-Jean-Baptiste Target et la défense de statut personnel à la fin de l'ancien régime," (doctoral thesis in law, Univ. of Paris, 1970).

16. Gauchet, esp. 166. This is, in fact, Gauchet's own interpretation of what he calls the "curious demonstration" of 22 August.

17. Lemay, ed., *Dictionnaire des constituants* 2:638–39.

18. The relevant work here includes Gauchet; Philippe Raynaud, "La déclaration des droits de l'homme," in *The Political Culture of the French Revolution*, vol. 2 of *The French Revolution and the Creation of Modern Political Culture*, ed. Colin Lucas (Oxford, 1988), 139–49; and Blandine Barret-Kriegel, *Les droits de l'homme et le droit naturel* (Paris, 1989).

19. Raynaud, "La déclaration," 140.

20. On these issues see particularly Gauchet, 36–59, and Barret-Kriegel, *Les droits*, 71–87.

21. Much of the most interesting recent material on this theme is collected in Keith Michael Baker, ed., *The Political Culture of the Old Regime* (Oxford, 1987). See also William Beik, *Absolutism and Society in Seventeenth-Century France: State Power and Provincial Aristocracy in Languedoc* (Cambridge, 1985).

22. Alexander Hamilton, James Madison, and John Jay, *The Federalist Papers*, Clinton Rossiter, ed. (New York, 1961), 323. Interestingly, Madison went on to write that there were only two methods of guarding against this danger. One was division of powers. The other, which "prevails in all governments possessing an hereditary or self-appointing authority," consisted of "creating a will in the community independent of the majority—that is, of the society itself." (323–24). A reference to the parlements?

23. Leonard W. Levy, "The Bill of Rights," in J. Jackson Barlow, Leonard W. Levy, and Ken Masugi, eds., *The American Founding: Essays on the Formation of the Constitution* (New York, 1988), 295–327; quotations from 314. The Federalists originally opposed a bill of rights, arguing in part, as Gordon Wood writes, that "the courts, as 'in all well-regulated communities,' would protect the common law liberties of the people and determine 'the extent of legislative powers' even in the absence of a specific bill." Gordon Wood, *The Creation of the American Republic, 1776–1787* (Chapel Hill, NC, 1969), 538, and more generally 536–43.

24. For an introduction to this burgeoning subject, see Keith Michael Baker, *Inventing the French Revolution: Essays on French Political Culture in the Eighteenth Century* (Cambridge, 1990), esp. 167–99; Chartier, *Cultural Origins*, esp. 20–37; and Mona Ozouf, "L'opinion publique," in Baker, ed., *The Political Culture of the Old Regime*, 419–34.

25. Barristers (*avocats*) were lawyers who made oral arguments in trials

and gave advice in cases where questions of law (as opposed to questions of fact) were at stake. As in modern England, they were a separate group from the solicitors (*procureurs*), who handled the technical and factual aspects of cases. They were also separate from the notaries (*notaires*), who had responsibility for conveyancing, wills, contracts, and the like.

26. Maza, "Le tribunal de la nation," 76–77.

27. On the legal profession in the Old Regime, see most recently Bell, "Lawyers and Politics in Paris." See also Maurice Gresset, *Gens de justice à Besançon de la conquête par Louis XIV à la Révolution française*, 2 vols. (Paris, 1978); Lenard R. Berlanstein, *The Barristers of Toulouse in the Eighteenth Century (1740–1793)* (Baltimore, 1975); and Albert Poirot, "Le milieu socio-professionel des avocats au parlement de Paris à la veille de la Révolution" (unpub. thesis, Ecole des Chartes, 1977).

28. See Bell, "Lawyers and Politics," 147–208.

29. Chrétien-Guillaume de Lamoignon de Malesherbes, "Mémoires sur les avocats" (1775), quoted in Pierre Grosclaude, *Malesherbes Témoin et Interprète de son temps* (Paris, 1961), 304.

30. François Bluche, *Les magistrats du Parlement de Paris* (Paris, 1985), 19.

31. See André-Jean Arnaud, *Les origines doctrinales du code civil français* (Paris, 1969), passim. On the question of lawyers' practical skills, see Mark Osiel, "Lawyers as Monopolists, Aristocrats and Entrepeneurs," *Harvard Law Review* 103, no. 8 (1990): 2009–66. On lawyers' education, see Poirot, "Le milieu socio-professional," 6–14.

32. Voltaire to Charles Augustin Feriol, 6 Sept. 1762, in *Les oeuvres complètes de Voltaire*, Theodore Besterman, ed., 134 vols. (Oxford, 1970–76), 109:203; Montesquieu, *Lettres persanes* (Paris, 1964), 123.

33. [Guy-Charles Aubry, André Blonde, Gabriel-Nicolas Maultrot, Claude Mey et al.], *Maximes du droit public françois*, 2 vols. (Amsterdam, 1775).

34. For background on the case, see Edmond Préclin, *Les jansénistes du 18e siècle et la constitution civile du clergé* (Paris, 1929), 54–61.

35. See ibid., and Jean Egret, *Louis XV et l'opposition parlementaire* (Paris, 1970), 9–25. On Jansenism, see most recently Catherine-Laurence Maire, "L'église et la nation: Du dépôt de la vérité au dépôt des lois, la trajéctoire janséniste au XVIIIe siècle," *Annales* 46, no. 5 (1991): 1177–1205.

36. On the history of the *ordre des avocats* in general, see Bell, "Lawyers and Politics," esp. 79–109. On its early history, see also Roland Delachenal, *Histoire des avocats au Parlement de Paris, 1300–1600* (Paris, 1885), esp. 120–36. On Jansenism in the bar, see the suggestive analysis of Marc Fumaroli, *L'âge de l'éloquence: Rhétorique et 'res literaria' de la Renaissance au seuil de l'époque classique* (Geneva, 1980), esp. 475–92 and 585–646.

37. This process is described in Bell, "Lawyers and Politics," 79–109.

38. For the best analysis of this movement, see Dale Van Kley, *The Damiens Affair and the Unraveling of the Old Regime, 1750–1770* (Princeton, NJ, 1984), esp. 166–225.

39. "My task," one of them said ingratiatingly, "will be less to persuade the judges I have the honor of addressing, than to make our adversaries blush." BN, JF 2298, fol. 102, printed text, 2. The lawyers were Louis Chevallier, Philippes Guillet de Blaru, and Claude-Joseph Prévost. For biographical information on these men and information on their political goals, see Bell, "Lawyers and Politics," 87, 110–11, 139. Prévost was the secretary of the Order of Barristers for two decades and played a major role in developing its institutional strength and autonomy.

40. BN, Départment des Imprimés, cote Ld⁴,802: *Plaidoyers de Mr. Joly, en faveur des trois chanoines, & des trois Curez de Reims, pour être déchargés de la Sentence d'excommunication prononcée contr'eux, le 17. juin 1715, au sujet de la Constitution Unigenitus* (n.p., [1716]), 19.

41. Van Kley, *The Damiens Affair*, 173.

42. The *mémoires* and *plaidoyers* may be found in the BN, JF 2298; and Département des Imprimés, cote Ld⁴, 773, 800, 801, 802, 812, 913, 933, 934, 935, and 936. For full titles, see the *Catalogue de l'Histoire de France*. See also the accompanying material in the BSP-LP 19: 407–8, 414.

43. *Avocat général* Guillaume-François Joly de Fleury commented scathingly on the speed and carelessness of the reconstructions: "I have rarely seen published writings with so many typographical errors, and even more errors of judgement (at least in the *plaidoyer* attributed to me). I don't know how they could have made me speak so poorly." Handwritten note in BN, JF 2298, fol. 48. The printed texts are collected in *Plaidoyers de Mr. Joly*. Compare with the handwritten drafts of Joly's *plaidoyer* in BN, JF 2298, fols. 136 ff.; and Prévost's *plaidoyer* in BSP-LP 19:1111 ff. (printed copy in BN, JF 2298, fols. 102 ff.)

44. "The *mémoires* gave all the more pleasure because they were the first openly-produced works which clearly opposed the *constitution* [i.e. *Unigenitus*] and the measures taken to implement it." J. Cadry and J. Jouail, *Histoire du livre des Réflexions morales et de la Constitution Unigenitus*, 4 vols. (Amsterdam, 1723), 1:692.

45. *Plaidoyers de Mr. Joly*, 2–4, 19; BN, JF 2298, fol. 102.

46. Entry in Louis Moréri, *Le grand dictionnaire historique* (Paris, 1759), 3:604.

47. "The acts of Censorship which emanate from these powers are abusive if they tend to trouble public order, to prevent the execution of the Laws, or to challenge the authority of the Magistrates." *Plaidoyers de Mr. Joly*, 4.

48. On the *appel*, see Moïse Cagnac, *De l'appel comme d'abus dans l'ancien droit français* (Paris, 1906), 19–27. On the ordinances of Louis XIV, see Barthélémy Auzanet, "Lettre de Maître Barthelemy Auzanet, écrite à un de ses amis," in *Oeuvres de M. Barthelemy Auzanet, ancien avocat au Parlement* (Paris, 1708), unpaginated.

49. Maire, "L'église et la nation," 1187. Maire associates the "secularization" of the notion of the "depository of truth" with a particular crisis in the

history of French Jansenism: the Council of Embrun of 1727. The evidence presented here suggests that it can be dated at least ten years earlier. See BN, JF 2298, fol. 102, printed text, 2.

50. Jules Flammermont, ed., *Remontrances du Parlement de Paris au XVIIIe siècle*, 3 vols. (Paris, 1888), 1:232–40. On Prévost, see the description by Louis-Adrien Le Paige in BSP-LP 460: no. 23.

51. BN, Ld⁴,773: Claude-Joseph Prévost, *Mémoire pour les trois docteurs et curez de Reims, au sujet des poursuites contre eux faites pour raison de la Constitution Unigenitus* (Paris, 1716), 11–13.

52. See Ernst H. Kantorowicz, *The King's Two Bodies: A Study in Medieval Political Theology* (Princeton, NJ, 1957); and, for its French incarnation, Ralph E. Giesey, *The Royal Funeral Ceremony in Renaissance France* (Geneva, 1960). On the repudiation of the notion of the king's two bodies, particularly in the notorious *lit de justice* of 1610, see Sarah Hanley, *The Lit de Justice of the Kings of France: Constitutional Ideology in Legend, Ritual and Discourse* (Princeton, NJ, 1983).

53. Prévost, *Mémoire*, 7.

54. "The *parlement* of Paris, true *parlement* of the Kingdom . . . born with the State, and whose establishment relates to and is intrinsic to the establishment of the Monarchy." Ibid., 10. In a sense, this *mémoire* can be seen as a bridge between two ages of *parlementaire* constitutionalism. In invoking the political language of the king's two bodies, Prévost reached out to a vision of monarchy largely abandoned by the Parlement itself, but still cherished in the bar. By suggesting that the Parlement and the monarchy had common origins (a theme he pursued in unpublished works on the *lit de justice*), he paved the way for his protégé, the great *éminence grise* of the Parlement, Adrien-Louis Le Paige, and thus for the great *parlementaire* offensives of the 1750s and 1760s.

55. In general, on the history of Jansenism in this period, see Georges Hardy, *Le Cardinal de Fleury et le mouvement janséniste* (Paris, 1924). On the conclusion of the 1716 case, see Préclin, *Les jansénistes*, 61.

56. In general on the barristers' practice, see the article "avocat" in the *Encyclopédie méthodique, ou par ordre de matières; par une société de gens de lettres, de savans et d'artistes: Jurisprudence* (Paris, 1783–87).

57. See, for instance, BN, Ld⁴,930: Louis Chevallier, *Plaidoyé de M. Louis Chevalier, ancien avocat au Parlement, Pour la Mere Denise-Elisabeth de Sallo Abesse perpetuelle du Monastere des Cordelieres de la Nativité de Jesus du Fauxbourg S. Germain à Paris, Appellante comme d'abus de la Sentence du Pere le Jeune Provincial des Cordeliers, du 21 de May 1715* (Soleure, 1717).

58. Ibid., 42.

59. In 1718, it began the first in a long series of strikes designed to support the Parlement in its own intensifying battles with the Crown. Claude-Joseph Prévost and his colleagues assured compliance from their sometimes-reluctant membership by disbarring anyone who opposed them. The victims included Nicolas-François Fessart, who had defended archbishop Mailly in

the 1716 case and earned venomous rebuke from the opposing counsel. See Bell, "Lawyers and Politics," 109–21. For Fessart's disbarral, see handwritten notes in *tableau des avocats* of 1729, Collection Boucher d'Argis, Bibliothèque des Avocats à la Cour d'Appel de Paris. For the rebuke, see BN, Ld⁴,933: Louis Chevallier, *Mémoire pour Maistres Jean-François de Beyne* (Paris, 1717), 10.

60. BN, JF 97, fol. 268: *Consultation de MM. les Avocats au Parlement de Paris sur l'effet des Arrests des Parlements . . . en matiere d'Appelle comme d'Abus des Censures Ecclésiastiques* (Paris, 1718), 5. The case also involved a priest who had fallen afoul of archbishop Mailly.

61. [Jacques-Charles Aubry], *Consultation de MM. les Avocats du Parlement de Paris au sujet du jugement rendu à Ambrun contre M. l'Evêque de Senez* (n.p. [1727]), 18. Aubry was aided by a Jansenist theologian, the abbé Boursier. For more on this case, see Préclin, *Les jansénistes*, 119–22; Hardy, *Le Cardinal de Fleury*, 91–101; Maire, "L'église et la nation," 1184–85.

62. [François de Maraimberg], *Mémoire pour les sieurs Samson Curé d'Olivet, Coüet curé de Darvoi, Gaucher Chanoine de Jargeau, Diocése d'Orléans, & autres Ecclesiastiques de différens Diocèses, Appelans comme d'abus* (Paris, 1730), 3.

63. *Requête de MM. les avocats au Parlement de Paris, au sujet de l'arrêt du Conseil d'Etat du Roi, du 30 octobre, 1730* (Paris, 1730), 1. For a discussion of the incident, see David A. Bell, "Des stratégies d'opposition sous Louis XV: L'affaire des avocats de 1730–31," *Histoire, économie et société* 9, no. 4 (1990): 567–90.

64. Archives des Affaires Étrangères, Correspondance Politique: Rome, 729, fol. 79; and ibid., 715, fols. 406–7. For a complete account of the "affair of the council of Embrun," based on newly-discovered sources, see Bell, "Lawyers and Politics," 147–56.

65. The composition of the briefs always lay in the hands of a small, wealthy, heavily noble group of zealous Jansenists who directed the Order of Barristers. These men also regularly drew support from a large percentage of their colleagues, including a disproportionate number of the wealthiest and most influential barristers. In the single case of a priest suspended by the bishop of Cambrai in 1740, 126 barristers (perhaps one-third of those in active practice) affixed their signatures to at least one *mémoire*. See Bell, "Lawyers and Politics," 151–52, 209–34. For the most complete collection of the briefs, see BSP-LP 414.

66. See Lucien Karpik, "Lawyers and Politics in France, 1814–1950: The State, the Market and the Public," *Law and Social Inquiry* 13, no. 4 (1988): 707–36.

67. *Maximes du droit public françois*, esp. 2:324–26.

68. "The subject enjoys his natural liberty up to the point that the public good, and the general interest do not constrain that liberty. This liberty consists of being able to do what he shall wish to do." Ibid. 1:210. Cf. 1:166, 183.

69. Ibid. 2:1–149. Incidentally, the work ended with a historical section

that, in attempting to revive the notion of the coronation oath as the renewal of some sort of social contract, sought to refute many of the long-standing royal arguments against the idea of the "king's two bodies." Ibid. 2, esp. 393–408.

70. Ibid. 2:245.

71. Maire, "L'église et la nation," 1187.

72. On this issue, see particularly the analysis of Peter Campbell, "The Conduct of Politics in France in the Time of the Cardinal Fleury, 1723–43," (Ph.D. diss., Univ. of London, 1985), 24. For interesting reflections on the heavy legacy of the religious wars in the eighteenth century, see J.G.A. Pocock, "Conservative Enlightenment and Democratic Revolutions: The American and French Cases in British Perspective," *Government and Opposition* 24, no. 1 (1989): 1–37.

73. Maire, "L'église et la nation," 1197. For a striking illustration of the comparison between Jansenists and beleaguered prophets, see *L'hérésie imaginaire des avocats, ou les Jérémies du temps* (n.p., [1731]).

74. Wood, *The Creation of the American Republic*, 152; Montesquieu, *The Spirit of the Laws*, Jean Brethe de la Gressaye, ed., 4 vols. (Paris, 1955), 1:115; 2:65–66. In general on the connection between Montesquieu and the *parlementaire* tradition, see Elie Carcassonne, *Montesquieu et le problème de la constitution au XVIIIe siècle* (Paris, 1926).

75. See most recently: Dale Van Kley, "The Jansenist Constitutional Legacy in the French Pre-Revolution," in Baker, ed., *The Political Culture of the Old Regime*, 169–201; Dale Van Kley, "The Religious Origins of the Patriot and Ministerial Parties in Pre-Revolutionary France: Controversy over the Chancellor's Constitutional *Coup*, 1771–1775," in Thomas Kselman, ed., *Belief in History* (South Bend, IN, 1991); Shanti Singham, "'A Conspiracy of Twenty Million Frenchmen': Public Opinion, Patriotism, and the Assault on Absolutism during the Maupeou Years, 1770–1775," (Ph.D. diss., Princeton, 1991).

76. Baker, *Inventing the French Revolution*, 120. In fact, these remonstrances drew heavily on Malesherbes's earlier, unpublished "Mémoires sur les avocats."

77. Sarah Maza has also made the case, drawing on the work of Peter Brooks, that in the 1770s and the 1780s, the *mémoires judiciaires* adopted a "melodramatic" form that was implicitly democratic. See Maza, "Domestic Melodrama as Political Ideology: The Case of the Comte de Sanois," *AHR* 94, no. 5 (1989): 1257–63.

78. See David A. Bell, "Lawyers into Demagogues: Chancellor Maupeou and the Transformation of Legal Practice in France, 1771–1789," *Past and Present* 130 (1991): 107–41.

79. These positions are described fully in Bell, "Lawyers and Politics," 330–49. On Linguet, see most recently Darline Gay Levy's excellent work, *The Ideas and Careers of Simon Nicolas Henri Linguet* (Urbana, IL, 1980).

80. Target's defense of the Order was entitled *La censure, lettre à * * * * (n.p., [1775]). Its fierce defense of the Order often contradicts his series of pam-

phlets against Chancellor Maupeou entitled *Lettres d'un homme à un autre homme* (n.p., [1771]).

81. Gérard Walter, *Robespierre*, 2 vols. (Paris, 1961), 1:49–55.

82. The sources on these cases, and Voltaire's role in them, is endless, but for concise treatments that focus on the barristers, see Baron Francis Delbeke, *L'action politique et sociale des avocats: Leur part dans la préparation de la Révolution française* (Louvain, 1927), and Maza, *Private Lives*, esp. chap. 2.

83. See Charles H. O'Brien, "Jansenists and Civil Toleration in France, 1775–1778: Le Paige, Giudi and Robert de Saint-Vincent," in Roland Crahay, ed., *La tolérance civile: Colloque international organisé à l'Université de Mons* (Brussels, 1982), 183–93; Jeffrey Merrick, *The Desacralization of the French Monarchy in the Eighteenth Century* (Baton Rouge, LA, 1990), 135–64.

84. Voltaire, *Oeuvres* 109:154, 202-3. On Élie's position in the bar, see Bibliothèque des Avocats, Collection Gaultier du Breuil, no. 15, 17; [Louis Petit de Bachaumont, Mathieu-François Pidansat de Mairobert, et. al.], *Mémoires secrets pour servir à l'histoire de la république des lettres*, 36 vols. (London, 1777–89), 31:28; Voltaire, *Oeuvres* 113:237–38, 245.

85. See notably Jean-Baptise-Jacques Élie de Beaumont, *Mémoire à consulter et consultation pour Pierre-Paul Sirven, Commissaire à Terrier dans le Diocèse de Castres, présentement à Genève, accusé d'avoir fait mourrir sa seconde fille, pour l'empêcher de se faire Catholique; & pour ses deux filles* (Paris, 1767). On the use of melodrama in *mémoires judiciaires*, see Maza, "Le tribunal de la nation," 80–87.

86. Pierre Firmin de Lacroix, *Mémoire pour le sieur Pierre-Paul Sirven, Feudiste, Habitant de Castres, Appellant, Contre les Consuls & Communauté de Mazamet, Seigneurs-Jusiticiers de Mazamet, Hautpoul & Hautpouloi, prenant le fait & cause de leur Procureur Jurisdictionnel, Intimés* (n.p., 1771). Some readers attributed the brief to Voltaire himself (see A. Corda and A. Trudon des Ormes, *Catalogue des factums*, 8 vols. [Paris, 1896–1904], s.v. Sirven), but Voltaire's correspondence belies this. On Firmin, see Voltaire to Élie de Beaumont, 4 Mar. 1770, in Voltaire, *Oeuvres* 120:70.

87. Lacroix, *Mémoire*, 127.

88. Voltaire to Marie Anne Ramond, 19 May 1770, in Voltaire, *Oeuvres* 120:203; Voltaire to Lacroix, 10 Dec. 1770, in ibid. 121:124.

89. See Egret, *Louis XV*, 182–202, and Bell, "Lawyers into Demagogues," passim.

90. On this point, see Durand Echeverria, *The Maupeou Revolution: A Study in the History of Libertarianism, France, 1770–1774* (Baton Rouge, LA, 1985), 84–87.

91. Séguier's attack—a condemnation of a brief by the liberal magistrate Dupaty—is reprinted in A. Clair and Clapier, *Le barreau français: collection des chefs d'oeuvre de l'éloquence judiciaire en France*, 10 vols. (Paris, 1818), vol. 4.

92. Some barristers tried nonetheless to convince the judges, but at the

cost of basic intellectual inconsistency: a brief would invoke existing laws in one paragraph, and demand they be scrapped in the next. For Linguet, see Simon-Nicolas-Henri Linquet, *Aiguilloniana* (London, 1777), 20–21.

93. Ambroise Falconnet, "Essai sur le mémoires," in *Le barreau français: partie moderne*, 2 vols. (Paris, 1806–8), 1:xxxi.

94. Pierre-Louis Lacretelle, "Un Barreau Extérieur à la fin du XVIIe siècle," in *Oeuvres de P. L. Lacretelle ainé*, 5 vols. (Paris, 1823–24), 1:121–23.

95. Lacretelle, *Oeuvres* 2:112. On the case see Maza, "Domestic Melodrama as Political Ideology," passim.

96. This is described in Lacretelle's notes on his cases in *Oeuvres* 2:442–45. Compare this treatment to Cardinal Fleury's campaign against the barrister Aubry.

97. [Charles-Alexandre de Calonne], *Lettre d'un avocat à M. de la Cretelle concernant l'opinion émise par ce dernier sur les lettres de cachet* (n.p., [1786]), 2. The attribution to Calonne is in Antoine-Alexandre Barbier, *Dictionnaire des ouvrages anonymes* (repr. Hildesheim, 1963). It is possible that Lacretelle, after the Revolution, confused the case of the Compagnie des Indes and the Sanois affair, and that Calonne never composed a *mémoire* in the first (I have, in any case, been unable to locate it). Alternately, Barbier mistakenly attributed the *Lettre* to Calonne, when he really meant the elusive piece in the Compagnie des Indes case.

98. Compare Calonne's pamphlet with *Réponse du comte de Courcy à M. le Comte de Sanois & à M. de la Cretelle, son Défenseur* (Paris, 1786).

99. Jacobson, "Politics of Criminal Law Reform," 401–2; *Mémoires secrets* 32:210.

100. Armand Lods, "L'avocat Target défenseur des Protestants," *Bulletin de la société de l'histoire du protestantisme français* 43 (1883): 606. This article uses the full text of Target's journal, which was lost during the Second World War. See Hudault, "Jean-Baptiste Target," passim.

101. Élie de Beaumont originally took on the case, but died before it was resolved.

102. Quoted in Lods, "L'avocat Target," 607.

103. *Mémoires secrets* 35:345.

104. Guy-Jean-Baptiste Target, *Consultation sur l'affaire de la dame marquise d'Anglure, contre les sieurs Petit, au conseil des Dépêches, Dans laquelle l'on traite du mariage & de l'état des Protestans* (Paris, 1787), 75, 103.

105. Ibid., 28, 164.

106. Maza, *Private Lives*, chap. 5. Maza reads the attack on "absolute" judges as an indirect attack on an "absolute" king. This interpretation, however, may not be justified, for it assumes an hostility to an entire regime on the part of men who did not yet imagine it could be overthrown, and who tended to see judges and king as irreconcilably opposed.

107. Michel de Servan, "Discours sur l'administration de la justice criminelle" (1766), reprinted in *Oeuvres édites et inédites de Servan*, Xavier de Portrets, ed., 5 vols. (Paris, 1825), 2:75; Target, *Mémoire*, 162.

108. Michel de Servan argued that even a single, absolute legislator, when

he legislated properly, represented the wills of the entire public. Servan, "Discours," 74.

109. Nicolas Bergasse, *Rapport du comité de constitution, sur l'organisation du pouvoir judiciaire, présentée à l'assemblée nationale par M. Bergasse* (Paris, 1789).

110. *AP* (17 Aug. 1789), 8:448.

111. For Martineau's Jansenist sympathies, see his signature of numerous *mémoires judiciaires* in BSP-LP 414.

Chapter 7

1. The most comprehensive reconstruction of the debate over religious rights appears in de Baecque, 164–81. An older analysis of the debate is N. Weiss, "Les séances des 22 et 23 août 1789 à l'Assemblée nationale," *BSHPF* 38 (1889): 561–75. This may be supplemented by Rials, 236–47. The Edict of 1787 is reproduced as the Édit du Roi concernant ceux qui ne font pas profession de la Religion Catholique. [17] Novembre 1787, in Isambert et al. 29:472–82. A brief summary of the circumstances surrounding the edict of 1787 appears in Burdette C. Poland, *French Protestantism and the French Revolution: A Study in Church and State, Thought and Religion* (Princeton, NJ, 1957), 79–81. Detailed analyses of the edict and its consequences were published in a special number of the *BSHPF* 134 (1988), "Actes des journées d'études sur l'Édit de 1787 (Paris, 9–10 Oct. 1987)," André Encrevé and Claude Lauriol, eds.

2. See Denis Lacorne, *L'invention de la République: le modèle américain* (Paris, 1991), 78–79.

3. Ibid., 190–95.

4. Henri Dubief, "La réception de l'édit du 17 novembre 1787 par les parlements," *BSHPF* 134:281–95.

5. *AP* 7:687–93. *Table des cahiers des États-généraux;* Louis Mazoyer, "La question protestante dans les cahiers des États-généraux," *BSHPF* 80 (1931): 41–73; Poland, *French Protestantism,* 95–99.

6. Marcel Gauchet lists 38 (Rials, 320–22). Most have been reproduced in Rials, 576–749, and de Baecque, 79–82, 86–88, 128–30, 220–92.

7. Article XII. *Essai sur la déclaration des droits de l'homme en société, soumis à l'Assemblée nationale par M. le duc de Lévis* (Aug. 1789); in de Baecque, 236.

8. "Préliminaire de la constitution françoise. Article premier. Du droit naturel & imprescriptible des hommes en société. Sur la liberté des pensées et des opinions," *Projet du préliminaire de la constitution françoise, présenté par M. Rabaut de Saint-Étienne* (Versailles, 1789); in Rials, 682.

9. [Abbé Sieyès], *Déclaration des droits de l'homme en société* (Versailles, 1789); in Rials, 614–21.

10. Article 14. *Déclaration des droits de l'homme et du citoyen, par M. Mounier* (Versailles, [1789]); in Rials, 608.

11. Article 12. *Déclaration des droits de l'homme remise dans les bureaux de l'Assemblée nationale par M. Peytion de Villeneuve, député de Chartres* (Paris, [1789]); in Rials, 726.

12. Articles 16, 17, 18. *Projet de déclaration des droits de l'homme et du citoyen, discuté dans le sixième Bureau de l'Assemblée nationale* (Versailles, n.d.); in Rials, 623; in de Baecque, 269.

13. Oliver J. Frederiksen, "The Bureaus of the French Constituent Assembly of 1789: An Early Experiment in the Group Conference Method," *Political Science Quarterly* 51 (1936): 418–37; Philip Dawson, "Le sixième Bureau de l'Assemblée nationale et son projet de déclaration des droits de l'homme," *AHRF* 232 (1978): 161–79.

14. Antoine de Baecque, "'Le choc des opinions': le débat des droits de l'homme, juillet-août 1789," in de Baecque, 29.

15. *Projet de déclaration;* Rials, 623; in de Baecque, 269.

16. In de Baecque, 165.

17. *AP* (22 Aug. 1789), 8:473; de Baecque, 166.

18. *AP* (22 Aug. 1789), 8:473; de Baecque, 167.

19. *AP* (23 Aug. 1789), 8:475–76; de Baecque, 168–71.

20. *AP* (23 Aug. 1789), 8:476–78; de Baecque, 172–75.

21. *AP* (23 Aug. 1789), 8:478; de Baecque, 175.

22. *AP* (23 Aug. 1789), 8:479; de Baecque, 176.

23. *AP* (23 Aug. 1789), 8:479; de Baecque, 176–77. At the very moment Rabaut Saint-Étienne addressed the Assembly, pogroms were exploding in Alsace and Jews were fleeing to Basel and other Swiss towns.

24. *AP* (23 Aug. 1789), 8:479; de Baecque, 177.

25. For example, Count François-Henri Virieu noted: "Religious sects have troubled the earth because their advocates have manifested their opinions, published their doctrines, and taken up a partisan manner. They should be contained through legal subordination." *Courrier de Provence* 1, letter no. 31, 22-23 Aug. 1789. Castellane tried to blunt these fears by blaming the religious wars on ambitious political chieftains willing to exploit the ignorance of the majority. Had the sixteenth-century leadership advocated the principles embedded in his motion, according to Castellane, "Everyone would [then] have freely served God according to his conscience, and we would not have had Catholics and Protestants, Frenchmen against Frenchmen, mutually massacring each other and for so long lay waste to the land we inhabit." De Baecque, 180.

26. *AP* (23 Aug. 1789), 8:480; de Baecque, 180–81.

27. De Baecque, 205–6.

28. Cited in Rials, 246–47. In the *Courrier de Provence*, Mirabeau wrote: "We cannot hide our grief that the National Assembly, instead of eradicating the germ of intolerance, seems to have reserved it in a Declaration of the Rights of Man."

29. *Journal d'Adrien Duquesnoy, député du Tiers État de Bar-le-Duc sur l'Assemblée constituante, 3 mai 1789–3 avril 1790,* ed. Robert de Crèvecoeur (Paris, 1894), 311.

30. Gauchet, 174.

31. Richard Mowery Andrews, "Boundaries of Citizenship: The Penal Regulation of Speech in Revolutionary France," *French Politics and Society* 7 (1989): 95.

32. Règlement du Conseil pour la librairie et imprimerie de Paris. 28 Feb. 1723; Isambert et al. 21:216–51.

33. Raymond Birn, "The Pamphlet Press and the Estates-General of 1789," *Studies on Voltaire and the Eighteenth Century* 287 (Oxford, 1991): 59–69. Carla Hesse, *Publishing and Cultural Politics in Revolutionary Paris, 1789–1810* (Berkeley, 1991), chap. 1.

34. This was particularly true with respect to early revolutionary newspapers. See Claude Labrosse and Pierre Rétat, *Naissance du journal révolutionnaire* (Lyon, 1989), chap. 1.

35. *AP* 7:656–64. *Table des cahiers des États-généraux.*

36. Article 15. *Déclaration des droits de l'homme et du citoyen, par M. Mounier;* in Rials, 608.

37. *Projet de déclaration des droits de l'homme en société. Présenté par MM. du Comité chargé de l'examen des déclarations des droits* (Versailles, [1789]); in Rials, 748.

38. Article 19. *Projet de déclaration des droits de l'homme et du citoyen;* in Rials, 623; in de Baecque, 269.

39. *Moniteur universel* 46 (24 Aug. 1789): 374; de Baecque, 183. La Rochefoucauld's motion was based largely upon Article 14 of the Virginia Declaration of Rights, which he had translated and published in 1783 along with the other American declarations.

40. De Baecque, 184.

41. *AP* (24 Aug. 1789), 8:483–84; de Baecque, 184.

42. *Moniteur universel* 46 (24 Aug. 1789): 380; de Baecque, 186.

43. Édit contenant règlement sur les imprimeurs et libraires de Paris. Aug. 1686. Isambert et al. 20:6–20.

44. Réglement du Conseil pour la librairie et imprimerie de Paris. 28 Feb. 1723; in Isambert et al. 21:216–51. Arrêt du Conseil d'État qui ordonne que le règlement fait pour les imprimeurs et librairies de la ville de Paris sera exécuté dans tout le royaume. 24 Mar. 1744. BN, Fonds français, MS. 22062, fol. 85. Arrêts du Conseil portant règlement sur les privilèges en librairie, portant suppression et création de différentes chambres syndicales dans le royaume, qui réglent les formalités à observer pour la réception des libraires et imprimeurs, portant établissement de deux ventes publiques de librairie, concernant les contrefaçons de livres et portant règlement de discipline pour les compagnons imprimeurs. 30 Aug. 1777; in Isambert et al. 26:108–28.

45. Lists of censors can also be found in A.-M. Lottin, *Catalogue chronologique des libraires et des libraires-imprimeurs de Paris* (Paris, 1789). On the administration of censorship, see William Hanley, "The Policing of Thought: Censorship in Eighteenth-Century France," *Studies on Voltaire and the Eighteenth Century* 183 (Oxford, 1980): 265–95; Raymond Birn, "Book Production and Censorship in France," in *Books and Society in*

History, ed. Kenneth E. Carpenter (New York, 1983), 145–71; H. de Beaumont, "L'administration de la librairie et la censure des livres de 1700 à 1750" (*École nationale des chartes: positions des thèses*, Paris, 1966), 72–78; Catherine Blangonnet, "Recherches sur les censeurs royaux au temps de Malesherbes (1750–1763)" (*École nationale des chartes: positions des thèses*, Paris, 1975), 15–22; Daniel Roche, "Censorship and the Publishing Industry," in *Revolution in Print: The Press in France, 1775–1800*, Robert Darnton and Daniel Roche, eds. (Berkeley, 1989), 3–26.

46. Henri-Jean Martin, "La direction des lettres," in Roger Chartier and Henri-Jean Martin, eds., *Histoire de l'édition française* 2 (Paris, 1990): 73–87.

47. Françoise Weil, "Les livres de permission tacite en France au XVIIIe Siècle," *Gutenberg Jahrbuch* 61 (1986): 211–27.

48. Detailed case studies of the assertions in the previous two paragraphs may be found in Chartier and Martin, *Histoire de l'édition française* 2: 71–146, 329–492.

49. BN, Fonds français, MSS 21897–21926, 21981–22003, 22039–22040.

50. BN, Nouvelles acquisitions françaises, MS. 3345, fol. 140. (Dec. 1757.)

51. In this respect the work of Robert Darnton is exemplary. See his *Literary Underground of the Old Regime* (Cambridge, MA, 1982) and *Édition et sédition: l'univers de la littérature clandestine au XVIIIe siècle* (Paris, 1991).

52. The most comprehensive document collections in France are in the BN (Collection Anisson-Duperron and Archives de la chambre syndicale des imprimeurs et libraires). The Archives de la Bastille in the Bibliothèque de l'Arsenal (Paris) are a treasure-trove of police records, and it is safe to say that every major archive or research library in Paris contains useful documentary evidence. The most important archive outside France covering the trade in French-language books is the municipal library of Neuchâtel, Switzerland. In the United States good collections of printed laws and decrees pertaining to the French book trade are in The New York Public Library and the Newberry Library, Chicago.

53. H.-J. Martin, "*L'Histoire de Charles XII*, les *Lettres philosophiques* et la censure," "L'affaire de *De l'Esprit*," and "Rousseau et Malesherbes," in *Histoire de l'édition française* 2:94–98; Daniel Roche, "La police du livre" and "La censure," ibid., 88–94, 99–109.

54. Birn, "Censorship in France," 154–63.

55. Eric Walter, "Les auteurs et le champ littéraire," *Histoire de l'édition française* 2:391.

56. Raymond Birn, "Malesherbes and the Call for a Free Press," in Darnton and Roche, *Revolution in Print*, 55.

57. Denis Diderot, *Lettre historique et politique sur le commerce de la librairie* (published as *Sur la liberté de la presse*), ed. Jacques Proust (Paris, 1964), 81–83.

58. Arthur M. Wilson, *Diderot* (New York, 1972), 332–42; D. W. Smith, *Helvétius: A Study in Persecution* (Oxford, 1965), 11–35.

59. Déclaration portant défenses à toutes personnes de quelque état et condition qu'elles soient de composer ni faire composer, imprimer et distribuer aucuns écrits contre le règle des ordonnances, sous les peines y mentionnées. 16 Apr. 1757; Isambert et al. 22:272–73.

60. C.-G. Lamoignon de Malesherbes, *Mémoires sur la librairie et sur la liberté de la presse,* ed. Graham E. Rodmell (Chapel Hill, NC, 1979). See Pierre Grosclaude, *Malesherbes: témoin et interprète de son temps* (Paris, [1961]), 163–86; and Birn, "Malesherbes and the Call for a Free Press," 57–61.

61. Malesherbes, "Second mémoire sur la librairie," *Mémoires,* 99.

62. Malesherbes, "Troisième mémoire sur la librairie," *Mémoires,* 118.

63. Ibid., 129–34.

64. Malesherbes, "Quatrième mémoire sur la librairie," *Mémoires,* 136–74.

65. BN, Fonds français, MSS 22095-22101. Jeremy Popkin and Dale Van Kley, "The Pre-Revolutionary Debate," intro. to sec. 5 of *The French Revolution Research Collection,* ed. Colin Lucas (Oxford, 1990), 1–17. Jeremy Popkin, "Pamphlet Journalism at the End of the Old Regime," *Eighteenth-Century Studies* 22 (1989): 351–67.

66. Theodore Besterman, *Voltaire* (New York, 1969), 525–27. Wilson, *Diderot,* 685–86. Raymond Trousson, *Rousseau et sa fortune littéraire* (St.-Médard-en-Jalles, 1971), 47–58; Robert Darnton, "Readers Respond to Rousseau: The Fabrication of Romantic Sensitivity," in Darnton, *The Great Cat Massacre and Other Episodes in French Cultural History* (New York, 1984), 215–56.

67. Daniel Roche, "La censure," in *Histoire de l'édition française* 2:106. Isabelle Lehu, "La diffusion du livre clandestin à Paris de 1750 à 1789" (thesis Univ. de Paris I, 1979), 135–40.

68. "Fragments sur la liberté de la presse (1776)," *OEuvres de Condorcet,* ed. A. Condorcet O'Connor and M.-F. Arago (Paris, 1847), 11:304–7.

69. Marie-Joseph Chénier, *Dénonciation des inquisiteurs de la pensée* (Paris, 1789).

70. Malesherbes, *Mémoires,* 217–310.

71. Birn, "Malesherbes and the Call for a Free Press," 50–66; Birn, "The Pamphlet Press," 59–69; Hesse, *Publishing and Cultural Politics,* chap. 1.

72. Malesherbes, *Mémoires,* 225–26, 299.

73. Ibid., 289–93.

74. Hesse, *Publishing and Cultural Politics,* 25; Birn, "The Pamphlet Press," 59–61.

75. Carla Hesse, "Economic Upheavals in Publishing," in Darnton and Roche, *Revolution in Print,* 69–97.

76. Chapter 5, Article 17: "No person may be sought out or pursued for writings which he will have had printed or published on whatever subject, as long as he has not intentionally advocated disobedience for the law, upsetting of the constituted powers, resistance to their acts, or other deeds considered crimes or legal offenses. Censuring the acts of the constituted powers is permitted; but purposeful slandering of public officials and the uprightness

of their intentions as they exercise their functions may be pursued legally by those who are the object. Slander and injury against all persons relative to the actions of their private life will be punished in accordance with the legal process." *Les constitutions de la France depuis 1789,* Jacques Godechot, ed. (Paris, 1979), 60–61.

77. Articles 1, 2, 4, 6. Édit portant révocation de l'Édit de Nantes. Oct. 1685; Isambert et al. 19:532–33.

78. Articles 9, 11. Ibid., 533–34.

79. Édit du Roi portant que les enfans des religionnaires seront mis, à compter de 5 ans, entre les mains de leurs parens catholiques, et s'ils n'en ont pas, en celles des Catholiques qui seront nommés par les juges pour être élevés dans la R. C. A. et R. Jan. 1686. Isambert et al. 19:543–44.

80. Déclaration sur l'édit d'octobre 1685, contenant règlement pour l'instruction des nouveaux convertis et de leurs enfans. 13 Dec. 1698. Isambert et al. 20:316.

81. Déclaration concernant la religion. 14 May 1724. Isambert et al. 21:261–262.

82. Ibid.

83. Joseph Dedieu, *Histoire politique des Protestants français (1715–1794)* (Paris, 1925), 1:chap. 2.

84. Ibid., 147.

85. Ibid., 215–27. Saint-Priest pointed out that acceptance of the fiction of *nouveaux convertis* as lapsed Catholics carried with it the obligation of granting them the sacraments, including that of marriage. See Jeffrey W. Merrick, *The Desacralization of the French Monarchy in the Eighteenth Century* (Baton Rouge, LA, 1990), 148.

86. BN, Collection JF, MS. 1671, fols. 144–245. A printed version of the *Mémoire de M. Joly de Fleury* is excerpted in [C.-G. Lamoignon de Malesherbes], *Premier mémoire sur le mariage des Protestans, en 1785* [1786].

87. Dedieu, *Histoire politique* 1:407–9.

88. Charles H. O'Brien, "The Jansenist Campaign for Toleration of Protestants in Late Eighteenth-Century France: Sacred or Secular?" *JHI* 46 (1985): 530–35.

89. Augustin Gazier, *Histoire générale du mouvement janséniste depuis ses origines jusqu'à nos jours* (Paris, 1927), 2:chaps. 18, 21, 23.

90. In this vein Dale Van Kley stresses the emergence, in the 1750s, of Jansenist juridical positions which had the king act as political magistrate who kept the peace and protected familial honor by ordering priests to administer the sacraments. By the same token, Jansenist thinking would have the king as magistrate order his judges to respect natural law contracts by registering marriages. Such contracts took precedence over any sacrament. Conversations with Van Kley, February 1992.

91. [Maultrot and Tailhé], *Questions sur la tolérance chrétienne* (n.p., 1758), reprinted as *Essai sur la tolérance chrétienne* (n.p., 1760). See Charles H. O'Brien, "Jansenists and Civil Toleration in Mid-Eighteenth Century France," *Theologische Zeitschrift* 37 (1981): 71–93.

92. [Louis Guidi], *Lettre à l'auteur de l'écrit intitulé "La légitimité et la nécessité de la loi du silence"* (n.p., 1759); *Lettre à un ami* (n.p., 1765); *Dialogue entre un évêque et un curé, sur les mariages des Protestans* (n.p., 1775); *Suite du dialogue sur les mariages des Protestans, ou réponse de M. le curé de *** à l'auteur d'une brochure intitulée, "Les Protestans déboutés de leurs prétentions"* (1776); *Dialogue sur l'état civil des Protestans en France, entre un président du parlement, un conseiller d'État et le curé de St.**** (n.p., 1779).

93. Charles H. O'Brien, "Jansenists and Civil Toleration in France, 1775–1778: Le Paige, Guidi, and Robert de Saint-Vincent," in *La tolérance civile*, Roland Crahay, ed. (Brussels, 1982), 183–99.

94. *Mémoire théologique et politique au sujet des mariages clandestins des Protestans de France*, 2d ed. (n.p., 1756). Recent research identifies a Protestant group in Paris as authoring the pamphlet. See the intervention of Daniel Robert in the "Actes des journées d'études sur l'Édit de 1787," *BSHPF* 134:215.

95. Arrêt du Conseil suivi de lettres patentes portant que les baptêmes et mariages des religionnaires seront célébrés par des ministres choisis par les intendans, à charge par lesdits ministres de ne pas faire de prêches ni exercices autres que ce qui est marqué dans leurs livres. 15 Sept. 1685. Isambert et al. 19:529.

96. *Mémoire théologique et politique au sujet des mariages clandestins des Protestans de France*, 111.

97. [Abbé de Caveyrac], *Mémoire politico-critique où l'on examine s'il est de l'intérêt de l'église et de l'état d'établir pour les Calvinistes du royaume une nouvelle forme de se marier* (n.p., 1756); *La voix du vrai patriote catholique opposé à celle des faux patriotes tolérants* (n.p., 1756); *Sentiments des Catholiques de France sur le mémoire au sujet des mariages clandestins des Protestans* (n.p., 1756); *Lettre d'un patriote sur la tolérance civile des Protestans de France et sur les avantages qui en résulteraient pour le royaume* (n.p., 1756).

98. John Woodbridge, "La conspiration du prince de Conti (1755–1757)," *Dix-huitième siècle* 17 (1985): 97–109.

99. John Pappas, "La répression contre les Protestants dans la seconde moitié du [dix-huitième] siècle, d'après les registres de l'ancien régime," *Dix-huitième siècle* 17 (1985): 111–28.

100. David D. Bien, *The Calas Affair: Persecution, Toleration, and Heresy in Eighteenth-Century Toulouse* (Princeton, NJ, 1960), 84–85, 92–115, 151–155.

101. Elisabeth Labrousse, "Note à propos de la conception de la tolérance au XVIIIe siècle," *Studies on Voltaire and the Eighteenth Century* 56 (Geneva, 1967): 799–811. Geoffrey Adams, "Myths and Misconceptions: The Philosophe View of the Huguenots in the Age of Louis XV," *Historical Reflections/Réflexions historiques* 1 (1974): 59–79. Professor Adams has recently published his findings in more comprehensive form: *Huguenots and French Opinion, 1685–1787* (Waterloo, ON, 1992).

102. *De l'esprit des loix*, Roger Callois, ed. (Paris, 1951), bk. 25, chaps. 9–10.

103. *Encyclopédie, ou dictionnaire raisonné des sciences, des arts et des métiers, par une société de gens de lettres* (Neufchastel [Paris], 1765), 8:843–44; Wilson, *Diderot*, 433–34.

104. Jaucourt's article is reproduced in Douglas H. Gordon and Norman L. Torrey, *The Censoring of Diderot's Encyclopédie and the Re-established Text* (New York, 1947), 95–106. See also, Madeleine F. Morris, *Le chevalier de Jaucourt, un ami de la terre* (Geneva, 1979).

105. *Traité sur la tolérance à l'occasion de la mort de Jean Calas*, in *Oeuvres complètes de Voltaire* 25, *Mélanges* (Paris, 1879), 13–118. René Pomeau, *La religion de Voltaire* (Paris, 1969), 326–41. Graham Garget, "Voltaire and Protestantism," *Studies on Voltaire and the Eighteenth Century* 188 (Oxford, 1980): chap. 7.

106. Adams, "Myths and Misconceptions," 69–70. Garget, *Voltaire and Protestantism*, 315–24. Rousseau's position is particularly revealing. In October 1761 a fellow Protestant, Jean Ribotte, urged him to intervene in favor of the pastor François Rochette, who had been arrested for holding an illegal outdoor service and was taken to Toulouse for trial, and for three brothers named Grenier who unsuccessfully attempted to set Rochette free and were arrested in turn. Rousseau rejected Ribotte's request, expressing dissatisfaction with outdoor Calvinist assemblies and pointing out that the Grenier brothers' action amounted to rebellion. The Parlement of Toulouse found pastor Rochette and the Greniers guilty and sentenced them to death, and the four were executed. The following year, in a note written for the penultimate chapter of *The Social Contract*, Rousseau composed a lengthy plea advocating legitimation of Protestant marriages. During the printing of the book he took fright, modified the passage, and finally insisted on having it removed. An uncancelled copy apparently was smuggled out of his publisher's workshop, and several pirated editions of *The Social Contract* contained the note. At the same time, while working on *The Social Contract* Rousseau received a new plea from Ribotte asking him to write a pamphlet in favor of Jean Calas, a Protestant accused of having murdered his son to prevent his conversion to Catholicism. Initially Rousseau refused; he had second thoughts, but these were cut short by his own persecution in June 1762. At length, however, in his *Lettre à Christophe de Beaumont* (1763), Rousseau made his case for Protestant civil rights in France. See *Oeuvres complètes de Jean-Jacques Rousseau*, ed. Bernard Gagnebin and Marcel Raymond (Paris, 1969), 4:978–79; Maurice Cranston, *The Noble Savage: Jean-Jacques Rousseau, 1754–1762* (Chicago, 1991), 299–300, 322; *Correspondance complète de Jean-Jacques Rousseau*, R.A. Leigh, ed. (Geneva and Oxford, 1965–1991), 9:137–39, 200–201, 304–7, 363; 10:61, 170, 212, 256; 12:202; R.A. Leigh, "Rousseau, His Publishers and the *Contrat social*," *Bulletin of the John Rylands University Library of Manchester* 66, 2 (Spring, 1984): 219–20; R.A. Leigh, "The Impact of Rousseau's *Contrat social* in Eighteenth-Century France: Mornet's Private Libraries Revisited," in *Unsolved Problems in the Bibliography of J.-J. Rousseau*, J.T.A. Leigh, ed. (Cambridge, 1990), 21.

107. Michel Perronet, "Les assemblées du clergé et les Protestants," *Dix-huitième siècle* 17:143–50.

108. Dedieu, *Histoire politique* 1:404.

109. See, for example, the anonymous pamphlet *Observations d'un mag-istrat sur un mémoire recemment publié concernant l'état civil à donner aux Protestans en France* (n.d., n.p.). Recently Barbara de Negroni has postu-lated an intriguing thesis linking the disastrous fate of Rousseau's *Émile* with renewed resistance towards granting civil status to French Protestants during the early 1760s. See de Negroni, ed., *Jean-Jacques Rousseau/Chré-tien-Guillaume de Lamoignon de Malesherbes: Correspondance* (Paris, 1991), 128–30.

110. Pierre Gilbert de Voisins, *Mémoires sur les moyens de donner aux Protestans un état civil en France* [1767] (Paris, 1787). In January 1762 Gilbert de Voisins already had addressed reports to the Conseil des Dépêches protecting the religious status of Lutherans in Alsace then under attack from Catholic bishops in the province. His "Affaire des religions d'Alsace" exists in the AN, MS. U-873.

111. Gilbert de Voisins, *Mémoires sur les moyens*, 60–77, 94–126.

112. Malesherbes best exemplifies this school. See, for example, his *Mé-moire sur la situation présente des affaires* (n.p., 1788). See too Elisabeth Badinter, *Les "Remontrances" de Malesherbes, 1771–1775* (Paris, 1978) and George A. Kelly, "The Political Thought of Lamoignon de Malesherbes," *Po-litical Theory* 7 (1979): 485–508.

113. Grosclaude, *Malesherbes*, 373–87.

114. Dedieu, *Histoire politique* 2:149–60, 166. Henri Dubief, "La récep-tion de l'Édit de 1787 par les parlements," *BSHPF* 134:282.

115. Anne-Robert-Jacques Turgot, *Mémoire sur la tolérance* (1774). M.-J.-A.-N. Caritat, marquis de Condorcet, "Recueil des pièces sur l'état des Pro-testans en France" (1781), in O'Connor and Arago, *OEuvres de Condorcet* 5:399–573. [G.-J.-B. Target], *Consultation sur l'affaire de la dame marquise d'Anglure contre les sieurs Petit, au Conseil des Dépêches, dans laquelle l'on traite du mariage et de l'état des Protestans* (Paris, 1787).

116. *Nouvelles ecclésiastiques* (2 Jan. 1783). See O'Brien, "The Jansenist Campaign," 526–29.

117. Michel Peronnet, "Loménie de Brienne, archévêque de Toulouse, principal ministre du roi et l'édit des non-Catholiques de novembre 1787," *BSHPF* 134:263–80.

118. Concerning Robert de Saint-Vincent's Jansenist credentials, see Dale Van Kley, *The Damiens Affair and the Unraveling of the Ancien Régime 1750–1770* (Princeton, NJ, 1983), 60, 126–27, 151. For Robert de Saint-Vin-cent's position on toleration during the 1770s, see O'Brien, "Jansenists and Civil Toleration," 192.

119. Malesherbes, *Premier mémoire sur le mariage des Protestans, en 1785* [1786] and *Second mémoire sur le mariage des Protestans, en 1786* (London, 1787). See Grosclaude, *Malesherbes*, 581–602.

120. Grosclaude, *Malesherbes*, 373–87.

121. AN, MS. H. 1639. "Mémoire sur les affaires de religion" [1776].

122. BN, Fonds français, MS. 10625. "Mémoire sur le mariage des Protestants" [1779].

123. C.-C. Rulhière's *Éclaircissemens historiques sur les causes de la révocation de l'Édit de Nantes et sur l'état des protestants en France depuis le commencement du règne de Louis XIV jusqu'à nos jours* (n.p., 1788), 2 vols., would become the essential public text justifying the Edict of Toleration.

124. "Mémoire sur l'état des Protestans en France" [1784–85], described in Grosclaude, *Malesherbes*, 583–84.

125. Malesherbes, *Premier mémoire sur le mariage des Protestans, en 1785*, 4.

126. Ibid., 31–94.

127. The idea of a civil cult, alluded to by Malesherbes, and again, during the debates of 22–23 August 1789, by Rabaut Saint-Étienne, would find fuller expression in the assembly wrangling over the Civil Constitution of the Clergy and especially the oath upholding it. *AP* (27 Nov.-26 Dec. 1790), 21:8–38, 74–110, 638–41, 677–79, 734–35, 750–53. This fact notwithstanding, the leading authority of the cult of Rousseau finds the philosopher's conception of a civil religion to have been the least emphasized of his political ideas until the apparent *failure* of the Civil Constitution in December 1791: "Between 1789 and 1791, nearly all patriots were convinced that religious sentiment in its traditional form would get along well with the Revolution, and might even serve it." R. Barny, *Rousseau dans la Révolution: le personnage de Jean-Jacques et les débuts du culte révolutionnaire*, "Studies on Voltaire and the Eighteenth Century" 246 (Oxford, 1986): 169.

128. Malesherbes, *Second mémoire sur le mariage des Protestants, en 1786*.

129. Between 1784 and 1787, Rabaut Saint-Étienne was a tireless pamphleteer in favor of toleration. See, for example, his *Le roi doit modifier les lois portées contre les Protestants* (London, 1784). Best known as the politician called on by Louis XVI to form a ministry following the dismissal of Necker on 11 July 1789, Breteuil two years earlier had supported Malesherbes's cause with his *Mémoire ou rapport général sur la situation des Calvinistes en France, sur les causes de cette situation et sur les moyens d'y rémédier*. The *mémoire* was published in its entirety by Rulhière in his *Éclaircissemens historiques* 2:19–136.

130. "L'Édit de Louis XVI sur l'état civil des Protestants: discours du conseiller Robert de Saint-Vincent dans la séance du Parlement de Paris du 9 février 1787," *BSHPF* 5 (1857): 423–44. The Parlement of Paris did issue some remonstrances extending the number of judicial offices from which Protestants were to be banned and expressing the established religion clause in more positive terms than the original wording had it. The royal ministry made no substantive changes and on 29 January 1788 the Parlement of Paris registered the edict by a vote of 97 to 17. Jules Flammermont, *Remontrances du Parlement de Paris* (Paris, 1898), 3:694–95. Henri Dubief, "La réception de l'édit du 17 novembre 1787 par les parlements," *BSHPF* 134:282–85.

131. The volume mentioned above, *La tolérance civile* (n. 93), analyzes the *Toleranzpatent* from various angles and offers an instructive comparison with the French edict.

132. Édit du roi concernant ceux qui ne font pas profession de la religion catholique. [17] Nov. 1787. Isambert et al. 29:472–82.

133. See, for example, [abbé Proyart], *Lettre à un magistrat du Parlement de Paris, au sujet de l'Édit sur l'état civil des Protestans* (Avignon, 1787); *Seconde lettre à un magistrat du Parlement de Paris sur l'Édit concernant l'état civil des Protestans* (Avignon, 1787); [père Bonnaud], *Discours à lire en présence du roi* (n.p., 1787); *Le secret révélé, ou lettre à un magistrat de province sur les protestans, par C ***, avocat* (n.p., n.d.).

134. Dubief, "La réception de l'édit du 17 novembre 1787 par les parlements," 281–95; Michel Peronnet, "Loménie de Brienne, archevêque de Toulouse, principal ministre du roi et l'Édit des non-Catholiques de novembre 1787," *BSHPF* 134: 276–77; "Le clergé catholique et les Protestants français (1770, 1780, 1788)," *BSHPF* 36 (1887): 531–39; "Protestation de l'évêque de La Rochelle contre l'Édit de Louis XVI accordant l'état civil aux non-Catholiques. Réquisitoire du procureur du Roi et arrêt du conseil contre le mandement dudit évêque (1788)," *BSHPF* 7 (1858): 157–69.

135. Cited in Christian Chene, "Le contenu et l'accueil de l''Édit de tolérance' de novembre 1787," *BSHPF* 134:137.

136. "Lettre de Rabaut Saint-Étienne sur l'Édit de tolérance de 1787," *BSHPF* 33 (1884): 363.

137. "Observations de Rabaut Saint-Étienne sur l'édit de Louis XVI restituant l'état civil aux non-Catholiques (1787)," *BSHPF* 13 (1867): 343–44.

138. [Rabaut Saint-Étienne], "Instructions aux pasteurs du Languedoc au sujet de l'Édit de tolérance," *BSHPF* 36 (1887): 549–50.

139. Daniel Ligou and Philippe Joutard suggest that even Rabaut Saint-Étienne might have had second thoughts about encouraging "wilderness" belief. His liberal Protestantism, as well as that of his fellow urban sophisticates, was a far cry from the Calvinist fundamentalism of the rural Cévennes and probably was closer to John Locke than to John Calvin. It seems evident, nevertheless, that Rabaut Saint-Étienne would have preferred settling doctrinal issues in a political atmosphere of freely competing views than in one which restrained a Protestantism differing from his own. See Daniel Ligou and Philippe Joutard, "Les déserts," *Histoire des Protestants en France*, ed. Robert Mandrou et al. (Toulouse, 1977), 233–36.

140. Isambert et al. 29:472. Back in December 1787 Rabaut Saint-Étienne had pointed out that the Edict of Toleration promised more than it delivered, and he suggested that it would have been preferable for the preamble to keep silent about natural rights. "Lettre de Rabaut Saint-Étienne sur l'Édit de tolérance de 1787."

141. *AP* (24 Aug. 1789), 8:480; de Baecque, 199.

142. The fears of National Assembly delegates in August 1789 that armed conflict between Protestants and Catholics was possible proved justified the following spring. Fighting erupted in Montauban in May 1790. While the

Assembly debated the Civil Constitution of the Clergy, unrest spread to Toulouse, Perpignan, and, most especially, Nîmes, where more than two hundred fatalities were recorded. This notwithstanding, until establishment of the de-Christianization movement in autumn 1793, revolutionary governments treated Protestantism generously. By mid-1790 Protestant public worship was a *fait accompli* throughout France, though the complete secularization of civil status by virtue of civil guardianship of birth, marriage, and death records was not finalized until September 1792. As Shanti Marie Singham shows in chapter 3, the civil and religious status of Jews was quite different from that of Protestants. As recognized corporate communities in the Old Régime, Sephardim and Ashkenazim possessed their own civil registers and observed Jewish religious customs. However, it was only in September 1791 that they obtained civil rights as French citizens. See Dedieu, *Histoire politique* 2:329–40; Poland, *French Protestantism*, 115–40; Zosa Szajkowski, *Jews and the French Revolutions of 1789, 1830, and 1848* (New York, 1970), 358–87; Robert Badinter, *"Libres et égaux:" l'emancipation des Juifs, 1789–1791* (Paris, 1989).

CHAPTER 8

1. Hippolyte Taine, *Les origines de la France contemporaine* (Paris, 1878), 2:386. This translation and all subsequent ones in this chapter are my own except where indicated.

2. William Sewell, *Work and Revolution in France: The Language of Labor from the Old Regime to 1848* (Cambridge, 1980), 114.

3. Ibid., 136.

4. Marcel Garaud, *Histoire générale du droit privé français 2: La Révolution et la propriété foncière* (Paris, 1958).

5. While conceived along different lines, my findings correspond well with those of Germain Sicard, "Le droit de propriété," in Geneviève Kubé, ed., *Propriété et révolution: Actes du Colloque de Toulouse, 12–14 octobre 1989* (Paris and Toulouse, 1990), 17–26.

6. John P. Dawson, "The Codification of the French Customs," *Michigan Law Review* 38 (1940): 765–800.

7. Joseph Van Kan, *Les efforts de codification en France: Etude historique et psychologique* (Paris, 1929).

8. Charles Lefebvre, *L'ancien droit des successions*, 2 vols. (Paris, 1912).

9. Pierre-Jean-Jacques-Guillaume Guyot, *Répertoire universel et raisonné de jurisprudence* (Paris, 1775–86), 16:14.

10. Robert-Joseph Pothier, *Traité du droit de domaine de propriété* (Paris and Orléans, 1772), 1:18.

11. Pierre Richelet, *Dictionnaire françois* (Geneva, 1679–80), 225; Antoine Furetière, Dictionnaire universel (The Hague and Rotterdam, 1690), 3:n.p.

12. Edouard Meynial, "Notes sur la formation de la théorie du domaine divisé," *Mélanges Fitting* (Montpellier, 1907), 2:409–61.

13. Sicard, "Le droit," 19–20.

14. Pothier, *Traité* 1:5. See also Pierre-Paul Henrion de Pansey, *Traité des fiefs de Dumoulin* (Paris, 1778), 392–93; and François Hervé, *Théorie des matières féodales et censuelles* (Paris, 1785–88), 1:375–77.

15. Jean-Louis Thireau, *Charles du Moulin, 1500–1566* (Geneva, 1980), 241.

16. Jean-Etienne-Marie de Portalis, *Discours, rapports, et travaux*, ed. Frédéric Portalis (Paris, 1844), 215.

17. Jean Bodin, *Les six livres de la république*, 4th ed. (Paris, 1579), 272ff.

18. Charles Loyseau, *Traité des seigneuries*, 11, in *Les oeuvres du maistre Charles Loyseau* (Paris, 1666).

19. Ibid., 4.

20. Ibid., 16.

21. Claude Fleury, *Droit publique de France*, ed. J. B. Dargon (Paris, 1769), 1:9.

22. Cf. Thireau, *Charles du Moulin.*

23. Loyseau, *Traité*, 5.

24. Fleury, *Droit* 1:5–9.

25. Pierre de Caseneuve, *Instruction pour le franc-alleu de la province de Languedoc* (n.p., 1640), 69.

26. William Church, *Constitutional Thought in Sixteenth-Century France* (Cambridge, MA, 1941), 331–32.

27. Loyseau, *Traité*, 69.

28. Ibid., 5.

29. See Paul Louis-Lucas, *Etude sur la vénalité des charges et fonctions publiques*, 2 vols. (Paris, 1883).

30. Loyseau, *Traité*, 97.

31. Sarah Hanley, *The "Lit de justice" of the Kings of France: Constitutional Ideology in Legend, Ritual, and Discourse* (Princeton, NJ, 1983), 176.

32. Herbert Rowen, *The King's State: Proprietary Dynasticism in Early Modern France* (New Brunswick, NJ, 1980), chaps. 3 and 4.

33. Bosquet, *Dictionnaire raisonné des domaines et des droits domainiaux* (Rouen, 1763), 1:513–20.

34. Church, *Constitutional Thought.*

35. Bodin, *Six livres*, 854ff.

36. Church, *Constitutional Thought*, 331–33.

37. Martin Wolfe, "Jean Bodin on Taxes: The Sovereignty-Taxes Paradox," *Political Science Quarterly* 83 (1968): 268–84.

38. Myron Gilmore, "Authority and Property in the Seventeenth Century: The First Edition of the *Traité des seigneuries*," *Harvard Library Bulletin* 4 (1950): 258–65.

39. Gaines Post, *Studies in Medieval Legal Thought: Public Law and the State, 1100–1322* (Princeton, NJ, 1964), chap. 5.

40. Loyseau, *Traité*, 16.

41. François Olivier-Martin, *L'organisation corporative de la France de l'ancien régime* (Paris and Liége, 1938), 207–8, 230–31; Charles de Lavie, *Des corps politiques et de leurs gouvernements* (Lyon, 1764), 2:127.

42. Lavie, *Des corps* 2:102.

43. Isambert et al. 23:370–78.

44. Lavie, *Des corps* 2:127.

45. Loyseau, *Cinq livres du droit des offices*, 63, in *Oeuvres*. For the remonstrance, see Jules Flammermont, ed., *Remontrances du Parlement de Paris au XVIIIe siècle* (Paris, 1888–98), 3:350.

46. Steven Kaplan, *Bread, Politics, and Political Economy in the Reign of Louis XV* (The Hague, 1976), 1:62–63.

47. Fleury, *Droit* 1:10.

48. Michael Sonenscher, "Journeymen, the Courts and the French Trades, 1781–1791," *Past and Present* 114 (1987): 77–109. For a more general discussion, see id., *Work and Wages: Natural Law, Politics, and the Eighteenth-Century French Trades* (Cambridge, 1989), chap. 2.

49. Flammermont, *Remontrances*, 3:309.

50. Loyseau, *Traité*, 11.

51. For what follows I have relied primarily on Emile Chénon, *Etude sur l'histoire des alleux en France* (Paris, 1888), and E. Andt, "Sur la théorie de la directe universelle présenté par l'edit de 1692," *Revue historique de droit français et étranger* ser. 4, 1 (1922): 604–36. I am also indebted to Harold Ellis's discussion of the allod in *Boulainvilliers and the French Monarchy: Aristocratic Politics in Early Eighteenth-Century France* (Ithaca, NY, 1988), 32ff.

52. Quoted in Chénon, *Etude*, 203.

53. Louis Chantereau-Lefebvre, *Traité des fiefs et de leur origine* (Paris, 1662), 1:154.

54. Isambert et al. 16:317.

55. Auguste Galland, *Contre le franc-alleu sans titre* (Paris, 1629), 99.

56. Isambert et al. 20:166–68.

57. Victor-Bénigne Flour de Saint-Génis, *Histoire documentaire et philosophique de l'administration des domaines des origines à 1903* 2 (Le Havre, 1903).

58. On this racket, see David D. Bien, "Office, Corps, and a System of State Credit: The Uses of Privilege under the Ancien Régime," in Keith Michael Baker, ed., *The French Revolution and the Making of Modern Political Culture* (Oxford, 1987), 1:89–114.

59. Guillaume-François Le Trosne, *De l'administration provinciale et de la réforme de l'impôt* (Basle, 1779), 563–66.

60. Caseneuve, *Instruction*, 122, 89.

61. Ibid., 3.

62. Pierre de Caseneuve, *Le franc-alleu de la province de Languedoc* (Toulouse, 1645), 114–17. This work is an enlarged second edition of the *Instruction*.

63. Ibid., 84.

64. Caseneuve, *Instruction*, 68–70.

65. Quoted in François Loirette, "The Defense of the Allodium in Seven-

teenth-Century Agenais: An Episode in Local Resistance to Encroaching Royal Power," in Raymond Kierstead, ed. and trans., *State and Society in Seventeenth-Century France* (New York, 1975), 182.

66. *L'avocat national, ou Lettre d'un patriot au sieur Bouquet* (n.p., n.d.), 119, 127.

67. Quoted in Flour de Saint-Génis, *Histoire documentaire* 2:747.

68. Quoted in William Doyle, *The Parlement of Bordeaux and the End of the Old Regime, 1771–1790* (London, 1974), 255.

69. Louis Petit de Bachaumont, *Mémoires secrètes* (London, 1788), 32:144.

70. Robert Boutruche, *Une société provinciale en lutte contre le régime féodal: L'alleu en Bordelais et en Bazadais du XIe au XVIIIe siècle* (Rodez, 1947).

71. Bosquet, *Dictionnaire* 2:129–32.

72. *AP* 1:224.

73. Louis Hordret, *Histoire des droits anciens et des prérogatives et franchises de la ville de Saint Quentin* (Paris and St. Quentin, 1781), 309.

74. Hervé, *Théorie* 6:156–57.

75. Ibid., 104, 125. Montesquieu also feared misuse of royal domainial rights. He insisted that in the wake of the Frankish conquest, the king had not disposed of all land as his fief and had not become universal seigneur until fiefs had become inheritable and therefore protected from arbitrary royal disposition. If the king had enjoyed the right to depose his own vassals, Montesquieu argued, he "would have had a power almost as arbitrary as that of the sultan in Turkey; which is contrary to all history." Charles de Secondat, baron de La Brède et de Montesquieu, *The Spirit of the Laws* (Paris, 1990), 2:303.

76. Hervé, *Théorie* 6:157.

77. Ibid., 241ff.

78. Boutruche, *Société*, 143ff.

79. J. Q. C. Mackrell, *The Attack on Feudalism in the Eighteenth Century* (Toulouse and Toronto, 1973).

80. Most recently by Hilton Root, *Peasant and King in Burgundy: Agrarian Foundation of French Absolutism* (Berkeley, 1987). These suits had been noted before by other historians, such as Robert Forster in *The House of Saulx-Tavanes: Versailles and Burgundy, 1700–1830* (Baltimore, 1971). Root gives them a different interpretation.

81. George Weulersse's books on the subject, most notably *Le mouvement physiocratique en France de 1756 à 1760*, 2 vols. (Paris, 1910), provide a basic background. See also Elizabeth Fox-Genovese, *The Origins of Physiocracy: Economic Revolution and Social Order in Eighteenth-Century France* (Ithaca, NY, 1976). On the reform of the grain trade, see Kaplan, *Bread*.

82. André Morellet, *Réfutation de l'ouvrage qui a pour titre "Dialogues sur le commerce des bleds"* (London, 1770), 109.

83. Denis Diderot, *Oeuvres complètes* (n.p., 1971), 8:760.

84. In general, I am sympathetic to the view of Warren J. Samuels, "The Physiocratic View of Property and the State," *Quarterly Journal of Economics* 75 (1961): 96–111, but I think he exaggerates the extent to which natural rights become absorbed by social rights in physiocratic thought. For a very different interpretation, see Elizabeth Fox-Genovese, "Physiocracy and Propertied Individualism: The Unfolding of Bourgeois Property in Unfree Labor Systems" in Elizabeth Fox-Genovese and Eugene D. Genovese, *Fruits of Merchant Capital: Slavery and Bourgeois Property in the Rise and Expansion of Capitalism* (New York, 1983), 272–98.

85. Pierre-Paul-François-Joachim-Henri Le Mercier de la Rivière, *Les voeux d'un françois* (Paris, 1788), 24–25.

86. Pierre-Paul-François-Joachim-Henri Le Mercier de la Rivière, *Essais sur les maximes et lois fondamentales de la monarchie françoise* (Paris and Versailles, 1789), 9.

87. Pierre-Samuel Dupont de Nemours, *De l'origine et des progrès d'une science nouvelle*, in Eugene Daire, ed., *Les physiocrates* (Paris, 1846), 356.

88. *Manifeste aux Normans* (n.p., n.d.) 7. Cf. also Voltaire's comment in his *L'homme aux quarante écus* (Paris, 1826), 6: "What would happen if the power that presides over the 'essential order of societies' took my land in its entirety?"

89. Anne-Robert-Jacques de Turgot, *Les oeuvres de Turgot*, ed. Eugène Daire (Paris, 1844), 253.

90. Victor Riquetti, marquis de Mirabeau, *L'ami des hommes, ou Traité de la population* (Avignon, 1756), 1:pt. 1, 126.

91. Turgot, *Oeuvres*, 253.

92. Le Trosne, *De l'administration*, 570. "I find that the greatest obstacle to the abolition of feudalism is that it has status as property and that it constitutes patrimony. With that title, it is respectable."

93. Pierre-François Boncerf, *Les inconvéniens des droits féodaux* (n.p., n.d.), 21.

94. *Encyclopédie méthodique: Finances* (Paris and Liége, 1785), 2:112.

95. Joseph Renauldon, *Traité historique et pratique des droits seigneuriaux* (Paris, 1765), iii–iv.

96. Hervé, *Théorie* 1:368–69, 386. See Régine Robin, "Fief et seigneurie dans le droit et l'idéologie juridique à la fin du XVIIIe siècle," *AHRF* 206 (1971): 554–602.

97. Renauldon, *Traité*, 5, 196-97.

98. Pansey, *Traité*, 3–6.

99. *L'avocat national*, 112.

100. Flammermont, *Remontrances* 2:575.

101. Jacob-Nicolas Moreau, *Leçons de moral, de politique, et de droit public* (Versailles, 1773), 82–83, 178–79, 200.

102. Isambert et al. 24:140.

103. Text in Rials, 573–74.

104. Beatrice Hyslop, *French Nationalism in 1789 according to the General Cahiers* (New York, 1934), 94.

105. *AP* 3:744; 4:85; 5:598.   106. Ibid. 4:107.

107. Ibid. (17 June 1789), 8:129.   108. Ibid. (17 July 1789), 8:229.

109. Rials, 531, 549, 610.

110. Georges Michon, *Essai sur l'histoire du parti feuillant: Adrien Duport* (Paris, 1924), 42–43.

111. *AP* (6 Aug. 1789), 8:353–56.

112. Keith Michael Baker, *Inventing the French Revolution: Essays on French Political Culture in the Eighteenth Century* (Cambridge, 1990), chap. 11.

113. Bertrand Barère de Vieuzac, *Le point du jour* (Paris, 1789), 2:220.

114. Stanislaus-Marie-Adélaide, comte de Clermont-Tonnerre, *Analyse raisonnée de la Constitution française* (Paris, 1791), 63–66.

115. *AP* (18 Aug. 1789), 8:451.   116. Ibid. 4:222.

117. Ibid. (4 Apr. 1791), 24:544.   118. Ibid. (2 Nov. 1789), 9:643.

119. Ibid. (23 Oct. 1789), 9:486.   120. Ibid. (30 Oct. 1789), 9:610.

121. Ibid. (13 Oct. 1789), 9:422.

122. The literature on the subject is, of course, vast and no bibliographic survey is possible here. Aside from Garaud, *Histoire*, I have found still very useful, Philippe Sagnac, *La législation civile de la Révolution française, (1789–1804)* (Paris, 1898).

123. *Moniteur* (10 Feb. 1790), 3:331.

124. In this I believe André Lichtenberger's old thesis is still correct. See his *Le socialisme au XVIIIe siècle: Etude sur les idées socialistes dans les écrivains français du XVIIIe siècle avant la Révolution* (Paris, 1895) and *Le socialisme et la Révolution française* (Paris, 1899).

125. Maximilien Robespierre, *Oeuvres complètes de Robespierre*, ed. Gustave Laurent (Nancy, 1939), 4:116–17.

126. *Moniteur* (24 Apr. 1793), 16:213.

127. *AP* (2 Nov. 1789), 9:643; *Moniteur* (10 Feb. 1790), 3:331.

128. Antoine-Louis Séguier, *La constitution renversée* (n.p., n.d.), 16–17.

129. *AP* 5:494.

130. See the report of François-Dénis Tronchet in *AP* (12 Sept. 1789), 8:621ff.

131. *Moniteur* (10 Feb. 1790), 3:331.   132. *AP* 2:470 and 3:27.

133. Ibid. (6 Aug. 1789), 8:356.   134. Ibid. (12 Sept. 1789), 8:625.

135. Pierre Caron, ed., *Recueil des textes législatifs et administratifs concernants la suppression des droits féodaux* (Paris, 1924), 31.

136. Ibid., 49, 130.

137. Philippe Sagnac and Pierre Caron, eds., *Les comités des droits féodaux et de législation et l'abolition du régime seigneurial, (1789–1793)* (Paris, 1907), 742–46.

138. Michael P. Fitzsimmons, *The Parisian Order of Barristers and the French Revolution* (Cambridge, MA, 1987), 67.

139. *Moniteur* (12 June 1794), 20:695.

140. Caron, *Recueil*, 179, 181, 191–92, 194, 197–98.

141. C. Michallet, *Le mystère des droits féodaux dévoilé* (Trévoux, 1791).

142. Ibid., 24ff, 53; Antoine-Jean-François Lautour-Duchatel, "Rapport et projet de decret concernant la suppression, sans indemnité, de divers droits féodaux" (Le Havre, 1792); Address of Jean-Baptiste Mailhe in *Moniteur* (10 June 1792), 12:615.

143. Michallet, *Le mystère*, 184.

144. Lautour-Duchatel, "Rapport," 16.

145. Michallet, *Le mystère*, pref., 2.; Lautour-Duchatel, "Rapport," 9–10.

146. Michallet, *Le mystère*, pref.

147. Auguste-Antoine-Joseph Prouveur, "Opinion de M. Prouveur . . . sur la suppression, sans indemnité, des droits féodaux casuels" (Paris, n.d.), 5–8.

148. Sixte-François-Joseph Deusy, "Opinion de M. Deusy . . . concernant la suppression sans indemnité des droits féodaux fixes et casuels" (Paris, n.d.), 11–12, 19.

149. Albert Soboul, "Survivances 'féodales' dans la société rurale française au XIXᵉ siècle," *Annales* 23 (1968): 965–86.

150. Garaud, *Histoire* 2:229ff.   151. Caron, *Recueil*, 200–201, 208.

152. Ibid., 209.   153. Ibid., 218.

154. Colin Lucas, "The First Directory and the Rule of Law," *FHS* 10 (1977): 231–60.

155. Garaud, *Histoire* 2:238–40.

156. André-Jean Arnaud, *Les origins doctrinales du Code Civil Français* (Paris, 1969). For an enlightening essay on property doctrine in this period, see Donald R. Kelley and Bonnie Smith, "What was Property? Legal Dimensions of the Social Question in France (1789–1848)," *Proceedings of the American Philosophical Society* 128 (1984): 200–230.

157. Portalis, *Discours*, 200–218.

158. Ibid., 3–19.

159. J. E. D. Bernardi, *Institution au droit françois civil et criminel, ou tableau raisonné de l'état actuel de la jurisprudence françoise* (Paris, Year VII), xii.

160. Jean-Jacques de Cambacérès, "Rapport fait à la Convention Nationale . . . 9 août 1793" in P.-Antoine Fénet, ed., *Recueil complet des travaux préparatoires du code civil* (Paris, 1827), 1:14.

< >

Index

In this index an "f" after a number indicates a separate reference on the next page, and an "ff" indicates separate references on the next two pages. A continuous discussion over two or more pages is indicated by a span of page numbers, e.g., "57–59." *Passim* is used for a cluster of references in close but not consecutive sequence.

Library of Congress Cataloging-in-Publication Data

The French idea of freedom : the Old Regime and the
Declaration of Rights of 1789 / edited by Dale Van Kley.
  p. cm.—(The Making of modern freedom)
  Includes bibliographical references and index.
  ISBN 0-8047-2355-9:
    1. Human rights—France. 2. Liberty. 3. France—
Constitutional history. 4. France—Politics and
government—1789. 5. France. Déclaration des droits de
l'homme et du citoyen. I. Van Kley, Dale K., 1941– .
II. Series.
JC599.F8F74 1994
323'.0944—dc20   93-50946
                                                    CIP

♾ This book is printed on acid-free paper.

Original printing 1994
Last figure below indicates year of this printing:
05 04 03 02 01 00 99 98 97 96